JOHN WESLEY'S
JOURNAL

*From a scarce print by Bland, published in year
1765 and approved by Mr. Wesley*
JOHN WESLEY, AGED SIXTY-THREE

The Heart of
John Wesley's Journal

With an Introduction by HUGH PRICE
HUGHES, M.A., and an appreciation of the
Journal by AUGUSTINE BIRRELL, K.C.,
Edited by PERCY LIVINGSTONE PARKER

KEATS PUBLISHING, INC.
NEW CANAAN, CONNECTICUT

THE HEART OF JOHN WESLEY'S JOURNAL

Shepherd Illustrated Classic edition published 1979

Special contents of this edition copyright © 1979
by Keats Publishing, Inc.

All Rights Reserved

Library of Congress Catalog Card Number: 79-64828
ISBN: 0-87983-207-X

Printed in the United States of America

Shepherd Illustrated Classics are published by
Keats Publishing, Inc.,
36 Grove Street, New Canaan, Connecticut 06840

LIST OF ILLUSTRATIONS

EDITOR'S NOTE

WHEN *John Wesley prepared his Journal for publication he prefaced it with the following account of its origin :*

"*It was in pursuance of an advice given by Bishop Taylor, in his 'Rules for Holy Living and Dying,' that, about fifteen years ago, I began to take a more exact account than I had done before, of the manner wherein I spent my time, writing down how I had employed every hour.*

"*This I continued to do, wherever I was, till the time of my leaving England for Georgia. The variety of scenes which I then passed through induced me to transcribe, from time to time, the more material parts of my diary, adding here and there such little reflections as occurred to my mind.*

"*Of this Journal thus occasionally compiled, the following is a short extract : it not being my design to relate all those particulars which I wrote for my own use only, and which would answer no valuable end to others, however important they were to me.*"

Rev. John Telford, one of Wesley's biographers, says that "the earlier parts of the Journal were published in the interest of Methodism, that the calumny and slander then rife might be silenced by a plain narrative of the facts as to its founding, and its purpose. The complete Journals, still preserved in twenty-six bound volumes, have never been printed. Copious extracts were made by Wesley himself, and issued in twenty-one parts, the successive instalments being eagerly expected by a host of readers."

The published Journal makes four volumes, each about the size of the present book. But though I have had to curtail it by three-quarters I have tried to retain the atmosphere of tremendous activity which is one of its most remarkable features.

Mr. Birrell, in his " Appreciation," has focused in a very striking way the interest, actuality, and charm of Wesley's Journal, and all I have had to do was to select those portions which best illustrate them.

The wonder is that it has not been done before. Edward FitzGerald once wrote to Professor Norton, " Had I any interest with publishers I would get them to reprint parts of it," for he was a great lover of the Journal.

Writing to another friend about Wesley's " Journal," FitzGerald said, " If you don't know it, do know it. It is curious to think of this diary running coevally with Walpole's letters—diary—the two men born and dying too within a few miles of one another, and with such different lives to record. And it is remarkable to read pure, unaffected, undying English, while Addison and Johnson are tainted with a style which all the world imitated."

Macaulay's estimate of Wesley may also be recalled. Wesley, he said, was " a man whose eloquence and logical acuteness might have made him eminent in literature, whose genius for government was not inferior to that of Richelieu, and who, whatever his errors may have been, devoted all his powers in defiance of obloquy and derision, to what he sincerely considered as the highest good of his species."

Wesley is one of the most strenuous ethical figures in history, and literature has no other such record of personal endeavour as that contained in these pages. To make that record accessible to every one is the object of this edition.

INTRODUCTION

BY THE REV. HUGH PRICE HUGHES, M.A.

HE who desires to understand the real history of the English people during the seventeenth, eighteenth and nineteenth centuries should read most carefully three books: George Fox's " Journal," John Wesley's " Journal," and John Henry Newman's " Apologia pro Vitâ Suâ."

As Lord Hugh Cecil has recently said in a memorable speech, the Religious Question cannot be ignored. It is *the* Question; in the deepest sense it is the only Question. It has always determined the course of history everywhere. In all ages the sceptical literary class has tried to ignore it, as the Roman historians, poets, and philosophers ignored Christianity until the time when Christianity became triumphant and dominant throughout the Roman Empire.

But, however much ignored or boycotted by literary men, the growth or decline of religion ultimately settles everything. Has not Carlyle said that George Fox making his own clothes is the most remarkable event in our history? George Fox was the very incarnation of that Individualism which has played, and will yet play, so great a part in the making of modern England. If you want to understand " the dissidence of Dissent and the Protestantism of the Protestant religion," read the Journal of George Fox.

Then came John Wesley and his "helpers." They were the first preachers since the days of the Franciscan friars in the Middle Ages who ever reached the working classes. In England, as in France, Germany, and everywhere else, the Reformation was essentially a middle-class movement. It never captured either the upper classes or the working classes. That explains its limitations.

As Dr. Rigg has shown, Wesley's itineraries were deliberately planned to bring him into direct contact neither with the aristocracy nor with the dependent or poverty-stricken poor, but with the industrious self-supporting workmen in town and country. The ultimate result was that "the man in the street" became Methodist in his conception of Christianity, whatever his personal conduct and character might be. A profound French critic said, fifty years ago, that modern England was Methodist, and the remark applies equally to the United States and to our colonies. The doctrines of the Evangelical Revival permeated the English-speaking world.

Then Newman appeared on the scene and a tremendous change began. The Anglican Church revived, and revived in Newman's direction. We witness to-day on every side the vast results of the Newman era. Many of these results are beneficial in the extreme ; others cannot be welcome to those who belong to the schools of George Fox and John Wesley.

The whole future of the British Empire depends upon this question of questions—Will George Fox and John Wesley on the one hand, or John Henry Newman on the other, ultimately prevail ? And the best way to arrive at the true inwardness of the issue is to read, ponder, and inwardly digest Wesley's "Journal" and Newman's "Apologia."

It is a great advantage that Mr. Parker has secured permission to republish Mr. Augustine Birrell's "Appreciation." That brilliant writer demonstrates, that there is no book in existence that gives you so exact and vivid a description of the eighteenth century in England as Wesley's "Journal." It is an incalculably more varied and complete account of the condition of the people of England than Boswell's "Johnson." As Mr. Birrell says, Wesley was himself "the greatest force of the eighteenth century in England. No man lived nearer the centre than John Wesley. Neither Clive nor Pitt, neither Mansfield nor Johnson. No single figure influenced so many minds, no single voice touched so many hearts. No other man did such a life's work for England." Wesley has demonstrated that a true prophet of God has more influence than all the politicians and soldiers and millionaires put together. He is the incalculable and unexpected element that is always putting all the devices of the clever to naught.

I do not understand what Mr. Birrell means by saying that "as a writer Wesley has not achieved distinction. He was no Athanasius, no Augustine ; he was ever a preacher." It is true that Wesley's main business was not to define metaphysical theology, but to cultivate friendly relations with Christians of all schools, and to save living men from sin. But he gave a death-blow to the destructive dogma of limited salvation with which the names of Augustine and Calvin will be for ever associated.

No doubt, like Oliver Cromwell, Wesley was essentially

a "man of action," and he deliberately sacrificed the niceties of literary taste to the greater task of making Englishmen on both sides of the Atlantic real Christians. Even so, the style of some of his more literary productions is a model of lucidity and grace.

But my main point here is to echo Mr. Birrell's final statement, that "we can learn better from Wesley's 'Journal' than from anywhere else what manner of man Wesley was, and the character of the times during which he lived and moved and had his being." My co-religionists and all who love the most characteristic qualities of modern English life are under a deep debt of obligation to my friend Mr. Parker and his publishers for giving them an opportunity of studying the eventful eighteenth century of English history at its centre and fountain-head.

The fact that this edition of the work has been condensed is no drawback. The "Journal," as originally published, was itself condensed by Wesley. The Book Room has in its possession large unpublished portions of the manuscript, much of which will be included in the standard edition which the Methodist Editor has now in hand; but for popular purposes Mr. Parker's edition will answer all important ends, and will give English readers for the first time an opportunity of reading in a handy form one of the most important, instructive, and entertaining books ever published in the English language.

Of course Mr. Parker alone is responsible for the selection of the portions of the "Journal" which appear in this volume.

HUGH PRICE HUGHES

AN APPRECIATION OF
JOHN WESLEY'S JOURNAL*

BY AUGUSTINE BIRRELL, K.C.

JOHN WESLEY, born as he was in 1703 and dying as he did in 1791, covers as nearly as mortal man may, the whole of the eighteenth century, of which he was one of the most typical and certainly the most strenuous figure.

He began his published Journal on October 14, 1735, and its last entry is under date Sunday, October 24, 1790, when in the morning he explained to a numerous congregation in Spitalfields Church "The Whole Armour of God," and in the afternoon enforced to a still larger audience in St. Paul's, Shadwell, the great truth, "One thing is needful," the last words of the Journal being "I hope many even then resolved to choose the better part."

Between those two Octobers there lies the most amazing record of human exertion ever penned or endured.

I do not know whether I am likely to have among my readers any one who has ever contested an English or Scottish county in a parliamentary election since household suffrage. If I have, that tired soul will know

* Reprinted in part from *Miscellanies*, by Augustine Birrell (Elliot Stock), by permission of the author and the publisher.

how severe is the strain of its three weeks, and how impossible it seemed at the end of the first week that you should be able to keep it going for another fortnight, and how when the last night arrived you felt that had the strife been accidentally prolonged another seven days you must have perished by the wayside.

Contesting the Three Kingdoms

Well, John Wesley contested the three kingdoms in the cause of Christ during a campaign which lasted forty years.

He did it for the most part on horseback. He paid more turnpikes than any man who ever bestrode a beast. Eight thousand miles was his annual record for many a long year, during each of which he seldom preached less frequently than five thousand times. Had he but preserved his scores at all the inns where he lodged, they would have made by themselves a history of prices. And throughout it all he never knew what depression of spirits meant—though he had much to try him, suits in chancery and a jealous wife.

In the course of this unparalleled contest Wesley visited again and again the most out of the way districts —the remotest corners of England—places which to-day lie far removed even from the searcher after the picturesque.

To-day, when the map of England looks like a grid-iron of railways, none but the sturdiest of pedestrians, the most determined of cyclists can retrace the steps of Wesley and his horse, and stand by the rocks and the natural amphitheatres in Cornwall and Northumberland in Lancashire and Berkshire, where he preached his gospel to the heathen.

Exertion so prolonged, enthusiasm so sustained, argues a remarkable man, while the organisation he created, the system he founded, the view of life he promulgated, is still a great fact among us.   No other name than Wesley's lies embalmed as his does.   Yet he is not a popular figure.   Our standard historians have dismissed him curtly.   The fact is, Wesley puts your ordinary historian out of conceit with himself.

How much easier to weave into your page the gossip of Horace Walpole, to enliven it with a heartless jest of George Selwyn's, to make it blush with sad stories of the extravagance of Fox, to embroider it with the rhetoric of Burke, to humanise it with the talk of Johnson, to discuss the rise and fall of administrations, the growth and decay of the constitution, than to follow John Wesley into the streets of Bristol, or on to the bleak moors near Burslem, when he met, face to face in all their violence, all their ignorance, and all their generosity the living men, women, and children who made up the nation.

A Book of Plots, Plays and Novels

It has perhaps also to be admitted that to found great organisations is to build your tomb—a splendid tomb, it may be, a veritable sarcophagus, but none the less a tomb.   John Wesley's chapels lie a little heavily on John Wesley.   Even so do the glories of Rome make us forgetful of the grave in Syria.

It has been said that Wesley's character lacks charm, that mighty antiseptic.   It is not easy to define charm, which is not a catalogue of qualities, but a mixture. Let no one deny charm to Wesley who has not read his Journal.   Southey's Life is a dull, almost a stupid book

which happily there is no need to read. Read the
Journal, which is a book full of plots and plays and
novels, which quivers with life and is crammed full of
character.

Wesley's Family Stock

John Wesley came of a stock which had been much
harassed and put about by our unhappy religious difficulties. Politics, business, and religion are the three
things Englishmen are said to worry themselves about.
The Wesleys early took up with religion. John Wesley's
great-grandfather and grandfather were both ejected
from their livings in 1662, and the grandfather was so
bullied and oppressed by the Five Mile Act that he
early gave up the ghost. Whereupon his remains were
refused what is called Christian burial, though a holier
and more primitive man never drew breath. This poor,
persecuted spirit left two sons according to the flesh,
Matthew and Samuel; and Samuel it was who in his
turn became the father of John and Charles Wesley.

Samuel Wesley, though minded to share the lot, hard
though that lot was, of his progenitors, had the modera-
tion of mind, the Christian conservatism which ever
marked the family, and being sent to a dissenting college,
became disgusted with the ferocity and bigotry he happened there to encounter. Those were the days of the
Calf's Head Club and feastings on the 29th of January,
graceless meals for which Samuel Wesley had no stomach.
His turn was for the things that are "quiet, wise, and
good." He departed from the dissenting seminary and
in 1685 entered himself as a poor scholar at Exeter
College, Oxford. He brought £2 6s. with him, and as
for prospects, he had none. Exeter received him.

REV. SAMUEL WESLEY
Father of John Wesley

REV. JOHN WESLEY
Grandfather of John Wesley

During the eighteenth century our two universities, famous despite their faults, were always open to the poor scholar who was ready to subscribe, not to boat clubs or cricket clubs, but to the Thirty-nine Articles. Three archbishops of Canterbury during the eighteenth century were the sons of small tradesmen. There was, in fact, much less snobbery and money-worship during the century when the British empire was being won than during the century when it is being talked about.

Samuel Wesley was allowed to remain at Oxford, where he supported himself by devices known to his tribe, and when he left the university to be ordained he had clear in his pouch, after discharging his few debts, £10 15s. He had thus made £8 9s. out of his university, and had his education, as it were, thrown in for nothing. He soon obtained a curacy in London and married a daughter of the well-known ejected clergyman, Dr. Annesley, about whom you may read in another eighteenth-century book "The Life and Errors of John Dunton."

Wesley's Mother

The mother of the Wesleys was a remarkable woman, though cast in a mould not much to our minds nowadays. She had nineteen children, and greatly prided herself on having taught them, one after another, by frequent chastisements to, what do you think? to cry softly. She had theories of education and strength of will, and of arm too, to carry them out.

She knew Latin and Greek, and though a stern, forbidding, almost an unfeeling, parent, she was successful in winning and retaining not only the respect but the affection of such of her huge family as lived to grow up. But out of the nineteen, thirteen early succumbed. Infant mortality was one of the great facts of the eighteenth century whose Rachels had to learn to cry softly over their dead babes. The mother of the Wesleys thought more of her children's souls than of their bodies.

A Domestic Squall

The revolution of 1688 threatened to disturb the early married life of Samuel Wesley and his spouse.

The husband wrote a pamphlet in which he defended revolution principles, but the wife secretly adhered to the old cause; nor was it until a year before Dutch William's death that the rector made the discovery that the wife of his bosom, who had sworn to obey him and regard him as her over-lord, was not in the habit of saying Amen to his fervent prayers on behalf of his suffering sovereign. An explanation was demanded and the truth extracted, namely, that in the opinion of the rector's wife her true king lived over the water. The rector at once refused to live with Mrs. Wesley any longer until she recanted. This she refused to do, and for a twelvemonth the couple dwelt apart, when William III. having the good sense to die, a reconciliation became possible. If John Wesley was occasionally a little pig-headed, need one wonder?

The story of the fire at Epworth Rectory and the miraculous escape of the infant John was once a tale as well known as Alfred in the neat-herd's hut, and pictures of it still hang up in many a collier's home.

John Wesley received a sound classical education at Charterhouse and Christ Church, and remained all his life very much the scholar and the gentleman. No company was too good for John Wesley, and nobody knew better than he did that had he cared to carry his powerful intelligence, his flawless constitution, and his infinite capacity for taking pains into any of the markets of the world, he must have earned for himself place, fame, and fortune.

Coming, however, as he did of a theological stock, having a saint for a father and a notable devout woman for a mother, Wesley from his early days learned to regard religion as the business of his life, just as the younger Pitt came to regard the House of Commons as the future theatre of his actions.

"My Jack is Fellow of Lincoln"

After a good deal of heart-searching and theological talk with his mother, Wesley was ordained a deacon by the excellent Potter, afterward Primate, but then (1725) Bishop of Oxford. In the following year Wesley was elected a Fellow of Lincoln, to the great delight of his father. "Whatever I am," said the good old man, "my Jack is Fellow of Lincoln."

. . . . .

Wesley's motive never eludes us. In his early manhood, after being greatly affected by Jeremy Taylor's "Holy Living and Dying" and the "Imitatio Christi," and by Law's "Serious Call" and "Christian Perfection," he met "a serious man" who said to him, "Sir, you wish to serve God and go to heaven. Remember you cannot serve Him alone. You must therefore find companions or make them. The Bible knows nothing of solitary religion."

He was very confident, this serious man, and Wesley never forgot his message. "You must find companions

or make them.   The Bible knows nothing of solitary
religion."   These words for ever sounded in Wesley's
ears, determining his theology, which rejected the stern
individualism of Calvin, and fashioning his whole polity,
his famous class meetings and generally gregarious
methods.

> Therefore to him it was given
> Many to save with himself.

We may continue the quotation and apply to Wesley the
words of Mr. Arnold's memorial to his father:

> Languor was not in his heart,
> Weakness not in his word,
> Weariness not on his brow.

If you ask what is the impression left upon the reader
of the Journal as to the condition of England question,
the answer will vary very much with the tenderness of
the reader's conscience and with the extent of his
acquaintance with the general behaviour of mankind at
all times and in all places.

No Sentimentalist

Wesley himself is no alarmist, no sentimentalist, he
never gushes, seldom exaggerates, and always writes on
an easy level.   Naturally enough he clings to the super-
natural and is always disposed to believe in the *bona
fides* of ghosts and the diabolical origin of strange noises,
but outside this realm of speculation, Wesley describes
things as he saw them.   In the first published words of
his friend, Dr. Johnson, " he meets with no basilisks
that destroy with their eyes, his crocodiles devour their
prey without tears, and his cataracts fall from the rocks
without deafening the neighbouring inhabitants."

Wesley's humour is of the species donnish, and his modes and methods quietly persistent.

Wesley's Humour

"On Thursday, May 20 (1742), I set out.   The next afternoon I stopped a little at Newport-Pagnell and then rode on till I overtook a serious man with whom I immediately fell into conversation.   He presently gave me to know what his opinions were, therefore I said nothing to contradict them.   But that did not content him.   He was quite uneasy to know 'whether I held the doctrines of the decrees as he did'; but I told him over and over 'We had better keep to practical things lest we should be angry at one another.'   And so we did for two miles till he caught me unawares and dragged me into the dispute before I knew where I was.   He then grew warmer and warmer; told me I was rotten at heart and supposed I was one of John Wesley's followers. I told him 'No.   I am John Wesley himself.'   Upon which

Improvisum aspris Veluti qui sentibus anguem
Presset——

he would gladly have run away outright.   But being the better mounted of the two I kept close to his side and endeavoured to show him his heart till we came into the street of Northampton."

What a picture have we here of a fine May morning in 1742, the unhappy Calvinist trying to shake off the Arminian Wesley!   But he cannot do it!   *John Wesley is the better mounted of the two*, and so they scamper together into Northampton.

The England described in the Journal is an England still full of theology; all kinds of queer folk abound;

strange subjects are discussed in odd places. There was drunkenness and cock-fighting, no doubt, but there were also Deists, Mystics, Swedenborgians, Antinomians, Necessitarians, Anabaptists, Quakers, nascent heresies, and slow-dying delusions. Villages were divided into rival groups, which fiercely argued the nicest points in the aptest language. Nowadays in one's rambles a man is as likely to encounter a grey badger as a black Calvinist.

England in Wesley's Day

The clergy of the Established Church were jealous of Wesley's interference in their parishes, nor was this unnatural—he was not a Nonconformist but a brother churchman. What right had he to be so peripatetic? But Wesley seldom records any instance of gross clerical misconduct. Of one drunken parson he does indeed tell us, and he speaks disapprovingly of another whom he found one very hot day consuming a pot of beer in a lone ale-house. I am bound to confess I have never had any but kindly feelings toward that thirsty ecclesiastic. What, I wonder, was he thinking of as Wesley rode by—*Libres Méditations d'un Solitaire Inconnu*—unpublished!

When Wesley, with that dauntless courage of his, a courage which never forsook him, which he wore on every occasion with the delightful ease of a soldier, pushed his way into fierce districts, amid rough miners dwelling in their own village communities almost outside the law, what most strikes one with admiration, not less in Wesley's Journal than in George Fox's (a kindred though earlier volume), is the essential fitness for freedom of our rudest populations. They were coarse and brutal and savage, but rarely did they fail to recognise the high character and lofty motives of the dignified mortal who had travelled so far to speak to them.

The Mobs He Met

Wesley was occasionally hustled, and once or twice pelted with mud and stones, but at no time were his sufferings at the hands of the mob to be compared with the indignities it was long the fashion to heap upon the heads of parliamentary candidates. The mob knew and appreciated the difference between a Bubb Dodington and a John Wesley.

I do not think any ordinary Englishman will be much horrified at the demeanour of the populace. If there was disturbance it was usually quelled. At Norwich two soldiers who disturbed a congregation were seized and carried before their commanding officer, who ordered them to be soundly whipped. In Wesley's opinion they richly deserved all they got. He was no sentimentalist, although an enthusiast.

Where the reader of the Journal will be shocked is when his attention is called to the public side of the country—to the state of the gaols—to Newgate, to Bethlehem, to the criminal code—to the brutality of so many of the judges, and the harshness of the magistrates, to the supineness of the bishops, to the extinction in high places of the missionary spirit—in short, to the heavy slumber of humanity.

Wesley was full of compassion, of a compassion wholly free from hysterics and like exaltative. In public affairs his was the composed zeal of a Howard. His efforts to penetrate the dark places were long in vain. He says in his dry way: " They won't let me go to Bedlam because they say I make the inmates mad, or into Newgate because I make them wicked." The reader of the Journal will be at no loss to see what these sapient magistrates meant.

Wesley was a terribly exciting preacher, quiet though his manner was. He pushed matters home without flinching. He made people cry out and fall down, nor did it surprise him, that they should.

*　　*　　*　　*　　*

Ever a Preacher

If you want to get into the last century, to feel its pulses throb beneath your finger, be content sometimes to leave the letters of Horace Walpole unturned, resist the drowsy temptation to waste your time over the learned triflers who sleep in the seventeen volumes of Nichols, nay even deny yourself your annual reading of Boswell or your biennial retreat with Sterne, and ride up and down the country with the greatest force of the eighteenth century in England.

No man lived nearer the centre than John Wesley. Neither Clive nor Pitt, neither Mansfield nor Johnson. You cannot cut him out of our national life. No single figure influenced so many minds, no single voice touched so many hearts. No other man did such a life's work for England.

As a writer he has not achieved distinction, he was no Athanasius, no Augustine, he was ever a preacher and an organiser, a labourer in the service of humanity ; but happily for us his Journals remain, and from them we can learn better than from anywhere else what manner of man he was, and the character of the times during which he lived and moved and had his being.

AUGUSTINE BIRRELL.

WESLEY'S LAST HOURS

BY ONE WHO WAS PRESENT *

On Thursday [February 24th, 1791] Mr. Wesley paid his last visit to that lovely place and family, Mr. Wolff's, at Balaam, which I have often heard him speak of with pleasure and much affection. Here Mr. Rogers said he was cheerful, and seemed nearly as well as usual, till Friday, about breakfast time, when he seemed very heavy.

About eleven o'clock Mrs. Wolff brought him home: I was struck with his manner of getting out of the coach, and going into the house, but more so as he went upstairs, and when he sat down in the chair. I ran for some refreshment, but before I could get anything for him he had sent Mr. R—— out of the room, and desired not to be interrupted for half-an-hour by any one, adding, not even if Joseph Bradford come.

Mr. Bradford came a few minutes after, and as soon as the limited time was expired, went into the room; immediately after he came out and desired me to mull some wine with spices and carry it to Mr. Wesley: he

* This account (condensed) was written by Betsy Ritchie, one of the saints of early Methodism. At the time she was about thirty-nine, and for the last two months of Wesley's life was his constant companion.

drank a little and seemed sleepy. In a few minutes he was seized with sickness, threw it up, and said, " I must lie down." We immediately sent for Dr. Whitehead : on his coming in Mr. Wesley smiled and said, " Doctor, they are more afraid than hurt." He lay most of the day, with a quick pulse, burning fever and extremely sleepy.

Saturday the 26th, he continued much the same ; spoke but little, and if roused to answer a question, or take a little refreshment (which was seldom more than a spoonful at a time) soon dozed again.

On Sunday morning, with a little of Mr. Bradford's help, Mr. Wesley got up, took a cup of tea, and seemed much better. Many of our friends were all hopes : yet Dr. Whitehead said, he was not out of danger from his present complaints.

Monday the 28th, his weakness increased apace and his friends in general being greatly alarmed, Dr. Whitehead was desirous they should call in another physician. Mr. Bradford mentioned his desire to our Honoured Father, which he absolutely refused, saying, " Dr. Whitehead knows my condition better than any one ; I am perfectly satisfied and will not have any one else." He slept most of the day, spoke but little ; yet that little testified how much his whole heart was taken up in the case of the Churches, the glory of God, and the things pertaining to that kingdom to which he was hastening. Once in a low, but very distinct manner, he said, " There is no way into the holiest but by the blood of Jesus." Had he had strength at the time, it seemed as if he would have said more.

Tuesday, March 1st, after a very restless night (though, when asked whether he was in pain, he generally answered " No," and never complained through his whole illness, except once, when he said that he felt a pain in his left breast, when he drew his breath), he began singing:

"All glory to God in the sky,
And peace upon earth be restor'd."

[Having sung two verses] his strength failed, but after lying still awhile he called on Mr. Bradford to give him a pen and ink; he brought them, but the right hand had well-nigh forgot its cunning, and those active fingers which had been the blessed instruments of spiritual consolation and pleasing instruction to thousands, could no longer perform their office. Some time after, he said to me, "I want to write": I brought him a pen and ink, and on putting the pen into his hand, and holding the paper before him, he said, "I cannot." I replied, "Let me write for you, sir; tell me what you would say." "Nothing," returned he, "but that God is with us." In the forenoon he said, "I will get up." While his things were getting ready, he broke out in a manner which, considering his extreme weakness, astonished us all, in these blessed words:

"I'll praise my Maker while I've breath,
And when my voice is lost in death,
  Praise shall employ my nobler pow'rs;
My days of praise shall ne'er be past,
While life, and thought, and being last,
  Or immortality endures."

Which were also the last words our Reverend and dear Father ever gave out in the City Road Chapel, viz., on Tuesday evening before preaching from, "We through the Spirit wait," &c.

When he got into his chair, we saw him change for death: but he, regardless of his dying frame, said, with a weak voice, " Lord, Thou givest strength to those that can speak, and to those that cannot : Speak, Lord, to all our hearts, and let them know that Thou loosest tongues." He then sang :

> " To Father, Son, and Holy Ghost,
> Who sweetly all agree."

Here his voice failed him, and after gasping for breath, he said, " Now we have done—Let us all go." We were obliged to lay him down on the bed from which he rose no more : but after lying still, and sleeping a little, he called me to him and said, " Betsy, you Mr. Bradford, &c., pray and praise." We knelt down, and truly our hearts were filled with the divine presence; the room seemed to be filled with God.

A little after he spoke to Mr. Bradford about the key and contents or his bureau ; while he attended to the directions given him, Mr. Wesley called me and said, "I would have all things ready for my Executors, Mr. Wolff, Mr. Horton, and Mr. Marriott "—here his voice again failed ; but taking breath he added, " Let me be buried in nothing but what is woollen, and let my corpse be carried in my coffin into the Chapel." Then, as if done with all below, he again begged we would pray and praise.

The next pleasing awful scene was the great exertion he made in order to make Mr. B. (who had not left the room) understand that he fervently desired a sermon he had written on the Love of God should be scattered abroad, and given away to everybody. Something else he wished to say, but, alas ! his speech failed ; and those lips which used to feed many were no longer able (except when particular strength was given) to convey their accustomed sounds.

A little after, Mr. Horton coming in, we hoped that if
he had anything of moment on his mind, which he wished
to communicate, he would again try to tell us what it
was, and that either Mr. Horton, or some of those who
were most used to hear our dear Father's dying voice
would be able to interpret his meaning; but though he
strove to speak, we were still unsuccessful: finding we
could not understand what he said, he paused a little,
and then with all the remaining strength he had, cried
out, "The best of all is, God is with us";—and then,
as if to assert the faithfulness of our promise-keeping
Jehovah, and comfort the hearts of his weeping friends,
lifting up his dying arm in token of victory, and raising
his feeble voice with a holy triumph not to be expressed,
again repeated the heart-reviving words, "The best of all
is, God is with us!"

Some time after, giving him something to wet his
parched lips, he said, "It will not do, we must take the
consequence; never mind the poor carcase." Pausing a
little, he cried, "The clouds drop fatness!" and soon
after, "The Lord is with us, the God of Jacob is our
refuge!" He then called us to prayer. Mr. Broadbent
was again the mouth of our full hearts, and though Mr
Wesley was greatly exhausted by these exertions, he
appeared still more fervent in spirit. Most of the night
following, though he was often heard attempting to repeat
the psalm before-mentioned, he could only get out,

"I'll praise —— I'll praise —— !"

On Wednesday morning we found the closing scene
drew near. Mr. Bradford, his faithful friend, and most
affectionate son, prayed with him, and the last word he
was heard to articulate was, "Farewell!" A few minutes

before ten, while Miss Wesley, Mr. Horton, Mr. Brackenbury, Mr. and Mrs. Rogers, Dr. Whitehead, Mr. Broadbent, Mr. Whitfield, Mr, Bradford, and E. R. were
kneeling around his bed ; according to his often expressed
desire, without a lingering groan, this man of God
gathered up his feet in the presence of his brethren !

DEATH OF JOHN WESLEY

IMPORTANT WESLEY DATES

Wesley Born	June 17, 1703
Epworth Parsonage Burned	1709
Goes to Charterhouse School	1714
Enters Christ Church, Oxford	1720
Ordained Deacon	1725
Wesley's First Sermon, Preached at S. Leigh	1725
Elected Fellow of Lincoln College	1726
Left Oxford to Assist his Father	1727
Holy Club Started	1727
Ordained Priest	1728
Returned to Oxford as Tutor	1729
Went to Georgia	1735
Published "Journal" Begins	Oct. 14, 1735
Returned to England	1738
Met Peter Böhler	Feb. 7, 1738
Famous Meeting in Aldersgate Street when Wesley's "heart was strangely warmed"	May 24, 1738
Wesley Begins Open Air Preaching	1739
Foundery (the Cradle of Methodism) Taken	1739
First Methodist Preaching-place Built at Bristol	1739
Lay Preachers Employed	1741
Methodist Classes Established at Bristol	1742
First Conference (London)	1744
Wesley Married	1751
City Road Chapel Built	1778

Wesley's Wife Died 1781

Wesley's Last Field Preaching (at Winchelsea) Oct. 6, 1790

Last Entry in his Journal . . . . Oct. 24, 1790

Last Sermon in City Road . . . . Feb. 22, 1791

His Last Sermon (Leatherhead) . . . Feb. 23, 1791

His Last Letter (to Wilberforce) . . . Feb. 24, 1791

Returned to City Road House to Die . . Feb. 25, 1791

Wesley Died in his Eighty-eighth Year . . March 2, 1791

PROGRESS OF METHODISM

When Wesley died in 1791, there were in England about 79,000 Methodists, Members of Society Classes, and 312 Ministers in Circuits. In America and Canada there were about 40,000 or 50,000 Methodists. Total 119,000.

At the Œcumenical Methodist Conference held in London in 1901, the marvellous growth of Methodism— the result of Wesley's work—was shown in the following figures; they indicate the extent of Methodism throughout the world: Ministers, 48,334; Local Preachers, 104,786; Churches, 89,087; Members, 7,659,285; Sunday Schools, 81,228: Teachers and Officers, 861,392; Scholars 7,077,079; and Adherents, 24,899,421.

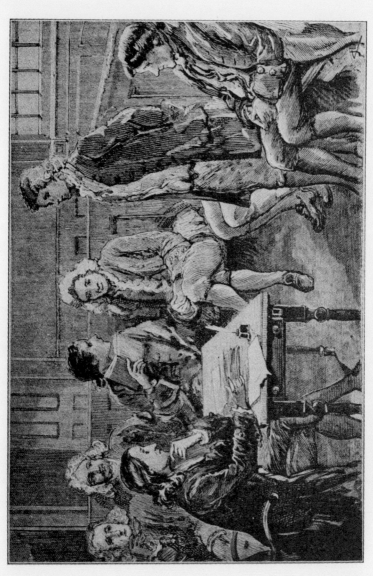

FIRST METHODIST "CLASS MEETING" CALLED BY THAT NAME

Introduction to the Shepherd
Classics Edition

Few persons have ever lived who exerted more positive influence on their time than John Wesley. His prodigious life and work, spanning most of the eighteenth century, epitomized and gave direction to an evangelical revival that changed the face of England, setting in motion forces of righteousness that have had reverberations to the ends of the earth.

Born at Epworth, June 17, 1703, he was the second surviving son of Samuel and Susanna Wesley, and the fifteenth of nineteen children. In the Anglican vicar's home where he grew up, he learned early the importance of sound doctrine and vigorous piety.

At the age of ten, John went to London to attend the Charterhouse School, and seven years later, he entered Christ Church College, Oxford. After graduation he offered himself to become a priest of the Church of England, and was ordained a deacon in 1725. For a while he assisted his father in pastoral work, but meeting with meager success, he returned to his scholarly pursuits at the University, where he had been made a teaching fellow at Lincoln College.

Here Wesley joined his brother, Charles, along with a few other students, in a closely knit fellowship of earnest souls seeking God's will. The group met regularly for study and worship, practiced fasting twice a week, and engaged themselves in a number of benevolent services to the poor. Because of their vigorous discipline they were dubbed in derision "the holy club" or "Methodists."

Following his father's death in 1735, John accepted

an appointment as a missionary to the colonists and Indians living in Georgia. However, his strict adherence to order did not set well with the more easy-going frontiersmen of the new world. A courtship rejection by one of the ladies of the colony added to his difficulties. Finally, after nearly two years of frustration, the broken Wesley returned to England. Typifying his anguish, on shipboard he wrote in his *Journal*, "I went to America to convert the Indians; but O! Who shall convert me?"

Back in London, his longing for spiritual reality eventually led to a little Moravian prayer meeting on Aldersgate Street. There on May 24, 1738, about a quarter before nine, while a layman was reading from Luther's Preface to the Book of Romans, "describing the change which God works in the heart through faith in Christ," Wesley felt his heart "strangely warmed," and received assurance that he was delivered from the law of sin and death. This experience kindled a fire in his life which was to set a nation aflame.

England was in desperate circumstances. Centuries of turmoil had left the people bitter and restless. Poverty was everywhere. Society reeked with moral decay. Making the situation more tragic, the apathetic established church was completely discredited and out of touch with the working masses.

Into this generation of despair, seething on the verge of revolution, John Wesley began to herald a Gospel of free and full salvation—a deliverance which any man can know now through simple faith in the finished work of Jesus Christ. Sophisticated churchmen closed their doors to his preaching. But Wesley, seeing all the world as his parish, "submitted to be more vile," and began to proclaim in the streets and fields the glad tidings of salvation.

Soon the soft-spoken Oxford don in clerical garb, standing scarcely five feet four inches tall, with his long, silken hair blowing in the wind, became a familiar sight across the land. Multitudes were arrested by his message, especially the poor, the outcasts of society, and those disenchanted with the cold religious institutions of the day.

The genius of Wesley, however, was not so much in his preaching, as in the way he followed up those whose hearts were awakened. Persons wanting further instruction were organized into classes, and in turn, these were formed into "circuits" of preaching points largely shepherded by laymen. By this means the growing movement was not restrained by lack of discipline and leadership.

For fifty years Wesley carried his ministry to the people. Hazardous conditions never deterred him from his mission "to reform the nation and to spread scriptural holiness over the land." It is estimated that he traveled 250,000 miles on horseback. During this period he preached 42,000 sermons, an average of more than 15 a week. Still at the age of 87, his eyes dim, his right hand shaking with a lingering fever almost every day, he wrote in his *Journal*: "Blessed be God, I do not slack my labor."

Part of his energy was given to reading and study, particularly the Bible which he revered as the very Word of God. Out of this came a profusion of writings on a wide variety of subjects. Altogether he authored over 400 publications, including Gospel tracts, sermons, appeals, hymns, textbooks, histories, Bible commentaries, and even a medical handbook entitled *Primitive Physick*.

During his undergraduate days in college, in pursuance of the advice of Bishop Taylor in his *Rules for Holy Living and Dying*, Wesley began the practice of recording how he employed the hours of the day. Extracts from these notes were published at different times during his life. From these portions of his *Journal* the present volume was compiled by P. L. Parker in 1902. Though an abbreviated anthology, it seeks to capture the high moments in the larger narrative, and preserves its vivid style and atmosphere.

As a self-portrait of Wesley, this remarkable composition shows better than anything else the manner of man he was, and the temper of the times in which he lived. In its pages you ride up and down the thoroughfares of England; you feel the fresh winds of the countryside on your cheek as he preaches in the open air. There is nothing artificial, nothing far-fetched about the account, but with unassuming honesty, it bears the heart of a man who was determined to make full proof of his ministry.

A few months before Wesley died on March 2, 1791, the last entry in his *Journal* noted that he had exhorted a large congregation in Spitalfields to "put on the whole armor of God." Then in the afternoon, to a still more crowded church at Shadwell, he recorded that he spoke on the truth, "One thing is needful," adding the comment, "and I hope many, even then, resolved to choose the better part."

This was the obsession of his life—the burning desire that every person yield themselves fully to the claims of Christ. As you read here what this commitment meant to the apostle of Methodism, may something of that same urgency be felt to "put on the whole armor of God," and so to "choose the better part."

Robert E. Coleman
Wilmore, Kentucky
July, 1979

JOHN WESLEY'S
JOURNAL

WESLEY'S JOURNAL

THE first entry in Wesley's Journal is that of October 14, 1735. But the following letter, which Wesley published with the first edition of his Journal, precedes it, as it describes the incidents which led to the formation of the Holy Club and to the social activities from which, as the Journal shows, Methodism has evolved.

The letter was written from Oxford in 1732 to Mr. Morgan, whose son is mentioned. It runs thus:

Wesley Begins his Work

In November 1729, at which time I came to reside at Oxford, your son [Mr. Morgan], my brother, myself, and one more, agreed to spend three or four evenings in a week together. Our design was to read over the classics, which we had before read in private, on common nights, and on Sunday some book in divinity. In the summer following, Mr. M. told me he had called at the gaol, to see a man who was condemned for killing his wife; and that, from the talk he had with one of the debtors, he verily believed it would do much good, if any one would be at the pains of now and then speaking with them.

This he so frequently repeated, that on August 24, 1730, my brother and I walked with him to the castle. We were so well satisfied with our conversation there, that we agreed to go thither once or twice a week; which we had not done long, before he desired me to go with him to see a poor woman in the town, who was sick. In this employment too, when we came to reflect upon it, we believed it would be worth while to spend an hour or two in a week; provided the minister of the parish, in which any such person was, were not against it. But that we might not depend wholly on our own judgments, I wrote an account to my father of our whole design; withal begging that he, who had lived seventy years in the world, and seen as much of it as most private men have ever done, would advise us whether we had yet gone too far, and whether we should now stand still, or go forward.

Origin of the Holy Club

In pursuance of [his] directions, I immediately went to Mr. Gerard, the Bishop of Oxford's chaplain, who was likewise the person that took care of the prisoners when any were condemned to die (at other times they were left to their own care): I proposed to him our design of serving them as far as we could, and my own intention to preach there once a month, if the bishop approved of it. He much commended our design, and said he would answer for the bishop's approbation, to whom he would take the first opportunity of mentioning it. It was not long before he informed me he had done so, and that his lordship not only gave his permission, but was greatly pleased with the undertaking, and hoped it would have the desired success.

Soon after, a gentleman of Merton College, who was one of our little company, which now consisted of five persons, acquainted us that he had been much rallied the day before for being a member of the Holy Club;

and that it was become a common topic of mirth at his college, where they had found out several of our customs, to which we were ourselves utter strangers. Upon this I consulted my father again.

.   .   .   .   .

Upon [his] encouragement we still continued to meet together as usual; and to confirm one another, as well as we could, in our resolutions, to communicate as often as we had opportunity (which is here once a week); and do what service we could to our acquaintance, the prisoners, and two or three poor families in the town.

Wesley Sails for America

1735. Tuesday, October 14.—Mr. Benjamin Ingham, of Queen's College, Oxford; Mr. Charles Delamotte, son of a merchant, in London, who had offered himself some days before; my brother, Charles Wesley, and myself, took boat for Gravesend, in order to embark for Georgia.

Our end in leaving our native country was not to avoid want (God having given us plenty of temporal blessings), nor to gain the dung or dross of riches or honour; but singly this—to save our souls; to live wholly to the glory of God. In the afternoon we found the "Simmonds" off Gravesend, and immediately went on board.

Fri. 17.—I began to learn German, in order to converse with the Germans, six-and-twenty of whom we had on board. On Sunday, the weather being fair and calm, we had the morning service on quarter-deck. I now first preached extempore, and then administered the Lord's supper to six or seven communicants.

Mon. 20.—Believing the denying ourselves, even in the smallest instances, might, by the blessing of God, be helpful to us, we wholly left off the use of flesh and wine, and confined ourselves to vegetable food—chiefly rice and biscuit.

Tues. 21.—We sailed from Gravesend. When we were past about half the Goodwin Sands, the wind suddenly failed. Had the calm continued till ebb, the ship had probably been lost. But the gale sprung up again in an hour, and carried us into the Downs.

We now began to be a little regular. Our common way of living was this : From four in the morning till five each of us used private prayer. From five to seven we read the Bible together, carefully comparing it (that we might not lean to our own understandings) with the writings of the earliest ages. At seven we break-fasted. At eight were the public prayers. From nine to twelve I usually learned German, and Mr. Delamotte, Greek. My brother writ sermons, and Mr. Ingham instructed the children. At twelve we met to give an account to one another what we had done since our last meeting, and what we designed to do before our next. About one we dined.

Life on Board

The time from dinner to four we spent in reading to those whom each of us had taken in charge, or in speaking to them severally, as need required. At four were the evening prayers ; when either the second lesson was explained (as it always was in the morning), or the children were catechised and instructed before the congregation. From five to six we again used private prayer. From six to seven I read in our cabin to two or three of the passengers (of whom there were about eighty English on board), and each of my brethren to a few more in theirs.

At seven I joined with the Germans in their public service, while Mr. Ingham was reading between the decks to as many as desired to hear. At eight we met again to exhort and instruct one another. Between nine and ten we went to bed, where neither the roaring of the sea nor the motion of the ship could take away the refreshing sleep which God gave us.

Fri. 31.—We sailed out of the Downs. At eleven at night I was waked by a great noise. I soon found there was no danger. But the bare apprehension of it gave me a lively conviction what manner of men those ought to be who are every moment on the brink of eternity.

Sat. Nov. 1.—We came to St. Helen's harbour, and the next day into Cowes road. The wind was fair, but we waited for the man-of-war which was to sail with us. This was a happy opportunity of instructing our fellow travellers.

Sun. 23.—At night I was awaked by the tossing of the ship and roaring of the wind, and plainly showed I was unfit, for I was unwilling, to die.

Wed. Dec. 10.—We sailed from Cowes, and in the afternoon passed the Needles. Here the ragged rocks, with the waves dashing and foaming at the foot of them, and the white side of the island rising to such a height, perpendicular from the beach, gave a strong idea ot " Him that spanneth the heavens, and holdeth the waters in the hollow of His hand ! "

1736. Thur. Jan. 15.—Complaint being made to Mr. Oglethorpe, of the unequal distribution of the water among the passengers, he appointed new officers to take charge of it. At this the old ones and their friends were highly exasperated against us, to whom they imputed the change,

Sat. 17.—Many people were very impatient at the
contrary wind.   At seven in the evening they were quieted
by a storm.   It rose higher and higher till nine.   About
nine the sea broke over us from stem to stern; burst
through the windows of the state cabin, where three or
four of us were, and covered us all over, though a bureau
sheltered me from the main shock.   About eleven I lay
down in the great cabin, and in a short time fell asleep,
though very uncertain whether I should wake alive, and
much ashamed of my unwillingness to die.   O how pure
in heart must he be, who would rejoice to appear before
God at a moment's warning !   Toward morning, " He
rebuked the winds and the sea, and there was a great
calm."

Memorable Atlantic Storms

Fri. 23.—In the evening another storm began.   In
the morning it increased, so that they were forced to let
the ship drive.   I could not but say to myself, " How is
it that thou hast no faith ? " being still unwilling to die.
About one in the afternoon, almost as soon as I had
stepped out of the great cabin-door, the sea did not
break as usual, but came with a full, smooth tide over
the side of the ship.   I was vaulted over with water in
a moment, and so stunned that I scarce expected to lift
up my head again, till the sea should give up her dead.
But thanks be to God, I received no hurt at all.   About
midnight the storm ceased.

Sun. 25.—At noon our third storm began.   At four
it was more violent than before.   At seven I went to
the Germans.   I had long before observed the great
seriousness of their behaviour.   Of their humility they
had given a continual proof, by performing those servile
offices for the other passengers, which none of the

English would undertake; for which they desired, and would receive no pay, saying, "it was good for their proud hearts," and "their loving Saviour had done more for them." And every day had given them an occasion of showing a meekness, which no injury could move. If they were pushed, struck, or thrown down, they rose again and went away; but no complaint was found in their mouth. There was now an opportunity of trying whether they were delivered from the spirit of fear, as well as from that of pride, anger and revenge.

In the midst of the psalm wherewith their service began, the sea broke over, split the mainsail in pieces, covered the ship, and poured in between the decks, as if the great deep had already swallowed us up. A terrible screaming began among the English. The Germans calmly sung on. I asked one of them afterwards, "Was you not afraid?" He answered, "I thank God, no." I asked, "But were not your women and children afraid?" He replied, mildly, "No; our women and children are not afraid to die."

Fri. 30.—We had another storm, which did us no other harm than splitting the fore-sail. Our bed being wet, I laid me down on the floor, and slept sound till morning. And, I believe, I shall not find it needful to go to bed (as it is called) any more.

Sun. Feb. 1.—We spoke with a ship of Carolina; and Wednesday, 4, came within soundings. About noon, the trees were visible from the masts, and in the afternoon from the main deck. In the evening lesson were these words: "A great door, and effectual, is opened." O let no one shut it!

Thur. 5.—Between two and three in the afternoon, God brought us all safe into the Savannah river. We cast anchor near Tybee Island, where the groves of pines, running along the shore, made an agreeable prospect, showing, as it were, the bloom of spring in the depth of winter.

Wesley Arrives in Georgia

Fri. 6.—About eight in the morning, we first set foot on American ground. It was a small uninhabited island, over against Tybee. Mr. Oglethorpe led us to a rising ground, where we all kneeled down to give thanks. He then took boat for Savannah. When the rest of the people were come on shore, we called our little flock together to prayers.

Sat. 7.—Mr. Oglethorpe returned from Savannah with Mr. Spangenberg, one of the pastors of the Germans. I soon found what spirit he was of; and asked his advice with regard to my own conduct. He said, "My brother, I must first ask you one or two questions. Have you the witness within yourself? Does the Spirit of God bear witness with your spirit, that you are a child of God?" I was surprised, and knew not what to answer. He observed it, and asked, "Do you know Jesus Christ?" I paused, and said, "I know he is the Saviour of the world." "True," replied he; "but do you know he has saved you?" I answered, "I hope he has died to save me." He only added, "Do you know yourself?" I said, "I do." But I fear they were vain words.

Sat. 14.—About one, Tomo Chachi, his nephew Thleeanouhee, his wife Sinauky, with two more women, and two or three Indian children, came on board. As soon as we came in, they all rose and shook us by the hand; and Tomo Chachi (one Mr. Musgrove interpreted) spoke as follows:

"I am glad you are come. When I was in England, I desired that some would speak the great word to me

and my nation then desired to hear it; but now we are
all in confusion. Yet I am glad you are come. I will
go up and speak to the wise men of our nation; and I
hope they will hear. But we would not be made
Christians as the Spaniards make Christians: we would
be taught, before we are baptized."

I answered, "There is but One, He that sitteth in
heaven, who is able to teach man wisdom. Though we
are come so far, we know not whether He will please to
teach you by us or no. If He teaches you, you will learn
wisdom, but we can do nothing." We then withdrew.

Thur. 19.—My brother and I took boat, and, passing
by Savannah, went to pay our first visit in America to
the poor heathens.

Begins his Ministry at Savannah

Sun. March 7.—I entered upon my ministry at
Savannah, by preaching on the epistle for the day,
being the thirteenth of the first of Corinthians. In the
second lesson (Luke xviii.) was our Lord's prediction of
the treatment which he himself (and, consequently, his
followers) was to meet with from the world. "Verily I
say unto you, There is no man that hath left house, or
friends, or brethren, or wife, or children, for the kingdom
of God's sake, who shall not receive manifold more in
this present time, and in the world to come life everlasting."

Yet, notwithstanding these declarations of our Lord—
notwithstanding my own repeated experience—notwithstanding the experience of all the sincere followers of
Christ whom I have ever talked with, read or heard of;
nay, and the reason of the thing evincing to a demonstration that all who love not the light must hate Him
who is continually labouring to pour it in upon them;

I do here bear witness against myself, that when I saw the number of people crowding into the church, the deep attention with which they received the word, and the seriousness that afterwards sat on all their faces; I could scarce refrain from giving the lie to experience and reason and Scripture all together.

I could hardly believe that the greater, the far greater part of this attentive, serious people would hereafter trample under foot that word, and say all manner of evil falsely of him that spake it.

Mon. 15.—Mr. Quincy going for Carolina, I removed into the minister's house. It is large enough for a larger family than ours, and has many conveniences, besides a good garden.

Tues. 30.—Mr. Ingham, coming from Frederica, brought me letters, pressing me to go thither. The next day Mr. Delamotte and I began to try, whether life might not as well be sustained by one sort as by variety of food. We chose to make the experiment with bread; and were never more vigorous and healthy than while we tasted nothing else.

"I Waked under Water"

Sun. April 4.—About four in the afternoon I set out for Frederica, in a pettiawga—a sort of flat-bottomed barge. The next evening we anchored near Skidoway Island, where the water, at flood, was twelve or fourteen foot deep. I wrapped myself up from head to foot, in a large cloak, to keep off the sand flies, and lay down on the quarter-deck. Between one and two I waked under water, being so fast asleep that I did not find where I was till my mouth was full of it. Having left my cloak, I know not how, upon deck, I swam round to the other side of the pettiawga, where a boat was tied.

and climbed up by the rope without any hurt, more than wetting my clothes.

Sat. 17.—Not finding, as yet, any door open for the pursuing our main design, we considered in what manner we might be most useful to the little flock at Savannah. And we agreed: 1. To advise the more serious among them to form themselves into a sort of little society, and to meet once or twice a week, in order to reprove, instruct, and exhort one another. 2. To select out of these a smaller number for a more intimate union with each other, which might be forwarded, partly by our conversing singly with each, and partly by inviting them all together to our house; and this, accordingly, we determined to do every Sunday in the afternoon.

Mon. May 10.—I began visiting my parishioners in order, from house to house; for which I set apart (the time when they cannot work, because of the heat, viz.) from twelve till three in the afternoon.

Thur. June 17.—An officer of a man-of-war, walking just behind us, with two or three of his acquaintance, cursed and swore exceedingly; but upon my reproving him, seemed much moved, and gave me many thanks.

Tues. 22.—Observing much coldness in M. ——'s behaviour, I asked him the reason of it. He answered, " I like nothing you do. All your sermons are satires upon particular persons, therefore I will never hear you more; and all the people are of my mind, for we won't hear ourselves abused.

" Beside, they say, they are Protestants. But as for you, they cannot tell what religion you are of. They never heard of such a religion before. They do not know what to make of it. And then your private behaviour: all the quarrels that have been here since you came, have been 'long of you. Indeed there is neither man nor woman in the town, who minds a word you say. And so you may preach long enough; but nobody will come to hear you."

He was too warm for hearing an answer. So I had nothing to do but to thank him for his openness, and walk away.

Talks to the Indians

Wed. 30.—I hoped a door was opened for going up immediately to the Choctaws, the least polished, that is, the least corrupted, of all the Indian nations. B. pun my informing Mr. Oglethorpe of our design, he objected, not only the danger of being intercepted or killed by the French there; but much more, the inexpediency of leaving Savannah destitute of a minister. These objections I related to our brethren in the evening, who were all of opinion, "We ought not to go yet."

Thur. July 1.—The Indians had an audience; and another on Saturday, when Chicali, their head-man, dined with Mr. Oglethorpe. After dinner, I asked the grey-headed old man, what he thought he was made for. He said, "He that is above knows what he made us for. We know nothing. We are in the dark. But white men know much. And yet white men build great houses, as if they were to live for ever. But white men cannot live for ever. In a little time, white men will be dust as well as I." I told him, "If red men will learn the good book, they may know as much as white men. But neither we nor you can understand that book, unless we are taught by Him that is above: and He will not teach, unless you avoid what you already know is not good." He answered, "I believe that. He will not teach us while our hearts are not white. And our men do what they know is not good: they kill their own children. And our women do what they know is not good : they kill the child before it is born. Therefore He that is above does not send us the good book."

Mon. 26.—My brother and I set out for Charlestown, in order to his embarking for England ; but the wind being contrary, we did not reach Port-Royal, forty miles from Savannah, till Wednesday evening. The next morning we left it. But the wind was so high in the afternoon, as we were crossing the neck of St. Helena's sound, that our oldest sailor cried out, " Now every one must take care for himself." I told him, " God would take care for us all." Almost as soon as the words were spoken, the mast fell. I kept on the edge of the boat, to be clear of her when she sunk (which we expected every moment), though with little prospect of swimming ashore, against such a wind and sea. But " how is it that thou hadst no faith ? " The moment the mast fell, two men caught it, and pulled it into the boat ; the other three rowed with all their might, and "God gave command to the wind and seas "; so that in an hour we were safe on land.

Fearless of Rains and Dews

Mon. Aug. 2.—I set out for the Lieutenant-Governor's seat, about thirty miles from Charlestown, to deliver Mr. Oglethorpe's letters. It stands very pleasantly, on a little hill, with a vale on either side, in one of which is a thick wood ; the other is planted with rice and Indian corn. I designed to have gone back by Mr. Skeen's, who has about fifty Christian negroes. But my horse tiring, I was obliged to return the straight way to Charles-town.

I had sent the boat we came in back to Savannah,

expecting a passage thither myself in Colonel Bull's. His not going so soon, I went to Ashley-Ferry on Thursday, intending to walk to Port-Royal. But Mr. Belinger not only provided me a horse, but rode with me himself ten miles, and sent his son with me to Cumbee-Ferry, twenty miles farther; whence, having hired horses and a guide, I came to Beaufort (or Port Royal) the next evening. We took boat in the morning; but, the wind being contrary, and very high, did not reach Savannah till Sunday, in the afternoon.

Finding Mr. Oglethorpe was gone, I stayed only a day at Savannah; and leaving Mr. Ingham and Dela-motte there, set out on Tuesday morning for Frederica. In walking to Thunderbolt I was in so heavy a shower, that all my clothes were as wet as if I had gone through the river. On which occasion I cannot but observe that vulgar error, concerning the hurtfulness of the rains and dews of America. I have been thoroughly wet with these rains more than once; yet without any harm at all. And I have lain many nights in the open air, and received all the dews that fell; and so, I believe, might any one, if his constitution was not impaired by the softness of a genteel education.

Desires to Go Among the Indians

Tues. Nov. 23.—Mr. Oglethorpe sailed for England, leaving Mr. Ingham, Mr. Delamotte, and me, at Savannah; but with less prospect of preaching to the Indians than we had the first day we set foot in America. Whenever I mentioned it, it was immediately replied, " You cannot leave Savannah without a minister."

To this indeed my plain answer was, " I know not that I am under any obligation to the contrary. I never promised to stay here one month. I openly declared both before, at, and ever since my coming hither, that I neither would nor could take charge of the English any longer than till I could go among the Indians." If it was said, " But did not the trustees of Georgia appoint you to be minister of Savannah ? " I replied, " They did; but it was not done by my solicitation: it was done without either my desire or knowledge. Therefore I cannot conceive that appointment to lay me under any obligation of continuing there any longer than till a door is opened to the heathens; and this I expressly declared at the time I consented to accept of that appointment."

But though I had no other obligation not to leave Savannah now, yet that of love I could not break through: I could not resist the importunate request of the more serious parishioners, " to watch over their souls yet a little longer, till some one came who might supply my place." And this I the more willingly did, because the time was not come to preach the Gospel of peace to the heathens; all their nations being in a ferment; and Paustoobee and Mingo Mattaw having told me, in terms, in my own house, " Now our enemies are all about us, and we can do nothing but fight; but if the beloved ones should ever give us to be at peace, then we would hear the great word."

Wed. Dec. 23.—Mr. Delamotte and I, with a guide, set out to walk to the Cowpen. When we had walked two or three hours, our guide told us plainly, he did not know where we were. However, believing it could not be far off, we thought it best to go on. In an hour or two we came to a cypress-swamp, which lay directly across our way : there was not time to walk back to Savannah before night; so we walked through it, the water being about breast high.

By the time we had gone a mile beyond it, we were
out of all path; and it being now past sunset, we sat
down, intending to make a fire, and to stay there till
morning; but finding our tinder wet, we were at a stand.
I advised to walk on still; but my companions, being
faint and weary, were for lying down, which we accordingly did about six o'clock; the ground was as wet as
our clothes, which, it being a sharp frost, were soon
froze together; however, I slept till six in the morning.
There fell a heavy dew in the night, which covered us
over as white as snow. Within an hour after sunrise,
we came to a plantation; and in the evening, without
any hurt, to Savannah.

Begins to Learn Spanish

1737. Fri. March 4.—I writ the trustees for Georgia
an account of our year's expense, from March 1, 1736, to
March 1, 1737; which, deducting extraordinary expenses,
such as repairing the parsonage house, and journeys to
Frederica, amounted, for Mr. Delamotte and me, to
£44 4s. 4d.

Mon. April 4.—I began learning Spanish, in order to
converse with my Jewish parishioners; some of whom
seem nearer the mind that was in Christ than many of
those who call him Lord.

Tues. 12.—Being determined, if possible, to put a
stop to the proceedings of one in Carolina, who had
married several of my parishioners without either banns
or licence, and declared he would do so still, I set out
in a sloop for Charlestown. I landed there on Thursday,
and related the case to Mr. Garden, the Bishop of London's
Commissary, who assured me, he would take care no
such irregularity should be committed for the future.

Sun. July 3.—Immediately after the holy communion,

I mentioned to Mrs. Williamson (Mr. Causton's niece) some things which I thought reprovable in her behaviour. At this she appeared extremely angry; said she did not expect such usage from me; and at the turn of the street, through which we were walking home, went abruptly away. The next day Mrs. Causton endeavoured to excuse her; told me she was exceedingly grieved for what had passed the day before, and desired me to tell her in writing what I disliked; which I accordingly did the day following.

But first I sent Mr. Causton the following note:

" SIR,

" To this hour you have shown yourself my friend; I ever have and ever shall acknowledge it. And it is my earnest desire that He who hath hitherto given me this blessing, would continue it still.

" But this cannot be, unless you will allow me one request, which is not so easy an one as it appears: do not condemn me for doing, in the execution of my office, what I think it my duty to do.

" If you can prevail upon yourself to allow me this, even when I act without respect of persons, I am persuaded there will never be, at least not long, any misunderstanding between us. For even those who seek it shall, I trust, find no occasion against me, ' except it be concerning the law of my God.'

" I am, &c.

" July 5, 1737."

Wed. 6.—Mr. Causton came to my house with Mr. Bailiff Parker and Mr. Recorder, and warmly asked, " How could you possibly think I should condemn you for executing any part of your office?" I said short, " Sir, what if I should think it the duty of my office to

repel one of your family from the holy communion?"
He replied, "If you repel me or my wife, I shall require
a legal reason.   But I shall trouble myself about none
else.   Let them look to themselves."

Warrant for Wesley's Arrest

Sun. Aug. 7.—I repelled Mrs. Williamson from the
holy communion.   And Monday, 8, Mr. Recorder, of
Savannah, issued out the warrant following:

"Georgia.   Savannah ss.

"*To all Constables, Tithingmen, and others, whom these
may concern :*

"YOU, and each of you, are hereby required to take
the body of John Wesley, Clerk:

" And bring him before one of the Bailiffs of the said
town to answer the complaint of William Williamson and
Sophia, his wife, for defaming the said Sophia, and refusing to administer to her the sacrament of the Lord's
supper in a public congregation without cause; by
which the said William Williamson is damaged one
thousand pound sterling; and for so doing, this is your
warrant, certifying what you are to do in the premises.
Given under my hand and seal the 8th day of August,
Anno. Dom. 1737.   THO. CHRISTIE."

Tues. 9.—Mr. Jones, the constable, served the
warrant, and carried me before Mr. Bailiff Parker and
Mr. Recorder.   My answer to them was, that the giving
or refusing the Lord's supper being a matter purely
ecclesiastical, I could not acknowledge their power to
interrogate me upon it.   Mr. Parker told me: "However, you must appear at the next Court, holden for
Savannah."   Mr. Williamson, who stood by, said:
"Gentlemen, I desire Mr. Wesley may give bail for his

appearance." But Mr. Parker immediately replied : " Sir, Mr. Wesley's word is sufficient."

Thur. 11.—Mr. Causton came to my house, and, among many other sharp words, said : " Make an end of this matter ; thou hadst best. My niece to be used thus ! I have drawn the sword, and I will never sheath it till I have satisfaction."

Soon after, he added: " Give the reasons of your repelling her before the whole congregation." I answered: " Sir, if you insist upon it, I will ; and so you may be pleased to tell her." He said, " Write to her, and tell her so yourself." I said, " I will "; and after he went I wrote as follows :

" *To Mrs. Sophia Williamson.*

" AT Mr. Causton's request, I write once more. The rules whereby I proceed are these :

" ' So many as intend to be partakers of the holy communion, shall signify their names to the curate, at least some time the day before.' This you did not do.

" ' And if any of these have done any wrong to his neighbours, by word or deed, so that the congregation be thereby offended, the curate shall advertise him that in any wise he presume not to come to the Lord's table until he hath openly declared himself to have truly repented.'

" If you offer yourself at the Lord's table on Sunday, I will advertise you (as I have done more than once) wherein you have done wrong. And when you have openly declared yourself to have truly repented, I will administer to you the mysteries of God.

" JOHN WESLEY.

" August 11, 1737."

Mr. Delamotte carrying this, Mr. Causton said, among many other warm sayings : " I am the person that am injured. The affront is offered to me; and I will espouse the cause of my niece. I am ill-used, and I will have satisfaction, if it be to be had in the world."

Which way this satisfaction was to be had, I did not yet conceive; but on Friday and Saturday it began to appear: Mr. Causton declared to many persons that " Mr. Wesley had repelled Sophy from the holy communion purely out of revenge, because he had made proposals of marriage to her which she rejected, and married Mr. Williamson."

The Jury's Charge against Wesley

Tues. 16.—Mrs. Williamson swore to and signed an affidavit insinuating much more than it asserted; but asserting that Mr. Wesley had many times proposed marriage to her, all which proposals she had rejected. Of this I desired a copy. Mr. Causton replied : " Sir, you may have one from any of the newspapers in America."

On Thursday and Friday was delivered out a list of twenty-six men, who were to meet as a grand jury on Monday, the 22nd. But this list was called in the next day, and twenty-four names added to it. Of this grand jury (forty-four of whom only met), one was a Frenchman, who did not understand English; one a Papist, one a professed infidel, three Baptists, sixteen or seventeen others Dissenters, and several others who had personal quarrels against me, and had openly vowed revenge.

To this grand jury, on Monday, the 22nd, Mr. Causton gave a long and earnest charge, " to beware of spiritual tyranny, and to oppose the new, illegal authority which was usurped over their consciences." Then Mrs. Williamson's affidavit was read; after which,

Mr. Causton delivered to the grand jury a paper, entitled :

" A list of grievances, presented by the grand jury for Savannah, this   day of August, 1737."

This the majority of the grand jury altered in some particulars, and on Thursday, September 1, delivered it again to the court, under the form of two present-ments, containing ten bills, which were then read to the people.

Herein they asserted, upon oath, " That John Wesley, clerk, had broken the laws of the realm, contrary to the peace of our Sovereign Lord the King, his crown and dignity.

" 1. By speaking and writing to Mrs. Williamson, against her husband's consent.

" 2. By repelling her from the holy communion.

" 3. By not declaring his adherence to the Church England.

" 4. By dividing the morning service on Sundays.

" 5. By refusing to baptize Mr. Parker's child, other-wise than by dipping, except the parents would certify it was weak, and not able to bear it.

" 6. By repelling William Gough from the holy communion.

" 7. By refusing to read the burial service over the body of Nathaniel Polhill.

" 8. By calling himself Ordinary of Savannah.

" 9. By refusing to receive William Aglionby as a godfather, only because he was not a communicant.

" 10. By refusing Jacob Matthews for the same reason ; and baptizing an Indian trader's child with only two sponsors." (This, I own, was wrong ; for I ought, at all hazards, to have refused baptizing it till he had procured a third.)

Fri. Sep. 2.—Was the third court at which I appeared since my being carried before Mr. P. and the Recorder.

I now moved for an immediate hearing on the first bill, being the only one of a civil nature; but it was refused. I made the same motion in the afternoon, but was put off till the next court-day.

On the next court-day I appeared again, as also at the two courts following, but could not be heard, because (the Judge said) Mr. Williamson was gone out of town.

The sense of the minority of the grand jurors themselves (for they were by no means unanimous) concerning these presentments may appear from the following paper, which they transmitted to the trustees:

To the Honourable the Trustees for Georgia.

"Whereas two presentments have been made: the one of August 23, the other of August 31, by the grand jury for the town and county of Savannah, in Georgia, against John Wesley, Clerk.

"We, whose names are underwritten, being members of the said grand jury, do humbly beg leave to signify our dislike of the said presentments; being, by many and divers circumstances, thoroughly persuaded in ourselves that the whole charge against Mr. Wesley is an artifice of Mr. Causton's, designed rather to blacken the character of Mr. Wesley, than to free the colony from religious tyranny, as he was pleased, in his charge to us, to term it. But as these circumstances will be too tedious to trouble your Honours with, we shall only beg leave to give the reasons of our dissent from the particular bills. . . . .

Fri. Oct. 7.—I consulted my friends, whether God did not call me to return to England. The reason for which I left it had now no force; there being no possibility, as

yet, of instructing the Indians; neither had I, as yet,
found or heard of any Indians on the continent of
America, who had the least desire of being instructed.
And as to Savannah, having never engaged myself, either
by word or letter, to stay there a day longer than I
should judge convenient, nor ever taken charge of the
people any otherwise than as in my passage to the
heathens, I looked upon myself to be fully discharged
therefrom, by the vacating of that design. Besides, there
was a probability of doing more service to that unhappy
people in England, than I could do in Georgia, by representing, without fear or favour, to the trustees the real
state the colony was in.   After deeply considering these
things, they were unanimous, "that I ought to go; but
not yet." So I laid the thoughts of it aside for the
present; being persuaded, that when the time was
come, God would "make the way plain before my face."

Why Wesley Left Georgia

Thur. Nov. 3.—I appeared again at the court, holden
on that day; and again, at the court held Tuesday,
November 22.   On which day Mr. Causton desired to
speak with me.   He then read me some affidavits which
had been made September 15, last past; in one of which
it was affirmed, that I then abused Mr. Causton in his
own house, calling him liar, villain, and so on.   It was
now likewise repeated before several persons, which
indeed I had forgot, that I had been reprimanded at the
last court, for an enemy to, and hinderer of, the public
peace.

I again consulted my friends, who agreed with me,
that the time we looked for was now come.   And the
next morning, calling on Mr. Causton, I told him, I
designed to set out for England immediately.   I set up

an advertisement in the Great Square to the same effect and quietly prepared for my journey.

Fri. Dec. 2.—I proposed to set out for Carolina about noon, the tide then serving. But about ten, the magistrates sent for me, and told me, I must not go out of the province; for I had not answered the allegations laid against me. I replied, "I have appeared at six or seven courts successively, in order to answer them. But I was not suffered so to do, when I desired it time after time." Then they said, however, I must not go, unless I would give security to answer those allegations at their court. I asked, "What security?" After consulting together about two hours, the Recorder showed me a kind of bond, engaging me, under a penalty of fifty pounds, to appear at their court when I should be required. He added, "But Mr. Williamson too has desired of us that you should give bail to answer his action." I then told him plainly, "Sir, you use me very ill, and so you do the trustees. I will give neither any bond, nor any bail at all. You know your business, and I know mine."

In the afternoon, the magistrates published an order, requiring all the officers and sentinels to prevent my going out of the province; and forbidding any person to assist me so to do. Being now only a prisoner at large, in a place where I know by experience, every day would give fresh opportunity to procure evidence of words I never said, and actions I never did; I saw clearly the hour was come for leaving this place : and as soon as evening prayers were over, about eight o'clock, the tide then serving, I shook off the dust of my feet, and left Georgia, after having preached the Gospel there (not as I ought, but as I was able) one year and nearly nine months.

Sat. 3.—We came to Purrysburg early in the morning, and endeavoured to procure a guide to Port-Royal. But none being to be had, we set out without one, an hour before sunrise. After walking two or three hours, we met with an old man, who led us into a small path, near which was a line of blazed trees (that is, marked by cutting off part of the bark), by following which, he said, we might easily come to Port-Royal in five or six hours.

Lost in the Woods

We were four in all; one of whom intended to go to England with me; the other two to settle in Carolina. About eleven we came into a large swamp, where we wandered about till near two. We then found another blaze, and pursued it, till it divided into two: one of these we followed through an almost impassable thicket, a mile beyond which it ended. We made through the thicket again, and traced the other blaze till that ended too. It now grew toward sunset; so we sat down, faint and weary, having had no food all day, except a gingerbread cake, which I had taken in my pocket. A third of this we had divided among us at noon; another third we took now; the rest we reserved for the morning; but we had met with no water all the day. Thrusting a stick into the ground, and finding the end of it moist, two of our company fell a digging with their hands, and, at about three feet depth, found water. We thanked God, drank, and were refreshed. The night was sharp: however, there was no complaining among us; but after having commended ourselves to God, we lay down close together, and (I at least) slept till near six in the morning.

Sun. 4.—God renewing our strength, we arose neither

faint nor weary, and resolved to make one trial more, to find out a path to Port-Royal. We steered due east; but finding neither path nor blaze, and the woods growing thicker and thicker, we judged it would be our best course to return, if we could, by the way we came. The day before, in the thickest part of the woods, I had broke many young trees, I knew not why, as we walked along: these we found a great help in several places, where no path was to be seen; and between one and two God brought us safe to Benjamin Arieu's house, the old man we left the day before.

In the evening I read French prayers to a numerous family, a mile from Arieu's; one of whom undertook to guide us to Port-Royal. In the morning we set out. About sunset, we asked our guide, if he knew where he was; who frankly answered, "No." However, we pushed on till, about seven, we came to a plantation; and the next evening, after many difficulties and delays, we landed on Port-Royal island.

Wed. 7.—We walked to Beaufort; where Mr. Jones, the minister of Beaufort, with whom I lodged during my short stay here, gave me a lively idea of the old English hospitality. On Thursday Mr. Delamotte came; with whom, on Friday, the 9th, I took boat for Charles-Town. After a slow passage, by reason of contrary winds, and some conflict (our provisions falling short) with hunger as well as cold, we came thither early in the morning, on Tuesday, the 13th.

Farewell to America

Thur. 22.—I took my leave of America (though, if it please God, not for ever), going on board the "Samuel," Captain Percy, with a young gentleman who had been a few months in Carolina, one of

my parishioners of Savannah, and a Frenchman, late
of Purrysburg, who was escaped thence with the skin
of his teeth.

Sat. 24.—We sailed over Charles-Town bar, and
about noon lost sight of land.

The next day the wind was fair, but high, as it was
on Sunday, 25, when the sea affected me more than
it had done in the sixteen weeks of our passage to
America. I was obliged to lie down the greatest part
of the day, being easy only in that posture.

Mon. 26.—I began instructing a Negro lad in the
principles of Christianity. The next day I resolved
to break off living delicately, and return to my old
simplicity of diet; and after I did so, neither my stomach
nor my head much complained of the motion of the
ship.

1738. Sun. Jan. 1.—All in the ship, except the captain
and steersman, were present both at the morning and
evening service, and appeared as deeply attentive as
even the poor people of Frederica did, while the word
of God was new to their ears. And it may be, one
or two among these likewise may " bring forth fruit with
patience."

Mon. 2.—Being sorrowful and very heavy (though I
could give no particular reason for it), and utterly
unwilling to speak close to any of my little flock (about
twenty persons), I was in doubt whether my neglect of
them was not one cause of my own heaviness. In the
evening, therefore, I began instructing the cabin-boy;
after which I was much easier.

I went several times the following days, with a design
to speak to the sailors, but could not. I mean, I was
quite averse from speaking; I could not see how to
make an occasion, and it seemed quite absurd to speak

without. Is not this what men commonly mean by, " I could not speak?" And is this a sufficient cause of silence, or no? Is it a prohibition from the good spirit? or a temptation from nature, or the evil one?

Sat. 7.—I began to read and explain some passages of the Bible to the young Negro. The next morning, another Negro who was on board desired to be a hearer too. From them I went to the poor Frenchman, who, understanding no English, had none else in the ship with whom he could converse. And from this time, I read and explained to him a chapter in the Testament every morning.

The Voyage to England

Fri. 13.—We had a thorough storm, which obliged us to shut all close; the sea breaking over the ship continually. I was at first afraid; but cried to God, and was strengthened. Before ten, I lay down: I bless God, without fear. About midnight we were awaked by a confused noise of seas and wind and men's voices, the like to which I had never heard before. The sound of the sea breaking over and against the sides of the ship, I could compare to nothing but large cannon, or American thunder. The rebounding, starting, quivering motion of the ship much resembled what is said of earthquakes.

The captain was upon deck in an instant. But his men could not hear what he said. It blew a proper hurricane; which beginning at south-west, then went west, north-west, north, and, in a quarter an hour, round by the east to the south-west point again. At the same time the sea running, as they term it, mountain-high, and that from many different points at once, the ship would not obey the helm; nor indeed could the steers-

man, through the violent rain, see the compass. So he
was forced to let her run before the wind, and in half an
hour the stress of the storm was over.

Tues. 24.—We spoke with two ships, outward-bound,
from whom we had the welcome news of our wanting
but one hundred and sixty leagues of the Land's-end.
My mind was now full of thought; part of which I writ
down as follows :

"I went to America, to convert the Indians; but O!
who shall convert me ? who, what is he that will deliver
me from this evil heart of mischief? I have a fair
summer religion. I can talk well; nay, and believe
myself, while no danger is near; but let death look me
in the face, and my spirit is troubled. Nor can I say,
'To die is gain!'

> 'I have a sin of fear, that when I've spun
> My last thread, I shall perish on the shore!'

"I think, verily, if the Gospel be true, I am safe : for
I not only have given, and do give, all my goods to feed
the poor; I not only give my body to be burned,
drowned, or whatever God shall appoint for me; but
I follow after charity (though not as I ought, yet as I
can), if haply I may attain it. I now believe the Gospel
is true. 'I show my faith by my works,' by staking my
all upon it. I would do so again and again a thousand
times, if the choice were still to make.

"Whoever sees me, sees I would be a Christian.
Therefore 'are my ways not like other men's ways.'
Therefore I have been, I am, I am content to be, 'a
by-word, a proverb of reproach.' But in a storm I
think, 'What, if the Gospel be not true? Then thou
art of all men most foolish. For what hast thou given
thy goods, thy ease, thy friends, thy reputation, thy
country, thy life? For what art thou wandering over

the face of the earth?—A dream! a cunningly-devised
fable!'

"O! who will deliver me from this fear of death?
What shall I do? Where shall I fly from it? Should
I fight against it by thinking, or by not thinking of it?
A wise man advised me some time since, 'Be still and
go on.' Perhaps this is best, to look upon it as my
cross; when it comes, to let it humble me, and quicken
all my good resolutions, especially that of praying without ceasing; and at other times, to take no thought
about it, but quietly to go on 'in the work of the
Lord.'"

Lands at Deal

We went on with a small, fair wind, till Thursday in
the afternoon; and then sounding, found a whitish sand
at seventy-five fathom: but having had no observation
for several days, the captain began to be uneasy, fearing
we might either get unawares into the Bristol Channel,
or strike in the night on the rocks of Scilly.

Sat. 28.—Was another cloudy day; but about ten in
the morning, the wind continuing southerly, the clouds
began to fly just contrary to the wind, and, to the surprise of us all, sunk down under the sun, so that at
noon we had an exact observation; and by this we
found we were as well as we could desire, about eleven
leagues south of Scilly.

Sun. 29.—We saw English land once more; which,
about noon, appeared to be the Lizard-Point. We ran
by it with a fair wind; and at noon, the next day, made
the west end of the Isle of Wight.

Here the wind turned against us, and in the evening
blew fresh, so that we expected (the tide being likewise
strong against us) to be driven some leagues backward

in the night : but in the morning, to our great surprise, we saw Beachy-Head just before us, and found we had gone forwards near forty miles.

Toward evening was a calm ; but in the night a strong north wind brought us safe into the Downs. The day before, Mr. Whitefield had sailed out, neither of us then knowing anything of the other. At four in the morning we took boat, and in half an hour landed at Deal: it being Wednesday, February 1, the anniversary festival in Georgia for Mr. Oglethorpe's landing there.

It is now two years and almost four months since I left my native country, and in order to teach the Georgian Indians the nature of Christianity: but what have I learned myself in the mean time? Why (what I the least of all suspected), that I who went to America to convert others, was never myself converted to God.* "I am not mad," though I thus speak ; but "I speak the words of truth and soberness " ; if haply some of those who still dream may awake, and see, that as I am, so are they.

In London Again

Wednesday, Feb. 1.—After reading prayers and explaining a portion of Scripture to a large company at the inn, I left Deal, and came in the evening to Feversham.

I here read prayers, and explained the second lesson to a few of those who were called Christians, but were indeed more savage in their behaviour than the wildest Indians I have yet met with.

Fri. 3.—I came to Mr. Delamotte's, at Blendon, where I expected a cold reception. But God had prepared the way before me ; and I no sooner mentioned

---

* I am not sure of this.

my name, than I was welcomed in such a manner as constrained me to say : " Surely God is in this place, and I knew it not ! Blessed be ye of the Lord! Ye have shown more kindness in the latter end than in the beginning."

In the evening I came once more to London, whence I had been absent two years and near four months.

Many reasons I have to bless God, though the design I went upon did not take effect, for my having been carried into that strange land, contrary to all my preceding resolutions. Hereby I trust He hath in some measure "humbled me and proved me, and shown me what was in my heart." Hereby I have been taught to "beware of men." Hereby I am come to know assuredly that if "in all our ways we acknowledge God, he will," where reason fails, " direct our path " by lot, or by the other means which he knoweth. Hereby I am delivered from the fear of the sea, which I had both dreaded and abhorred from my youth.

Hereby God has given me to know many of his servants ; particularly those of the Church of Hernhuth. Hereby my passage is opened to the writings of holy men in the German, Spanish, and Italian tongues. I hope, too, some good may come to others hereby. All in Georgia have heard the word of God. Some have believed, and began to run well. A few steps have been taken towards publishing the glad tidings both to the African and American heathens. Many children have learned "how they ought to serve God," and to be useful to their neighbour. And those whom it most concerns have an opportunity of knowing the true state of their infant colony, and laying a firmer foundation of peace and happiness to many generations.

Sat. 4.—I told my friends some of the reasons which

a little hastened my return to England. They all agreed it would be proper to relate them to the trustees of Georgia.

Accordingly, the next morning I waited on Mr. Oglethorpe, but had not time to speak on that head. In the afternoon I was desired to preach at St. John the Evangelist's. I did so on those strong words, " If any man be in Christ, he is a new creature." I was afterwards informed many of the best in the parish were so offended, that I was not to preach there any more.

Mon. 6.—I visited many of my old friends, as well as most of my relations. I find the time is not yet come when I am to be "hated of all men." O may I be prepared for that day !

Wesley Meets Peter Böhler

Tues. 7.—(A day much to be remembered.) At the house of Mr. Weinantz, a Dutch merchant, I met Peter Böhler, Schulius Richter, and Wensel Neiser, just then landed from Germany. Finding they had no acquaintance in England, I offered to procure them a lodging, and did so near Mr. Hutton's, where I then was. And from this time I did not willingly lose any opportunity of conversing with them while I stayed in London.

Wed. 8.—I went to Mr. Oglethorpe again, but had no opportunity of speaking as I designed. Afterwards I waited on the Board of Trustees, and gave them a short but plain account of the state of the colony : an account, I fear, not a little differing from those which they had frequently received before, and for which I have reason to believe some of them have not forgiven me to this day.

Sun. 12.—I preached at St. Andrew's, Holborn, on : " Though I give all my goods to feed the poor, and though I give my body to be burned, and have not charity, it profiteth me nothing." O hard sayings ! Who can hear them? Here too, it seems, I am to preach no more.

Fri. 17.—I set out for Oxford with Peter Böhler, where we were kindly received by Mr. Sarney, the only one now remaining here of many who, at our embarking for America, were used to " take sweet counsel together," and rejoice in " bearing the reproach of Christ."

Sat. 18.—We went to Stanton-Harcourt. The next day I preached once more at the castle, in Oxford, to a numerous and serious congregation.

All this time I conversed much with Peter Böhler, but I understood him not; and least of all when he said, " My brother, my brother, that philosophy of yours must be purged away."

Mon. 20.—I returned to London. On Tuesday I preached at Great St. Helen's, on : " If any man will come after me, let him deny himself, and take up his cross daily, and follow me."

Sun. 26.—I preached at six, at St. Lawrence's ; at ten, in St. Catherine Cree's church ; and in the afternoon, at St. John's, Wapping. I believe it pleased God to bless the first sermon most, because it gave most offence ; being, indeed, an open defiance of that mystery of iniquity which the world calls " prudence," grounded on those words of St. Paul to the Galatians, " As many as desire to make a fair show in the flesh, they constrain you to oe circumcised ; only lest they should suffer persecution for the cross of Christ."

Mon. 27.—I took coach for Salisbury, and had several opportunities of conversing seriously with my fellow travellers.

Tues. 28.—I saw my mother once more. The next day I prepared for my journey to my brother at Tiverton.

PETER BÖHLER
*John Wesley regarded Böhler as the
instrument of his conversion*

But on Thursday morning, March 2, a message that my brother Charles was dying at Oxford, obliged me to set out for that place immediately. Calling at an odd house in the afternoon, I found several persons there who seemed well-wishers to religion, to whom I spake plainly; as I did in the evening both to the servants and strangers at my inn.

Wesley's Four Resolutions

With regard to my own behaviour, I now renewed and wrote down my former resolutions.

1. To use absolute openness and unreserve with all I should converse with.

2. To labour after continual seriousness, not willingly indulging myself in any the least levity of behaviour, or in laughter; no, not for a moment.

3. To speak no word which does not tend to the glory of God; in particular, not to talk of worldly things. Others may, nay, must. But what is that to thee? And,

4. To take no pleasure which does not tend to the glory of God; thanking God every moment for all I do take, and therefore rejecting every sort and degree of it, which I feel I cannot so thank him in and for.

Sat. March 4.—I found my brother at Oxford, recovering from his pleurisy; and with him Peter Böhler; by whom, in the hand of the great God, I was, on Sunday, the 5th, clearly convinced of unbelief, of the want of that faith whereby alone we are saved.

Immediately it struck into my mind, "Leave off preaching. How can you preach to others, who have not faith yourself?" I asked Böhler whether he thought I should leave it off or not. He answered, "By no means." I asked, "But what can I preach?" He

said, " Preach faith till you have it; and then, because
you have it, you will preach faith."

Accordingly, Monday, 6, I began preaching this new
doctrine, though my soul started back from the work.
The first person to whom I offered salvation by faith
alone, was a prisoner under sentence of death. His
name was Clifford. Peter Böhler had many times
desired me to speak to him before. But I could not
prevail on myself so to do; being still, as I had been
many years, a zealous asserter of the impossibility of a
death-bed repentance.

Incidents on the Manchester Road

Tues. 14.—I set out for Manchester with Mr. Kinchin,
Fellow of Corpus Christi, and Mr. Fox, late a prisoner
in the city prison.

About eight, it being rainy and very dark, we lost our
way; but before nine, came to Shipston, having rode
over, I know not how, a narrow foot-bridge, which lay
across a deep ditch near the town. After supper I read
prayers to the people of the inn, and explained the
second lesson; I hope not in vain.

The next day we dined at Birmingham; and, soon
after we left it, were reproved for our negligence there,
in letting those who attended us go, without either
exhortation or instruction, by a severe shower of hail.

In the evening we came to Stafford. The mistress of
the house joined with us in family prayer. The next
morning one of the servants appeared deeply affected,
as did the ostler, before we went. Soon after breakfast,
stepping into the stable, I spake a few words to those
who were there. A stranger who heard me said, " Sir,
I wish I was to travel with you"; and when I went into
the house, followed me, and began abruptly, "Sir, I

believe you are a good man, and I come to tell you a little of my life." The tears stood in his eyes all the time he spoke; and we hoped not a word which was said to him was lost.

At Newcastle, whither we came about ten, some to whom we spoke at our inn were very attentive; but a gay young woman waited on us, quite unconcerned: however, we spoke on. When we went away, she fixed her eyes and neither moved nor said one word, but appeared as much astonished as if she had seen one risen from the dead.

Coming to Holms-Chapel about three, we were surprised at being shown into a room where a cloth and plates were laid. Soon after two men came in to dinner, Mr. Kinchin told them, if they pleased, that gentleman would ask a blessing for them. They stared and, as it were, consented; but sat still while I did it, one of them with his hat on. We began to speak on turning to God, and went on, though they appeared utterly regardless. After a while their countenances changed, and one of them stole off his hat, and laying it down behind him, said, all we said was true; but he had been a grievous sinner, and not considered it as he ought; but he was resolved, with God's help, now to turn to him in earnest. We exhorted him and his companion, who now likewise drank in every word, to cry mightily to God, that he would " send them help from his holy place."

Late at night we reached Manchester.

Companions on Horseback

Fri. 17.—Early in the morning we left Manchester, taking with us Mr. Kinchin's brother, for whom we came, to be entered at Oxford. We were fully determined to lose no opportunity of awakening, instructing, or exhorting, any whom we might meet within our journey. At Knutsford, where we first stopped, all we spake to thankfully received the word of exhortation. But at Talk-on-the-hill, where we dined, she with whom we were was so much of a gentlewoman, that for near an hour our labour seemed to be in vain. However, we spoke on. Upon a sudden, she looked as one just awaked out of a sleep. Every word sunk into her heart. Nor have I seen so entire a change both in the eyes, face, and manner of speaking, of any one in so short a time.

About five, Mr. Kinchin riding by a man and woman double-horsed, the man said, " Sir, you ought to thank God it is a fair day ; for if it rained, you would be sadly dirty with your little horse.' Mr. Kinchin answered, " True : and we ought to thank God for our life, and health, and food, and raiment, and all things." He then rode on, Mr. Fox following, the man said, " Sir, my mistress would be glad to have some more talk with that gentleman." We stayed, and when they came up, began to search one another's hearts. They came to us again in the evening, at our inn at Stone, where I explained both to them and many of their acquaintance who were come together, that great truth—godliness hath the promise both of this life and of that which is to come.

Tues. 21.—Between nine and ten we came to Hedgeford. In the afternoon one overtook us, whom we soon found more inclined to speak than to hear. However, we spoke, and spared not. In the evening we overtook a young man, a Quaker, who afterwards came to us, to our inn at Henley, whither he sent for the rest of his family, to join with us in prayer ; to which I added, as usual, the exposition of the second lesson. Our other companion went with us a mile or two in the morning; and then not only spoke less than the day before, but took in good part a serious caution against talkativeness and vanity.

An hour after we were overtook by an elderly gentleman, who said he was going to enter his son at Oxford. We asked, "At what college?" He said he did not know; having no acquaintance there on whose recommendation he could depend. After some conversation, he expressed a deep sense of the good providence of God; and told us he knew God had cast us in his way, in answer to his prayer. In the evening we reached Oxford, rejoicing in our having received so many fresh instances of that great truth, "In all thy ways acknowledge Him, and He shall direct thy paths."

Preaches in Oxford Castle

Thur. 23.—I met Peter Böhler again, who now amazed me more and more, by the account he gave of the fruits of living faith—the holiness and happiness which he affirmed to attend it. The next morning I began the Greek Testament again, resolving to abide by "the law and the testimony"; and being confident that God would hereby show me whether this doctrine was of God.

Mon. 27.—Mr. Kinchin went with me to the castle, where, after reading prayers, and preaching on, "It is appointed unto men once to die," we prayed with the condemned man, first in several forms of prayer, and then in such words as were given us in that hour. He kneeled down in much heaviness and confusion, having "no rest in" his "bones, by reason of" his "sins." After a space he rose up, and eagerly said, "I am now ready to die. I know Christ has taken away my sins;

and there is no more condemnation for me." The same composed cheerfulness he showed when he was carried to execution; and in his last moments he was the same, enjoying a perfect peace, in confidence that he was "accepted in the Beloved."

Sun. April 2.—Being Easter-day, I preached in our college chapel, on, "The hour cometh, and now is, when the dead shall hear the voice of the Son of God, and they that hear shall live." I preached in the afternoon, first at the castle, and then at Carfax, on the same words. I see the promise; but it is afar off.

Believing it would be better for me to wait for the accomplishment of it in silence and retirement, on Monday 3, I complied with Mr. Kinchin's desire, and went to him at Dummer, in Hampshire. But I was not suffered to stay here long; being earnestly pressed to come up to London, if it were only for a few days. Thither, therefore, I returned, on Tuesday, 18th.

Talks with Böhler

I asked P. Böhler again, whether I ought not to refrain from teaching others. He said, "No; do not hide in the earth the talent God hath given you." Accordingly, on Tuesday 25, I spoke clearly and fully at Blendon to Mr. Delamotte's family, of the nature and fruits of faith. Mr. Broughton and my brother were there. Mr. Broughton's great objection was, he could never think that I had not faith, who had done and suffered such things. My brother was very angry, and told me, I did not know what mischief I had done by talking thus. And, indeed, it did please God then to kindle a fire, which I trust shall never be extinguished.

On Wednesday 26, the day fixed for my return to

Oxford, I once more waited on the trustees for Georgia; but, being straitened for time, was obliged to leave the papers for them, which I had designed to give into their own hands. One of these was the instrument whereby they had appointed me minister of Savannah; which, having no more place in those parts, I thought it not right to keep any longer.

P. Böhler walked with me a few miles, and exhorted me not to stop short of the grace of God. At Gerard's Cross I plainly declared to those whom God gave into my hands, the faith as it is in Jesus: as I did next day to a young man I overtook on the road, and in the evening to our friends at Oxford. A strange doctrine, which some, who did not care to contradict, yet knew not what to make of; but one or two, who were thoroughly bruised by sin, willingly heard, and received it gladly.

In the day or two following, I was much confirmed in the "truth that is after godliness," by hearing the experiences of Mr. Hutchins, of Pembroke College, and Mrs. Fox: two living witnesses that God can (at least, if he does not always) give that faith whereof cometh salvation in a moment, as lightning falling from heaven.

Mon. May 1.—The return of my brother's illness obliged me again to hasten to London. In the evening I found him at James Hutton's, better as to his health than I expected; but strongly averse from what he called "the new faith."

This evening our little society began, which afterwards met in Fetter-lane.

Wed. 3.—My brother had a long and particular conversation with Peter Böhler. And it now pleased God to open his eyes; so that he also saw clearly what was

the nature of that one true living faith, whereby alone,
" through grace, we are saved."

Thur. 4.—Peter Böhler left London, in order to
embark for Carolina. O what a work hath God begun,
since his coming into England! such an one as shall
never come to an end, till heaven and earth pass
away.

Sun. 7.—I preached at St. Lawrence's in the morning; and afterwards at St. Katherine Cree's church. I
was enabled to speak strong words at both; and was
therefore the less surprised at being informed, I was not
to preach any more in either of those churches.

Sun. 14.—I preached in the morning at St. Ann's,
Aldersgate; and in the afternoon at the Savoy Chapel,
free salvation by faith in the blood of Christ. I was
quickly apprised, that at St. Ann's, likewise, I am to
preach no more.

Fri. 19.—My brother had a second return of his
pleurisy. A few of us spent Saturday night in prayer.
The next day, being Whitsunday, after hearing Dr.
Heylyn preach a truly Christian sermon (on, " They
were all filled with the Holy Ghost ": " And so," said
he, " may all you be, if it is not your own fault "), and
assisting him at the holy communion (his curate being
taken ill in the church), I received the surprising news
that my brother had found rest to his soul. His bodily
strength returned also from that hour. " Who is so great
a God as our God ? "

I preached at St. John's, Wapping, at three, and at
St. Bennett's, Paul's-wharf, in the evening. At these
churches, likewise, I am to preach no more. At St.
Antholin's I preached on the Thursday following.

Monday, Tuesday, and Wednesday, I had continual sorrow and heaviness in my heart.

Wed. May 24.—I think it was about five this morning that I opened my Testament on those words, "There are given unto us exceeding great and precious promises, even that ye should be partakers of the divine nature" (2 Peter i. 4). Just as I went out, I opened it again on those words, "Thou art not far from the kingdom of God." In the afternoon I was asked to go to St. Paul's. The anthem was, "Out of the deep have I called unto thee, O Lord : Lord, hear my voice. O let thine ears consider well the voice of my complaint. If thou, Lord, wilt be extreme to mark what is done amiss, O Lord, who may abide it? For there is mercy with thee ; therefore shalt thou be feared. O Israel, trust in the Lord : for with the Lord there is mercy, and with Him is plenteous redemption. And He shall redeem Israel from all his sins."

"I Felt my Heart Strangely Warmed"

In the evening I went very unwillingly to a society in Aldersgate-street, where one was reading Luther's preface to the Epistle to the Romans. About a quarter before nine, while he was describing the change which God works in the heart through faith in Christ, I felt my heart strangely warmed. I felt I did trust in Christ, Christ alone, for salvation ; and an assurance was given me that He had taken away my sins, even mine, and saved me from the law of sin and death.

I began to pray with all my might for those who had in a more especial manner despitefully used me and persecuted me. I then testified openly to all there what I now first felt in my heart. But it was not long before the enemy suggested, "This cannot be faith ; for

where is thy joy?" Then was I taught that peace and
victory over sin are essential to faith in the Captain of
our salvation; but that, as to the transports of joy that
usually attend the beginning of it, especially in those
who have mourned deeply, God sometimes giveth, sometimes withholdeth them, according to the counsels ot
his own will.

After my return home, I was much buffeted with
temptations; but cried out, and they fled away. They
returned again and again. I as often lifted up my eyes,
and He "sent me help from his holy place." And
herein I found the difference between this and my former
state chiefly consisted. I was striving, yea, fighting with
all my might under the law, as well as under grace.
But then I was sometimes, if not often, conquered;
now, I was always conqueror.

Thur. 25.—The moment I awaked, "Jesus, Master,"
was in my heart and in my mouth; and I found all my
strength lay in keeping my eye fixed upon him, and my
soul waiting on him continually. Being again at St.
Paul's in the afternoon, I could taste the good word of
God in the anthem, which began, "My song shall be
always of the loving-kindness of the Lord: with my
mouth will I ever be showing forth thy truth from one
generation to another." Yet the enemy injected a fear,
"If thou dost believe, why is there not a more sensible
change?" I answered (yet not I), "That I know not.
But this I know, I have 'now peace with God.' And I
sin not to-day, and Jesus my Master has forbid me to
take thought for the morrow."

Wed. June 7.—I determined, if God should permit,
to retire for a short time into Germany. I had fully
proposed, before I left Georgia, so to do, if it should
please God to bring me back to Europe. And I now

clearly saw the time was come. My weak mind could not bear to be thus sawn asunder. And I hoped the conversing with those holy men who were themselves living witnesses of the full power of faith, and yet able to bear with those that are weak, would be a means, under God, of so establishing my soul, that I might go on from faith to faith, and from strength to strength."

[The next three months Wesley spent in Germany visiting the Moravians.]

Wesley Preaches in Newgate Gaol

Sun. September 17 (London).—I began again to declare in my own country the glad tidings of salvation, preaching three times, and afterwards expounding the holy Scripture, to a large company in the Minories. On Monday I rejoiced to meet with our little society, which now consisted of thirty-two persons.

The next day I went to the condemned felons, in Newgate, and offered them free salvation. In the evening I went to a society in Bear Yard, and preached repentance and remission of sins. The next evening I spoke the truth in love at a society in Aldersgate Street : some contradicted at first, but not long ; so that nothing but love appeared at our parting.

Fri. Nov. 3.—I preached at St. Antholin's : Sunday, 5, in the morning, at St. Botolph's, Bishopsgate ; in the afternoon, at Islington ; and in the evening, to such a congregation as I never saw before, at St. Clement's, in the Strand. As this was the first time of my preaching here, I suppose it is to be the last.

Sun. Dec. 3 (Oxford).—I began reading prayers at Bocardo (the city prison), which had been long discontinued. In the afternoon I received a letter, earnestly desiring me to publish my account of Georgia ; and another, as earnestly dissuading me from it, "because it would bring much trouble upon me." I consulted God in His word, and received two answers: the first, Ezek. xxxiii. 2–6 : the other, "Thou therefore endure hardship, as a good soldier of Jesus Christ."

Tues. 5.—I began reading prayers and preaching in Gloucester Green workhouse; and on Thursday, in that belonging to St. Thomas's parish. On both days I preached at the castle. At St. Thomas's was a young woman, raving mad, screaming and tormenting herself continually. I had a strong desire to speak to her. The moment I began she was still. The tears ran down her cheeks all the time I was telling her, "Jesus of Nazareth is able and willing to deliver you."

Mon. 11.—Hearing Mr. Whitefield was arrived from Georgia, I hastened to London from Oxford; and on Tuesday, 12, God gave us once more to take sweet counsel together.

Wesley Begins Field-preaching

1739. March 15.—During my stay [in London] I was fully employed; between our own society in Fetter Lane, and many others, where I was continually desired to expound; so that I had no thought of leaving London, when I received, after several others, a letter from Mr. Whitefield, and another from Mr. Seward, entreating me, in the most pressing manner, to come to Bristol without delay. This I was not at all forward to do.

Wed. 28.—My journey was proposed to our society in Fetter Lane. But my brother Charles would scarce bear the mention of it; till appealing to the oracles of God, he received those words as spoken to himself, and answered not again: "Son of man, behold, I take from thee the desire of thine eyes with a stroke: yet shalt thou not mourn or weep, neither shall thy tears run down." Our other brethren, however, continuing the dispute, without any probability of their coming to one conclusion, we at length all agreed to decide it by lot. And by this it was determined I should go.

Thur. 29.—I left London, and in the evening expounded to a small company at Basingstoke. Saturday, 31. In the evening I reached Bristol, and met Mr. Whitefield there. I could scarce reconcile myself at first to this strange way of preaching in the fields, of which he set me an example on Sunday; having been all my life (till very lately) so tenacious of every point relating to decency and order, that I should have thought the saving of souls almost a sin, if it had not been done in a church.

April 1.—In the evening (Mr. Whitefield being gone) I begun expounding our Lord's sermon on the mount (one pretty remarkable precedent of field-preaching, though I suppose there were churches at that time also), to a little society which was accustomed to meet once or twice a week in Nicholas Street.

Mon. 2.—At four in the afternoon, I submitted to be more vile, and proclaimed in the highways the glad tidings of salvation, speaking from a little eminence in a ground adjoining to the city, to about three thousand people. The Scripture on which I spoke was this (is it possible any one should be ignorant, that it is fulfilled in every true minister of Christ?) " The Spirit of the Lord is upon me, because he hath anointed me to preach the Gospel to the poor ; he hath sent me to heal the broken-hearted ; to preach deliverance to the captives, and recovery of sight to the blind; to set at liberty them that are bruised, to proclaim the accceptable year of the Lord."

Sun. 8.—At seven in the morning I preached to about a thousand persons at Bristol, and afterwards to about fifteen hundred on the top of Hannam-mount in Kingswood. I called to them, in the words of the evangelical Prophet, "Ho! every one that thirsteth, come ye to the waters; come, and buy wine and milk without money and without price." About five thousand were in the afternoon at Rose-green (on the other side of Kingswood); among whom I stood and cried, in the name of the Lord, "If any man thirst, let him come unto me and drink. He that believeth on me, as the Scripture hath said, out of his belly shall flow rivers of living water."

Tues. 17.—At five in the afternoon I was at a little society in the Back Lane. The room in which we were was propped beneath, but the weight of people made the floor give way; so that in the beginning of the expounding, the post which propped it fell down with a great noise. But the floor sunk no further; so that, after a little surprise at first, they quietly attended to the things that were spoken.

Mon. May 7.—I was preparing to set out for Pensford, having now had leave to preach in the church, when I received the following note :

"Sir,—Our minister, having been informed you are beside yourself, does not care you should preach in any of his churches."—I went, however; and on Priestdown, about half a mile from Pensford, preached Christ our "wisdom, righteousness, sanctification, and redemption."

Tues. 8.—I went to Bath, but was not suffered to be in the meadow where I was before, which occasioned the offer of a much more convenient place, where I preached Christ to about a thousand souls.

Wed. 9.—We took possession of a piece of ground near St. James's churchyard, in the Horse Fair, Bristol, where it was designed to build a room large enough to contain both the societies of Nicholas and Baldwin Street, and such of their acquaintance as might desire to be present with them, at such times as the Scripture was expounded. And on Saturday, 12, the first stone was laid with the voice of praise and thanksgiving.

The First Methodist Building

I had not at first the least apprehension or design of being personally engaged, either in the expense of this work, or in the direction of it, having appointed eleven feoffees, on whom I supposed these burdens would fall, of course; but I quickly found my mistake. First, with regard to the expense : for the whole undertaking must have stood still, had not I immediately taken upon my-self the payment of all the workmen; so that before I knew where I was, I had contracted a debt of more than a hundred and fifty pounds. And this I was to dis-charge how I could; the subscriptions of both societies not amounting to one quarter of the sum.

And as to the direction of the work, I presently received letters from my friends in London, Mr. White-field in particular, backed with a message by one just come from thence, that neither he nor they would have anything to do with the building, neither contribute any-thing towards it, unless I would instantly discharge all feoffees, and do everything in my own name. Many reasons they gave for this; but one was enough, viz., "that such feoffees always would have it in their power to control me; and, if I preached not as they liked, to turn me out of the room I had built." I accordingly yielded to their advice, and calling all the feoffees together, cancelled (no man opposing) the instrument made before, and took the whole management into my own hands. Money, it is true, I had not, nor any human prospect or probability of procuring it ; but I knew " the earth is the Lord's, and the fulness thereof," and in his name set out, nothing doubting.

Sun. 13.—My ordinary employment, in public, was now as follows : Every morning I read prayers and preached at Newgate. Every evening I expounded a portion of Scripture at one or more of the societies. On Monday, in the afternoon, I preached abroad, near Bristol ; on Tuesday, at Bath and Two Mile Hill alternately ; on Wednesday, at Baptist Mills ; every other Thursday, near Pensford ; every other Friday, in another part of Kingswood ; on Saturday in the afternoon, and Sunday morning, in the Bowling-green (which lies near the middle of the city) ; on Sunday, at eleven, near Hannam-mount ; at two, at Clifton ; and at five on Rose-green. And hitherto, as my days, so my strength hath been.

Wesley's Living Arguments

Sun. 20.—Seeing many of the rich at Clifton church, my heart was much pained for them, and I was earnestly desirous that some even of them might " enter into the kingdom of heaven." But full as I was, I knew not where to begin in warning them to flee from the wrath to come till my Testament opened on these words : " I came not to call the righteous, but sinners to repentance " ; in applying which my soul was so enlarged that methought I could have cried out (in another sense than poor vain Archimedes), " Give me where to stand, and I will shake the earth." God's sending forth lightning with the rain did not hinder about fifteen hundred from staying at Rose-green. Our Scripture was, " It is the glorious God that maketh the thunder. The voice of the Lord is mighty in operation; the voice of the Lord is a glorious voice." In the evening he spoke to three whose souls were all storm and tempest, and immediately there was a great calm.

During this whole time I was almost continually asked, either by those who purposely came to Bristol to inquire concerning this strange work, or by my old or new correspondents, " How can these things be? " And innumerable cautions were given me (generally grounded on gross misrepresentations of things), not to regard visions or dreams, or to fancy people had remission of sins because of their cries, or tears, or bare outward professions. To one who had many times wrote to me on this head, the sum of my answer was as follows:

" The question between us turns chiefly, if not wholly, on matter of fact. You deny that God does now work these effects; at least, that he works them in this manner. I affirm both, because I have heard these things with my own ears, and have seen with my eyes. I have seen (as far as a thing of this kind can be seen) very many persons changed in a moment from the spirit of fear, horror, despair, to the spirit of love, joy, and peace; and from sinful desire, till then reigning over them, to a pure desire of doing the will of God. These are matters of fact, whereof I have been, and almost daily am, an eye or ear witness.

What I have to say touching visions or dreams, is this: I know several persons in whom this great change was wrought in a dream, or during a strong represen-tation to the eye of their mind, of Christ either on the cross or in the glory. This is the fact; let any judge of it as they please. And that such a change was then wrought appears (not from their shedding tears only, or falling into fit, or crying out; these are not the fruits, as you seem to suppose, whereby I judge, but) from the whole tenor of their life, till then many ways wicked; from that time holy, just, and good.

" I will show you him that was a lion till then, and is now a lamb; him that was a drunkard, and is now exemplarily sober; the whoremonger that was, who now abhors the very 'garment spotted by the flesh.' These are my living arguments for what I assert, viz., 'that God does now, as aforetime, give remission of sins and the gift of the Holy Ghost even to us and to our children; yea, and that always suddenly as far as I have known, and often in dreams or in the visions of God.' If it be not so, I am found a false witness before God. For these things I do, and by his grace, will testify."

Beau Nash Argues with Wesley

Tues. June 5.—There was great expectation at Bath of what a noted man was to do to me there; and I was much entreated not to preach, because no one knew what might happen. By this report I also gained a much larger audience, among whom were many of the rich and great. I told them plainly, the Scripture had concluded them all under sin—high and low, rich and poor, one with another. Many of them seemed to be a little surprised, and were sinking apace into seriousness, when their champion appeared, and coming close to me, asked by what authority I did these things.

I replied, " By the authority of Jesus Christ, conveyed to me by the (now) Archbishop of Canterbury, when he laid hands upon me, and said, 'Take thou authority to preach the Gospel.'" He said, "This is contrary to Act of Parliament: this is a conventicle." I answered,

"Sir, the conventicles mentioned in that Act (as the preamble shows) are seditious meetings; but this is not such; here is no shadow of sedition; therefore it is not contrary to that Act." He replied, "I say it is: and, beside, your preaching frightens people out of their wits."

"Sir, did you ever hear me preach?" "No." "How, then, can you judge of what you never heard?" "Sir, by common report." "Common report is not enough. Give me leave, Sir, to ask, Is not your name Nash?" "My name is Nash." "Sir, I dare not judge of you by common report: I think it not enough to judge by." Here he paused awhile, and, having recovered himself, said, "I desire to know what this people comes here for": on which one replied, "Sir, leave him to me: let an old woman answer him. You, Mr. Nash, take care of your body; we take care of our souls; and for the food of our souls we come here." He replied not a word, but walked away.

As I returned, the street was full of people, hurrying to and fro, and speaking great words. But when any of them asked, "Which is he?" and I replied, "I am he," they were immediately silent. Several ladies following me into Mr. Merchant's house, the servant told me there were some wanted to speak to me. I went to them, and said, "I believe, ladies, the maid mistook: you only wanted to look at me." I added, "I do not expect that the rich and great should want either to speak with me, or to hear me; for I speak the plain truth—a thing you hear little of, and do not desire to hear." A few more words passed between us, and I retired.

Mon. 11.—I received a pressing letter from London (as I had several others before), to come thither as soon as possible; our brethren in Fetter Lane being in great confusion for want of my presence and advice. I therefore preached in the afternoon on these words: "I take you to record this day, that I am pure from the blood of all men; for I have not shunned to declare unto you all the counsel of God." After sermon I commended them to the grace of God, in whom they had believed. Surely God hath yet a work to do in this place. I have not found such love, no, not in England; nor so childlike, artless, teachable, a temper, as He hath given to this people.

Yet, during this whole time, I had many thoughts concerning the unusual manner of my ministering among them. But after frequently laying it before the Lord, and calmly weighing whatever objections I heard against it, I could not but adhere to what I had some time since wrote to a friend, who had freely spoken his sentiments concerning it. An extract of that letter I here subjoin that the matter may be placed in a clear light.

"All the World my Parish"

"You say, you cannot reconcile some parts of my behaviour with the character I have long supported. No, nor ever will. Therefore I have disclaimed that character on every possible occasion. I told all in our ship, all at Savannah, all at Frederica, and that over and over, in express terms, 'I am not a Christian; I only follow after, if haply I may attain it.'

.   .   .   .   .

"If you ask on what principle I acted, it was this: 'A desire to be a Christian; and a conviction that whatever I judge conducive thereto, that I am bound to do; wherever I judge I can best answer this end, thither it is my duty to go.' On this principle I set out for America; on this I visited the Moravian church; and on the same am I ready now (God being my helper) to go to Abyssinia or China, or whithersoever it shall please God, by this conviction, to call me.

"As to your advice that I should settle in college, I have no business there, having now no office, and no pupils. And whether the other branch of your proposal be expedient for me, viz., 'to accept of a cure of souls,' it will be time enough to consider when one is offered to me.

"But, in the meantime, you think I ought to sit still; because otherwise I should invade another's office, if I interfered with other people's business and intermeddled with souls that did not belong to me. You accordingly ask, 'How is it that I assemble Christians who are none of my charge, to sing psalms, and pray, and hear the Scriptures expounded?' and think it hard to justify doing this in other men's parishes, upon catholic principles?

"Permit me to speak plainly. If by catholic principles you mean any other than scriptural, they weigh nothing with me; I allow no other rule, whether of faith or practice, than the holy Scriptures. But on scriptural principles, I do not think it hard to justify whatever I do. God in Scripture commands me, according to my power, to instruct the ignorant, reform the wicked, confirm the virtuous. Man forbids me to do this in another's parish; that is, in effect, to do it at all; seeing I have now no parish of my own, nor probably ever shall. Whom then shall I hear, God or man?

.   .   .   .   .

"I look upon all the world as my parish; thus far I mean, that, in whatever part of it I am, I judge it meet, right, and my bounden duty, to declare unto all that are willing to hear, the glad tidings of salvation. This is the work which I know God has called me to; and sure I am that his blessing attends it. Great encouragement have I, therefore, to be faithful in fulfilling the work he hath given me to do. His servant I am, and, as such, am employed according to the plain direction of his word, 'As I have opportunity, doing good unto all men'; and his providence clearly concurs with his word; which has disengaged me from all things else, that I might singly attend on this very thing, 'and go about doing good.'"

•   •   •   •   •

Susanna Wesley and her Son

Wed. 13.—After receiving the holy communion at Islington, I had once more an opportunity of seeing my mother, whom I had not seen since my return from Germany.

I cannot but mention an odd circumstance here. I had read her a paper in June last year, containing a short account of what had passed in my own soul, till within a few days of that time. She greatly approved it, and said she heartily blessed God, who had brought me to so just a way of thinking. While I was in Germany a copy of that paper was sent (without my knowledge) to one of my relations. He sent an account of it to my mother, whom I now found under strange fears concerning me, being convinced "by an account taken from one of my own papers, that I had greatly erred from the faith." I could not conceive what paper that should be; but, on inquiry, found it was the same I had read her myself. How hard is it to form a true judgment of any person or thing from the account of a prejudiced relater! yea, though he be ever so honest a man : for he who gave this relation was one of unquestionable veracity. And yet by his sincere account of a writing which lay before his eyes, was the truth so totally disguised, that my mother knew not the paper she had heard from end to end, nor I that I had myself wrote.

Thur. 14.—I went with Mr. Whitefield to Blackheath, where were, I believe, twelve or fourteen thousand people. He a little surprised me, by desiring me to preach in his stead; which I did (though nature recoiled) on my favourite subject, "Jesus Christ, who of God is made unto us wisdom, righteousness, sanctification, and redemption."

I was greatly moved with compassion for the rich that were there, to whom I made a particular application. Some of them seemed to attend, while others drove away their coaches from so uncouth a preacher.

Sun. 17.—I preached, at seven, in Upper-Moorfields, to (I believe) six or seven thousand people, on, "Ho, every one that thirsteth, come ye to the waters."

At five I preached on Kennington Common, to about fifteen thousand people, on those words, "Look unto me, and be ye saved, all ye ends of the earth."

Mon. 18.—I left London early in the morning, and the next evening reached Bristol, and preached (as I had appointed, if God should permit) to a numerous congregation. My text now also was, "Look unto me and be ye saved, all ye ends of the earth." Howell Harris called upon me an hour or two after. He said, he had been much dissuaded from either hearing or seeing me, by many who said all manner of evil of me. "But," said he, "as soon as I heard you preach, I quickly found what spirit you was of. And before you had done, I was so overpowered with joy and love, that I had much ado to walk home."

Sun. 24.—As I was riding to Rose-green, in a smooth, plain part of the road, my horse suddenly pitched upon his head, and rolled over and over. I received no other hurt than a little bruise on one side; which for the present I felt not, but preached without pain to six or seven thousand people on that important direction, " Whether ye eat or drink, or whatever you do, do all to the glory of God."

Talks with Whitefield

Fri. July 6.—In the afternoon I was with Mr. Whitefield, just come from London, with whom I went to Baptist Mills, where he preached concerning "the Holy Ghost, which all who believe are to receive"; not without a just, though severe, censure of those who preach as if there were no Holy Ghost.

Sat. 7.—I had an opportunity to talk with him of those outward signs which had so often accompanied the inward work of God. I found his objections were chiefly grounded on gross misrepresentations of matter of fact. But the next day he had an opportunity of informing himself better: for no sooner had he begun (in the application of his sermon) to invite all sinners to believe in Christ, than four persons sunk down close to him, almost in the same moment. One of them lay without either sense or motion. A second trembled exceedingly. The third had strong convulsions all over his body, but made no noise, unless by groans. The fourth, equally convulsed, called upon God, with strong cries and tears. From this time, I trust, we shall all suffer God to carry on his own work in the way that pleaseth him.

Fri. 13.—On Friday, in the afternoon, I left Bristol with Mr. Whitefield, in the midst of heavy rain. But the clouds soon dispersed, so that we had a fair, calm evening, and a serious congregation at Thornbury.

Tues. 17.—I rode to Bradford, five miles from Bath, whither I had been long invited to come. I waited on the minister, and desired leave to preach in his church. He said, it was not usual to preach on the week days; but if I could come thither on a Sunday, he should be glad of my assistance. Thence I went to a gentleman in the town, who had been present when I preached at Bath, and, with the strongest marks of sincerity and affection, wished me good luck in the name of the Lord. But it was past. I found him now quite cold. He began disputing on several heads; and at last told me plainly, one of our own college had informed him they always took me to be a little crack-brained at Oxford.

However, some persons who were not of his mind, having pitched on a convenient place (called Bear Field, or Bury Field), on the top of the hill under which the town lies; I there offered Christ to about a thousand people, for "wisdom, righteousness, sanctification, and redemption." Thence I returned to Bath, and preached on, "What must I do to be saved?" to a larger audience than ever before.

I was wondering the "god of this world" was so still; when, at my return from the place of preaching, poor R——d Merchant told me, he could not let me preach any more in his ground. I asked him why; he said, the people hurt his trees, and stole things out of his ground. "And besides," added he, "I have already, by letting thee be there, merited the displeasure of my neighbours." O fear of man! Who is above thee, but they who indeed "worship God in spirit and in truth?"

Not even those who have one foot in the grave! Not
even those who dwell in rooms of cedar; and who have
heaped up gold as the dust, and silver as the sand of
the sea.

Press-gang Disturbs the Sermon

Sat. 21.—I began expounding, a second time, our
Lord's sermon on the mount.   In the morning, Sunday,
22, as I was explaining, " Blessed are the poor in spirit,"
to about three thousand people, we had a fair opportunity of showing all men, what manner of spirit we were
of : for in the middle of the sermon the press-gang came,
and seized on one of the hearers (ye learned in the law,
what becomes of Magna Charta, and of English liberty
and property?   Are not these mere sounds, while, on
any pretence, there is such a thing as a press-gang
suffered in the land ?), all the rest standing still and
none opening his mouth or lifting up his hand to resist
them.

Mon. Sept. 3 (London).—I talked largely with my
mother, who told me that, till a short time since, she
had scarce heard such a thing mentioned, as the having
forgiveness of sins now, or God's Spirit bearing witness
with our spirit : much less did she imagine that this was
the common privilege of all true believers.   " Therefore," said she, " I never durst ask for it myself.   But
two or three weeks ago, while my son Hall was pro-
nouncing those words, in delivering the cup to me,
' The blood of our Lord Jesus Christ, which was given
for thee,' the words struck through my heart, and I
knew God for Christ's sake had forgiven me all my
sins."

I asked whether her father (Dr. Annesley) had not
the same faith; and, whether she had not heard him

preach it to others.   She answered, he had it himself;
and declared, a little before his death, that for more than
forty years he had no darkness, no fear, no doubt at all
of his being "accepted in the Beloved."   But that,
nevertheless, she did not remember to have heard him
preach, no, not once, explicitly upon it: whence she
supposed he also looked upon it as the peculiar blessing
of a few; not as promised to all the people of God.

The New Name of Methodism

Sun. 9.—I declared to about ten thousand, in Moorfields, what they must do to be saved.   My mother went
with us, about five, to Kennington, where were supposed
to be twenty thousand people.   I again insisted on that
foundation of all our hope, " Believe in the Lord Jesus,
and thou shalt be saved."   From Kennington I went to
a society at Lambeth.   The house being filled, the rest
stood in the garden.   The deep attention they showed
gave me a good hope that they will not all be forgetful
hearers.

Sun. 16.—I preached at Moorfields to about ten
thousand, and at Kennington Common to, I believe,
near twenty thousand, on those words of the calmer Jews
to St. Paul, "We desire to hear of thee what thou
thinkest; for as concerning this sect, we know that
everywhere it is spoken against."   At both places I
described the real difference between what is generally
called Christianity and the true old Christianity, which,
under the new name of Methodism, is now also everywhere spoken against.

Sun. 23.—I declared to about ten thousand, in Moorfields, with great enlargement of spirit, " The kingdom
of God is not meat and drink; but righteousness, and
peace, and joy in the Holy Ghost."   At Kennington I

enforced to about twenty thousand that great truth, " One thing is needful." Thence I went to Lambeth, and showed (to the amazement, it seemed, of many who were present) how " he that is born of God doth not commit sin."

Mon. 24.—I preached once more at Plaistow, and took my leave of the people of that place. In my return, a person galloping swiftly rode full against me, and overthrew both man and horse; but without any hurt to either. Glory be to Him who saves both man and beast !

An Accident and a Long Sermon

Thur. 27.—I went in the afternoon to a society at Deptford, and thence, at six, came to Turner's Hall : which holds (by computation) two thousand persons. The press both within and without was very great. In the beginning of the expounding, there being a large vault beneath, the main beam which supported the floor broke. The floor immediately sunk, which occasioned much noise and confusion among the people. But two or three days before, a man had filled the vault with hogsheads of tobacco. So that the floor, after sinking a foot or two, rested upon them, and I went on without interruption.

Sun. Oct. 7.—About eleven I preached at Runwick, seven miles from Gloucester. The church was much crowded, though a thousand or upwards stayed in the churchyard. In the afternoon I explained further the same words, " What must I do to be saved ? " I believe some thousands were then present, more than had been in the morning.

Between five and six I called on all who were present (about three thousand) at Stanley, on a little green, near the town, to accept of Christ, as their only " wisdom, righteousness, sanctification, and redemption." I was strengthened to speak as I never did before ; and continued speaking near two hours : the darkness of the night, and a little lightning, not lessening the number, but increasing the seriousness, of the hearers. I concluded the day by expounding part of our Lord's sermon on the mount, to a small, serious company at Ebly.

Wesley in Wales

Mon. 15.—Upon a pressing invitation, some time since received, I set out for Wales. About four in the afternoon I preached on a little green, at the foot of the Devauden (a high hill, two or three miles beyond Chepstow), to three or four hundred plain people, on " Christ our wisdom, righteousness, sanctification, and redemption." After sermon, one who I trust is an old disciple of Christ, willingly received us into his house : whither many following, I showed them their need of a Saviour, from these words, " Blessed are the poor in spirit." In the morning I described more fully the way to salvation —"Believe in the Lord Jesus, and thou shalt be saved " : and then, taking leave of my friendly host, before two came to Abergavenny.

I felt in myself a strong aversion to preaching here. However, I went to Mr. W—— (the person in whose ground Mr. Whitefield preached), to desire the use of it He said, with all his heart—if the minister was not willing to let me have the use of the church : after whose refusal (for I wrote a line to him immediately), he invited me to his house. About a thousand people stood patiently (though the frost was sharp, it being after sunset), while, from Acts xxviii. 22, I simply described the plain, old religion of the Church of England, which is now almost everywhere spoken against, under the new name of Methodism.

Fri. 19.—I preached in the morning at Newport on "What must I do to be saved?" to the most insensible, ill-behaved people I have ever seen in Wales. One ancient man, during a great part of the sermon, cursed and swore almost incessantly; and, towards the conclusion, took up a great stone, which he many times attempted to throw. But that he could not do.—Such the champions, such the arms against field-preaching!

At four I preached at the Shire Hall of Cardiff again, where many gentry, I found, were present. Such freedom of speech I have seldom had, as was given me in explaining those words, "The kingdom of God is not meat and drink; but righteousness, and peace, and joy in the Holy Ghost." At six almost the whole town (I was informed) came together; to whom I explained the six last beatitudes: but my heart was so enlarged, I knew not how to give over, so that we continued three hours.

Sat. 20.—I returned to Bristol. I have seen no part of England so pleasant for sixty or seventy miles together as those parts of Wales I have been in. And most of the inhabitants are indeed ripe for the Gospel.

"A Terrible Sight"

Tues. 23.—In riding to Bradford I read over Mr. Law's book on the new birth. Philosophical, speculative, precarious: Behmenish, void, and vain!

"O what a fall is there!"

At eleven I preached at Bearfield to about three thousand, on the spirit of nature, of bondage, and of adoption.

Returning in the evening, I was exceedingly pressed

to go back to a young woman in Kingswood. (The fact I nakedly relate, and leave every man to his own judgment of it.) I went. She was nineteen or twenty years old; but, it seems, could not write or read. I found her on the bed, two or three persons holding her. It was a terrible sight. Anguish, horror, and despair, above all description, appeared in her pale face. The thousand distortions of her whole body showed how the dogs of hell were gnawing her heart. The shrieks intermixed were scarce to be endured. But her stony eyes could not weep. She screamed out, as soon as words could find their way, "I am damned, damned; lost for ever! Six days ago you might have helped me. But it is past. I am the devil's now. I have given myself to him. His I am. Him I must serve. With him I must go to hell. I will be his. I will serve him. I will go with him to hell. I cannot be saved. I will not be saved. I must, I will, I will be damned !" She then began praying to the devil. We began:

"Arm of the Lord, awake, awake !"

She immediately sunk down as asleep; but, as soon as we left off, broke out again, with inexpressible vehemence: "Stony hearts, break! I am a warning to you. Break, break, poor stony hearts! Will you not break? What can be done more for stony hearts? I am damned that you may be saved. Now break, now break, poor stony hearts! You need not be damned, though I must." She then fixed her eyes on the corner of the ceiling, and said: "There he is: ay, there he is! Come, good devil, come! Take me away. You said you would dash my brains out: come, do it quickly. I am yours. I will be yours. Come just now. Take me away."

We interrupted her by calling again upon God : on which she sunk down as before : and another young woman began to roar out as loud as she had done. My brother now came in, it being about nine o'clock. We continued in prayer till past eleven ; when God in a moment spoke peace into the soul, first of the first tormented, and then of the other. And they both joined in singing praise to Him who had " stilled the enemy and the avenger."

"Yonder Comes Wesley, Galloping"

Sat. 27.—I was sent for to Kingswood again, to one of those who had been so ill before. A violent rain began just as I set out, so that I was thoroughly wet in a few minutes. Just at that time the woman (then three miles off) cried out, " Yonder comes Wesley, galloping as fast as he can." When I was come, I was quite cold and dead, and fitter for sleep than prayer. She burst out into a horrid laughter, and said, "No power, no power ; no faith, no faith. She is mine ; her soul is mine. I have her, and will not let her go."

We begged of God to increase our faith. Meanwhile her pangs increased more and more ; so that one would have imagined, by the violence of the throes, her body must have been shattered to pieces. One who was clearly convinced this was no natural disorder, said, " I think Satan is let loose. I fear he will not stop here." And added, " I command thee, in the name of the Lord Jesus, to tell if thou hast commission to torment any other soul." It was immediately answered, " I have. L——y C——r and S——h J——s." (Two who lived at some distance, and were then in perfect health.)

We betook ourselves to prayer again ; and ceased not

till she began, about six o'clock, with a clear voice and composed, cheerful look :

"Praise God, from whom all blessings flow."

Sun. 28.—I preached once more at Bradford, at one in the afternoon. The violent rains did not hinder more, I believe, than ten thousand from earnestly attending to what I spoke on those solemn words : " I take you to record this day that I am pure from the blood of all men. For I have not shunned to declare unto you all the counsel of God."

Returning in the evening, I called at Mrs. J——'s, in Kingswood. S——h J——s and L——y C——r were there. It was scarce a quarter of an hour before L——y C——r fell into a strange agony ; and presently after, S——h J——s. The violent convulsions all over their bodies were such as words cannot describe. Their cries and groans were too horrid to be borne, till one of them, in a tone not to be expressed, said : " Where is your faith now ? Come, go to prayers. I will pray with you. ' Our Father, which art in heaven.' " We took the advice, from whomsoever it came, and poured out our souls before God, till L——y C——r's agonies so increased, that it seemed she was in the pangs of death. But in a moment God spoke : she knew his voice ; and both her body and soul were healed.

We continued in prayer till near one, when S——h J——'s voice was also changed, and she began strongly to call upon God. This she did for the greatest part of the night. In the morning we renewed our prayers, while she was crying continually, " I burn ! I burn ! O what shall I do ? I have a fire within me. I cannot bear it. Lord Jesus ! Help ! "—Amen, Lord Jesus ! when thy time is come.

Tues. Nov. 27.—I writ Mr. D. (according to his request) a short account of what had been done in Kingswood, and of our present undertaking there. The account was as follows:

"Few persons have lived long in the west of England who have not heard of the colliers of Kingswood; a people famous, from the beginning hitherto, for neither fearing God nor regarding man: so ignorant of the things of God, that they seemed but one remove from the beasts that perish; and therefore utterly without desire of instruction, as well as without the means of it.

The Colliers of Kingswood

"Many last winter used tauntingly to say of Mr. Whitefield, 'If he will convert heathens, why does not he go to the colliers of Kingswood?' In spring he did so. And as there were thousands who resorted to no place of public worship, he went after them into their own wilderness, 'to seek and save that which was lost.' When he was called away others went into 'the highways and hedges, to compel them to come in.' And, by the grace of God, their labour was not in vain. The scene is already changed. Kingswood does not now, as a year ago, resound with cursing and blasphemy. It is no more filled with drunkenness and uncleanness, and the idle diversions that naturally lead thereto. It is no longer full of wars and fightings, of clamour and bitterness, of wrath and envyings. Peace and love are there. Great numbers of the people are mild, gentle, and easy to be entreated. They 'do not cry, neither strive'; and hardly is their 'voice heard in the streets'; or, indeed, in their own wood; unless when they are at their usual evening diversion—singing praise unto God their Saviour.

"That their children too might know the things which make for their peace, it was some time since proposed to build a house in Kingswood; and after many foreseen and unforeseen difficulties, in June last the foundation was laid. The ground made choice of was in the middle of the wood, between the London and Bath roads, not far from that called Two Mile Hill, about three measured miles from Bristol.

"Here a large room was begun for the school, having four small rooms at either end for the schoolmasters (and, perhaps, if it should please God, some poor children) to lodge in. Two persons are ready to teach, so soon as the house is fit to receive them, the shell of which is nearly finished; so that it is hoped the whole will be completed in spring or early in the summer.

"It is true, although the masters require no pay, yet this undertaking is attended with great expense."

Wesley's Correspondents

1740. Thur. Jan. 3.—I left London, and the next evening came to Oxford, where I spent the two following days in looking over the letters which I had received for the sixteen or eighteen years last past. How few traces of inward religion are here! I found but one among all my correspondents who declared (what I well remember, at that time I knew not how to understand), that God had "shed abroad his love in his heart," and given him the "peace that passeth all understanding." But who believed his report? Should I conceal a sad truth, or declare it for the profit of others? He was expelled out of his society, as a madman; and, being disowned by his friends, and despised and forsaken of all men, lived obscure and unknown for a few months, and then went to Him whom his soul loved.

Mon. 21.—I preached at Hannam, four miles from Bristol. In the evening I made a collection in our congregation for the relief of the poor, without Lawford's gate; who, having no work (because of the severe frost), and no assistance from the parish wherein they lived, were reduced to the last extremity. I made another collection on Thursday; and a third on Sunday; by which we were enabled to feed a hundred, sometimes a hundred and fifty, a day, of those whom we found to need it most.

A Sermon and a Riot

Tues. April 1 (Bristol).—While I was expounding the former part of the twenty-third chapter of the Acts (how wonderfully suited to the occasion! though not by my choice), the floods began to lift up their voice. Some or other of the children of Belial had laboured to disturb us several nights before: but now it seemed as if all the host of the aliens were come together with one consent. Not only the court and the alleys, but all the street, upwards and downwards, was filled with people, shouting, cursing and swearing, and ready to swallow the ground with fierceness and rage. The mayor sent order that they should disperse. But they set him at nought. The chief constable came next in person, who was, till then, sufficiently prejudiced against us. But they insulted him also in so gross a manner, as I believe fully opened his eyes. At length the mayor sent several of his officers, who took the ringleaders into custody, and did not go till all the rest were dispersed. Surely he hath been to us " the minister of God for good."

Wed. 2.—The rioters were brought up to the court, the quarter sessions being held that day. They began to excuse themselves by saying many things of me. But the mayor cut them all short, saying, "What Mr. Wesley is, is nothing to you. I will keep the peace; I will have no rioting in this city."

Calling at Newgate in the afternoon, I was informed that the poor wretches under sentence of death were earnestly desirous to speak with me; but that it could not be; Alderman Beecher having just then sent an express order that they should not. I cite Alderman Beecher to answer for these souls at the judgment-seat of Christ.

Sun. Sept. 14 (London).—As I returned home in the evening, I had no sooner stepped out of the coach than the mob, who were gathered in great numbers about my door, quite closed me in. I rejoiced and blessed God, knowing this was the time I had long been looking for; and immediately spake to those that were next me of "righteousness, and judgment to come." At first not many heard, the noise round about us being exceeding great. But the silence spread farther and farther, till I had a quiet, attentive congregation; and when I left them, they all showed much love, and dismissed me with many blessings.

Preaching Incidents

Sun. 28.—I began expounding the sermon on the mount, at London. In the afternoon I described to a numerous congregation at Kennington, the life of God in the soul. One person who stood on the mount made a little noise at first; but a gentleman, whom I knew not, walked up to him, and, without saying one word, mildly took him by the hand and led him down. From that time he was quiet till he went away.

When I came home I found an innumerable mob round the door, who opened all their throats the moment they saw me. I desired my friends to go into the house; and then walking into the midst of the people, proclaimed, " the name of the Lord, gracious and merciful, and repenting him of the evil." They stood staring one at another. I told them they could not flee from the face of this great God : and therefore besought them, that we might all join together in crying to Him for mercy. To this they readily agreed : I then commended them to his grace, and went undisturbed to the little company within.

Tues. 30.—As I was expounding the twelfth of the Acts, a young man, with some others, rushed in, cursing and swearing vehemently; and so disturbed all near him, that, after a time, they put him out. I observed it, and called to let him come in, that our Lord might bid his chains fall off. As soon as the sermon was over, he came and declared before us all that he was a smuggler, then going on that work; as his disguise, and the great bag he had with him, showed. But he said, he must never do this more; for he was now resolved to have the Lord for his God.

Wesley's Labour Colony

Tues. Nov. 25 (London).—After several methods proposed for employing those who were out of business, we determined to make a trial of one which several of our brethren recommended to us. Our aim was, with as little expense as possible, to keep them at once from want and from idleness, in order to which, we took twelve of the poorest, and a teacher, into the society-room, where they were employed for four months, till spring came on, in carding and spinning of cotton. And the design answered : they were employed and maintained with very little more than the produce of their own labour.

Fri. 28.—A gentleman came to me full of good-will, to exhort me not to leave the Church ; or (which was the same thing in his account) to use extemporary prayer; which, said he, " I will prove to a demonstration to be no prayer at all.   For you cannot do two things at once.   But thinking how to pray, and praying, are two things.   *Ergo*, you cannot both think and pray at once."   Now, may it not be proved by the self-same demonstration, that praying by a form is no prayer at all ? *e.g.* " You cannot do two things at once.   But reading and praying are two things.   *Ergo*, you cannot both read and pray at once."   Q.E.D.

Dispute with Whitefield

1741.   Sun. Feb. 1.—A private letter, wrote to me by Mr. Whitefield, having been printed without either his leave or mine, great numbers of copies were given to our people, both at the door and in the Foundery itself.   Having procured one of them, I related (after preaching) the naked fact to the congregation, and told them, " I will do just what I believe Mr. Whitefield would, were he here himself."   Upon which I tore it in pieces before them all.   Every one who had received it, did the same.   So that in two minutes there was not a whole copy left.

Sat. March 28.—Having heard much of Mr. White-field's unkind behaviour, since his return from Georgia, I went to him to hear him speak for himself, that I might know how to judge.   I much approved of his plainness of speech.   He told me, he and I preached two different gospels; and therefore he not only would not join with, or give me the right hand of fellowship, but was resolved publicly to preach against me and my brother, wheresoever he preached at all.   Mr. Hall (who went with me) put him in mind of the promise he had made but a few days before, that, whatever his private opinion was, he would never publicly preach against us. He said, that promise was only an effect of human weakness, and he was now of another mind.

Mon. April 6.—I had a long conversation with Peter Böhler. I marvel how I refrain from joining these men. I scarce ever see any of them but my heart burns within me. I long to be with them; and yet I am kept from them.

Thur. May 7.—I reminded the United Society that many of our brethren and sisters had not needful food; many were destitute of convenient clothing; many were out of business, and that without their own fault; and many sick and ready to perish: that I had done what in me lay to feed the hungry, to clothe the naked, to employ the poor, and to visit the sick; but was not, alone, sufficient for these things; and therefore desired all whose hearts were as my heart:

1. To bring what clothes each could spare to be distributed among those that wanted most.

2. To give weekly a penny, or what they could afford, for the relief of the poor and sick.

My design, I told them, is to employ for the present all the women who are out of business, and desire it, in knitting.

To these we will first give the common price for what work they do; and then add, according as they need.

Twelve persons are appointed to inspect these, and to visit and provide things needful for the sick.

Each of these is to visit all the sick within their district every other day; and to meet on Tuesday evening, to give an account of what they have done, and consult what can be done farther.

WESLEY'S INTERVIEW WITH WHITEFIELD

Fri. 8.—I found myself much out of order. However, I made shift to preach in the evening: but on Saturday my bodily strength quite failed, so that for several hours I could scarce lift up my head. Sunday, 10. I was obliged to lie down most part of the day, being easy only in that posture. Yet in the evening my weakness was suspended, while I was calling sinners to repentance. But at our love-feast which followed, beside the pain in my back and head, and the fever which still continued upon me, just as I began to pray, I was seized with such a cough, that I could hardly speak. At the same time came strongly into my mind, "These signs shall follow them that believe." I called on Jesus aloud, to "increase my faith," and to "confirm the word of his grace." While I was speaking my pain vanished away; the fever left me; my bodily strength returned; and for many weeks I felt neither weakness nor pain. "Unto thee, O Lord, do I give thanks."

Wesley at Northampton and Nottingham

Mon. June 8.—I set out from Enfield Chace for Leicestershire. In the evening we came to Northampton: and the next afternoon to Mr. Ellis's at Markfield, five or six miles beyond Leicester.

For these two days I had made an experiment which I had been so often and earnestly pressed to do—speaking to none concerning the things of God, unless my heart was free to it. And what was the event? Why, 1. That I spoke to none at all for fourscore miles together; no, not even to him that travelled with me in the chaise, unless a few words at first setting out. 2. That I had no cross either to bear or to take up, and commonly, in an hour or two, fell fast asleep. 3. That I had much respect shown me wherever I came; every one behaving to me, as to a civil, good-natured gentleman. O how pleasing is all this to flesh and blood! Need ye "compass sea and land" to make "proselytes" to this?

Sun. 14.—I rode to Nottingham, and at eight preached at the market-place, to an immense multitude of people, on, "The dead shall hear the voice of the Son of God; and they that hear shall live." I saw only one or two who behaved lightly, whom I immediately spoke to; and they stood reproved. Yet, soon after, a man behind me began aloud to contradict and blaspheme; but upon my turning to him, he stepped behind a pillar, and in a few minutes disappeared.

In the afternoon we returned to Markfield. The church was so excessive hot (being crowded in every corner), that I could not, without difficulty, read the evening service. Being afterwards informed that abundance of people were still without, who could not possibly get into the church, I went out to them, and explained that great promise of our Lord, "I will heal their backslidings: I will love them freely." In the evening I expounded in the church, on her who "loved much, because she had much forgiven."

Mon. 15.—I set out for London, and read over in the way that celebrated book, Martin Luther's "Comment on the Epistle to the Galatians." I was utterly ashamed. How have I esteemed this book, only because I heard it so commended by others; or, at best, because I had read some excellent sentences occasionally quoted from it! But what shall I say, now I judge for myself? now I see with my own eyes? Why, not only that the author makes nothing out, clears up not one considerable difficulty; that he is quite shallow in his remarks on many passages, and muddy and confused almost on all; but that he is deeply tinctured with mysticism throughout, and hence often dangerously wrong.

An Ox in the Congregation

Fri. July 10.—I rode to London, and preached at Short's Gardens, on, "the name of Jesus Christ of Nazareth." Sunday 12. While I was showing, at Charles' Square, what it is "to do justly, to love mercy, and to walk humbly with our God," a great shout began. Many of the rabble had brought an ox, which they were vehemently labouring to drive in among the people. But their labour was in vain; for in spite of them all, he ran round and round, one way and the other, and at length broke through the midst of them clear away, leaving us calmly rejoicing and praising God.

Sat. 25 (Oxford).—It being my turn (which comes about once in three years), I preached at St. Mary's, before the University. The harvest truly is plenteous. So numerous a congregation (from whatever motives they came) I have seldom seen at Oxford. My text was the confession of poor Agrippa, "Almost thou persuadest me to be a Christian." I have "cast my bread upon the waters." Let me "find it again after many days!"

Wed. Aug. 26 (London).—I was informed of a remarkable conversation, at which one of our sisters was present a day or two before; wherein a gentleman was assuring his friends, that he himself was in Charles Square, when a person told Mr. Wesley to his face, that he, Mr. Wesley, had paid twenty pounds already, on being convicted for selling Geneva; and that he now kept two Popish priests in his house. This gave occasion to another to mention what he had himself heard, at an eminent Dissenting teacher's, viz., that it was beyond dispute, Mr. Wesley had large remittances from Spain, in order to make a party among the poor; and that as soon as the Spaniards landed, he was to join them with twenty thousand men.

Wesley at Cardiff

Thur. Oct. 1.—We set out for Wales; but missing our passage over the Severn in the morning, it was sunset before we could get to Newport.   We inquired there if we could hire a guide to Cardiff; but there was none to be had.   A lad coming in quickly after, who was going (he said) to Lanissan, a little village two miles to the right of Cardiff, we resolved to go thither.   At seven we set out : it rained pretty fast, and there being neither moon nor stars, we could neither see any road, nor one another, nor our own horses' heads; but the promise of God did not fail; he gave his angels charge over us; and soon after ten we came safe to Mr. Williams's house at Lanissan.

Fri. 2.—We rode to Fonmon castle.   We found Mr. Jones's daughter ill of the small-pox; but he could cheerfully leave her and all the rest in the hands of Him in whom he now believed.   In the evening I preached at Cardiff, in the shire-hall, a large and convenient place, on, " God hath given unto us eternal life, and this life is in his Son."   There having been a feast in the town that day, I believed it needful to add a few words upon imtemperance : and while I was saying, " As for you, drunkards, you have no part in this life; you abide in death; you choose death and hell "; a man cried out vehemently, " I am one; and thither I am going."   But I trust God at that hour began to show him and others "a more excellent way."

Sun. Nov. 22 (Bristol).—Being not suffered to go to church as yet [after a serious fever], I communicated at home. I was advised to stay at home some time longer; but I could not apprehend it necessary : and therefore, on Monday, 23, went to the new room, where we praised God for all his mercies. And I expounded, for about an hour (without any faintness or weariness), on, "What reward shall I give upon the Lord for all the benefits that he hath done unto me? I will receive the cup of salvation, and call upon the name of the Lord."

I preached once every day this week, and found no inconvenience by it. Sunday, 29. I thought I might go a little farther. So I preached both at Kingswood and at Bristol; and afterwards spent near an hour with the society, and about two hours at the love-feast. But my body could not yet keep pace with my mind. I had another fit of my fever the next day; but it lasted not long, and I continued slowly to regain my strength.

A Curious Interruption

Mon. Dec. 7.—I preached on, "Trust ye in the Lord Jehovah; for in the Lord is everlasting strength." I was showing, what cause we had to trust in the Captain of our salvation, when one in the midst of the room cried out, "Who was your captain the other day, when you hanged yourself? I know the man who saw you when you was cut down." This wise story, it seems, had been diligently spread abroad, and cordially believed by many in Bristol. I desired they would make room for the man to come nearer. But the moment he saw the way open, he ran away with all possible speed, not so much as once looking behind him.

Sat. 12.—In the evening one desired to speak with me. I perceived him to be in the utmost confusion, so

that for awhile he could not speak.   At length, he said,
" I am he that interrupted you at the new room, on
Monday.   I have had no rest since, day or night, nor
could have till I had spoken to you.   I hope you will
forgive me, and that it will be a warning to me all the
days of my life."

Wesley's Congregation Stoned

1742. Mon. Jan. 25 (London).—While I was explaining at Long Lane, " He that committeth sin is of
the devil " ; his servants were above measure enraged :
they not only made all possible noise (although, as I had
desired before, no man stirred from his place, or answered them a word) ; but violently thrust many persons
to and fro, struck others, and break down part of the
house.   At length they began throwing large stones
upon the house, which, forcing their way wherever they
came, fell down, together with the tiles, among the
people, so that they were in danger of their lives.   I
then told them, " You must not go on thus ; I am
ordered by the magistrate, who is, in this respect, to us
the minister of God, to inform him of those who break
the laws of God and the King : and I must do it if you
persist herein ; otherwise I am a partaker of your sin."

When I ceased speaking they were more outrageous
than before.   Upon this I said, " Let three or four
calm men take hold of the foremost, and charge a constable with him, that the law may take its course."   They
did so, and brought him into the house, cursing and
blaspheming in a dreadful manner.   I desired five or
six to go with him to Justice Copeland, to whom they
nakedly related the fact.   The justice immediately
bound him over to the next sessions at Guildford.

I observed when the man was brought into the house,

that many of his companions were loudly crying out, " Richard Smith, Richard Smith!" who, as it afterwards appeared, was one of their stoutest champions. But Richard Smith answered not; he was fallen into the hands of One higher than they. God had struck him to the heart; as also a woman, who was speaking words not fit to be repeated, and throwing whatever came to hand, whom He overtook in the very act. She came into the house with Richard Smith, fell upon her knees before us all, and strongly exhorted him, never to turn back, never to forget the mercy which God had shown to his soul. From this time we had never any considerable interruption or disturbance at Long Lane; although we withdrew our persecution, upon the offender's submission and promise of better behaviour.

Tues. 26.—I explained at Chelsea the faith which worketh by love. I was very weak when I went into the room; but the more " the beasts of the people" increased in madness and rage, the more was I strengthened, both in body and soul; so that I believe few in the house, which was exceeding full, lost one sentence of what I spoke. Indeed they could not see me, nor one another at a few yards distance, by reason of the exceeding thick smoke, which was occasioned by the wild-fire, and things of that kind, continually thrown into the room. But they who could praise God in the midst of the fires were not to be affrighted by a little smoke.

Mon. Feb. 15.—Many met together to consult on a proper method for discharging the public debt; and it was at length agreed, 1. That every member of the society, who was able, should contribute a penny a week. 2. That the whole society should be divided into little companies or classes—about twelve in each class. And 3. That one person in each class should receive the contribution of the rest, and bring it in to the Stewards, weekly.

Fri. March 10.—I rode once more to Pensford at the earnest request of several serious people. The place where they desired me to preach was a little green spot, near the town. But I had no sooner begun than a great company of rabble, hired (as we afterwards found) for that purpose, came furiously upon us, bringing a bull, which they had been baiting, and now strove to drive in among the people. But the beast was wiser than his drivers; and continually ran either on one side of us or the other, while we quietly sang praise to God, and prayed for about an hour. The poor wretches, finding themselves disappointed, at length seized upon the bull, now weak and tired, after having been so long torn and beaten both by dogs and men; and, by main strength, partly dragged, and partly thrust, him in among the people.

A Bull in the Congregation

When they had forced their way to the little table on which I stood, they strove several times to throw it down, by thrusting the helpless beast against it, who, of himself, stirred no more than a log of wood. I once or twice put aside his head with my hand, that the blood might not drop upon my clothes; intending to go on as soon as the hurry should be a little over. But the table falling down, some of our friends caught me in their arms, and carried me right away on their shoulders; while the rabble wreaked their vengeance on the table, which they tore bit from bit. We went a little way off, where I finished my discourse, without any noise or interruption.

Sun. 21.—In the evening I rode to Marshfield, and on Tuesday, in the afternoon, came to London. Wednesday, 24. I preached for the last time in the French chapel at Wapping, on "If ye continue in my word, then are ye my disciples indeed."

Thur. 25.—I appointed several earnest and sensible men to meet me, to whom I showed the great difficulty I had long found of knowing the people who desired to be under my care. After much discourse, they all agreed, there could be no better way to come to a sure, thorough knowledge of each person, than to divide them into classes, like those at Bristol, under the inspection of those in whom I could most confide. This was the origin of our classes at London, for which I can never sufficiently praise God; the unspeakable usefulness of the institution having ever since been more and more manifest.

Fri. April 9.—We had the first watch-night in London. We commonly choose for this solemn service the Friday night nearest the full moon, either before or after, that those of the congregation who live at a distance, may have light to their several homes. The service begins at half an hour past eight, and continues till a little after midnight. We have often found a peculiar blessing at these seasons. There is generally a deep awe upon the congregation, perhaps in some measure owing to the silence of the night, particularly in singing the hymn with which we commonly conclude :

> "Hearken to the solemn voice,
> The awful midnight cry !
> Waiting souls, rejoice, rejoice,
> And feel the Bridegroom nigh."

Sun. May 9.—I preached in Charles Square to the largest congregation I have ever seen there. Many of the baser people would fain have interrupted, but they found, after a time, it was lost labour. One, who was more serious, was (as she afterwards confessed) exceedingly angry at them. But she was quickly rebuked, by a stone which light upon her forehead, and struck her down to the ground. In that moment her anger was at an end, and love only filled her heart.

Wed. 12.—I waited on the Archbishop of Canterbury with Mr. Whitefield, and again on Friday; as also on the Bishop of London. I trust if we should be called to appear before princes, we should not be ashamed.

Wesley Was "the Better Mounted"

Mon. 17.—I had designed this morning to set out for Bristol; but was unexpectedly prevented. In the afternoon I received a letter from Leicestershire, pressing me to come without delay, and pay the last office of friendship to one whose soul was on the wing for eternity. On Thursday, 20, I set out. The next afternoon I stopped a little at Newport-Pagnell, and then rode on till I overtook a serious man, with whom I immediately fell into conversation.

He presently gave me to know what his opinions were: therefore I said nothing to contradict them. But that did not content him: he was quite uneasy to know whether I held the doctrine of the decrees as he did; but I told him over and over, " We had better keep to practical things, lest we should be angry at one another." And so we did for two miles, till he caught me unawares, and dragged me into the dispute before I knew where I was. He then grew warmer and warmer; told me I was rotten at heart, and supposed I was one of John Wesley's followers. I told him, " No, I am John Wesley himself." Upon which he would gladly have run away outright. But being the better mounted of the two, I kept close to his side, and endeavoured to show him his heart, till we came into the street of Northampton.

Thur. 27.—We came to Newcastle about six; and, after a short refreshment, walked into the town. I was surprised : so much drunkenness, cursing, and swearing (even from the mouths of little children), do I never remember to have seen and heard before, in so small a compass of time. Surely this place is ripe for Him who " came not to call the righteous, but sinners to repentance."

Sun. 30.—At seven I walked down to Sandgate, the poorest and most contemptible part of the town ; and, standing at the end of the street with John Taylor, began to sing the hundredth Psalm, Three or four people came out to see what was the matter ; who soon increased to four or five hundred. I suppose there might be twelve or fifteen hundred, before I had done preaching ; to whom I applied those solemn words, " He was wounded for our transgressions, He was bruised for our iniquities ; the chastisement of our peace was upon Him ; and by His stripes we are healed."

A Big Crowd at Newcastle

Observing the people, when I had done, to stand gaping and staring upon me, with the most profound astonishment, I told them, " If you desire to know who I am, my name is John Wesley. At five in the evening, with God's help, I design to preach here again."

At five, the hill on which I designed to preach was covered, from the top to the bottom. I never saw so large a number of people together, either at Moorfields, or at Kennington Common. I knew it was not possible for the one half to hear, although my voice was then strong and clear ; and I stood so as to have them all in view, as they were ranged on the side of the hill. The word of God which I set before them was, " I will heal

their backsliding, I will love them freely." After
preaching, the poor people were ready to tread me
under foot, out of pure love and kindness. It was some
time before I could possibly get out of the press. I
then went back another way than I come; but several
were got to our inn before me; by whom I was
vehemently importuned to stay with them, at least, a
few days; or, however, one day more. But I could not
consent; having given my word to be at Birstal, with
God's leave, on Tuesday night.

Wesley on his Father's Tombstone

Sat. June 5.—It being many years since I had been
in Epworth before, I went to an inn, in the middle of
the town, not knowing whether there were any left in it
now who would not be ashamed of my acquaintance.
But an old servant of my father's, with two or three
poor women, presently found me out. I asked her,
"Do you know any in Epworth who are in earnest to
be saved?" She answered, "I am, by the grace of
God; and I know I am saved through faith." I asked,
"Have you then the peace of God? Do you know that
He has forgiven your sins?" She replied, "I thank
God, I know it well. And many here can say the same
thing."

Sun. 6.—A little before the service began, I went to
Mr. Romley, the curate, and offered to assist him either
by preaching or reading prayers. But he did not care to
accept of my assistance. The church was exceeding full
in the afternoon, a rumour being spread that I was to
preach. But the sermon on, "Quench not the Spirit," was
not suitable to the expectation of many of the hearers.
Mr. Romley told them, one of the most dangerous ways
of quenching the Spirit was by enthusiasm; and en-

EPWORTH CHURCH

WESLEY PREACHING ON HIS FATHER'S TOMB

larged on the character of an enthusiast, in a very florid and oratorical manner. After sermon John Taylor stood in the churchyard, and gave notice, as the people were coming out, " Mr. Wesley, not being permitted to preach in the church, designs to preach here at six o'clock."

Accordingly at six I came, and found such a congregation as I believe Epworth never saw before. I stood near the east end of the church, upon my father's tombstone, and cried, " The kingdom of heaven is not meat and drink; but righteousness, and peace, and joy in the Holy Ghost."

"Let them Convert the Scolds"

Wed. 9.—I rode over to a neighbouring town, to wait upon a justice of peace, a man of candour and understanding; before whom (I was informed) their angry neighbours had carried a whole waggon-load of these new heretics. But when he asked what they had done, there was a deep silence; for that was a point their conductors had forgot. At length one said, " Why, they pretended to be better than other people; and besides, they prayed from morning to night." Mr. S. asked, " But have they done nothing besides ? " " Yes, sir," said an old man : " an't please your worship, they have *converted* my wife. Till she went among them, she had such a tongue! And now she is as quiet as a lamb." " Carry them back, carry them back," replied the justice, " and let them convert all the scolds in the town."

Sat. 12.—I preached on the righteousness of the law and the righteousness of faith. While I was speaking, several dropped down as dead; and among the rest, such a cry was heard, of sinners groaning for the righteousness of faith, as almost drowned my voice. But many of these soon lifted up their heads with joy, and broke out into thanksgiving; being assured they now had the desire of their soul—the forgiveness of their sins.

I observed a gentleman there, who was remarkable for not pretending to be of any religion at all. I was informed he had not been at public worship of any kind for upwards of thirty years. Seeing him stand as motionless as a statue, I asked him abruptly, " Sir, are you a sinner ? " He replied, with a deep and broken voice, " Sinner enough "; and continued staring upwards till his wife and a servant or two, who were all in tears, put him into his chaise and carried him home.

Sun. 13.—At seven I preached at Haxey, on, " What must I do to be saved ? " Thence I went to Wroote, of which (as well as Epworth) my father was rector for several years. Mr. Whitelamb offering me the church, I preached in the morning on, " Ask, and it shall be given you " : in the afternoon, on the difference between the righteousness of the law and the righteousness of faith. But the church could not contain the people, many of whom came from far, and, I trust, not in vain.

At six I preached for the last time in Epworth church-yard (being to leave the town the next morning), to a vast multitude gathered together from all parts, on the beginning of our Lord's Sermon on the Mount. I con-tinued among them for near three hours, and yet we scarce knew how to part. O let none think his labour of love is lost because the fruit does not immediately appear ! Near forty years did my father labour here ; but he saw little fruit of all his labour. I took some pains among this people too; and my strength also seemed spent in vain; but now the fruit appeared.

There were scarce any in the town on whom either my father or I had taken any pains formerly but the seed, sown so long since, now sprung up, bringing forth repentance and remission of sins.

Death of Wesley's Mother

I left Bristol in the evening of Sunday, July 18, and on Tuesday came to London. I found my mother on the borders of eternity. But she had no doubt or fear; nor any desire but (as soon as God should call) "to depart and be with Christ."

Fri. 23.—About three in the afternoon I went to my mother, and found her change was near. I sat down on the bed-side. She was in her last conflict; unable to speak, but I believe quite sensible. Her look was calm and serene, and her eyes fixed upward, while we commended her soul to God. From three to four the silver cord was loosing, and the wheel breaking at the cistern; and then without any struggle, or sigh, or groan, the soul was set at liberty. We stood round the bed, and fulfilled her last request, uttered a little before she lost her speech: "Children, as soon as I am released, sing a psalm of praise to God."

Sun. August 1.—Almost an innumerable company of people being gathered together, about five in the afternoon, I committed to the earth the body of my mother, to sleep with her fathers. The portion of Scripture from which I afterwards spoke was, "I saw a great white throne, and Him that sat on it, from whose face the earth and the heaven fled away; and there was found no place for them. And I saw the dead, small and great, stand before God; and the books were opened: and the dead were judged out of those things which were written in the books, according to their

works." It was one of the most solemn assemblies I
ever saw, or expect to see on this side eternity.

We set up a plain stone at the head of her grave,
inscribed with the following words :

𝕳𝖊𝖗𝖊 𝖑𝖎𝖊𝖘 𝖙𝖍𝖊 𝕭𝖔𝖉𝖞

OF

MRS. SUSANNAH WESLEY,

THE YOUNGEST AND LAST SURVIVING DAUGHTER OF
DR. SAMUEL ANNESLEY.

In sure and steadfast hope to rise,
And claim her mansion in the skies,
A Christian here her flesh laid down,
The cross exchanging for a crown.

True daughter of affliction, she,
Inured to pain and misery,
Mourn'd a long night of griefs and fears,
A legal night of seventy years.

The Father then reveal'd his Son,
Him in the broken bread made known,
She knew and felt her sins forgiven,
And found the earnest of her heaven.

Meet for the fellowship above,
She heard the call, " Arise, my love ! "
" I come," her dying looks replied,
And lamb-like, as her Lord, she died.

Mrs. Wesley as Preacher

I cannot but further observe, that even she (as well as
her father, and grandfather, her husband, and her three
sons) had been, in her measure and degree, a preacher
of righteousness. This I learned from a letter, wrote
long since to my father; part of which I have here
subjoined :

February 6, 1711–12.

" —— As I am a woman, so I am also mistress of a
large family. And though the superior charge of the

SUSANNAH WESLEY

souls contained in it lies upon you ; yet, in your absence, I cannot but look upon every soul you leave under my care, as a talent committed to me under a trust, by the great Lord of all the families both of heaven and earth. And if I am unfaithful to him or you in neglecting to improve these talents, how shall I answer unto him, when he shall command me to render an account of my stewardship ?

" As these, and other such like thoughts, made me at first take a more than ordinary care of the souls of my children and servants, so—knowing our religion requires a strict observation of the Lord's day, and not thinking that we fully answered the end of the institution by going to church, unless we filled up the intermediate spaces of time by other acts of piety and devotion—I thought it my duty to spend some part of the day, in reading to and instructing my family : and such time I esteemed spent in a way more acceptable to God, than if I had retired to my own private devotions.

" This was the beginning of my present practice. Other people's coming and joining with us was merely accidental. Our lad told his parents : they first desired to be admitted ; then others that heard of it begged leave also : so our company increased to about thirty ; and it seldom exceeded forty last winter.

" But soon after you went to London last, I light on the account of the Danish Missionaries. I was, I think, never more affected with anything; I could not forbear spending good part of that evening in praising and adoring the divine goodness for inspiring them with such ardent zeal for His glory. For several days I could think or speak of little else. At last it came into my mind, Though I am not a man nor a minister, yet if my heart were sincerely devoted to God, and I was inspired with a true zeal for his glory, I might do somewhat more than I do. I thought I might pray more for them, and might speak to those with whom I converse with more warmth of affection. I resolved to begin with my own children; in which I observe the following method : I take such a proportion of time as I can spare every night to discourse with each child apart. On Monday, I talk with Molly; on Tuesday, with Hetty; Wednesday, with Nancy; Thursday, with Jacky; Friday, with Patty; Saturday, with Charles; and with Emily and Suky together on Sunday.

She Speaks to Two Hundred

" With those few neighbours that then came to me, I discoursed more freely and affectionately. I chose the best and most awakening sermons we have. And I spent somewhat more time with them in such exercises, without being careful about the success of my undertaking. Since this, our company increased every night; for I dare deny none that ask admittance."

" Last Sunday I believe we had above two hundred. And yet many went away, for want of room to stand.

" We banish all temporal concerns from our society. None is suffered to mingle any discourse about them with our reading or singing. We keep close to the business of the day; and when it is over, all go home.

" I cannot conceive, why any should reflect upon you, because your wife endeavours to draw people to church, and to restrain them from profaning the Lord's day, by reading to them, and other persuasions. For my part, I value no censure upon this account. I have long since shook hands with the world. And I heartily wish, I had never given them more reason to speak against me.

" As to its looking particular, I grant it does. And so does almost anything that is serious, or that may any way advance the glory of God, or the salvation of souls.

" As for your proposal, of letting some other person read : alas ! you do not consider what a people these are. I do not think one man among them could read a sermon, without spelling a good part of it. Nor has any of our family a voice strong enough to be heard by such a number of people.

" But there is one thing about which I am much dissatisfied ; that is, their being present at family prayers. I do not speak of any concern I am under, barely because so many are present ; for those who have the honour of speaking to the Great and Holy God, need not be ashamed to speak before the whole world ; but because of my sex. I doubt if it is proper for me to present the prayers of the people to God. Last Sunday I would fain have dismissed them before prayers ; but they begged so earnestly to stay, I durst not deny them.

"To THE REV. MR. WESLEY,
" *In St. Margaret's Churchyard, Westminster.*"

How the Wesleys were Brought up

For the benefit of those who are entrusted, as she was, with the care of a numerous family, I cannot but add one letter more, which I received many years ago :

July 24, 1732.

" DEAR SON,—According to your desire, I have collected the principal rules I observed in educating my family ; which I now send you as they occurred to my mind, and you may (if you think they can be of use to any) dispose of them in what order you please.

" The children were always put into a regular method of living, in such things as they were capable of, from their birth; as in dressing, undressing, changing their linen, &c. The first quarter commonly passes in sleep. After that, they were, if possible, laid into their cradles awake, and rocked to sleep; and so they were kept rocking, till it was time for them to awake. This was done to bring them to a regular course of sleeping; which at first was three hours in the morning, and three in the afternoon: afterward two hours, till they needed none at all.

" When turned a year old (and some before), they were taught to fear the rod, and to cry softly; by which means they escaped abundance of correction they might otherwise have had; and that most odious noise of the crying of children was rarely heard in the house; but the family usually lived in as much quietness as if there had not been a child among them.

" As soon as they were grown pretty strong, they were confined to three meals a day. At dinner their little table and chairs were set by ours, where they could be overlooked; and they were suffered to eat and drink (small beer) as much as they would; but not to call for anything. If they wanted aught, they used to whisper to the maid which attended them, who came and spake to me; and as soon as they could handle a knife and fork, they were set to our table. They were never suffered to choose their meat, but always made to eat such things as were provided for the family.

" Mornings they had always spoon-meat; sometimes at nights. But whatever they had, they were never permitted to eat, at those meals, of more than one thing; and of that sparingly enough. Drinking or eating between meals was never allowed, unless in case of sickness; which seldom happened. Nor were they suffered to go into the kitchen to ask anything of the servants, when they were at meat: if it was known they did, they were certainly beat, and the servants severely reprimanded.

" At six, as soon as family prayers were over, they had their supper; at seven, the maid washed them; and, beginning at the youngest, she undressed and got them all to bed by eight; at which time she left them in their several rooms awake; for there was no such thing allowed of in our house, as sitting by a child till it fell asleep.

" They were so constantly used to eat and drink what was given them, that when any of them was ill, there was no difficulty in making them take the most unpleasant medicine: for they durst not refuse it, though some of them would presently throw it up. This I mention to show that a person may be taught to take anything, though it be never so much against his stomach.

"Conquer the Child's Will"

" In order to form the minds of children, the first thing to be done is to conquer their will, and bring them to an obedient temper. To inform the understanding is a work of time, and must with children proceed by slow degrees as they are able to bear it: but the subjecting the will is a thing which must be done at once; and the sooner the better. For by neglecting timely correction, they will contract a stubbornness and obstinacy which is hardly ever after conquered; and never, without using such severity as would be as painful to me as to the child. In the esteem of the world they pass for kind and indulgent, whom I call cruel, parents, who permit their children to get habits which they know must be afterwards broken. Nay, some are so stupidly fond, as in sport to teach their children to do things which, in a while after, they have severely beaten them for doing.

" Whenever a child is corrected, it must be conquered; and this will be no hard matter to do, if it be not grown headstrong by too much indulgence. And when the will of a child is totally subdued, and it is brought to revere and stand in awe of the parents, then a great many childish follies and inadvertences may be passed by. Some should be overlooked and taken no notice of, and others mildly reproved; but no wilful transgression ought ever to be forgiven children, without chastisement, less or more, as the nature and circumstances of the offence require.

" I insist upon conquering the will of children betimes, because this is the only strong and rational foundation of a religious education; without which both precept and example will be ineffectual. But when this is thoroughly done, then a child is capable of being governed by the reason and piety of its parents, till its own understanding comes to maturity, and the principles of religion have taken root in the mind.

" I cannot yet dismiss this subject. As self-will is the root of all sin and misery, so whatever cherishes this in children insures their after-wretchedness and irreligion; whatever checks and mortifies it promotes their future happiness and piety. This is still more evident, if we farther consider, that religion is nothing else than the doing the will of God, and not our own : that the one grand impediment to our temporal and eternal happiness being this self - will, no indulgences of it can be trivial, no denial unprofitable. Heaven or hell depends on this alone. So that the parent who studies to subdue it in his child, works together with God in the renewing and saving a soul. The parent who indulges it does the devil's work, makes religion impracticable, salvation unattainable; and does all that in him lies to damn his child, soul and body for ever.

They had Nothing they Cried For

" The children of this family were taught, as soon as they could speak, the Lord's prayer, which they were made to say at rising and bed-time constantly; to which, as they grew bigger, were added a short prayer for their parents, and some collects; a short catechism, and some portion of Scripture, as their memories could bear.

" They were very early made to distinguish the Sabbath from other days; before they could well speak or go. They were as soon taught to be still at family prayers, and to ask a blessing immediately after, which they used to do by signs, before they could kneel or speak.

" They were quickly made to understand they might have nothing they cried for, and instructed to speak handsomely for what they wanted, They were not suffered to ask even the lowest servant for aught without saying, ' Pray give me such a thing '; and the servant was chid, if she ever let them omit that word. Taking God's name in vain, cursing and swearing, profaneness, obscenity, rude, ill-bred names, were never heard among them. Nor were they ever permitted to call each other by their proper names without the addition of brother or sister.

" None of them were taught to read till five years old, except Kezzy, in whose case I was overruled; and she was more years learning than any of the rest had been months. The way of teaching was this: The day before a child began to learn, the house was set in order, every one's work appointed them, and a charge given that none should come into the room from nine till twelve, or from two till five; which, you know, were our school hours. One day was allowed the child wherein to learn its letters; and each of them did in that time know all its letters, great and small, except Molly and Nancy, who were a day and a half before they knew them perfectly; for which I then thought them very dull; but since I have observed how long many children are learning the horn-book, I have changed my opinion.

"But the reason why I thought them so then was, because the rest learned so readily; and your brother Samuel, who was the first child I ever taught, learned the alphabet in a few hours. He was five years old on February 10; the next day he began to learn, and as soon as he knew the letters, began at the first chapter of Genesis. He was taught to spell the first verse, then to read it over and over, till he could read it offhand without any hesitation, so on to the second, &c., till he took ten verses for a lesson, which he quickly did. Easter fell low that year, and by Whitsuntide he could read a chapter very well; for he read continually, and had such a prodigious memory, that I cannot remember ever to have told him the same word twice.

Keeping the Wesley Children in Order

"What was yet stranger, any word he had learned in his lesson, he knew, wherever he saw it, either in his Bible, or any other book; by which means he learned very soon to read an English author well.

"The same method was observed with them all. As soon as they knew the letters, they were put first to spell, and read one line, then a verse; never leaving till perfect in their lesson, were it shorter or longer. So one or other continued reading at school-time, without any intermission ; and before we left school, each child read what he had learned that morning ; and ere we parted in the afternoon, what they had learned that day.

" There was no such thing as loud talking or playing allowed of; but every one was kept close to their business, for the six hours of school : and it is almost incredible, what a child may be taught in a quarter of a year, by a vigorous application, if it have but a tolerable capacity, and good health. Every one of these, Kezzy excepted, could read better in that time, than the most of women can do as long as they live.

" Rising out of their places, or going out of the room, was not permitted, unless for good cause; and running into the yard, garden, or street, without leave, was always esteemed a capital offence.

" For some years we went on very well. Never were children in better order. Never were children better disposed to piety, or in more subjection to their parents ; till that fatal dispersion of them, after the fire, into several families. In those they were left at full liberty to converse with servants, which before they had always been restrained from; and to run abroad, and play with any children, good or bad. They soon learned to neglect a strict observation of the Sabbath, and got knowledge of several songs and bad things, which before they had no notion of. The civil behaviour which made them admired, when at home, by all which saw them, was, in great measure, lost ; and a clownish accent, and many rude ways, were learned, which were not reformed without some difficulty.

" When the house was rebuilt, and the children all brought home, we entered upon a strict reform; and then was begun the custom of singing psalms at beginning and leaving school, morning and evening. Then also that of a general retirement at five o'clock was entered upon; when the oldest took the youngest that could speak, and the second the next, to whom they read the Psalms for the day, and a chapter in the New Testament; as, in the morning, they were directed to read the Psalms and a chapter in the Old: after which they went to their private prayers, before they got their breakfast, or came into the family. And, I thank God, the custom is still preserved among us.

Susanna Wesley's "By-laws"

"There were several by-laws observed among us, which slipped my memory, or else they had been inserted in their proper place; but I mention them here, because I think them useful.

"1. It had been observed, that cowardice and fear of punishment often lead children into lying, till they get a custom of it, which they cannot leave. To prevent this, a law was made, That whoever was charged with a fault, of which they were guilty, if they would ingenuously confess it, and promise to amend, should not be beaten. This rule prevented a great deal of lying, and would have done more, if one in the family would have observed it. But he could not be prevailed on, and therefore was often imposed on by false colours and equivocations; which none would have used (except one), had they been kindly dealt with. And some, in spite of all, would always speak truth plainly.

"2. That no sinful action, as lying, pilfering, playing at church, or on the Lord's day, disobedience, quarrelling, &c., should ever pass unpunished.

"3. That no child should ever be chid, or beat twice,

for the same fault; and that if they amended, they should never be upbraided with it afterwards.

"4. That every signal act of obedience, especially when it crossed upon their own inclinations, should be always commended, and frequently rewarded, according to the merits of the cause.

"5. That if ever any child performed an act of obedience, or did anything with an intention to please, though the performance was not well, yet the obedience and intention should be kindly accepted; and the child with sweetness directed how to do better for the future.

"6. That propriety be inviolably preserved, and none suffered to invade the property of another in the smallest matter, though it were but of the value of a farthing, or a pin; which they might not take from the owner without, much less against, his consent. This rule can never be too much inculcated on the minds of children; and from the want of parents or governors doing it as they ought, proceeds that shameful neglect of justice which we may observe in the world.

"7. That promises be strictly observed; and a gift once bestowed, and so the right passed away from the donor, be not resumed, but left to the disposal of him to whom it was given; unless it were conditional, and the condition of the obligation not performed.

"8. That no girl be taught to work till she can read very well; and then that she be kept to her work with the same application, and for the same time, that she was held to in reading. This rule also is much to be observed; for the putting children to learn sewing before they can read perfectly, is the very reason why so few women can read fit to be heard, and never to be well understood."

Wed. December 1 (Newcastle).—We had several places

offered, on which to build a room for the society; but none was such as we wanted. And perhaps there was a providence in our not finding any as yet; for, by this means, I was kept at Newcastle, whether I would or no.

Sat. 4.—I was both surprised and grieved at a genuine instance of enthusiasm. J—— B——, of Tunfield Leigh, who had received a sense of the love of God a few days before, came riding through the town, hallooing and shouting, and driving all the people before him; telling them, God had told him he should be a king, and should tread all his enemies under his feet. I sent him home immediately to his work, and advised him to cry day and night to God, that he might be lowly in heart; lest Satan should again get an advantage over him.

Mr. Stephenson and Wesley

To-day a gentleman called and offered me a piece of ground. On Monday an article was drawn, wherein he agreed to put me into possession on Thursday, upon payment of thirty pounds.

Tues, 7.—I was so ill in the morning, that I was obliged to send Mr. Williams to the room. He afterwards went to Mr. Stephenson, a merchant in the town, who had a passage through the ground we intended to buy. I was willing to purchase it. Mr. Stephenson told him, "Sir, I do not want money; but if Mr. Wesley wants ground, he may have a piece of my garden, adjoining to the place you mention. I am at a word. For forty pounds he shall have sixteen yards in breadth, and thirty in length."

Wed. 8.—Mr. Stephenson and I signed an article, and I took possession of the ground. But I could not fairly go back from my agreement with Mr. Riddel: so I entered on his ground at the same time. The whole is

about forty yards in length; in the middle of which we
determined to build the house, leaving room for a small
courtyard before, and a little garden behind, the
building.

Mon. 13.—I removed into a lodging, adjoining to the
ground where we were preparing to build; but the
violent frost obliged us to delay the work. I never felt
so intense cold before. In a room where a constant fire
was kept, though my desk was fixed within a yard of the
chimney, I could not write for a quarter of an hour
together, without my hands being quite benumbed.

Newcastle's First Methodist Room

Mon. 20.—We laid the first stone of the house.
Many were gathered, from all parts, to see it; but none
scoffed or interrupted while we praised God, and prayed
that He would prosper the work of our hands upon us.
Three or four times in the evening, I was forced to
break off preaching, that we might pray and give thanks
to God.

Thur. 23.—It being computed that such a house as
was proposed could not be finished under £700,
many were positive it would never be finished at
all; others, that I should not live to see it covered.
I was of another mind; nothing doubting but, as it
was begun for God's sake, He would provide what was
needful for the finishing it.

1743. Sat. January 1.—Between Doncaster and
Epworth I overtook one who immediately accosted me
with so many and so impertinent questions, that I was
quite amazed. In the midst of some of them, concerning
my travels and my journey, I interrupted him, and asked,
"Are you aware that we are on a longer journey; that
we are travelling toward eternity?" He replied instantly,

"O, I find you! I find you! I know where you are! Is not your name Wesley? 'Tis pity! 'Tis great pity! Why could not your father's religion serve you? Why must you have a new religion?" I was going to reply; but he cut me short by crying out in triumph, "I am a Christian! I am a Christian! I am a Churchman! I am a Churchman! I am none of your Culamites"; as plain as he could speak; for he was so drunk, he could but just keep his seat. Having then clearly won the day, or, as his phrase was, "put them all down," he began kicking his horse on both sides and rode off as fast as he could.

Wesley Refused the Sacrament at Epworth

In the evening I reached Epworth. Sunday, 2. At five I preached on, "So is every one that is born of the Spirit." About eight I preached from my father's tomb on Heb. viii. 11. Many from the neighbouring towns asked, if it would not be well, as it was sacrament Sunday, for them to receive it. I told them, "By all means: but it would be more respectful first to ask Mr. Romley, the curate's leave." One did so, in the name of the rest; to whom he said, "Pray tell Mr. Wesley, I shall not give him the sacrament; for he is not fit."

How wise a God is our God! There could not have been so fit a place under heaven, where this should befall me first as my father's house, the place of my nativity, and the very place where, "according to the straitest sect of our religion," I had so long "lived a Pharisee!" It was also fit, in the highest degree, that he who repelled me from that very table, where I had myself so often distributed the bread of life, should be one who owed his all in this world to the tender love which my father had shown to his, as well as personally to himself.

Tues. 22.—I went to South-Biddick, a village of colliers seven miles south-east of Newcastle. The spot where I stood was just at the bottom of a semi-circular hill, on the rising sides of which many hundreds stood; but far more on the plain beneath. I cried to them, in the words of the prophet, " O ye dry bones, hear the word of the Lord ! " Deep attention sat on every face; so that here also I believed it would be well to preach weekly.

Wesley and the Cock-fighter

Wed. 23.—I met a gentleman in the streets cursing and swearing in so dreadful a manner, that I could not but stop him. He soon grew calmer; told me he must treat me with a glass of wine; and that he would come and hear me, only he was afraid I should say something against fighting of cocks.

April 1. (Being Good Friday.)—I had a great desire to visit a little village called Placey, about ten measured miles north of Newcastle. It is inhabited by colliers only, and such as had been always in the first rank for savage ignorance and wickedness of every kind. Their grand assembly used to be on the Lord's day; on which men, women, and children met together to dance, fight, curse and swear, and play at chuck ball, span-farthing, or whatever came next to hand. I felt great compassion for these poor creatures, from the time I heard of them first; and the more, because all men seemed to despair of them.

Between seven and eight I set out with John Healy, my guide. The north wind, being unusually high, drove the sleet in our face, which froze as it fell, and cased us over presently. When we came to Placey, we could very hardly stand. As soon as we were a little recovered I went into the square, and declared Him who "was wounded for our transgressions" and "bruised for our iniquities." The poor sinners were quickly gathered together and gave earnest heed to the things which were spoken. And so they did in the afternoon again, in spite of the wind and snow, when I besought them to receive Him for their King; to "repent and believe the Gospel."

Wesley in Seven Dials

Sun. May 29.—I began officiating at the chapel in West Street, near the Seven Dials, of which (by a strange chain of providences) we have a lease for several years. I preached on the Gospel for the day, part of the third chapter of St. John; and afterwards administered the Lord's Supper to some hundreds of communicants. I was a little afraid at first, that my strength would not suffice for the business of the day, when a service of five hours (for it lasted from ten to three) was added to my usual employment. But God looked to that: so I must think; and they that will call it enthusiasm may. I preached at the Great-gardens at five to an immense congregation, on, "Ye must be born again." Then the leaders met (who filled all the time that I was not speaking in public); and after them, the bands. At ten at night I was less weary than at six in the morning.

Sun. July 10 (Newcastle).—I preached at eight on Chowden Fell, on, "Why will ye die, O house of Israel?" Ever since I came to Newcastle the first time, my spirit had been moved within me, at the crowds of poor wretches, who were every Sunday, in the afternoon sauntering to and fro on the Sandhill. I resolved, if possible, to find them a better employ; and as soon as the service at All Saints was over, walked straight from the church to the Sandhill, and gave out a verse of a psalm. In a few minutes I had company enough; thousands upon thousands crowding together. But the prince of this world fought with all his might lest his kingdom should be overthrown. Indeed, the very mob of Newcastle, in the height of their rudeness, have commonly some humanity left. I scarce observed that they threw any thing at all; neither did I receive the least personal hurt: but they continued thrusting one another to and fro, and making such a noise, that my voice could not be heard: so that, after spending near an hour in singing and prayer, I thought it best to adjourn to our own house.

Wesley's Horses give Trouble

Mon. 18.—I set out from Newcastle with John Downes, of Horsley. We were four hours riding to Ferry Hill, about twenty measured miles. After resting there an hour we rode softly on; and, at two o'clock, came to Darlington. I thought my horse was not well; he thought the same of his; though they were both young, and very well the day before. We ordered the hostler to fetch a farrier, which he did without delay; but, before the men could determine what was the matter, both the horses lay down and died.

I hired a horse to Sandhutton, and rode on, desiring John Downes to follow me. Thence I rode to Borough-bridge on Tuesday morning, and then walked on to Leeds.

Mon. August 22 (London).—After a few of us had joined in prayer, about four I set out and rode softly to Snow Hill; where, the saddle slipping quite upon my mare's neck, I fell over her head, and she ran back into

Smithfield. Some boys caught her and brought her to me again, cursing and swearing all the way. I spoke plainly to them, and they promised to amend. I was setting forward, when a man cried, "Sir, you have lost your saddle-cloth." Two or three more would needs help me to put it on; but these, too, swore at almost every word. I turned to one and another, and spoke in love. They all took it well, and thanked me much. I gave them two or three little books, which they promised to read over carefully.

Before I reached Kensington, I found my mare had lost a shoe. This gave me an opportunity of talking closely, for near half an hour, both to the smith and his servant. I mention these little circumstances to show how easy it is to redeem every fragment of time (if I may so speak), when we feel any love to those souls for which Christ died.

Wesley Goes to Cornwall

Fri. 26.—I set out for Cornwall. In the evening I preached at the cross in Taunton, on, "The kingdom of God is not meat and drink; but righteousness, and peace, and joy in the Holy Ghost." A poor man had posted himself behind, in order to make some disturbance : but the time was not come; the zealous wretches who "deny the Lord that bought them" had not yet stirred up the people. Many cried out, "Throw down that rascal there; knock him down; beat out his brains" : so that I was obliged to entreat for him more than once, or he would have been but roughly handled.

Sat. 27.—I reached Exeter in the afternoon; but as no one knew of my coming, I did not preach that night, only to one poor sinner at the inn; who, after listening to our conversation for a while, looked earnestly at us, and asked, whether it was possible for one, who had in some measure known "the power of the world to come," and was "fallen away" (which she said was her case), to be "renewed again to repentance." We besought God in her behalf, and left her sorrowing; and yet not without hope.

Sun. 28.—I preached at seven to a handful of people. The sermon we heard at church was quite innocent of meaning: what that in the afternoon was, I know not; for I could not hear a single sentence.

From church I went to the castle; where were gathered together (as some imagined) half the grown persons in the city. It was an awful sight. So vast a congregation in that solemn amphitheatre! And all silent and still, while I explained at large, and enforced, that glorious truth, "Happy are they whose iniquities are forgiven, and whose sins are covered."

Mon. 29.—We rode forward. About sunset we were in the middle of the first great pathless moor beyond Launceston. About eight we were got quite out of the way; but we had not got far before we heard Bodmin bell. Directed by this we turned to the left and came to the town before nine.

Tues. 30.—In the evening we reached St. Ives. At seven I invited all guilty, helpless sinners, who were conscious they "had nothing to pay," to accept of free forgiveness. The room was crowded both within and without; but all were quiet and attentive.

Wed. 31.—I spoke severally with those of the society, who were about one hundred and twenty. Near an hundred of these had found peace with God: such is the blessing of being persecuted for righteousness' sake! As we were going to church at eleven, a large company at the market-place welcomed us with a loud huzza:

wit as harmless as the ditty sung under my window
(composed, one assured me, by a gentlewoman of their
own town),

> " Charles Wesley is come to town,
>   To try if he can pull the churches down."

In the evening I explained "the promise of the
Father." After preaching, many began to be turbulent;
but John Nelson went into the midst of them, spoke a
little to the loudest, who answered not again, but went
quietly away.

The Cornish Tinners

Sat. September 3.—I rode to the Three-cornered Down
(so called), nine or ten miles east of St. Ives, where we
found two or three hundred tinners, who had been
some time waiting for us. They all appeared quite
pleased and unconcerned; and many of them ran after
us to Gwennap (two miles east), where their number was
quickly increased to four or five hundred. I had much
comfort here, in applying these words, "He hath
anointed me to preach the Gospel to the poor." One
who lived near invited us to lodge at his house, and
conducted us back to the Green in the morning. We
came thither just as the day dawned.

I strongly applied those gracious words, "I will heal their
backslidings, I will love them freely," to five or six hundred
serious people. At Trezuthan Downs, five miles nearer
St. Ives, we found seven or eight hundred people, to
whom I cried aloud, "Cast away all your transgressions;
for why will ye die, O house of Israel?" After dinner
I preached again to about a thousand people, on Him
whom "God hath exalted to be a Prince and a Saviour."
It was here first I observed a little impression made on

two or three of the hearers; the rest, as usual, showing huge approbation, and absolute unconcern.

Fri. 9.—I rode in quest of St. Hilary Downs, ten or twelve miles south-east of St. Ives. And the Downs I found, but no congregation—neither man, woman, nor child. But by that I had put on my gown and cassock, about an hundred gathered themselves together, whom I earnestly called "to repent and believe the Gospel." And if but one heard, it was worth all the labour.

Sat. 10.—There were prayers at St. Just in the afternoon, which did not end till four. I then preached at the Cross, to, I believe, a thousand people, who all behaved in a quiet and serious manner.

At six I preached at Sennan, near the Land's End; and appointed the little congregation (consisting chiefly of old, grey-headed men) to meet me again at five in the morning. But on Sunday, 11, great part of them were got together between three and four o'clock: so between four and five we began praising God; and I largely explained and applied, "I will heal their backslidings; I will love them freely."

We went afterwards down, as far as we could go safely, toward the point of the rocks at the Land's End. It was an awful sight! But how will these melt away, when God shall arise to judgment! The sea between does indeed "boil like a pot." "One would think the deep to be hoary." But "though they swell, yet can they not prevail. He hath set their bounds, which they cannot pass."

Between eight and nine I preached at St. Just, on the green plain near the town, to the largest congregation (I was informed) that ever had been seen in these parts. I cried out, with all the authority of love, "Why will ye die, O house of Israel?" The people trembled, and were still. I had not known such an hour before in Cornwall.

In the Scilly Isles

Mon. 12.—I had had for some time a great desire to go and publish the love of God our Saviour, if it were but for one day, in the Isles of Scilly; and I had occasionally mentioned it to several. This evening three of our brethren came and offered to carry me thither, if I could procure the mayor's boat, which, they said, was the best sailer of any in the town. I sent, and he lent it me immediately. So the next morning, Tuesday, 13, John Nelson, Mr. Shepherd, and I, with three men and a pilot, sailed from St. Ives. It seemed strange to me to attempt going in a fisher-boat, fifteen leagues upon the main ocean; especially when the waves began to swell, and hang over our heads. But I called to my companions, and we all joined together in singing lustily and with a good courage:

"When passing through the watery deep,
  I ask in faith his promised aid;
The waves an awful distance keep,
  And shrink from my devoted head;
Fearless their violence I dare:
They cannot harm—for God is there."

About half an hour after one, we landed on St. Mary's, the chief of the inhabited islands.

We immediately waited upon the Governor, with the usual present, viz., a newspaper. I desired him, likewise, to accept of an "Earnest Appeal." The minister not being willing I should preach in the church, I preached, at six, in the streets, to almost all the town, and many soldiers, sailors, and workmen, on, "Why will ye die, O house of Israel?" It was a blessed time, so that I scarce knew how to conclude. After sermon I gave

them some little books and hymns, which they were so
eager to receive, that they were ready to tear both them
and me to pieces.

For what political reason such a number of workmen
were gathered together, and employed at so large an
expense, to fortify a few barren rocks, which whosoever
would take, deserves to have them for his pains, I could
not possibly devise: but a providential reason was easy
to be discovered. God might call them together to hear
the Gospel, which perhaps otherwise they might never
have thought of.

At five in the morning I preached again, on, "I will
heal their backslidings; I will love them freely." And
between nine and ten, having talked with many in private,
and distributed both to them and others between two and
three hundred hymns and little books, we left this barren,
dreary place, and set sail for St. Ives, though the wind
was strong, and blew directly in our teeth. Our pilot
said we should have good luck if we reached the land;
but he knew not Him whom the winds and seas obey.
Soon after three we were even with the Land's End, and
about nine we reached St. Ives.

Remarkable Service at Gwennap

Tues. 20.—At Trezuthan Downs I preached to two or
three thousand people, on the "highway" of the Lord,
the way of holiness. We reached Gwennap a little
before six, and found the plain covered from end to end.
It was supposed there were ten thousand people; to
whom I preached Christ our "wisdom, righteousness,
sanctification, and redemption." I could not conclude
till it was so dark we could scarce see one another. And
there was on all sides the deepest attention; none speaking, stirring, or scarce looking aside. Surely here, though

in a temple not made with hands, was God worshipped in "the beauty of holiness."

Wed. 21.—I was waked between three and four, by a large company of tinners, who, fearing they should be too late, had gathered round the house, and were singing and praising God. At five I preached once more, on, "Believe on the Lord Jesus Christ, and thou shalt be saved." They all devoured the word. O may it be health to their soul, and marrow unto their bones!

We rode to Launceston that day. Thursday, 22. As we were riding through a village called Sticklepath, one stopped me in the street, and asked abruptly, "Is not thy name John Wesley?" Immediately two or three more came up, and told me I must stop there. I did so; and before we had spoke many words, our souls took acquaintance with each other. I found they were called Quakers: but that hurt not me; seeing the love of God was in their hearts.

A Mob at Wednesbury

Thur. Oct. 20.—After preaching to a small, attentive congregation (at Birmingham), I rode to Wednesbury. At twelve I preached in a ground near the middle of the town, to a far larger congregation than was expected, on, "Jesus Christ, the same yesterday, and to-day, and for ever." I believe every one present felt the power of God: and no creature offered to molest us, either going or coming; but the Lord fought for us, and we held our peace.

I was writing at Francis Ward's, in the afternoon, when the cry arose, that the mob had beset the house. We prayed that God would disperse them; and it was so: one went this way, and another that; so that, in half an hour, not a man was left. I told our brethren, "Now

RIOT IN WEDNESBURY

is the time for us to go "; but they pressed me exceedingly
to stay. So, that I might not offend them, I sat down,
though I foresaw what would follow. Before five the mob
surrounded the house again, in greater numbers than
ever. The cry of one and all was, "Bring out the
minister; we will have the minister."

I desired one to take their captain by the hand, and
bring him into the house. After a few sentences inter-
changed between us, the lion was become a lamb. I
desired him to go and bring one or two more of the most
angry of his companions. He brought in two, who were
ready to swallow the ground with rage; but in two
minutes they were as calm as he. I then bade them
make way, that I might go out among the people.

As soon as I was in the midst of them, I called
for a chair; and standing up, asked, "What do any of
you want with me?" Some said, "We want you to go
with us to the justice." I replied, "That I will, with
all my heart." I then spoke a few words, which God
applied; so that they cried out, with might and main,
"The gentleman is an honest gentleman, and we will
spill our blood in his defence." I asked, "Shall we go
to the justice to-night, or in the morning?" Most
of them cried, "To-night, to-night"; on which I went
before, and two or three hundred followed; the rest
returning whence they came.

The night came on before we had walked a mile,
together with heavy rain. However, on we went to
Bentley Hall, two miles from Wednesbury. One or two
ran before, to tell Mr. Lane they had brought Mr.
Wesley before his worship. Mr. Lane replied, "What
have I to do with Mr. Wesley? Go and carry him back
again." By this time the main body came up, and began
knocking at the door. A servant told them Mr. Lane

was in bed. His son followed, and asked what was the matter. One replied, " Why, an't please you, they sing psalms all day; nay, and make folks rise at five in the morning. And what would your worship advise us to do?" "To go home," said Mr. Lane, "and be quiet."

Wesley in Danger

Here they were all at a full stop, till one advised, to go to Justice Persehouse, at Walsal. All agreed to this; so we hastened on, and about seven came to his house. But Mr. P—— likewise sent word, that he was in bed. Now they were at a stand again; but at last they all thought it the wisest course to make the best of their way home. About fifty of them undertook to convoy me. But we had not gone a hundred yards, when the mob of Walsal came, pouring in like a flood, and bore down all before them. The Darlaston mob made what defence they could; but they were weary, as well as out-numbered: so that in a short time, many being knocked down, the rest ran away, and left me in their hands.

To attempt speaking was vain; for the noise on every side was like the roaring of the sea. So they dragged me along till we came to the town; where seeing the door of a large house open, I attempted to go in; but a man, catching me by the hair, pulled me back into the middle of the mob. They made no more stop till they had carried me through the main street, from one end of the town to the other. I continued speaking all the time to those within hearing, feeling no pain or weariness. At the west end of the town, seeing a door half open, I made toward it, and would have gone in; but a gentle-man in the shop would not suffer me, saying, they would pull the house down to the ground. However, I stood at the door, and asked, "Are you willing to hear me speak?" Many cried out, "No, no! knock his brains out; down with him; kill him at once." Others said, "Nay, but we will hear him first." I began asking, "What evil have I done? Which of you all have I wronged in word or deed?" And continued speaking for above a quarter of an hour, till my voice suddenly failed: then the floods began to lift up their voice again; many crying out, "Bring him away! bring him away!"

In the mean time my strength and my voice returned, and I broke out aloud in prayer. And now the man who just before headed the mob, turned, and said, "Sir, I will spend my life for you: follow me, and not one soul here shall touch a hair of your head." Two or three of his fellows confirmed his words, and got close to me immediately. At the same time, the gentleman in the shop cried out, "For shame, for shame! Let him go."

An honest butcher, who was a little farther off, said it was a shame they should do thus; and pulled back four or five, one after another, who were running on the most fiercely. The people then, as if it had been by common consent, fell back to the right and left; while those three or four men took me between them, and carried me through them all. But on the bridge the mob rallied again: we therefore went on one side, over the mill-dam, and thence through the meadows; till, a little before ten, God brought me safe to Wednesbury; having lost only one flap of my waistcoat, and a little skin from one of my hands.

His Presence of Mind

I never saw such a chain of providences before; so many convincing proofs, that the hand of God is on

every person and thing, and overruling all as it seemeth
Him good.

The poor woman of Darlaston, who had headed that
mob, and sworn, that no one should touch me, when she
saw her followers give way, ran into the thickest of the
throng, and knocked down three or four men, one after
another.   But many assaulting her at once, she was soon
overpowered, and had probably been killed in a few
minutes (three men keeping her down and beating her
with all their might), had not a man called to one of
them, " Hold, Tom, hold ! "   " Who is there ? " said Tom :
" what, honest Munchin ?   Nay, then, let her go."   So
they held their hand, and let her get up and crawl home
as well as she could.

From the beginning to the end I found the same
presence of mind, as if I had been sitting in my own
study.   But I took no thought for one moment before
another; only once it came into my mind, that if they
should throw me into the river, it would spoil the papers
that were in my pocket.   For myself, I did not doubt
but I should swim across, having but a thin coat, and a
light pair of boots.

The circumstances that follow, I thought, were particularly remarkable : 1. That many endeavoured to throw
me down while we were going down-hill on a slippery
path to the town ; as well judging, that if I was once on
the ground, I should hardly rise any more.   But I made
no stumble at all, nor the least slip till I was entirely out
of their hands.   2. That although many strove to lay
hold on my collar or clothes, to pull me down, they
could not fasten at all : only one got fast hold of the
flap of my waistcoat, which was soon left in his hand ;
the other flap, in the pocket of which was a bank note,
was torn but half off.   3. That a lusty man just behind

struck at me several times, with a large oaken stick; with which if he had struck me once on the back part of my head, it would have saved him all farther trouble. But every time the blow was turned aside, I know not how; for I could not move to the right hand or left.

"What Soft Hair He Has"

4. That another came rushing through the press, and raising his arm to strike, on a sudden let it drop, and only stroked my head, saying, " What soft hair he has ! " 5. That I stopped exactly at the mayor's door, as if I had known it (which the mob doubtless thought I did), and found him standing in the shop, which gave the first check to the madness of the people.   6. That the very first men whose hearts were turned were the heroes of the town, the captains of the rabble on all occasions, one of them having been a prize-fighter at the bear-garden.

7. That from first to last, I heard none give a reviling word, or call me by any opprobrious name whatever ; but the cry of one and all was : " The Preacher ! The Preacher ! The Parson ! The Minister ! "   8. That no creature, at least within my hearing, laid anything to my charge, either true or false ; having in the hurry quite forgot to provide themselves with an accusation of any kind.   And, lastly, that they were as utterly at a loss, what they should do with me ; none proposing any determinate thing ; only, " Away with him ! Kill him at once ! "

By how gentle degrees does God prepare us for his will !   Two years ago a piece of brick grazed my shoulders.   It was a year after that the stone struck me between the eyes.   Last month I received one blow, and this evening two ; one before we came into the town, and one after we were gone out; but both were as nothing: for though one man struck me on the breast with all his might, and the other on the mouth with such a force that the blood gushed out immediately, I felt no more pain from either of the blows, than if they had touched me with a straw.

It ought not to be forgotten, that when the rest of the society made all haste to escape for their lives, four only would not stir, William Sitch, Edward Slater, John Griffiths, and Joan Parks : these kept with me, resolving to live or die together; and none of them received one blow, but William Sitch, who held me by the arm, from one end of the town to the other. He was then dragged away and knocked down; but he soon rose and got to me again. I afterwards asked him, what he expected when the mob came upon us? He said, "To die for Him who had died for us": and he felt no hurry or fear; but calmly waited till God should require his soul of him.

Wesley's Defenders

I asked J. Parks, if she was not afraid when they tore her from me? She said, "No; no more than I am now. I could trust God for you, as well as for myself. From the beginning I had a full persuasion that God would deliver you. I knew not how; but I left that to Him, and was as sure as if it were already done." I asked, if the report was true that she had fought for me. She said, "No; I knew God would fight for His children." And shall these souls perish at the last?

When I came back to Francis Ward's I found many of our brethren waiting upon God. Many also whom I never had seen before came to rejoice with us. And

the next morning, as I rode through the town in my
way to Nottingham, every one I met expressed such a
cordial affection, that I could scarce believe what I saw
and heard.

The Sleepy Magistrates' Proclamation

I cannot close this head without inserting as great a
curiosity in its kind as, I believe, was ever yet seen in
England; which had its birth within a very few days of
this remarkable occurrence at Walsal.

" *Staffordshire.*

" To all High-Constables, Petty-Constables, and other
  of his Majesty's Peace Officers, within the said
  County, and particularly to the Constable of
  Tipton " (near Walsal) :

"Whereas, we, his Majesty's Justices of the Peace
for the said County of Stafford, have received information that several disorderly persons, styling themselves
Methodist Preachers, go about raising routs and riots,
to the great damage of his Majesty's liege people, and
against the peace of our Sovereign Lord the King :

" These are, in his Majesty's name, to command you
and every one of you, within your respective districts, to
make diligent search after the said Methodist Preachers,
and to bring him or them before some of us his said
Majesty's Justices of the Peace, to be examined concerning their unlawful doings.

 " Given under our hands and seals, this   day
  of October, 1743.
      " J. Lane.
      " W. Persehouse."

N.B.—The very justices to whose houses I was carried,
and who severally refused to see me !

Sat. 22.—I rode from Nottingham to Epworth, and on Monday set out for Grimsby: but at Ferry we were at a full stop, the boatmen telling us we could not pass the Trent; it was as much as our lives were worth to put from shore before the storm abated. We waited an hour; but, being afraid it would do much hurt, if I should disappoint the congregation at Grimsby, I asked the men if they did not think it possible to get to the other shore: they said, they could not tell; but if we would venture our lives, they would venture theirs. So we put off, having six men, two women, and three horses, in the boat.

Wesley Nearly Drowned

Many stood looking after us on the river-side, in the middle of which we were, when, in an instant, the side of the boat was under water, and the horses and men rolling one over another. We expected the boat to sink every moment; but I did not doubt of being able to swim ashore. The boatmen were amazed as well as the rest; but they quickly recovered and rowed for life. And soon after, our horses leaping overboard, lightened the boat, and we all came unhurt to land.

They wondered what was the matter I did not rise (for I lay along in the bottom of the boat), and I wondered too, till, upon examination, I found that a large iron crow, which the boatmen sometimes used, was (none knew how) run through the string of my boot, which pinned me down that I could not stir; so that if the boat had sunk, I should have been safe enough from swimming any further.

The same day, and, as near as we could judge, the same hour, the boat in which my brother was crossing the Severn, at the New Passage, was carried away by the wind, and in the utmost danger of splitting upon the rocks. But the same God, when all human hope was past, delivered them as well as us.

Methodism on the Stage

Mon. 31.—We set out early in the morning, and in the evening came to Newcastle.

Wed. November 2.—The following advertisement was published :

FOR THE BENEFIT OF MR. ESTE.

By the Edinburgh Company of Comedians, on Friday, November 4, will be acted a Comedy, called,

THE CONSCIOUS LOVERS ;

To which will be added a Farce, called,

TRICK UPON TRICK, OR METHODISM DISPLAYED

On Friday, a vast multitude of spectators were assembled in the Moot Hall to see this. It was believed there could not be less than fifteen hundred people, some hundreds of whom sat on rows of seats built upon the stage. Soon after the comedians had begun the first act of the play, on a sudden all those seats fell down at once, the supporters of them breaking like a rotten stick. The people were thrown one upon another, about five foot forward, but not one of them hurt. After a short time the rest of the spectators were quiet, and the actors went on. In the middle of the second act, all the shilling seats gave a crack, and sunk several inches down. A great noise and shrieking followed ; and as many as could readily get to the door, went out, and returned no more. Notwithstanding this, when the noise was over, the actors went on with the play.

In the beginning of the third act the entire stage suddenly sunk about six inches : the players retired with great precipitation; yet in a while they began again. At the latter end of the third act, all the sixpenny seats, without any kind of notice, fell to the ground.   There was now a cry on every side; it being supposed that many were crushed in pieces : but, upon inquiry, not a single person (such was the mercy of God !) was either killed or dangerously hurt.   Two or three hundred remaining still in the hall, Mr. Este (who was to act the Methodist) came upon the stage and told them, for all this he was resolved the farce should be acted.   While he was speaking, the stage sunk six inches more; on which he ran back in the utmost confusion, and the people as fast as they could out of the door, none staying to look behind him.

Which is most surprising—that those players acted this farce the next week—or that some hundreds of people came again to see it ?

The First Conference

1744. Mon. June 18.—I left Epworth; and on Wednesday, 20, in the afternoon, met my brother in London.

Monday, 25, and the five following days, we spent in conference with many of our brethren (come from several parts), who desire nothing but to save their own souls, and those who hear them.   And surely, as long as they continue thus minded, their labour shall not be in vain in the Lord.

The next day we endeavoured to purge the society of all that did not walk according to the Gospel.   By this means we reduced the number of members to less than nineteen hundred.   But number is an inconsiderable circumstance.   May God increase them in faith and love !

Fri. Aug. 24.—(St. Bartholomew's day.) I preached, I suppose the last time, at St. Mary's [Oxford]. Be it so. I am now clear of the blood of these men. I have fully delivered my own soul.

The Beadle came to me afterwards, and told me the Vice-Chancellor had sent him for my notes. I sent them without delay, not without admiring the wise providence of God. Perhaps few men of note would have given a sermon of mine the reading, if I had put t into their hands; but by this means it came to be read, probably more than once, by every man of eminence in the University.

Wesley's Chancery Bill

Thur. Dec. 27.—I called on the solicitor whom I had employed in the suit lately commenced in Chancery; and here I first saw that foul monster, a Chancery bill! A scroll it was of forty-two pages, in large folio, to tell a story which needed not to have taken up forty lines! and stuffed with such stupid senseless, improbable lies (many of them, too, quite foreign to the question) as, I believe, would have cost the compiler his life in any heathen court of either Greece or Rome. And this is equity in a Christian country! This is the English method of redressing other grievances!

1745. Sat. Jan. 5.—I had often wondered at myself (and sometimes mentioned it to others), that ten thousand cares, of various kinds, were no more weight and burden to my mind, than ten thousand hairs were to my head. Perhaps I began to ascribe something of this to my own strength. And thence it might be, that on Sunday, 13, that strength was withheld, and I felt what it was to be troubled about many things. One, and another, hurrying me continually, it seized upon my spirit more and more, till I found it absolutely necessary to fly for my life; and that without delay. So the next day, Monday, 14, I took horse, and rode away for Bristol.

Between Bath and Bristol I was earnestly desired to turn aside, and call at the house of a poor man, William Shalwood. I found him and his wife sick in one bed, and with small hopes of the recovery of either. Yet (after prayer) I believed they would " not die, but live, and declare the loving-kindness of the Lord." The next time I called he was sitting below stairs, and his wife able to go abroad.

As soon as we came into the house at Bristol, my soul was lightened of her load, of that insufferable weight which had lain upon my mind, more or less, for several days. On Sunday, several of our friends from Wales, and other parts, joined with us in the great sacrifice ot thanksgiving. And every day we found more and more cause to praise God, and to give him thanks for His still increasing benefits.

Mon. Feb. 18.—I set out with Richard Moss from London for Newcastle.

Wesley's Effective Letter

Sun. March 3.—As I was walking up Pilgrim-street, hearing a man call after me, I stood still. He came up, and used much abusive language, intermixed with many oaths and curses. Several people came out to see what was the matter; on which he pushed me twice or thrice, and went away.

Upon inquiry, I found this man had signalized himself a long season, by abusing and throwing stones at any ot our family who went that way. Therefore I would not lose the opportunity, but on Monday, 4, sent him the tollowing note :

" ROBERT YOUNG,—I expect to see you, between this and Friday, and to hear from you, that you are sensible of your fault; otherwise, in pity to your soul, I shall be obliged to inform the magistrates of your assaulting me yesterday in the street.

" I am,

" Your real friend,

" JOHN WESLEY."

Within two or three hours, Robert Young came and promised a quite different behaviour. So did this gentle reproof, if not save a soul from death, yet prevent a multitude of sins.

Sat. April 6.—Mr. Stephenson, of whom I bought the ground on which our house is built, came at length, after delaying it more than two years, and executed the writings. So I am freed from one more care. May I in every thing make known my request to God !

Press Gang and Methodists

Wed. June 19 (Redruth).—Being informed here of what had befallen Mr. Maxfield, we turned aside toward Crowan church-town. But in the way we received information, that he had been removed from thence the night before. It seems, the valiant constables who guarded him, having received timely notice, that a body of five hundred Methodists were coming to take him away by force, had, with great precipitation, carried him two miles further, to the house of one Henry Tomkins.

Here we found him, nothing terrified by his adversaries. I desired Henry Tomkins to show me the warrant. It was directed by Dr. Borlase, and his father, and Mr. Eustick, to the constables and overseers of several parishes, requiring them to " apprehend all such able-bodied men as had no lawful calling or sufficient maintenance "; and to bring them before the aforesaid gentlemen at Marazion, on Friday, 21, to be examined, whether they were proper persons to serve his Majesty in the land-service.

It was indorsed, by the steward of Sir John St. Aubyn, with the names of seven or eight persons, most of whom were well known to have lawful callings, and a sufficient maintenance thereby. But that was all one: they were called "Methodists"; therefore, soldiers they must be. Underneath was added, "A person, his name unknown, who disturbs the peace of the parish."

A word to the wise. The good men easily understood, this could be none but the Methodist Preacher; for who "disturbs the peace of the parish" like one who tells all drunkards, whoremongers, and common swearers, "You are in the high road to hell"?

When we came out of the house, forty or fifty myrmidons stood ready to receive us. But I turned full upon them, and their courage failed: nor did they recover till we were at some distance. Then they began blustering again, and throwing stones; one of which struck Mr. Thompson's servant.

Fri. 21.—We rode to Marazion. (Vulgarly called Market-jew.) Finding the justices were not met, we walked up St. Michael's Mount. The house at the top is surprisingly large and pleasant. Sir John St. Aubyn had taken much pains, and been at a considerable expense, in repairing and beautifying the apartments; and when the seat was finished, the owner died!

About two, Mr. Thompson and I went into the room where the justices and commissioners were. After a few minutes, Dr. Borlase stood up and asked, whether we had any business. I told him, "We have." We desired to be heard concerning one who was lately apprehended at Crowan. He said, " Gentlemen, the business of Crowan does not come on yet. You shall be sent for when it does." So we retired, and waited in another room, till after nine o'clock. They delayed the affair of Mr. Maxfield (as we imagined they would) to the very last. About nine he was called. I would have gone in then; but Mr. Thompson advised to wait a little longer. The next information we received was, that they had sentenced him to go for a soldier. Hearing this, we went straight to the commission chamber. But the honourable gentlemen were gone.

They had ordered Mr. Maxfield to be immediately put on board a boat, and carried for Penzance. We were informed, they had first offered him to a Captain of a man-of-war, that was just come into the harbour. But he answered, " I have no authority to take such men as these, unless you would have me give him so much a week, to preach and pray to my people."

Reading the Riot Act

Sat. 22.—We reached St. Ives about two in the morning. At five I preached on, " Love your enemies "; and at Gwennap, in the evening, on, " All that will live godly in Christ Jesus shall suffer persecution."

We heard to-day, that as soon as Mr. Maxfield came to Penzance, they put him down into the dungeon; and that the mayor being inclined to let him go, Dr. Borlase had gone thither on purpose, and had himself read the Articles of War in the court, and delivered him to one who was to act as an officer.

Sat. 29.—I preached at St. Just again, and at Morva and Zennor on Sunday, 30. About six in the evening,

I began preaching at St. Ives, in the street, near John Nance's door. A multitude of people were quickly assembled, both high and low, rich and poor; and I observed not any creature to laugh or smile, or hardly move hand or foot. I expounded the Gospel for the day, beginning with, "Then drew near all the publicans and sinners for to hear Him." A little before seven came Mr. Edwards from the mayor, and ordered one to read the proclamation against riots. I concluded quickly after; but the body of the people appeared utterly unsatisfied, not knowing how to go away. Forty or fifty of them begged they might be present at the meeting of the society; and we rejoiced together for an hour in such a manner as I had never known before in Cornwall.

Tues. July 2.—I preached in the evening at St. Just. I observed not only several gentlemen there, who I suppose never came before, but a large body of tinners, who stood at a distance from the rest; and a great multitude of men, women, and children, beside, who seemed not well to know why they came. Almost as soon as we had done singing, a kind of gentlewoman began. I have seldom seen a poor creature take so much pains. She scolded, and screamed, and spit and stamped, and wrung her hands, and distorted her face and body all manner of ways. I took no notice of her at all, good or bad; nor did almost any one else. Afterwards I heard she was one that had been bred a Papist; and when she heard we were so, rejoiced greatly. No wonder she would be proportionably angry, when she was disappointed of her hope.

Mr. Eustick, a neighbouring gentleman, came, just as I was concluding my sermon. The people opening to the right and left, he came up to me, and said, "Sir, I have a warrant from Dr. Borlase, and you must go with me." Then, turning round, he said, "Sir, are you Mr. Shepherd? If so, you are mentioned in the warrant too. Be pleased, Sir, to come with me." We walked with him to a public-house, near the end of the town. Here he asked me, if I was willing to go with him to the doctor. I told him, just then, if he pleased. "Sir," said he, "I must wait upon you to your inn ; and in the morning, if you will be so good as to go with me, I will show you the way." So he handed me back to my inn and retired.

Wesley Seized for Soldier

Wed. 3.—I waited till nine; but no Mr. Eustick came. I then desired Mr. Shepherd to go and inquire for him at the house wherein he had lodged; he met him, coming, as he thought, to our inn. But after waiting some time, we inquired again, and learned he had turned aside to another house in the town. I went thither, and asked, "Is Mr. Eustick here?" After some pause, one said, "Yes"; and showed me into the parlour. When he came down, he said, "O Sir, will you be so good as to go with me to the doctor's?" I answered, "Sir, I came for that purpose." "Are you ready, Sir?" I answered, "Yes." "Sir, I am not quite ready. In a little time, Sir, in a quarter of an hour, I will wait upon you. I will come to William Chenhall's."

In about three quarters of an hour he came, and finding there was no remedy, he called for his horse, and put forward towards Dr. Borlase's house; but he was in no haste; so that we were an hour and a quarter riding three or four measured miles. As soon as we came into the yard, he asked a servant, "Is the doctor at home?" upon whose answering, "No, Sir, he is gone to church"; he presently said, "Well, Sir, I have executed my commission. I have done, Sir; I have no more to say."

About noon Mr. Shepherd and I reached St. Ives. After a few hours' rest, we rode to Gwennap. Finding the house would not contain one fourth of the people, I stood before the door. I was reading my text, when a man came, raging as if just broke out of the tombs; and, riding into the thickest of the people, seized three or four, one after another, none lifting up a hand against him. A second (gentleman, so called) soon came after, if possible, more furious than he; and ordered his men to seize on some others, Mr. Shepherd in particular. Most of the people, however, stood still as they were before, and began singing an hymn.

Upon this Mr. B. lost all patience, and cried out with all his might, " Seize him, seize him. I say, seize the Preacher for his Majesty's service." But no one stirring, he rode up and struck several of his attendants, cursing them bitterly for not doing as they were bid. Perceiving still that they would not move, he leaped off his horse, swore he would do it himself, and caught hold of my cassock, crying, "I take you to serve his Majesty." A servant taking his horse, he took me by the arm, and we walked arm in arm for about three quarters of a mile. He entertained me all the time, with the " wickedness of the fellows belonging to the society." When he was taking breath, I said, " Sir, be they what they will, I apprehend it will not justify you, in seizing me in this manner, and violently carrying me away, as you said, to serve his Majesty." He replied, " I seize you ! And violently carry you away ! No, Sir, no. Nothing like it. I asked you to go with me to my house, and you said you was willing; and if so, you are welcome; and if not, you are welcome to go where you please." I

answered, " Sir, I know not if it would be safe for me to
go back through this rabble." " Sir," said he, " I will go
with you myself." He then called for his horse, and
another for me, and rode back with me to the place
from whence he took me.

Dramatic Scenes at Falmouth

Thur. 4.—I rode to Falmouth.   About three in the
afternoon I went to see a gentlewoman who had been
long indisposed.   Almost as soon as I sat down, the
house was beset on all sides by an innumerable multitude
of people.   A louder or more confused noise could hardly
be at the taking of a city by storm.   At first Mrs. B. and
her daughter endeavoured to quiet them.   But it was
labour lost.   They might as well have attempted to still
the raging of the sea.   They were soon glad to shift for
themselves, and leave K. E. and me to do as well as we
could.   The rabble roared with all their throats, " Bring
out the Canorum!   Where is the Canorum ? " (an un-
meaning word which the Cornish generally use instead
of Methodist).

No answer being given, they quickly forced open the
outer door, and filled the passage.   Only a wainscot-
partition was between us, which was not likely to stand
long.   I immediately took down a large looking-glass
which hung against it, supposing the whole side would
fall in at once.   When they began their work with abundance of bitter imprecations, poor Kitty was utterly astonished, and cried out, " O Sir, what must we do ? "   I said,
" We must pray."   Indeed at that time, to all appearance,
our lives were not worth an hour's purchase.   She asked,
" But, Sir, is it not better for you to hide yourself ? to
get into the closet ? "   I answered, " No.   It is best for
me to stand just where I am."   Among those without,

were the crews of some privateers, which were lately come into harbour. Some of these, being angry at the slowness of the rest, thrust them away, and, coming up all together, set their shoulders to the inner door, and cried out, "Avast, lads, avast!" Away went all the hinges at once, and the door fell back into the room.

I stepped forward at once into the midst of them, and said, "Here I am. Which of you has anything to say to me. To which of you have I done any wrong? To you? Or you? Or you?" I continued speaking till I came, bare-headed as I was (for I purposely left my hat that they might all see my face), into the middle of the street, and then raising my voice, said, "Neighbours, countrymen! Do you desire to hear me speak?" They cried vehemently, "Yes, yes. He shall speak. He shall. Nobody shall hinder him." But having nothing to stand on, and no advantage of ground, I could be heard by few only. However, I spoke without intermission, and, as far as the sound reached, the people were still; till one or two of their captains turned about and swore, not a man should touch him.

Mr. Thomas, a clergyman, then came up, and asked, "Are you not ashamed to use a stranger thus?" He was soon seconded by two or three gentlemen of the town, and one of the aldermen; with whom I walked down the town, speaking all the time, till I came to Mrs. Maddern's house. The gentlemen proposed sending for my horse to the door, and desired me to step in and rest the mean time. But, on second thoughts, they judged it not advisable to let me go out among the people again: so they chose to send my horse before me to Penryn, and to send me thither by water; the sea running close by the back-door of the house in which we were.

I never saw before, no, not at Walsal itself, the hand of God so plainly shown as here. There I had many companions who were willing to die with me : here, not a friend, but one simple girl, who likewise was hurried away from me in an instant, as soon as ever she came out of Mrs. B.'s door. There I received some blows, lost part of my clothes, and was covered over with dirt : here, although the hands of perhaps some hundreds of people were lifted up to strike or throw, yet they were one and all stopped in the mid-way ; so that not a man touched me with one of his fingers; neither was anything thrown from first to last ; so that I had not even a speck of dirt on my clothes. Who can deny that God heareth the prayer, or that He hath all power in heaven and earth ?

"I Am John Wesley"

I took boat at about half an hour past five. Many of the mob waited at the end of the town, who, seeing me escaped out of their hands, could only revenge themselves with their tongues. But a few of the fiercest ran along the shore, to receive me at my landing. I walked up the steep narrow passage from the sea, at the top of which the foremost man stood. I looked him in the face, and said, "I wish you a good night." He spake not, nor moved hand or foot till I was on horseback. Then he said, "I wish you was in hell," and turned back to his companions.

As soon as I came within sight of Tolcarn (in Wendron parish), where I was to preach in the evening, I was met by many, running as it were for their lives, and begging me to go no further. I asked, "Why not ?" They said, "The churchwardens and con stables, and all the heads of the parish, are waiting for you at the top of the hill, and are resolved to have you : they have a special warrant from the justices met at Helstone, who will stay there till you are brought." I rode directly up the hill, and observing four or five horsemen, well dressed, went straight to them, and said, " Gentlemen, has any of you anything to say to me ?— I am John Wesley."

One of them appeared extremely angry at this, that I should presume to say I was " Mr. John Wesley." And I know not how I might have fared for advancing so bold an assertion, but that Mr. Collins, the minister of Redruth (accidently, as he said) came by. Upon his accosting me, and saying he knew me at Oxford, my first antagonist was silent, and a dispute of another kind began : whether this preaching had done any good. I appealed to matter of fact. He allowed (after many words), " People are the better for the present " ; but added, " To be sure, by and by they will be as bad, if not worse than ever."

When he rode away, one of the riders said, " Sir, I would speak with you a little; let us ride to the gate." We did so, and he said, " Sir, I will tell you the ground of this. All the gentlemen of these parts say, that you have been a long time in France and Spain, and are now sent hither by the Pretender ; and that these societies are to join him." Nay, surely " all the gentlemen in these parts " will not lie against their own conscience !

I rode hence to a friend's house, some miles off, and found the sleep of a labouring man is sweet. I was informed there were many here also who had an earnest desire to hear " this preaching," but they did not dare ; Sir —— V——n having solemnly declared, nay, and that in the face of the whole congregation, as they were coming out of church, "If any man of this parish dares hear these fellows, he shall not come to my Christmas-feast !"

Sat. 6.—I rode with Mr. Shepherd to Gwennap. Here also we found the people in the utmost consternation. Word was brought, that a great company of tinners, made drunk on purpose, were coming to do terrible things. I laboured much to compose their minds : but fear had no ears ; so that abundance of people went away. I preached to the rest, on, " Love your enemies." The event showed this also was a false alarm, an artifice of the devil, to hinder men from hearing the word of God.

Wesley Pushed from a High Wall

Sun. 7.—I preached, at five, to a quiet congregation, and about eight, at Stithians. Between six and seven in the evening we came to Tolcarn. Hearing the mob was rising again, I began preaching immediately. I had not spoke a quarter of an hour before they came in view. One Mr. Trounce rode up first, and began speaking to me, wherein he was roughly interrupted by his companions. Yet, as I stood on a high wall, and kept my eyes upon them, many were softened, and grew calmer and calmer ; which some of their champions observing, went round and suddenly pushed me down. I light on my feet, without any hurt ; and finding myself close to the warmest of the horsemen, I took hold of his hand and held it fast, while I expostulated the case. As for being convinced, he was quite above it : however, both he and his fellows grew much milder, and we parted very civilly.

Mon. 8.—I preached at five, on, " Watch and pray," to a quiet and earnest congregation. We then rode on to St. Ives, the most still and honourable post (so are the times changed) which we have in Cornwall.

Tues. 9.—I had just begun preaching at St. Just, when Mr. E. came once more, took me by the hand, and said, I must go with him. To avoid making a tumult, I went. He said, I had promised, last week, not to come again to St. Just for a month. I absolutely denied the having made any such promise. After about half an hour, he handed me back to my inn.

Riot Act and a Sermon

Wed. 10.—In the evening I began to expound (at Trevonan, in Morva), "Ho! every one that thirsteth, come ye to the waters." In less than a quarter of an hour, the constable and his companions came, and read the proclamation against riots. When he had done, I told him, "We will do as you require: we will disperse within an hour"; and went on with my sermon. After preaching, I had designed to meet the society alone. But many others also followed with such earnestness, that I could not turn them back: so I exhorted them all, to love their enemies, as Christ hath loved us. They felt what was spoken.

Thur. 25.—I came back safe, blessed be God, to Bristol. I found both my soul and body much refreshed in this peaceful place. Thursday, August 1, and the following days, we had our second Conference, with as many of our brethren that labour in the word as could be present.

Pelted by the Mob at Leeds

Mon. Sept. 9.—I left London, and the next morning called on Dr. Doddridge, at Northampton. It was about the hour when he was accustomed to expound a portion of Scripture to young gentlemen under his care. He desired me to take his place. It may be the seed was not altogether sown in vain.

Thur. 12.—I came to Leeds, preached at five, and at eight met the society; after which the mob pelted us with dirt and stones great part of the way home. The congregation was much larger next evening; and so was the mob at our return, and likewise in higher spirits, being ready to knock out all our brains for joy that the Duke of Tuscany was Emperor. What a melancholy consideration is this! that the bulk of the English nation will not suffer God to give them the blessings he would; because they would turn them into curses. He cannot, for instance, give them success against their enemies; for they would tear their own countrymen in pieces: he cannot trust them with victory, lest they should thank him by murdering those that are quiet in the land.

Great Excitement at Newcastle

Wed. 18.—About five we came to Newcastle, in an acceptable time. We found the generality of the inhabitants in the utmost consternation; news being just arrived, that, the morning before, at two o'clock, the Pretender had entered Edinburgh. A great concourse of people were with us in the evening, to whom I expounded the third chapter of Jonah; insisting particularly on that verse, "Who can tell, if God will return, and repent, and turn away from his fierce anger, that we perish not?"

Thur. 19.—The mayor (Mr. Ridley) summoned all the householders of the town to meet him at the town-hall; and desired as many of them as were willing, to set their hands to a paper, importing that they would, at the hazard of their goods and lives, defend the town against the common enemy. Fear and darkness were now on every side; but not on those who had seen the light of God's countenance. We rejoiced together in the evening with solemn joy, while God applied those words to many hearts, "Fear not ye; for I know that ye seek Jesus which was crucified."

Fri. 20.—The mayor ordered the townsmen to be under arms, and to mount guard in their turns, over and above the guard of soldiers, a few companies of whom had been drawn into the town on the first alarm. Now, also, Pilgrim-street gate was ordered to be walled up. Many began to be much concerned for us, because our house stood without the walls. Nay, but the Lord is a wall of fire unto all that trust in him.

I had desired all our brethren to join with us this day in seeking God by fasting and prayer. About one we met, and poured out our souls before him; and we believed he would send an answer of peace.

Wesley's Letter to the Mayor

Sat. 21.—The same day the action was, came the news of General Cope's defeat. Orders were now given for the doubling of the guard, and for walling up Pandon and Sally-port gates. In the afternoon I wrote the following letter:

"*To the Worshipful the Mayor of Newcastle.*

"SIR,—My not waiting upon you at the town-hall was not owing to any want of respect. I reverence you for your office' sake; and much more for your zeal in the execution of it. I would to God every magistrate in the land would copy after such an example! Much less was it owing to any disaffection to his Majesty King

George. But I knew not how far it might be either necessary or proper for me to appear on such an occasion. I have no fortune at Newcastle : I have only the bread I eat, and the use of a little room for a few weeks in the year.

"All I can do for his Majesty, whom I honour and love—I think not less than I did my own father—is this, I cry unto God, day by day, in public and in private, to put all his enemies to confusion : and I exhort all that hear me to do the same ; and, in their several stations, to exert themselves as loyal subjects; who, so long as they fear God, cannot but honour the King.

"Permit me, Sir, to add a few words more, out of the fulness of my heart. I am persuaded you fear God, and have a deep sense that His Kingdom ruleth over all. Unto whom, then (I may ask you), should we flee for succour, but unto Him whom, by our sins, we have justly displeased ? O, Sir, is it not possible to give any check to these overflowings of ungodliness ? to the open, flagrant wickedness, the drunkenness and profaneness, which so abound, even in our streets ? I just take leave to suggest this. May the God whom you serve direct you in this, and all things ! This is the daily prayer of, Sir,

"Your obedient servant, for Christ's sake,
"J. W."

Preaching under Difficulties.

Sun. 22.—The walls were mounted with cannon, and all things prepared for sustaining an assault. Meantime our poor neighbours, on either hand, were busy in removing their goods. And most of the best houses in our street were left without either furniture or inhabitants.

Those within the walls were almost equally busy in carrying away their money and goods; and more and more of the gentry every hour rode southward as fast as they could. At eight I preached at Gateshead, in a broad part of the street, near the Popish chapel, on the wisdom of God in governing the world. How do all things tend to the furtherance of the Gospel!

All this week the alarms from the north continued, and the storm seemed nearer every day. Many wondered we would still stay without the walls: others told us we must remove quickly; for if the cannon began to play from the top of the gates, they would beat all the house about our ears. This made me look how the cannons on the gates were planted; and I could not but adore the providence of God, for it was obvious, 1. They were all planted in such a manner, that no shot could touch our house. 2. The cannon on New-gate so secured us on one side, and those upon Pilgrim-street gate on the other, that none could come near our house, either way, without being torn in pieces.

On Friday and Saturday many messengers of lies terrified the poor people of the town, as if the rebels were just coming to swallow them up. Upon this the guards were increased, and abundance of country gentlemen came in, with their servants, horses, and arms. Among those who came from the north was one whom the mayor ordered to be apprehended, on suspicion of his being a spy. As soon as he was left alone he cut his own throat; but a surgeon coming quickly, sewed up the wound, so that he lived to discover those designs of the rebels, which were thereby effectually prevented.

Sun. 29.—Advice came that they were in full march southward, so that it was supposed they would reach Newcastle by Monday evening. At eight I called on a

multitude of sinners in Gateshead, to seek the Lord
while he might be found. Mr. Ellison preached another
earnest sermon, and all the people seemed to bend before
the Lord. In the afternoon I expounded part of the
lesson for the day—Jacob wrestling with the angel.
The congregation was so moved, that I began again and
again, and knew not how to conclude. And we cried
mightily to God to send his Majesty King George help
from his holy place, and to spare a sinful land yet a
little longer, if haply they might know the day of their
visitation.

The Blasphemous Troops

Tues. Oct. 8.—I wrote to General Husk as follows:

" A surly man came to me this evening, as he said,
from you. He would not deign to come up stairs to
me, nor so much as into the house; but stood in the
yard till I came, and then obliged me to go with him
into the street, where he said, ' You must pull down the
battlements of your house, or to-morrow the General
will pull them down for you.'

" Sir, to me this is nothing. But I humbly conceive
it would not be proper for this man, whoever he is, to
behave in such a manner to any other of his Majesty's
subjects, at so critical a time as this.

" I am ready, if it may be for his Majesty's service,
to pull not only the battlements, but the house down;
or to give up any part of it, or the whole, into your
Excellency's hands."

Sat. 26.—I sent Alderman Ridley the following letter:

" SIR,—The fear of God, the love of my country, and the
regard I have for his Majesty King George, constrain

me to write a few plain words to one who is no stranger to these principles of action.

"My soul has been pained day by day, even in walking the streets of Newcastle, at the senseless, shameless wickedness, the ignorant profaneness, of the poor men to whom our lives are entrusted. The continual cursing and swearing, the wanton blasphemy of the soldiers in general, must needs be a torture to the sober ear, whether of a Christian or an honest infidel. Can any that either fear God, or love their neighbour, hear this without concern? especially if they consider the interest of our country, as well as of these unhappy men themselves. For can it be expected, that God should be on their side who are daily affronting him to his face? And if God be not on their side, how little will either their number, or courage, or strength avail?

"Is there no man that careth for these souls? Doubtless there are some who ought so to do. But many of these, if I am rightly informed, receive large pay, and do just nothing.

"I would to God it were in my power, in any degree, to supply their lack of service. I am ready to do what in me lies, to call these poor sinners to repentance, once or twice a day (while I remain in these parts), at any hour, or at any place. And I desire no pay at all for doing this; unless what my Lord shall give at his appearing.

.   .   .   .

"Having myself no knowledge of the General, I took the liberty to make this offer to you. I have no interest herein; but I should rejoice to serve, as I am able, my King and country. If it be judged, that this will be of no real service, let the proposal die, and be forgotten. But I beg you, Sir, to believe, that I have the same

glorious cause, for which you have shown so becoming a
zeal, earnestly at heart; and that therefore I am, with
warm respect,

> " Sir,
>> " Your most obedient servant."

Sun. 27.—I received a message from Mr. Ridley, that
he would communicate my proposal to the General, and
return me his answer as soon as possible.

Having now delivered my own soul, on Monday,
Nov. 4, I left Newcastle.   Before nine we met several
expresses, sent to countermand the march of the army
into Scotland ; and to inform them, that the rebels had
passed the Tweed, and were marching southward.

Bonfires Everywhere

Tues. 5.—In the evening I came to Leeds, and found
the town full of bonfires, and people shouting, firing of
guns, cursing and swearing, as the English manner of
keeping holidays is.   I immediately sent word to some
of the magistrates, of what I had heard on the road.
This ran through the town, as it were, in an instant :
and I hope it was a token for good.   The hurry in the
streets was quashed at once—some of the bonfires
indeed remained ; but scarce any one was to be seen
about them, but a few children warming their hands.

Thur. 7.—I rode to Stayley Hall, in Cheshire, after
many interruptions in the way, by those poor tools of
watchmen, who stood with great solemnity at the end of
almost every village.   I preached there on Mark i. 15,
and rode on to Bradbury Green.

Fri. 8.—Understanding that a neighbouring gentleman,
Dr. C., had affirmed to many, that Mr. Wesley was now
with the Pretender, near Edinburgh, I wrote him a few

lines. It may be, he will have a little more regard to truth, or shame, for the time to come.

Wesley and Faith-healing

1746. Mon. March 17.—I took my leave of Newcastle, and set out with Mr. Downes and Mr. Shepherd. But when we came to Smeton, Mr. Downes was so ill, that he could go no further. When Mr. Shepherd and I left Smeton, my horse was so exceeding lame that I was afraid I must have lain by too. We could not discern what it was that was amiss; and yet he would scarce set his foot to the ground. By riding thus seven miles, I was thoroughly tired, and my head ached more than it had done for some months. (What I here aver is the naked fact: let every man account for it as he sees good.) I then thought, " Cannot God heal either man or beast, by any means, or without any ? " Immediately my weariness and head-ache ceased, and my horse's lameness in the same instant. Nor did he halt any more either that day or the next. A very odd accident this also !

Fri. May 30 (Bristol).—I light upon a poor, pretty, fluttering thing, lately come from Ireland, and going to be a singer at the play-house. She went in the evening to the chapel, and thence to the watch-night, and was almost persuaded to be a Christian. Her convictions continued strong for a few days; but then her old acquaintance found her, and we saw her no more.

Sun. July 6 (London).—After talking largely with both the men and women leaders, we agreed it would prevent great expense, as well of health as of time and of money, if the poorer people of our society could be persuaded to leave off drinking of tea. We resolved ourselves to begin and set the example. I expected some difficulty in breaking off a custom of six-and-twenty years' standing. And, accordingly, the three first days, my head ached, more or less, all day long, and I was half asleep from morning till night. The third day, on Wednesday, in the afternoon, my memory failed, almost entirely. In the evening I sought my remedy in prayer. On Thursday morning my head-ache was gone. My memory was as strong as ever. And I have found no inconvenience, but a sensible benefit in several respects, from that very day to this.

Thur. 17.—I finished the little collection which I had made among my friends for a lending-stock: it did not amount to thirty pounds; which a few persons afterwards made up fifty. And by this inconsiderable sum, above two hundred and fifty persons were relieved in one year.

Wesley Encounters Severe Weather

1747. Tues. Feb. 10 (London).—My brother returned from the north, and I prepared to supply his place there. Sunday, 15. I was very weak and faint; but on Monday, 16, I rose soon after three, lively and strong, and found all my complaints were fled away like a dream.

I was wondering, the day before, at the mildness of the weather; such as seldom attends me in my journeys. But my wonder now ceased: the wind was turned full north, and blew so exceeding hard and keen, that when we came to Hatfield, neither my companions nor I had much use of our hands or feet. After resting an hour, we bore up again through the wind and snow, which drove full in our faces. But this was only a squall. In Baldock-field the storm began in earnest. The large hail drove so vehemently in our faces, that we could not see, nor hardly breathe. However, before two o'clock we reached Baldock, where one met and conducted us safe to Potten.

About six I preached to a serious congregation. Tuesday, 17. We set out as soon as it was well light ; but it was really hard work to get forward; for the frost would not well bear or break; and the untracked snow covering all the roads, we had much ado to keep our horses on their feet. Meantime the wind rose higher and higher, till it was ready to overturn both man and beast. However, after a short bait at Bugden, we pushed on, and were met in the middle of an open field with so violent a storm of rain and hail, as we had not had before. It drove through our coats, great and small, boots, and everything, and yet froze as it fell, even upon our eye-brows; so that we had scarce either strength or motion left, when we came into our inn at Stilton.

We now gave up our hopes of reaching Grantham, the snow falling faster and faster. However, we took the advantage of a fair blast to set out, and made the best of our way to Stamford-heath. But here a new difficulty arose, from the snow lying in large drifts. Sometimes horse and man were well nigh swallowed np. Yet in less than an hour we were brought safe to Stamford. Being willing to get as far as we could, we made but a short stop here; and about sunset came, cold and weary, yet well, to a little town called Brig-casterton.

Wed. 18.—Our servant came up and said, " Sir, there is no travelling to-day. Such a quantity of snow has fallen in the night, that the roads are quite filled up." I told him, " At least we can walk twenty miles a day, with our horses in our hands." So in the name of God we set out. The north-east wind was piercing as a sword, and had driven the snow into such uneven heaps, that the main road was unpassable. However, we kept on, a-foot or on horseback, till we came to the White Lion at Grantham.

Some from Grimsby had appointed to meet us here; but not hearing anything of them (for they were at another house, by mistake), after an hour's rest, we set out straight for Epworth. On the road we overtook a clergyman and his servant; but the tooth-ache quite shut my mouth. We reached Newark about five.

Preaching to the Lead Miners

Tues. March 24.—I rode to Blanchland, about twenty miles from Newcastle. The rough mountains round about were still white with snow. In the midst of them is a small winding valley, through which the Derwent runs. On the edge of this the little town stands, which is indeed little more than a heap of ruins. There seems to have been a large cathedral church, by the vast walls which still remain. I stood in the churchyard, under one side of the building, upon a large tomb-stone, round which, while I was at prayers all the congregation kneeled down on the grass. They were gathered out of the lead-mines from all parts; many from Allandale, six miles off. A row of little children sat under the opposite wall, all quiet and still. The whole congregation drank in every word with such earnestness in their looks, I could not but hope that God will make this wilderness sing for joy.

Wed. June 24.—We rode (from Bristol) to Beercrocomb, hoping to reach Tavistock the next day. So we set out at three. The rain began at four. We reached Colestock, dropping wet, before seven. The rain ceased while we were in the house, but began when we took horse, and attended us all the way to Exeter. While we stayed here to dry our clothes, I took the opportunity of writing " A Word to a Freeholder." Soon after three we set out : but it was near eight before we could reach Oakhampton.

Fri. 26.—We came to Tavistock before noon ; but it being market-day, I did not preach till five in the evening. The rain began almost as soon as we began singing, and drove many out of the field. After preaching (leaving Mr. Swindells there) I went on for Plymouth-dock.

How Wesley Dealt with a Mob

Within two miles of Plymouth, one overtook and informed us, that, the night before, all the Dock was in an uproar; and a constable, endeavouring to keep the peace, was beaten and much hurt. As we were entering the Dock, one met us, and desired we would go the back-way : " For," said he, " there are thousands of people waiting about Mr. Hide's door." We rode up straight into the midst of them. They saluted us with three huzzas ; after which I alighted, took several of them by the hand, and began to talk with them. I would gladly have passed an hour among them ; and believe, if I had, there had been an end of the riot. But the day being far spent (for it was past nine o'clock), I was persuaded to go in. The mob then recovered their spirits, and fought valiantly with the doors and windows : but about ten they were weary, and went every man to his own home.

Sat. 27.—I preached at four, and then spoke severally to part of the society. As yet I have found only one person among them who knew the love of God, before my brother came. No wonder the devil was so still; for his goods were in peace.

About six in the evening, I went to the place where I preached the last year. A little before we had ended the hymn, came the Lieutenant, a famous man, with his retinue of soldiers, drummers, and mob. When the drums ceased, a gentleman barber began to speak: but his voice was quickly drowned in the shouts of the multitude, who grew fiercer and fiercer, as their numbers increased. After waiting about a quarter of an hour, perceiving the violence of the rabble still increasing, I walked down into the thickest of them, and took the captain of the mob by the hand. He immediately said, " Sir, I will see you safe home. Sir, no man shall touch you. Gentlemen, stand off: give back. I will knock the first man down that touches him." We walked on in great peace; my conductor every now and then stretching out his neck (he was a very tall man) and looking round, to see if any behaved rudely, till we came to Mr. Hide's door. We then parted in much love. I stayed in the street near half an hour after he was gone, talking with the people, who had now forgot their anger, and went away in high good humour.

Sun. 28.—I preached at five, on the Common, to a well-behaved, earnest congregation : and at eight near the room, on, " Seek ye the Lord, while He may be found." The congregation was much larger than before, and equally serious and attentive. At ten I went to church. Mr. Barlow preached an useful sermon, on, " God be merciful to me a sinner " ; and a thundering one in the afternoon, on, " Where their worm dieth not, and the fire is not quenched."

Mon. 29.—I took horse between three and four, and reached Perranwell, three miles beyond Truro, about six. I preached to a very large congregation at seven ; and the word was as the rain on the tender herb.

Tues. 30.—We came to St. Ives before Morning Prayers, and walked to church without so much as one huzza. How strangely has one year changed the scene in Cornwall! This is now a peaceable, nay, honourable station. They give us good words almost in every place. What have we done, that the world should be so civil to us ?

Wed. July 1.—I spoke severally to all those who had votes in the ensuing election. I found them such as I desired. Not one would even eat or drink at the expense of him for whom he voted. Five guineas had been given to W. C., but he returned them immediately. T. M. positively refused to accept any thing. And when he heard that his mother had received money privately, he could not rest till she gave him the three guineas, which he instantly sent back.

Thursday 2, was the day of election for Parliament-men. It was begun and ended without any hurry at all. I had a large congregation in the evening, among whom two or three roared for the disquietness of their heart : as did many at the meeting which followed ; particularly those who had lost their first love.

Thurs. Aug. 13 (Dublin).—We walked in the afternoon to see two persons that were sick near Phœnix Park. That part of it which joins to the city is sprinkled up and down with trees, not unlike Hyde Park. But about a mile from the town is a thick grove of old, tall oaks; and in the centre of this, a round, open green (from which are vistas of all four ways), with a handsome stone pillar in the midst, having a Phœnix on the top.

I continued reaching, morning and evening, to

many more than the house would contain, and had
more and more reason to hope they would not all be
unfruitful hearers.

Sun. Sept. 27 (London).—I preached in Moorfields,
morning and evening, and continued so to do till
November. I know no church in London (that in West-
street excepted) where there is so serious a congregation.

Mon. 28.—I talked with one who, a little time
before, was so overwhelmed with affliction, that she
went out one night to put an end to it all, by throwing
herself into the New River. As she went by the
Foundery (it being a watch-night), she heard some
people singing. She stopped, and went in ; she listened
awhile, and God spoke to her heart. She had no more
desire to put an end to her life; but to die to sin, and
live to God.

The Bargemen and their Clubs

Mon. Nov. 2.—I preached at Windsor at noon, and
in the afternoon rode to Reading. Mr. J. R. had just
sent his brother word, that he had hired a mob to pull
down his preaching-house that night. In the evening
Mr. S. Richards overtook a large company of bargemen
walking towards it, whom he immediately accosted, and
asked, if they would go with him and hear a good
sermon; telling them, " I will make room for you, if
you were as many more." They said, they would go
with all their hearts. " But neighbours," said he,
" would it not be as well to leave those clubs behind
you ? Perhaps some of the women may be frighted at
them." They threw them all away, and walked quietly
with him to the house, where he set them in a pew.

In the conclusion of my sermon, one of them who
used to be their captain, being the head taller than his

fellows, rose up, and looking round the congregation, said, "The gentleman says nothing but what is good; I say so; and there is not a man here that shall dare to say otherwise."

Remarkable Accident to Wesley

1748. Thur. Jan. 28.—I set out for Deverel Long-bridge. About ten o'clock we were met by a loaded waggon, in a deep, hollow way. There was a narrow path between the road and the bank: I stepped into this, and John Trembath followed me. When the waggon came near, my horse began to rear, and to attempt climbing up the bank. This frighted the horse which was close behind, and made him prance and throw his head to and fro, till the bit of the bridle catched hold of the cape of my great coat, and pulled me backward off my horse. I fell as exact on the path, between the waggon and the bank, as if one had taken me in his arms and laid me down there. Both our horses stood stock still, one just behind me, the other before; so, by the blessing of God, I rose unhurt, mounted again, and rode on.

Sat. Feb. 6.—I preached at eight in the morning at Bath, and in the evening at Coleford. The colliers of this place were " darkness " indeed; but now they are " light in the Lord."

Tues. 9.—I met about sixty of the society in Bristol, to consult about enlarging the room; and indeed securing it, for there was no small danger of its falling upon our heads. In two or three days, two hundred and thirty pounds were subscribed. We immediately procured experienced builders to make an estimate of the expense; and I appointed five stewards (besides those of the society) to superintend the work.

Fri. 12.—After preaching at Oakhill about noon, I rode to Shepton, and found them all under a strange consternation. A mob, they said, was hired, prepared, and made sufficiently drunk, in order to do all manner of mischief. I began preaching between four and five : none hindered or interrupted at all. We had a blessed opportunity, and the hearts of many were exceedingly comforted. I wondered what was become of the mob. But we were quickly informed : they mistook the place, imagining I should alight (as I used to do) at William Stone's house, and had summoned, by drum, all their forces together, to meet me at my coming : but Mr. Mr. Swindells innocently carrying me to the other end of the town, they did not find their mistake till I had done preaching : so that the hindering this, which was one of their designs, was utterly disappointed.

However, they attended us from the preaching-house to William Stone's, throwing dirt, stones, and clods, in abundance : but they could not hurt us ; only Mr. Swindells had a little dirt on his coat, and I a few specks on my hat.

A Shower of Stones

After we were gone into the house, they began throwing great stones, in order to break the door. But perceiving this would require some time, they dropped that design for the present. They first broke all the tiles on the pent-house over the door, and then poured in a shower of stones at the windows. One of their captains, in his great zeal, had followed us into the house, and was now shut in with us. He did not like this, and would fain have got out; but it was not possible; so he kept as close to me as he could, thinking himself safe when he was near me : but, staying a little behind—when I went up two pair of stairs, and stood close on one side, where we were a little sheltered —a large stone struck him on the forehead, and the blood spouted out like a stream. He cried out, " O Sir, are we to die to-night? What must I do? What must I do?" I said, "Pray to God. He is able to deliver you from all danger." He took my advice, and began praying in such a manner as he had scarce done ever since he was born.

Mr. Swindells and I then went to prayer; after which I told him, " We must not stay here; we must go down immediately." He said, " Sir, we cannot stir; you see how the stones fly about." I walked straight through the room, and down the stairs; and not a stone came in, till we were at the bottom. The mob had just broke open the door when we came into the lower room; and exactly while they burst in at one door, we walked out at the other. Nor did one man take any notice of us, though we were within five yards of each other.

A Horrible Proposition

They filled the house at once, and proposed setting it on fire. But one of them, happening to remember that his own house was next, with much ado persuaded them not to do it. Hearing one of them cry out, " They are gone over the grounds," I thought the advice was good; so we went over the grounds, to the farther end of the town, where Abraham Jenkins waited, and undertook to guide us to Oakhill.

I was riding on in Shepton Lane, it being now quite dark, when he cried out, "Come down: come down from the bank." I did as I was bid; but the bank being high, and the side very near perpendicular, I came down all at once, my horse and I tumbling one over another. But we both rose unhurt.

Sat. April 9.—I preached in Connaught, a few miles from Athlone. Many heard; but, I doubt, felt nothing.

The Shannon comes within a mile of the house where I preached. I think there is not such another river in Europe: it is here ten or twelve miles over, though scarce thirty miles from its fountain-head. There are many islands in it, once well inhabited, but now mostly desolate. In almost every one is the ruins of a church: in one, the remains of no less than seven. I fear, God hath still a controversy with this land, because it is defiled with blood.

Incidents in Ireland

Sun. 10 (Easter-day).—Never was such a congregation seen before at the sacrament in Athlone. I preached at three. Abundance of Papists flocked to hear; so that the priest, seeing his command did not avail, came in person at six, and drove them away before him like a flock of sheep.

Tues. 12.—I rode to Clara, where I was quickly informed, that there was to begin in an hour's time a famous cockfight, to which almost all the country was coming from every side. Hoping to engage some part of them in a better employ, I began preaching in the street, as soon as possible. One or two hundred stopped, and listened a while, and pulled off their hats, and forgot their diversion.

The congregation at Tullamore in the evening was larger than ever before, and deep attention sat on every face. Toward the latter end of the sermon, there began a violent storm of hail. I desired the people to cover their heads; but the greater part of them would not; nor did any one go away till I concluded my discourse.

Fri. 15.—I rode to Edinderry. Abundance of people

were quickly gathered together. Having been disturbed in the night by Mr. Swindells, who lay with me, and had a kind of apoplectic fit, I was not at all well about noon, when I began to preach, in a large walk, on one side of the town, and the sun shone hot upon my head, which had been aching all the day; but I forgot this before I had spoken long; and when I had finished my discourse, I left all my weariness and pain behind, and rode on, in perfect health to Dublin.

Sat. 23.—I read, some hours, an extremely dull book, Sir James Ware's "Antiquities of Ireland." By the vast number of ruins which are seen in all parts, I had always suspected what he shows at large, namely, that in ancient times it was more populous, tenfold, than it is now; many that were large cities, being now ruinous heaps; many shrunk into inconsiderable villages.

I visited one in the afternoon who was ill of a fever, and lay in a very close room. While I was near him, I found myself not well. After my return home, I felt my stomach out of order. But I imagined it was not worth any notice, and would pass off before the morning.

Wesley Lives on Apple-tea

Sun. 24.—I preached at Skinner's Alley at five; and on Oxmantown Green at eight. I was weak in body, but was greatly revived by the seriousness and earnestness of the congregation. Resolving to improve the opportunity, I gave notice of preaching there again in the afternoon; which I did to a congregation much more numerous, and equally attentive. As I came home I was glad to lie down, having a quinsey, attended with a fever. However, when the society met, I made a shift to creep in among them. Immediately my voice was restored. I spoke without pain, for near an hour

together.   And great was our rejoicing over each other ;
knowing that God would order all things well.

Mon. 25.—Finding my fever greatly increased, I judged
it would be best to keep my bed, and to live awhile on
apples and apple-tea.   On Tuesday I was quite well,
and should have preached, but that Dr. Rutty (who
had been with me twice) insisted on my resting for a
time.

I read to-day what is accounted the most correct
history of St. Patrick that is extant; and, on the
maturest consideration, I was much inclined to believe,
that St. Patrick and St. George were of one family.
The whole story smells strong of romance.

A Determined Preacher

Thursday, 28, was the day fixed for my going into the
country : but all about me began to cry out, " Sure, you
will not go to-day?   See how the rain pours down ! "
I told them, " I must keep my word, if possible."   But
before five, the man of whom I had bespoke an horse
sent word, his horse should not go out in such a day.
I sent one who brought him to a better mind.   So
about six I took horse.   About nine I called at Killcock.

Between one and two we came to Kinnegad.   My
strength was now pretty well exhausted; so that when
we mounted again, after resting an hour, it was as much
as I could do to sit my horse.   We had near eleven
Irish (measured) miles to ride, which are equal to
fourteen English.   I got over them pretty well in three
hours, and by six reached Tyrrel's Pass.

At seven I recovered my strength, so as to preach
and meet the society; which began now to be at a
stand, with regard to number, but not with regard to
the grace of God.

Fri. 29.—I rode to Temple Maqueteer, and thence toward Athlone. We came at least an hour before we were expected. Nevertheless we were met by many of our brethren. The first I saw, about two miles from the town, were a dozen little boys running with all their might, some bare-headed, some bare-footed and bare-legged: so they had their desire of speaking to me first, the others being still behind.

Zealous Protestants

Tues. May 3.—I rode to Birr, twenty miles from Athlone, and, the key of the sessions-house not being to be found, declared " the grace of our Lord Jesus Christ " in the street, to a dull, rude, senseless multitude. Many laughed the greater part of the time. Some went away just in the middle of a sentence. And yet when one cried out (a Carmelite friar, clerk to the priest), "You lie! you lie!" the zealous Protestants cried out, "Knock him down": and it was no sooner said than done. I saw some bustle, but knew not what was the matter, till the whole was over.

In the evening we rode to Balliboy. There being no house that could contain the congregation, I preached here also in the street. I was afraid, in a new place, there would be but few in the morning; but there was a considerable number, and such a blessing as I had scarce found since I landed in Ireland.

Sun. 15 (Dublin).—Finding my strength greatly restored, I preached at five, and at eight on Oxmantown Green. I expected to sail as soon as I had done; but the captain putting it off (as their manner is), gave me an opportunity of declaring the Gospel of peace to a still larger congregation in the evening. One of them, after listening some time, cried out, shaking his head,

" Ay, he is a Jesuit ; that's plain." To which a Popish priest, who happened to be near, replied aloud, " No, he is not ; I would to God he was."

Mon. 16.—Observing a large congregation in the evening, and many strangers among them, I preached more roughly than ever I had done in Dublin, on those awful words, " What shall it profit a man, if he shall gain the whole world, and lose his own soul ? "

Wed. 18.—We took ship. The wind was small in the afternoon, but exceeding high towards night. About eight I laid me down on the quarter-deck. I was soon wet from head to foot, but I took no cold at all. About four in the morning we landed at Holyhead, and in the evening reached Carnarvon.

Fri. August 12.—In riding to Newcastle, I finished the tenth Iliad of Homer. What an amazing genius had this man ! To write with such strength of thought, and beauty of expression, when he had none to go before him ! And what a vein of piety runs through his whole work, in spite of his pagan prejudices ! Yet one cannot but observe such improprieties intermixed, as are shocking to the last degree.

Wesley Protests Against Lawlessness

Thur. 25.—I rode with Mr. Grimshaw to Roughlee. At half-hour after twelve I began to preach. I had about half finished my discourse, when the mob came pouring down the hill like a torrent. After exchanging a few words with their captain, to prevent any contest, I went with him as he required. When we came to Barrowford, two miles off, the whole army drew up in battle array before the house into which I was carried, with two or three of my friends. After I had been detained above an hour, their captain went out, and I followed him, and desired him to conduct me whence I came. He said, he would : but the mob soon followed after; at which he was so enraged, that he must needs turn back to fight them, and so left me alone.

A farther account is contained in the following letter, which I wrote the next morning—

Widdop, Aug. 26, 1748.

" Sir,—Yesterday, between twelve and one o'clock, while I was speaking to some quiet people, without any noise or tumult, a drunken rabble came, with clubs and staves, in a tumultuous and riotous manner, the captain of whom, Richard B., by name, said he was a deputy-constable, and that he was come to bring me to you. I went with him ; but I had scarce gone ten yards, when a man of his company struck me with his fist in the face with all his might; quickly after, another threw his stick at my head : I then made a little stand; but another of your champions, cursing and swearing in the most shocking manner, and flourishing his club over his head, cried out, ' Bring him away ! '

" With such a convoy I walked to Barrowford, where they informed me you was ; their drummer going before, to draw all the rabble together from all quarters.

" When your deputy had brought me into the house, he permitted Mr. Grimshaw, the minister of Haworth, Mr. Colbeck, of Keighley, and one more, to be with me, promising that none should hurt them. Soon after you and your friends came in, and required me to promise, I would come to Roughlee no more. I told you, I would sooner cut off my hand, than make any such promise : neither would I promise that none of my friends should come. After abundance of rambling discourse (for I could keep none of you long to any one point), from about one o'clock till between three and four (in which one of you frankly said, 'No; we will not be like Gamaliel, we will proceed like the Jews'), you seemed a little satisfied with my saying, 'I will not preach at Roughlee at this time.' You then undertook to quiet the mob, to whom you went and spoke a few words, and their noise immediately ceased. I then walked out with you at the back-door.

Beaten by the Mob

"I should have mentioned that I had several times before desired you to let me go, but in vain; and that when I attempted to go with Richard B., the mob immediately followed, with oaths, curses, and stones; that one of them beat me down to the ground; and when I rose again, the whole body came about me like lions, and forced me back into the house.

"While you and I went out at one door, Mr. Grimshaw and Mr. Colbeck went out at the other. The mob immediately closed them in, tossed them to and fro with the utmost violence, threw Mr. Grimshaw down, and loaded them both with dirt and mire of every kind; not one of your friends offering to call off your bloodhounds from the pursuit.

"The other quiet, harmless people, who followed me at a distance, to see what the end would be, they treated still worse; not only by the connivance, but by the express order, of your deputy. They made them run for their lives, amidst showers of dirt and stones, without any regard to age or sex. Some of them they trampled in the mire, and dragged by the hair, particularly Mr. Mackford, who came with me from Newcastle. Many they beat with their clubs without mercy. One they forced to leap down (or they would have thrown him headlong) from a rock, ten or twelve feet high, into the river.   And when he crawled out, wet and bruised, they swore they would throw him in again, which they were hardly persuaded not to do.   All this time you sat well-pleased close to the place, not attempting in the least to hinder them.

" And all this time you was talking of justice and law !   Alas, Sir, suppose we were Dissenters (which I deny), suppose we were Jews or Turks, are we not to have the benefit of the laws of our country ?   Proceed against us by the law, if you can or dare ; but not by lawless violence ; not by making a drunken, cursing, swearing, riotous mob, both judge, jury, and executioner. This is flat rebellion against God and the King, as you may possibly find to your cost."

Defending Field Preaching

Between four and five we set out from Roughlee. But observing several parties of men upon the hills, and suspecting their design, we put on and passed the lane they were making for before they came.   One of our brothers, not riding so fast, was intercepted by them. They immediately knocked him down, and how it was that he got from amongst them he knew not.

Before seven we reached Widdop.   The news of what had passed at Barrowford made us all friends.   The person in whose house Mr. B. preached, sent and begged I would preach there ; which I did at eight, to such a congregation as none could have expected on so short a warning.   He invited us also to lodge at his house, and all jealousies vanished away.

Sun. 28.—I was invited by Mr. U., the Minister of Goodshaw, to preach in his church.   I began reading prayers at seven ; but perceiving the church would scarce contain half of the congregation, after prayers I went out, and standing on the churchyard wall, in a place shaded from the sun, explained and enforced those words in the second lesson, " Almost thou per suadest me to be a Christian."

I wonder at those who still talk so loud of the in-decency of field-preaching. The highest indecency is in St. Paul's Church, when a considerable part of the congregation are asleep, or talking, or looking about, not minding a word the preacher says. On the other hand, there is the highest decency in a churchyard or field, when the whole congregation behave and look as if they saw the Judge of all, and heard Him speaking from heaven.

Three Remarkable Shots with Stones

At one I went to the Cross in Bolton. There was a vast number of people, but many of them utterly wild. As soon as I began speaking, they began thrusting to and fro; endeavouring to throw me down from the steps on which I stood. They did so once or twice ; but I went up again, and continued my discourse. They then began to throw stones; at the same time some got upon the Cross behind me to push me down ; on which I could not but observe, how God overrules even the minutest circumstances. One man was bawling just at my ear, when a stone struck him on the cheek, and he was still. A second was forcing his way down to me, till another stone hit him on the forehead : it bounded back, the blood ran down, and he came no farther. The third, being got close to me, stretched out his hand, and in the instant a sharp stone came upon the joints of his fingers. He shook his hand, and was very quiet till I concluded my discourse and went away.

Sat. Oct. 22.—I spent an hour in observing the various works of God in the Physic Garden at Chelsea. It would be a noble improvement of the design, if some able and industrious person were to make a full and accurate inquiry into the use and virtues of all these plants : without this, what end does the heaping them thus together answer, but the gratifying an idle curiosity ?

Mon. Nov. 21.—I set out for Leigh, in Essex. It had rained hard in the former part of the night, which was succeeded by a sharp frost ; so that most of the road was like glass ; and the north-east wind set just in our face. However, we reached Leigh by four in the afternoon. Here was once a deep open harbour ; but the sands have long since blocked it up, and reduced a once flourishing town to a small ruinous village. I preached to most of the inhabitants of the place in the evening ; to many in the morning, and then rode back to London.

Wesley in Wales

1749. Mon. April 3.—I set out for Ireland. We waited more than four hours at the passage ; by which delay, I was forced to disappoint a large congregation at Newport. About three I came to Pedras, near Carphilly. The congregation had waited some hours. I began immediately, wet and weary as I was ; and we rejoiced over all our labours.

In the evening, and the next morning (Tues. 4), I preached at Cardiff. O what a fair prospect was here some years ago ! Surely this whole town would have known God, from the least even to the greatest, had it not been for men leaning to their own understanding, instead of " the law and the testimony."

At twelve I preached at Lanmais, to a loving, earnest

people, who do not desire to be any wiser than God. In the evening I preached at Fonmon, the next morning at Cowbridge. How is the scene changed since I was here last, amidst the madness of the people, and the stones flying on every side! Now all is calm; the whole town is in good humour, and flock to hear the glad tidings of salvation. In the evening I preached at Lantrissent.

Thursday, 6. We rode to a hard-named place on the top of a mountain. I scarce saw any house near: however, a large number of honest, simple people soon came together; but few could understand me: so Henry Lloyd, when I had done, repeated the substance of my sermon in Welsh. The behaviour of the people recompensed us for our labour in climbing up to them.

Marries his Brother

About noon we came to Aberdare, just as the bell was ringing for a burial. This had brought a great number together, to whom, after the burial, I preached in the church. We had almost continued rain from Aberdare to the great rough mountain that hangs over the vale of Brecknock: but as soon as we gained the top of this, we left the clouds behind us. We had a mild, fair, sunshiny evening the remainder of our journey.

Fri. 7.—We reached Garth. Saturday, 8. I married my brother and Sarah Gwynne. It was a solemn day, such as becomes the dignity of a Christian marriage.

Wed. 12.—We came to Holyhead between one and two. But all the ships were on the Irish side. One came in the next day, but could not go out, the wind being quite contrary. In this journey I read over Statius's Thebais. I wonder one man should write so well and so ill. Sometimes he is scarce inferior to Virgil; sometimes as low as the dullest parts of Ovid.

In the evening I preached on, " Be ye also ready." The poor people now seemed to be much affected; and equally so the next night: so that I was not sorry that the wind was contrary.

Sat. 15.—We went on board at six, the wind then standing due east. But no sooner were we out of the harbour, than it turned south-west, and blew a storm. Yet we made forward, and about one o'clock came within two or three leagues of land. The wind then wholly failed; a calm suddenly following a storm, produced such a motion as I never felt before. But it was not long before the wind sprung up west, which obliged us to stand away for the Skerries. When we wanted a league of shore it fell calm again, so that there we rolled about till past sunset.

But in the night we got back into Dublin Bay, and landed soon after three at Dunleary, about seven English miles from the city. Leaving William Tucker to follow me in a chaise, I walked straight away, and came to Skinner's Alley a little before the time of preaching. I preached on, " Beloved, if God so loved us, we ought also to love one another." In the afternoon, and again in the evening (in our own garden), I preached on, " Let us come boldly unto the throne of grace, that we may obtain mercy, and find grace to help in time of need."

On Thursday and Friday I examined the classes, and was much comforted among them. I left about four hundred in the society; and, after all the stumbling-blocks laid in the way, I found four hundred and forty-nine.

Mon. 24.—The cold which I had had for some days growing worse and worse, and the swelling which began in my cheek increasing greatly, and paining me much, I sent for Dr. Rutty. But, in the mean time, I applied boiled nettles, which took away the pain in a moment. Afterwards I used warm treacle, which so abated the swelling, that before the doctor came I was almost well. However, he advised me not to go out that day. But I had appointed to read the letters in the evening. I returned home as early as I could, and found no inconvenience.

Methodists Lease an Abbey

Fri. May 12.—Before nine we came to Nenagh. I had no design to preach; but one of the dragoons quartered there, would take no denial : so I ordered a chair to be carried out, and went to the market-place. Presently such a congregation was gathered round me as I had not seen since I left Athlone. To these I spake, as I was able, the whole counsel of God; and then rode cheerfully on to Limerick.

Between six and seven I preached at Mardyke (an open place without the walls), to about two thousand people; not one of whom I observed either to laugh, or to look about, or to mind anything but the sermon.

Some years since an old abbey here was rebuilt, with a design to have public service therein. But that design failing, only the shell of it was finished. Of this (lying useless) the society has taken a lease. Here I preached in the morning, Saturday, 13, to six or seven hundred people.

We then went to prayers at the cathedral, an ancient and venerable pile. In the afternoon I walked round the walls of the town, scarce so large as Newcastle-upon-Tyne. And the fortifications are much in the same repair; very sufficient to keep out the wild Irish.

14.—(Being Whit-Sunday). Our church was more than full in the morning, many being obliged to stand without. I hardly knew how the time went, but continued speaking till near seven o'clock. I went at eleven to the cathedral. I had been informed it was a custom here, for the gentry especially, to laugh and talk all the time of divine service; but I saw nothing of it. The whole congregation, rich and poor, behaved suitably to the occasion.

In the evening I preached to a numerous congregation, on, "If any man thirst, let him come unto me and drink." We afterwards met the society. Six or seven prisoners of hope were set at liberty this day.

Mon. 15.—A company of revellers and dancers had in the afternoon taken possession of the place where I used to preach. Some advised me to go to another place; but I knew it needed not. As soon as ever I came in sight, the holiday mob vanished away.

Wesley and the Soldiers' Class

Wed. 17.—I met the class of soldiers, eight of whom were Scotch Highlanders. Most of these were brought up well; but evil communications had corrupted good manners. They all said, from the time they entered into the army, they had grown worse and worse. But God had now given them another call, and they knew the day of their visitation.

Mon. 22.—The more I converse with this people, the more I am amazed. That God hath wrought a great work among them, is manifest; and yet the main of them, believers and unbelievers, are not able to give a rational account of the plainest principles of religion. It is plain, God begins His work at the heart; then "the inspiration of the Highest giveth understanding."

Wed. 24.—About eight, several of us took boat for Newtown, six miles from Limerick. After dinner we took boat, in order to return. The wind was extremely high. We endeavoured to cross over to the leeward side of the river; but it was not possible. The boat being small, and over-loaded, was soon deep in water; the more so, because it leaked much, and the waves washed over us frequently; and there was no staying to empty it, all our men being obliged to row with all their strength. After they had toiled about an hour, the boat struck upon a rock, the point of which lay just under the water. It had four or five shocks, the wind driving us on before we could get clear. But our men wrought for life; and about six o'clock God brought us safe to Limerick.

A Ridiculous Question

Mon. June 5.—I rode to Blarney, three miles wide of Cork, where many of the society met me. I spent some time with them in exhortation and prayer, and then went on to Rathcormuck.

I was a little surprised at the acuteness of a gentleman here, who in conversation with Colonel Barry, about late occurrences, said, he had heard, there was a people risen up that placed all religion in wearing long whiskers; and seriously asked, whether these were not the same who were called Methodists.

Tues. 13.—We rode over to Gloster, a beautiful seat built by an Englishman, who had scarce finished his house, and laid out his gardens, when he was called to his everlasting home. Sir L—— P—— and his lady dined with us, whether coming by accident or design I know not. About five I preached in the stately saloon, to a little company of plain, serious people; the fine ones looking on, and some of them seeming to be a little affected. I expounded at Birr about seven, in the strongest manner I could, the story of Dives and Lazarus.

Wed. 14.—We designed to dine at Ferbane, about twelve miles from Birr. We stopped at the first inn in the town; but they did not care to entertain heretics; neither did the people at the second inn; I alighted at the third, and went in, without asking any questions.

About seven I preached at Athlone. It being the time of the general review, abundance of soldiers and many officers were present. They all behaved with the utmost decency. But a gentleman of the town did not; which had like to cost him dear. Many swords were drawn; but the officers interposed, and it went no farther.

Wed. July 19.—I finished the translation of " Martin Luther's Life." Doubtless he was a man highly favoured of God, and a blessed instrument in His hand. But O! what pity that he had no faithful friend! None that would, at all hazards, rebuke him plainly and sharply, for his rough, untractable spirit, and bitter zeal for opinions, so greatly obstructive of the work of God!

A Rough Voyage

Thur. 20.—About ten at night we embarked [from Dublin] for Bristol, in a small sloop. I soon fell asleep. When I awaked in the morning, we were many leagues from land, in a rough, pitching sea. Toward evening the wind turned more against us, so that we made little way. About ten we were got between the Bishop and his Clerks (the rocks so called) and the Welsh shore; the wind blew fresh from the south; so that the captain, fearing we should be driven on the rocky coast, steered back again to sea. On Saturday morning we made the Bishop and his Clerks again, and beat to and fro all the day. About eight in the evening it blew hard, and we had a rolling sea: notwithstanding which, at four on Sunday morning, we were within sight of Minehead. The greatest part of the day we had a dead calm; but in the evening the wind sprung up, and carried us into Kingroad. On Monday morning we landed at the quay in Bristol.

Tues. 25.—I rode over to Kingswood, and inquired particularly into the state of our school there. I was concerned to find that several of the rules had been habitually neglected: I judged it necessary, therefore, to lessen the family; suffering none to remain therein, who were not clearly satisfied with them, and determined to observe them all.

Wed. Sept. 6.—I reached Newcastle; and after resting a day, and preaching two evenings and two mornings, with such a blessing as we have not often found, on Friday set out to visit the northern societies. I began with that at Morpeth, where I preached at twelve, on one side of the market-place. It was feared the market would draw the people from the sermon; but it was just the contrary: they quitted their stalls, and there was no buying or selling till the sermon was concluded.

At Alnwick likewise I stood in the market-place in the evening, and exhorted a numerous congregation to be always ready for death, for judgment, for heaven. I felt what I spoke; as I believe did most that were present, both then and in the morning, while I besought them to "present" themselves, "a living sacrifice, holy, acceptable to God."

Sat. 9.—I rode slowly forward to Berwick. I was myself much out of order; but I would not lose the opportunity of calling, in the evening, all that were "weary and heavy-laden," to Him who hath said, "I will give you rest."

Tues. 26.—I had a solemn and delightful ride to Keswick, having my mind stayed on God.

Wed. 27.—I took horse at half an hour past three. There was no moon, or stars, but a thick mist; so that I could see neither road, nor anything else; but I went as right as if it had been noon-day. When I drew nigh Penruddock Moor, the mist vanished, the stars appeared, and the morning dawned; so I imagined all the danger was past; but when I was on the middle of the moor, the mist fell again on every side, and I quickly lost my way. I lifted up my heart. Immediately it cleared up, and I soon recovered the high-road. On Alstone Moor I missed my way again; and what, I believe, no stranger has done lately, rode through all the bogs, without any stop, till I came to the vale, and thence to Hinely Hill.

A large congregation met in the evening. I expounded part of the twentieth chapter of the Revelation. But O what a time was this! It was as though we were already standing before the "great white throne." God was no less present with us in prayer; when one just by me cried with a loud and bitter cry. I besought God to give us a token that all things should work together for good. He did so: he wrote pardon upon her heart; and we all rejoiced unto him with reverence.

Wed. Oct. 18.—I rode, at the desire of John Bennet, to Rochdale, in Lancashire. As soon as ever we entered the town, we found the streets lined on both sides with multitudes of people, shouting, cursing, blaspheming, and gnashing upon us with their teeth. Perceiving it would not be practicable to preach abroad, I

went into a large room, open to the street, and called
aloud, " Let the wicked forsake his way, and the un-
righteous man his thoughts." The word of God
prevailed over the fierceness of man. None opposed or
interrupted ; and there was a very remarkable change
in the behaviour of the people, as we afterwards went
through the town.

Remarkable Scenes at Bolton

We came to Bolton about five in the evening. We
had no sooner entered the main street, than we perceived the lions at Rochdale were lambs in comparison
of those at Bolton. Such rage and bitterness I scarce
ever saw before, in any creatures that bore the form of
men. They followed us in full cry to the house where
we went ; and as soon as we were gone in, took possession of all the avenues to it, and filled the street from
one end to the other.

After some time the waves did not roar quite so loud.
Mr. P—— thought he might then venture out. They
immediately closed in, threw him down, and rolled him
in the mire ; so that when he scrambled from them, and
got into the house again, one could scarce tell what or
who he was. When the first stone came among us
through the window, I expected a shower to follow ; and
the rather, because they had now procured a bell to call
their whole forces together. But they did not design to
carry on the attack at a distance : presently one ran up
and told us, the mob had burst into the house : he
added, that they had got J—— B—— in the midst of
them. They had ; and he laid hold on the opportunity
to tell them of " the terrors of the Lord."

Meantime D—— T—— engaged another part of
them with smoother and softer words. Believing the

time was now come, I walked down into the thickest of them. They had now filled all the rooms below. I called for a chair. The winds were hushed, and all was calm and still. My heart was filled with love, my eyes with tears, and my mouth with arguments. They were amazed, they were ashamed, they were melted down, they devoured every word. What a turn was this! O how did God change the counsel of the old Ahithophel into foolishness; and bring all the drunkards, swearers, Sabbath-breakers, and mere sinners in the place, to hear of His plenteous redemption!

Thur. 19.—Abundantly more than the house could contain were present at five in the morning, to whom I was constrained to speak a good deal longer than I am accustomed to do. Perceiving they still wanted to hear, I promised to preach again at nine, in a meadow near the town. Thither they flocked from every side; and I called aloud, "All things are ready; come unto the marriage." O how have a few hours changed the scene! We could now walk through every street of the town, and none molested or opened his mouth, unless to thank or bless us.

Wesley at Dudley and Birmingham

On Tuesday, 24, about noon, we came to Dudley. At one I went to the market-place, and proclaimed the name of the Lord to an huge, unwieldy, noisy multitude; the greater part of whom seemed in no wise to know "wherefore they were come together." I continued speaking about half an hour, and many grew serious and attentive, till some of Satan's servants pressed in, raging and blaspheming, and throwing whatever came to hand. I then retired to the house from which I came. The multitude poured after, and

covered over with dirt many that were near me ; but I
had only a few specks. I preached in Wednesbury at
four, to a nobler people, and was greatly comforted
among them : so I was likewise in the morning, Wednesday, 25. How does a praying congregation strengthen
the preacher !

After preaching again at one, I rode to Birmingham.
This had been long a dry uncomfortable place ; so I
expected little good here : but I was happily disappointed.
Such a congregation I never saw there before : not a
scoffer, nor a trifler, not an inattentive person (so far as
I could discern) among them ; and seldom have I known
so deep, solemn a sense of the power, and presence, and
love of God. The same blessing we had at the meeting
of the society ; and again at the morning preaching.
Will then God at length cause even this barren wilderness to blossom and bud as the rose ?

Wesley in Wales

1750. Sun. Jan. 28.—I read prayers (in London),
and Mr. Whitefield preached. How wise is God in
giving different talents to different preachers ! Even
the little improprieties both of his language and manner
were a means of profiting many, who would not have
been touched by a more correct discourse, or a more
calm and regular manner of speaking.

Tues. March 6 (Bristol).—I began writing a short
French Grammar. We observed Wednesday, 7, as a
day of fasting and prayer.

Sun. 11.—I should willingly have spent more time
in Bristol ; finding more and more proofs that God was
reviving His work ; but that the accounts I received
from Ireland made me think it my duty to be there as
soon as possible ; so, on Monday, 19, I set out with

Christopher Hopper for the New Passage. When we
came there, the wind was high, and almost full against
us : nevertheless we crossed in less than two hours, and
reached Cardiff before night ; where I preached at seven,
and found much refreshment.

Tues. 20.—Expecting to preach at Aberdare, sixteen
Welsh miles from Cardiff, I rode thither over the
mountains. But we found no notice had been given :
so, after resting an hour, we set out for Brecknock.
The rain did not intermit at all, till we came within
sight of it. Twice my horse fell down, and threw me
over his head ; but without any hurt, either to man or
beast.

Wed. 21.—We rode to Builth, where we found notice
had been given, that Howell Harris would preach at
noon. By this means a large congregation was assembled ;
but Howell did not come : so, at their request, I preached.
Between four and five Mr. Philips set out with us for
Royader. I was much out of order in the morning :
however, I held out to Llanidloes, and then lay down.
After an hour's sleep I was much better, and rode on to
Machynlleth.

About an hour and a half before we came to Dolgelly,
the heavy rain began. We were on the brow of the hill,
so we took all that came, our horses being able to go
but half a foot-pace. But we had amends made us at
our inn : John Lewis, and all his house, gladly joined
with us in prayer ; and all we spoke to appeared willing
to hear and to receive the truth in love.

Fri. 23.—Before we looked out, we heard the roaring
of the wind, and the beating of the rain. We took
horse at five. It rained incessantly all the way we rode.
And when we came on the great mountain, four miles
from the town (by which time I was wet from my neck

to my waist), it was with great difficulty I could avoid
being borne over my mare's head, the wind being ready
to carry us all away: nevertheless, about ten we came
safe to Dannabull, praising Him who saves both man
and beast.

Our horses being well tired, and ourselves thoroughly
wet, we rested the remainder of the day; the rather,
because several of the family understood English—an
uncommon thing in these parts. We spoke closely to
these; and they appeared much affected, particularly
when we all joined in prayer.

Waiting for the Irish Boat

Sat. 24.—We set out at five, and at six came to the
sands. But the tide was in, so that we could not pass:
so I sat down in a little cottage for three or four hours,
and translated Aldrich's " Logic." About ten we passed,
and before five came to Baldon Ferry, and found the
boat ready for us: but the boatmen desired us to stay
a while, saying, the wind was too high, and the tide too
strong. The secret was, they stayed for more passengers;
and it was well they did: for while we were walking to
and fro, Mr. Jenkin Morgan came; at whose house,
near half-way between the ferry and Holyhead, I had
lodged three years before. The night soon came on;
but our guide, knowing all the country, brought us safe
to his own door.

Sun. 25.—I preached at Howell Thomas's, in
Trefollwin parish, to a small, earnest congregation.

The wind being contrary, I accepted of the invitation
of an honest exciseman (Mr. Holloway), to stay at his
house till it should change. Here I was in a little,
quiet, solitary spot, where no human voice was heard,
but those of the family. On Tuesday I desired Mr.

Hopper to ride over to Holyhead, and inquire concerning our passage. He brought word, that we might probably pass in a day or two: so on Wednesday we both went thither. Here we overtook John Jane, who had set out on foot from Bristol with three shillings in his pocket. Six nights out of the seven since he set out, he had been entertained by utter strangers. He went by us we could not tell how, and reached Holyhead on Sunday, with one penny left.

By him we sent back our horses to Mr. Morgan's. I had a large congregation in the evening. It almost grieved me, I could give them but one sermon, now they were at length willing to hear. About eleven we were called to go on board, the wind being quite fair: and so it continued till we were just out of the harbour. It then turned west, and blew a storm. There was neither moon nor stars, but rain and wind enough; so that I was soon tired of staying on deck. But we met another storm below: for who should be there, but the famous Mr. Gr——, of Carnarvonshire—a clumsy, overgrown, hard-faced man; whose countenance I could only compare to that (which I saw in Drury Lane thirty years ago) of one of the ruffians in "Macbeth." I was going to lie down, when he tumbled in, and poured out such a volley of ribaldry, obscenity, and blasphemy, every second or third word being an oath, as was scarce ever heard at Billingsgate. Finding there was no room for me to speak, I retired into my cabin, and left him to Mr. Hopper. Soon after, one or two of his own company interposed, and carried him back to his cabin.

Thur. 29.—We wrought our way four or five leagues toward Ireland; but were driven back in the afternoon to the very mouth of the harbour; nevertheless the wind shifting one or two points, we ventured out

again; and by midnight we were got about half seas
over; but the wind then turning full against us, and
blowing hard, we were driven back again, and were glad,
about nine, to get into the bay once more.

In the evening I was surprised to see, instead of some
poor, plain people, a room full of men, daubed with
gold and silver. That I might not go out of their
depth, I began expounding the story of Dives and
Lazarus. It was more applicable than I was aware;
several of them (as I afterwards learned) being eminently
wicked men. I delivered my own soul; but they could
in nowise bear it. One and another walked away,
murmuring sorely. Four stayed till I drew to a close;
they then put on their hats, and began talking to one
another. I mildly reproved them; on which they rose
up and went away, railing and blaspheming. I had then
a comfortable hour with a company of plain, honest
Welshmen.

"Where is the Parson?"

In the night there was a vehement storm. Blessed
be God that we were safe on shore! Saturday, 31. I
determined to wait one week longer, and, if we could
not sail then, to go and wait for a ship at Bristol.
At seven in the evening, just as I was going down to
preach, I heard a huge noise, and took knowledge of the
rabble of gentlemen. They had now strengthened themselves with drink and numbers, and placed Captain
Gr—— (as they called him) at their head. He soon
burst open both the outward and inner door, struck old
Robert Griffith, our landlord, several times, kicked his
wife, and, with twenty full-mouthed oaths and curses,
demanded, "Where is the parson?" Robert Griffith
came up, and desired me to go into another room,

where he locked me in. The captain followed him quickly, broke open one or two doors, and got on a chair, to look on the top of a bed : but his foot slipping (as he was not a man made for climbing), he fell down backward all his length. He rose leisurely, turned about, and, with his troop, walked away.

I then went down to a small company of the poor people, and spent half an hour with them in prayer. About nine, as we were preparing to go to bed, the house was beset again. The captain burst in first. Robert Griffith's daughter was standing in the passage with a pail of water, with which (whether with design or in her fright, I know not) she covered him from head to foot. He cried as well as he could, "M—urder! Murder!" and stood very still for some moments. In the mean time Robert Griffith stepped by him and locked the door. Finding himself alone, he began to change his voice, and cry, "Let me out! Let me out!" Upon his giving his word and honour, that none of the rest should come in, they opened the door, and all went away together.

Wesley Interviews Mrs. Pilkington

Thur. April 12 (Dublin).—I breakfasted with one of the society, and found she had a lodger I little thought of. It was the famous Mrs. Pilkington, who soon made an excuse for following me up stairs. I talked with her seriously about an hour : we then sung, "Happy Magdalene." She appeared to be exceedingly struck: how long the impression may last, God knows.

Sun. May 20 (Cork).—Understanding the usual place of preaching would by no means contain those who desired to hear, about eight I went to Hammond's

Marsh. The congregation was large and deeply attentive. A few of the rabble gathered at a distance; but
by little and little they drew near, and mixed with the
congregation: so that I have seldom seen a more
quiet and orderly assembly at any church in England or
Ireland.

In the afternoon, a report being spread abroad that
the mayor designed to hinder my preaching on the
Marsh in the evening, I desired Mr. Skelton and Mr.
Jones to wait upon him, and inquire concerning it.
Mr. Skelton asked, if my preaching there would be
disagreeable to him; adding, "Sir, if it would, Mr.
Wesley will not do it." He replied warmly, "Sir, I'll
have no mobbing." Mr. Skeleton replied, "Sir, there
was none this morning." He answered, "There was.
Are there not churches and meeting-houses enough?
I will have no more mobs or riots." Mr. Skelton
replied, "Sir, neither Mr. Wesley nor they that heard
him made either mobs or riots." He answered plain,
"I will have no more preaching; and if Mr. Wesley
attempts to preach, I am prepared for him."

I began preaching in our own house soon after five.
Mr. Mayor meantime was walking in the 'Change, and
giving orders to the town-drummers and to his sergeants
—doubtless to go down and keep the peace! They
accordingly came down to the house, with an innumerable mob attending them. They continued drumming,
and I continued preaching, till I had finished my discourse. When I came out, the mob immediately closed
me in. Observing one of the sergeants standing by, I
desired him to keep the King's peace; but he replied,
"Sir, I have no orders to do that." As soon as I came
into the street, the rabble threw whatever came to hand;
but all went by me, or flew over my head; nor do I

remember that one thing touched me. I walked on straight through the midst of the rabble, looking every man before me in the face; and they opened on the right and left, till I came near Dant's Bridge. A large party had taken possession of this, one of whom was bawling out, "Now, hey for the Romans!" When I came up, they likewise shrunk back, and I walked through them to Mr. Jenkins's house; but a Papist stood just within the door, and endeavoued to hinder my going in; till one of the mob (I suppose aiming at me, but missing) knocked her down flat. I then went in, and God restrained the wild beasts, so that not one attempted to follow me.

But many of the congregation were more roughly handled, particularly Mr. Jones, who was covered with dirt, and escaped with his life almost by miracle. The main body of the mob then went to the house, brought out all the seats and benches, tore up the floor, the door, the frames of the windows, and whatever of wood-work remained; part of which they carried off for their own use, and the rest they burnt in the open street.

Finding there was no probability of their dispersing, I sent to Alderman Pembrock, who immediately desired Mr. Alderman Windthrop, his nephew, to go down to Mr. Jenkins, with whom I walked up the street, none giving me an unkind or disrespectful word.

Wesley Burnt in Effigy

Mon. 21.—I rode on to Bandon. From three in the afternoon till past seven, the mob of Cork marched in grand procession, and then burnt me in effigy near Dant's Bridge.

Wed. 23.—The mob was still patrolling the streets, abusing all that were called Methodists, and threatening to murder them and pull down their houses, if they did not leave this way.

Thur. 24.—They again assaulted Mr. Stockdale's house, broke down the boards he had nailed up against the windows, destroyed what little remained of the window-frames and shutters, and damaged a considerable part of his goods.

Fri. 25.—One Roger O'Ferrall fixed up an advertisement at the public Exchange, that he was ready to head any mob, in order to pull down any house that should dare to harbour a swaddler. (A name given to Mr. Cennick first by a Popish priest, who heard him speak of a child wrapped in swaddling clothes; and probably did not know the expression was in the Bible, a book he was not much acquainted with.)

At this time God gave us great peace at Bandon, notwithstanding the unwearied labours, both public and private, of good Dr. B.——, to stir up the people. But, Saturday, 26, many were under great apprehensions of what was to be done in the evening. I began preaching in the main street at the usual hour, but to more than twice the usual congregation. After I had spoke about a quarter of an hour, a clergyman, who had planted himself near me, with a very large stick in his hand, according to agreement, opened the scene. (Indeed his friends assured me he was in drink, or he would not have done it.) But, before he had uttered many words, two or three resolute women, by main strength, pulled him into a house; and, after expostulating a little, sent him away through the garden.

The next champion that appeared was one Mr. M——, a young gentleman of the town. He was attended by two others, with pistols in their hands. But his triumph too was but short; some of the people quickly bore him away, though with much gentleness and civility.

The third came on with greater fury; but he was encountered by a butcher of the town (not one of the Methodists), who used him as he would an ox, bestowing one or two hearty blows upon his head. This cooled his courage, especially as none took his part. So I quietly finished my discourse.

Visits to Kinsale and Cork

Mon. 28.—I rode to Kinsale, one of the pleasantest towns which I have seen in Ireland. At seven I preached at the Exchange, to a few gentry, many poor people, and abundance of soldiers. All behaved like men that feared God. After sermon came one from Cork, and informed us Mr. W—— had preached both morning and afternoon under the wall of the barracks; that the town-drummers came; but the soldiers assured them if they went to beat there they would be all cut in pieces; that then the mayor came himself, at the head of his mob, but could make no considerable disturbance; that he went and talked to the commanding officer, but with so little success, that the colonel came out and declared to the mob, they must make no riot there. Here is a turn of affairs worthy of God! Doth He not rule in heaven and earth?

Wed. 30.—I rode to Cork. By talking with Captain ——, I found there was no depending on the good offices of the colonel. He had told the captain with great openness, "If Mr. Wesley preached in the barracks, and the mob were to come and break the windows, I might have a long bill from the barrack-master." Break the windows! Nay, it is well if they had not broken the bones of all the soldiers.

A little before five I walked towards the barracks. The boys quickly gathered, and were more and more turbulent. But in a moment all was quiet. This, I afterwards found, was owing to Mr. W——, who snatched a stick out of a man's hand, and brandished it over his head, on which the whole troop valiantly ran away.

When we came over the south bridge, a large mob gathered; but before they were well formed we reached the barrack gate; at a small distance from which I stood and cried, " Let the wicked forsake his way." The congregation of serious people was large; the mob stood about a hundred yards off. I was a little surprised to observe, that almost all the soldiers kept together in a body near the gate, and knew not but the report might be true, that, on a signal given, they were all to retire into the barracks; but they never stirred until I had done. As we walked away, one or two of them followed us. Their numbers increased, until we had seven or eight before and a whole troop of them behind ; between whom I walked, through an immense mob, to Alderman Pembrock's door.

At an Irish Funeral

Thurs. 31.—I rode to Rathcormuck. There being a great burying in the afternoon, to which people came from all parts, Mr. Lloyd read part of the burial service in the church ; after which I preached on, " The end of all things is at hand." I was exceedingly shocked at (what I had only heard of before) the Irish howl which followed. It was not a song, as I supposed, but a dismal, inarticulate yell, set up at the grave by four shrill-voiced women, who (we understood) were hired for that purpose. But I saw not one that shed a tear ; for that it seems, was not in their bargain.

Wed. June 13.—I rode to Shronill again ; and in the morning, Thursday, 14, to Clonmell. After an hour's rest we set forward, but were obliged to stop in the afternoon, sooner than we designed, by my horse having a shoe loose. The poor man, at whose house we called, was not only patient of exhortation, but exceeding thankful for it. We afterwards missed our way ; so that it was near eight o'clock before we got over the ferry, a mile short of Waterford.

At the ferry was a lad who asked my name. When he heard it, he cried out, " O Sir, you have no business here ; you have nothing to do at Waterford. Butler has been gathering mobs there all this week ; and they set upon us so, that we cannot walk the streets. But if you will stay at that little house, I will go and bring B. M'Cullock to you."

We stayed some time, and then thought it best to go a little on our way toward Portarlington. But the ferryman would not come over : so that, after waiting till we were weary, we made our way through some grounds, and over the mountain, into the Carrick road ; and went on, about five miles, to a village where we found a quiet house. Sufficient for this day was the labour thereof. We were on horseback, with but an hour or two's intermission, from five in the morning, till within a quarter of eleven at night.

Fri. 15.—About two in the morning I heard people making a great noise, and calling me by my name. They were some of our friends from Waterford, who informed us, that, upon the lad's coming in, sixteen or eighteen of them came out, to conduct me into the town. Not finding me, they returned ; but the mob met them by the way, and pelted them with dirt and stones to their own doors.

JOHN WESLEY IN AN IRISH CABIN

We set out at four, and reached Kilkenny, about twenty-five old Irish miles, about noon. This is by far the most pleasant, as well as most fruitful country, which I have seen in all Ireland. Our way after dinner lay by Dunmore, the seat of the late Duke of Ormond. We rode through the park for about two miles, by the side of which the river runs. I never saw either in England, Holland, or Germany, so delightful a place. The walks, each consisting of four rows of ashes, the tufts of trees sprinkled up and down, interspersed with the smoothest and greenest lawns, are beautiful beyond description. And what hath the owner thereof, the Earl of Arran ? Not even the beholding it with his eyes.

Wesley Rides Ninety Miles

My horse tired in the afternoon ; so I left him behind, and borrowed that of my companion. I came to Aymo about eleven, and would very willingly have passed the rest of the night there ; but the good woman of the inn was not minded that I should. For some time she would not answer : at last she opened the door just wide enough to let out four dogs upon me. So I rode on to Ballybrittas, expecting a rough salute here too, from a large dog which used to be in the yard. But he never stirred, till the hostler waked and came out. About twelve I laid me down. I think this was the longest day's journey I ever rode ; being fifty old Irish, that is, about ninety English miles.

Thurs. 21.—I returned to Closeland, and preached in the evening to a little, earnest company. O who should drag me into a great city, if I did not know there is another world ! How gladly could I spend the remainder of a busy life in solitude and retirement !

Thur. Sept. 6.—I rode to Salisbury and preached at Winterburn in the evening; the next, at Reading; and, on Saturday, 8, came to London.

Here I had the following account from one of our preachers :—

"John Jane was never well after walking from Epworth to Hainton, on an exceeding hot day, which threw him into a fever. But he was in great peace and love, even to those who greatly wanted love to him. He was some time at Alice Shadforth's house, with whom he daily talked of the things of God. He was never without the love of God, spent much time in private prayer, and joined likewise with her in prayer several times in a day. On Friday, August 24, growing, as she thought, stronger in body, he sat in the evening by the fire-side : about six he fetched a deep sigh, and never spoke more. He was alive till the same hour on Saturday; at which, without any struggle, or any sign of pain, with a smile on his face, he passed away. His last words were, 'I find the love of God in Christ Jesus.'

He Left One Shilling and Fourpence

"All his clothes, linen and woollen, stockings, hat, and wig, are not thought sufficient to answer his funeral expenses, which amount to one pound seventeen shillings and threepence. All the money he had was one shilling and fourpence." Enough for any unmarried preacher of the Gospel to leave to his executors.

Mon. 17.—My brother set out for the north; but returned the next day, much out of order. How little do we know the counsels of God! But we know they are all wise and gracious.

Wed. 19.—When I came home in the evening, I found my brother abundantly worse. He had had no sleep for several nights ; and expected none, unless from opiates. I went down to our brethren below, and we made our request known to God. When I went up again he was in a sound sleep, which continued till the morning.

Fri. 21.—We had a watch-night at Spitalfields. I often wonder at the peculiar providence of God on these occasions. I do not know that in so many years one person has ever been hurt, either in London, Bristol, or Dublin, in going so late in the night to and from all parts of the town.

Sun. 23.—My brother being not yet able to assist, I had more employment to-day than I expected. In the morning I read prayers, preached, and administered the sacrament to a large congregation in Spitalfields. The service at West Street continued from nine till one. At five I called the sinners in Moorfields to repentance. And, when I had finished my work found more liveliness and strength than I did at six in the morning.

Wesley as Editor

Mon. 24.—I left London, and, the next morning, called at what is styled the Half-way House. Quickly after, as a young man was riding by the door, both horse and man tumbled over each other. As soon as he got up, he began cursing his horse. I spoke a few words, and he was calm. He told me, he did fear God once ; but for some time past he had cared for nothing. He went away full of good resolutions. God bring them to good effect !

I reached Kingswood in the evening ; and the next day selected passages of Milton for the eldest children to transcribe and repeat weekly.

Thur. 27.—I went into the school, and heard half the

children their lessons, and then selected passages of the
" Moral and Sacred Poems." Friday, 28. I heard the
other half of the children. Saturday, 29. I was with
them from four to five in the morning. I spent most
of the day in revising Kennet's " Antiquities," and
marking what was worth reading in the school.

Wed. Oct. 3.—I revised, for the use of the children,
Archbishop Potter's " Grecian Antiquities " ; a dry, dull,
heavy book. Thursday, 4. I revised Mr. Lewis's
" Hebrew Antiquities "; something more entertaining
than the other, and abundantly more instructive.

Sat. 6.—I nearly finished the abridgment of Dr. Cave's
" Primitive Christianity " ; a book wrote with as much
learning, and as little judgment, as any I remember to
have read in my whole life ; serving the ancient Christians
just as Xenophon did Socrates ; relating every weak
thing they ever said or did.

Thur. 11.—I prepared a short " History of England,"
for the use of the children ; and on Friday and Saturday
a short " Roman History," as an introduction to the
Latin historians.

Mon. 15.—I read over Mr. Holmes's " Latin
Grammar "; and extracted from it what was needful to
perfect our own.

In Canterbury Cathedral

Mon. Dec. 3.—I rode to Canterbury, and preached
on Rev. xx. A few turbulent people made a little noise,
as I found it was their custom to do. Perceiving more
of them were gathered the next night, I turned and
spoke to them at large. They appeared to be not a
little confounded, and went away as quiet as lambs.

Wed. 5.—I walked over the cathedral, and surveyed
the monuments of the ancient men of renown. One

would think such a sight should strike an utter damp upon human vanity. What are the great, the fair, the valiant now? the matchless warrior—the puissant monarch?—

> An heap of dust is all remains of thee!
> 'Tis all thou art, and all the proud shall be.

Mon. 10.—I rode to Leigh, in Essex, where I found a little company seeking God; and endeavoured to encourage them in "provoking one another to love and good works."

Mon. 17.—I set upon cleansing Augeas's stable; upon purging that huge work, Mr. Fox's "Acts and Monuments," from all the trash which that honest, injudicious writer has heaped together, and mingled with those venerable records, which are worthy to be had in everlasting remembrance.

1751. Wed. Jan. 30.—Having received a pressing letter from Dr. Isham, then the rector of our college, to give my vote at the election for a Member of Parliament, which was to be the next day, I set out early, in a severe frost, with the north-west wind full in my face. The roads were so slippery, that it was scarce possible for our horses to keep their feet: indeed one of them could not; but fell upon his head, and cut it terribly. Nevertheless, about seven in the evening, God brought us safe to Oxford. A congregation was waiting for me at Mr. Evans's, whom I immediately addressed in those awful words, "What is a man profited, if he shall gain the whole world, and lose his own soul?"

Thur. 31.—I went to the schools, where the Convocation was met: but I did not find the decency and order which I expected. The gentleman for whom I came to vote was not elected: yet I did not repent of my coming ; I owe much more than this to that generous, friendly man, who now rests from his labours.

I was much surprised wherever I went, at the civility of the people—gentlemen as well as others.   There was no pointing, no calling of names, as once ; no, nor even laughter.   What can this mean?   Am I become a servant of men ?   Or is the scandal of the cross ceased ?

Wesley Decides to Marry

Fri. Feb. 1.—We set out for London in another bitter morning, having such a wind (now got to the east, and so in our face again) as I hardly ever remember. But by five in the evening we were under shelter at the Foundery.   It being the night before appointed for a watch-night, we continued praying and praising God as usual, till about twelve o'clock : and I found no inconvenience, but a little faintness, which a few hours' sleep removed.

Sat. 2.—Having received a full answer from Mr. P——, I was clearly convinced that I ought to marry.   For many years I remained single because I believed I could be more useful in a single, than in a married state.   And I praise God, who enabled me so to do.   I now as fully believed, that in my present circumstances, I might be more useful in a married state ; into which, upon this clear conviction, and by the advice of my friends, I entered a few days after.

Wed. 6.—I met the single men, and showed them on how many accounts it was good for those who had received that gift from God, to remain " single for the kingdom of heaven's sake " ; unless where a particular case might be an exception to the general rule.

Sun. 10.—After preaching at five, I was hastening to take my leave of the congregation at Snowsfields, purposing to set out in the morning for the north; when, on the middle of London-bridge, both my feet slipped on the ice, and I fell with great force, the bone of my ankle lighting on the top of a stone. However, I got on, with some help, to the chapel, being resolved not to disappoint the people. After preaching, I had my leg bound up by a surgeon, and made a shift to walk to the Seven Dials. It was with much difficulty that I got up into the pulpit; but God then comforted many of our hearts.

I went back in a coach to Mr. B——'s, and from thence in a chair to the Foundery; but I was not able to preach, my sprain growing worse. I removed to Threadneedle Street; where I spent the remainder of the week, partly in prayer, reading, and conversation, partly in writing an " Hebrew Grammar," and " Lessons for Children."

Sun. 17.—I was carried to the Foundery, and preached, kneeling (as I could not stand), on part of the twenty-third Psalm; my heart being enlarged, and my mouth opened to declare the wonders of God's love.

Marriage and Preaching

Monday, 18, was the second day I had appointed for my journey; but I was disappointed again, not being yet able to set my foot to the ground. However, I preached (kneeling) on Tuesday evening, and Wednesday morning.

Sun. 24.—I preached, morning and evening, at Spitalfields.

Mon. Mar. 4.—Being tolerably able to ride, though not to walk, I set out for Bristol. I came thither on Wednesday, thoroughly tired; though, in other respects, better than when I set out.

Tues. 19.—Having finished the business for which I came to Bristol, I set out again for London; being desired by many to spend a few days there before I entered upon my northern journey. I came to London on Thursday, and, having settled all affairs, left it again on Wednesday, 27. I cannot understand, how a Methodist preacher can answer it to God, to preach one sermon, or travel one day less, in a married than in a single state. In this respect surely, " it remaineth, that they who have wives be as though they had none."

Wesley and his Barber

Thur. April 11 (Bolton).—The barber who shaved me said, " Sir, I praise God on your behalf. When you was at Bolton last, I was one of the most eminent drunkards in all the town; but I came to listen at the window, and God struck me to the heart. I then earnestly prayed for power against drinking; and God gave me more than I asked: he took away the very desire of it. Yet I felt myself worse and worse, till, on April 5 last, I could hold out no longer. I knew I must drop into hell that moment, unless God appeared to save me: and he did appear. I knew he loved me; and felt sweet peace. Yet I did not dare to say I had faith, till, yesterday was twelvemonth, God gave me faith; and his love has ever since filled my heart."

Mon. 22.—The rain stopped while I was preaching at the market-place in Morpeth. We rode from thence to Alnwick, where (it being too wet to preach at the Cross) some of our friends procured the Town Hall. This, being very large, contained the people well; only the number of them made it extremely hot.

Tues. 23.—We rode on to Berwick-upon-Tweed.

Wed. 24.—Mr. Hopper and I took horse between three and four, and about seven came to Old-camus. Whether the country was good or bad we could not see, having a thick mist all the way. The Scotch towns are like none which I ever saw, either in England, Wales, or Ireland : there is such an air of antiquity in them all, and such a peculiar oddness in their manner of building. But we were most surprised at the entertainment we met with in every place, so far different from common report. We had all things good, cheap, in great abundance, and remarkably well-dressed. In the afternoon we rode by Preston Field, and saw the place of battle, and Colonel Gardiner's house. The Scotch here affirm, that he fought on foot after he was dismounted, and refused to take quarter. Be it as it may, he is now " where the wicked cease from troubling, and where the weary are at rest."

Wesley's Impressions of Scotland

We reached Musselburgh between four and five. I had no intention to preach in Scotland; nor did I imagine there were any that desired I should. But I was mistaken. Curiosity (if nothing else) brought abundance of people together in the evening. And whereas in the kirk (Mrs. G—— informed me) there used to be laughing and talking, and all the marks of the grossest inattention : but it was far otherwise here : they remained as statues from the beginning of the sermon to the end.

Thur. 25.—We rode to Edinburgh ; one of the dirtiest cities I had ever seen, not excepting Cölen in Germany.

We returned to Musselburgh to dinner, whither we were followed in the afternoon by a little party of gentlemen from Edinburgh. I know not why any should complain of the shyness of the Scots toward strangers. All I spoke with were as free and open with me as the people of Newcastle or Bristol; nor did any person move any dispute of any kind, or ask me any question concerning my opinion.

I preached again at six, on, " Seek ye the Lord, while He may be found." I used great plainness of speech toward them; and they all received it in love: so that the prejudice which the devil had been several years planting was torn up by the roots in one hour. After preaching, one of the bailies of the town, with one of the elders of the kirk, came to me, and begged I would stay with them a while, if it were but two or three days, and they would fit up a far larger place than the school, and prepare seats for the congregation. Had not my time been fixed, I should gladly have complied.

Wesley's Remarkable Vitality

1752. Sun. March 15 (London).—While I was preaching at West Street in the afternoon, there was one of the most violent storms I ever remember. In the midst of the sermon great part of an house opposite to the chapel was blown down. We heard an huge noise, but knew not the cause; so much the more did God speak to our hearts: and great was the rejoicing of many in confidence of his protection. Between four and five I took horse, with my wife and daughter. The tiles were rattling from the houses on both sides; but they hurt not us. We reached Hayes about seven in the evening, and Oxford the next day.

Thur. April 16.—I walked over to Burnham. I had no thought of preaching there, doubting if my strength would allow of preaching always thrice a day, as I had

done most days since I came from Evesham. But
finding an house full of people, I could not refrain.
Still the more I use my strength, the more I have. I
am often much tired the first time I preach in a day; a
little the second time; but after the third or fourth, I
rarely feel either weakness or weariness.

Wed. 22.—I rode to Grimsby. The crowd was so
great in the evening, that the room was like an oven.
The next night I preached at the end of the town,
whither almost all the people, rich and poor, followed
me; and I had a fair opportunity of closely applying that
weighty question, " Lord, are there few that be saved?"

Fri. 24.—We rode by a fine seat; the owner of which
(not much above fourscore years old) says he desires
only to live thirty years longer; ten to hunt, ten to get
money (having at present but twenty thousand pounds
a year), and ten years to repent. O that God may not
say unto him, " Thou fool, this night shall thy soul be
required of thee!"

When I landed at the quay in Hull, it was covered
with people, inquiring, "Which is he? Which is he?"
But they only stared and laughed; and we walked unmolested to Mr. A——'s house.

I was quite surprised at the miserable condition of
the fortifications; far more ruinous and decayed than
those at Newcastle, even before the rebellion. It is well
there is no enemy near.

A Crowded Coach

I went to prayers at three in the old church—a grand
and venerable structure. Between five and six the coach
called, and took me to Mighton Car, about half a mile
from the town. An huge multitude, rich and poor,
horse and foot, with several coaches, were soon gathered

together; to whom I cried with a loud voice and a composed spirit, " What shall it profit a man, if he shall gain the whole world, and lose his own soul?" Some thousands of the people seriously attended; but many behaved as if possessed by Moloch. Clods and stones flew about on every side; but they neither touched nor disturbed me.

When I had finished my discourse, I went to take coach; but the coachman had driven clear away. We were at a loss, till a gentlewoman invited my wife and me to come into her coach. She brought some inconveniences on herself thereby; not only as there were nine of us in the coach, three on each side, and three in the middle; but also as the mob closely attended us, throwing in at the windows (which we did not think it prudent to shut) whatever came next to hand. But a large gentlewoman who sat in my lap, screened me, so that nothing came near me.

Wesley Sleeps in a Cellar

Mon. May 25.—We rode to Durham, and thence, through very rough roads, and as rough weather, to Barnard Castle. I was exceeding faint when we came in: however, the time being come, I went into the street, and would have preached; but the mob was so numerous and so loud, that it was not possible for many to hear. Nevertheless, I spoke on, and those who were near listened with huge attention. To prevent this, some of the rabble fetched the engine, and threw a good deal of water on the congregation; but not a drop fell on me. After about three quarters of an hour, I returned into the house.

Tues. June 9.—My lodging was not such as I should have chosen; but what Providence chooses is always

good. My bed was considerably under ground, the
room serving both for a bed-chamber and a cellar. The
closeness was more troublesome at first than the cool-
ness : but I let in a little fresh air, by breaking a pane
of paper (put by way of glass) in the window ; and then
slept sound till the morning.

Mon. 15.—I had many little trials in this journey, of
a kind I had not known before. I had borrowed a
young, strong mare, when I set out from Manchester.
But she fell lame before I got to Grimsby. I procured
another, but was dismounted again between Newcastle
and Berwick. At my return to Manchester, I took my
own : but she had lamed herself in the pasture. I
thought, nevertheless, to ride her four or five miles
to-day ; but she was gone out of the ground, and we
could hear nothing of her. However, I comforted
myself, that I had another at Manchester, which I
had lately bought. But when I came thither, I found
one had borrowed her too, and rode her away to
Chester.

Sat. 20.—I rode to Chester, and preached at six, in
the accustomed place, a little without the gates, near
St. John's church. One single man, a poor alehouse-
keeper, seemed disgusted, spoke a harmless word, and
ran away with all speed. All the rest behaved with the
utmost seriousness, while I declared " the grace of our
Lord Jesus Christ."

Round Chester Walls

Mon. 22.—We walked round the walls of the city,
which are something more than a mile and three quarters
in circumference. But there are many vacant spaces
within the walls, many gardens, and a good deal o
pasture-ground : so that I believe Newcastle-upon-Tyne,

within the walls, contains at least a third more houses than Chester.

The greatest convenience here is what they call " the Rows "; that is, covered galleries, which run through the main streets on each side, from east to west, and from north to south; by which means one may walk both clean and dry in any weather, from one end of the city to the other.

I preached, at six in the evening, in the square, to a vast multitude, rich and poor. The far greater part, the gentry in particular, were seriously and deeply attentive; though a few of the rabble, most of them drunk, laboured much to make a disturbance. One might already perceive a great increase of earnestness in the generality of the hearers.

Tues. Aug. 25.—I preached in the market-place at Kinsale. The next morning, at eight, I walked to the fort. On the hill above it we found a large, deep hollow, capable of containing two or three thousand people. On one side of this, the soldiers soon cut a place with their swords for me to stand, where I was screened both from the wind and sun, while the congregation sat on the grass before me. Many eminent sinners were present, particularly of the army; and I believe God gave them a loud call to repentance.

Sat. Sept. 23.—We reached Cork. Sunday, 24. In the evening I proposed to the society the building a preaching-house. The next day ten persons subscribed an hundred pounds; another hundred was subscribed in three or four days, and a piece of ground taken. I saw a double providence now in our not sailing last week. If we had, probably this house had never been built; and it is most likely we should have been cast away. Above thirty ships, we were informed, have been lost on these coasts in the late storm.

The wind being contrary still, on Monday, Oct. 2, I rode once more to Bandon. But though I came unexpected, the house was too small to contain one half of the congregation; so I preached in the street, both this evening, and at five on Tuesday morning; the moon giving us as much light as we wanted, till the sun supplied her place. I then returned to Cork. On Friday, 6, the ship being under sail, we took boat, and came to Cove in the evening. All the inns being full, we lodged at a private house; but we found one inconvenience herein: we had nothing to eat; for our provisions were on board, and there was nothing to be bought in the town; neither flesh, nor fish, nor butter, nor cheese. At length we procured some eggs and bread, and were well contented.

A Boiling Sea

Sun. 8.—We were called early by the pilot, and told we must rise and go on board. We did so, and found a large number of passengers: but the wind turning, most of them went on shore. At eleven I preached to those that were left. About six it blew a storm: but we were anchored in a safe harbour; so it neither hurt nor disturbed us.

Mon. 9.—Finding there was no probability of sailing soon, we went up to Mr. P——'s, near Passage. I preached there in the street about four, to most of the inhabitants of the town. They behaved very quietly; but very few seemed either convinced or affected.

Tues. 10.—We had another violent storm: it made Mr. P——'s house rock to and fro, though it was a new, strong house, and covered on all sides with hills, as well as with trees. We afterwards heard, that several ships were lost on the coast. Only one got into the harbour, but grievously shattered, her rigging torn in pieces, and her main-mast gone by the board.

Wed. 11.—I rode to Cork once more, and was very fully employed all the day. The next morning we returned to Cove, and about noon got out of the harbour. We immediately found the effects of the late storm, the sea still boiling like a pot. The moon set about eight, but the Northern Lights abundantly supplied her place. Soon after, God smoothed the face of the deep, and gave us a small, fair wind.

Fri. 13.—I read over Pascal's "Thoughts." What could possibly induce such a creature as Voltaire to give such an author as this a good word; unless it was, that he once wrote a satire? And so his being a satirist might atone even for his being a Christian.

Sat. 14.—About seven we sailed into Kingroad, and happily concluded our little voyage. I now rested a week at Bristol and Kingswood, preaching only morning and evening.

Wesley's Forgiveness

Sunday, 29, was an useful day to my soul. I found more than once trouble and heaviness; but I called upon the name of the Lord; and he gave me a clear, full approbation of his way, and a calm, thankful acquiescence in his will.

I cannot but stand amazed at the goodness of God. Others are most assaulted on the weak side of their soul; but with me it is quite otherwise; if I have any strength at all (and I have none but what I have received), it is in forgiving injuries; and on this very side am I assaulted, more frequently than on any other.

Yet leave me not here one hour to myself, or I shall betray myself and Thee!

In the remaining part of this (November), and in the following month, I prepared the rest of the books for the " Christian Library " ; a work by which I have lost about two hundred pounds. Perhaps the next generation may know the value of it.

1753. Sat. Jan. 20.—I advised one who had been troubled many years with a stubborn paralytic disorder, to try a new remedy. Accordingly, she was electrified, and found immediate help. By the same means I have known two persons cured of an inveterate pain in the stomach ; and another of a pain in his side, which he had had ever since he was a child. Nevertheless, who can wonder that many gentlemen of the faculty, as well as their good friends, the apothecaries, decry a medicine so shockingly cheap and easy, as much as they do quicksilver and tar-water?

Sat. Feb. 3.—I visited one in the Marshalsea prison ; a nursery of all manner of wickedness. O shame to man, that there should be such a place, such a picture of hell, upon earth! And shame to those who bear the name of Christ, that there should need any prison at all in Christendom!

Thur. 8.—A proposal was made for devolving all temporal business, books and all, entirely on the Stewards ; so that I might have no care upon me (in London at least) but that of the souls committed to my charge. O when shall it once be ! From this day?

In the afternoon I visited many of the sick ; but such scenes, who could see unmoved? There are none such to be found in a pagan country. If any of the Indians in Georgia were sick (which indeed exceeding rarely happened, till they learned gluttony and drunkenness from the Christians), those that were near him gave him whatever he wanted. O who will convert the English into honest Heathens!

On Friday and Saturday I visited as many more as I could. I found some in their cells under ground; others in their garrets, half starved both with cold and hunger, added to weakness and pain. But I found not one of them unemployed, who was able to crawl about the room. So wickedly, devilishly false is that common objection, "They are poor, only because they are idle." If you saw these things with your own eyes, could you lay out money in ornaments or superfluities?

Thur. 15.—I visited Mr. S——, slowly recovering from a severe illness. He expressed much love, and did not doubt, he said, inasmuch as I meant well, but that God would convince me of my great sin in writing books; seeing men ought to read no book but the Bible. I judged it quite needless to enter into a dispute with a sea captain, seventy-five years old.

Fri. March 16.—I returned to Bristol; and on Monday, 19, set out with my wife for the north.

Sat. 31.—I preached at Boothbank, where I met Mr. C——, late gardener to the Earl of W——. Surely it cannot be! Is it possible the earl should turn off an honest, diligent, well-tried servant, who had been in the family above fifty years, for no other fault than hearing the Methodists?

Sun. April 15.—I preached in the afternoon at Cockermouth, to well nigh all the inhabitants of the town. Intending to go from thence into Scotland, I inquired concerning the road, and was informed, I could not pass the arm of the sea which parts the two kingdoms, unless I was at Bonas, about thirty miles from Cockermouth, soon after five in the morning. At first

I thought of taking an hour or two's sleep, and setting out at eleven or twelve. But, upon farther consider a tion, we chose to take our journey first, and rest afterward. So we took horse about seven, and having a calm, moonshiny night, reached Bonas before one. After two or three hours' sleep, we set out again, without any faintness or drowsiness.

The Pay of Preaching

Our landlord, as he was guiding us over the Frith, very innocently asked, how much a year we got by preaching thus. This gave me an opportunity of explaining to him that kind of gain which he seemed utterly a stranger to. He appeared to be quite amazed, and spake not one word, good or bad, till he took his leave.

Presently after he went, my mare stuck fast in a quagmire, which was in the midst of the high road. But we could well excuse this; for the road all along, for near fifty miles after, was such as I never saw any natural road, either in England or Ireland; nay, far better, notwithstanding the continued rain, than the turnpike road between London and Canterbury.

We dined at Dumfries, a clean, well-built town, having two of the most elegant churches (one at each end of the town) that I have seen. We reached Thorny Hill in the evening. What miserable accounts pass current in England of the inns in Scotland! Yet here, as well as wherever we called in our whole journey, we had not only everything we wanted, but everything readily and in good order, and as clean as I ever desire.

Tues. 17.—We set out about four, and rode over several high, but extremely pleasant, mountains, to

Lead Hill ; a village of miners, resembling Placey, near Newcastle. We dined at a village called Lesmahaggy, and about eight in the evening reached Glasgow. A gentleman who had overtaken us on the road sent one with us to Mr. Gillies's house.

Wesley in Glasgow

Wed. 18.—I walked over the city, which I take to be as large as Newcastle-upon-Tyne. The University (like that of Dublin) is only one College, consisting of two small squares ; I think not larger, nor at all handsomer, than those of Lincoln College, in Oxford. The habit of the students gave me surprise. They wear scarlet gowns, reaching only to their knees. Most I saw were very dirty, some very ragged, and all of very coarse cloth. The high church is a fine building. The outside is equal to that of most cathedrals in England ; but it is miserably defaced within ; having no form, beauty, or symmetry left.

At seven in the evening Mr. G. began the service, at his own (the College) church. It was so full before I came, that I could not get in without a good deal of difficulty.

Thur. 19.—At seven I preached about a quarter of a mile from the town ; but it was an extremely rough and blustering morning ; and few people came either at the time or place of my preaching : the natural consequence of which was, that I had but a small congregation. About four in the afternoon, a tent, as they term it, was prepared ; a kind of moving pulpit, covered with canvass at the top, behind, and on the sides. In this I preached near the place where I was in the morning, to near six times as many people as before ; and I am persuaded what was spoken came to some of their hearts, " not in word only, but in power."

Fri. 20.—I had designed to preach at the same place ; but the rain made it impracticable. So Mr. G. desired me to preach in his church ; so I began between seven and eight. Surely with God nothing is impossible ! Who would have believed, five-and-twenty years ago, either that the minister would have desired it, or that I should have consented to preach in a Scotch kirk ?

Apprenticeship Customs

Wed. 25.—We came to Alnwick on the day whereon those who have gone through their apprenticeship are made free of the corporation. Sixteen or seventeen, we were informed, were to receive their freedom this day, and, in order thereto (such is the unparalleled wisdom of the present corporation, as well as of their forefathers), to walk through a great bog (purposely preserved for the occasion ; otherwise it might have been drained long ago), which takes up some of them to the neck, and many of them to the breast.

Tues. May 8.—I rode [from Stockton] to Robinhood's Bay, near Whitby. The town is very remarkably situated : it stands close to the sea, and is in great part built on craggy and steep rocks, some of which rise perpendicular from the water. And yet the land, both on the north, south, and west, is fruitful and well cultivated. I stood on a little rising near the quay, in a warm, still evening, and exhorted a multitude of people, from all parts, to " seek the Lord, while he may be found." They were all attention ; and most of them met me again at half an hour after four in the morning. I could gladly have spent some days here ; but my stages were fixed : so, on Wednesday, 9, I rode on to York.

Sun. July 8 (London).—After preaching at the chapel, morning and afternoon, I took horse with Mr. P——. We had designed to ride only two or three hours, in order to shorten the next day's journey. But a young man, who overtook us near Kingston, induced us to change our purpose. So we only rested about half an hour at Cobham; and leaving it between nine and ten, rode on softly in a calm, moonshiny night, and about twelve came to Godalming. We took horse again at half an hour past four, and reached Portsmouth about one.

After a little rest, we took a walk round the town, which is regularly fortified; and is, I suppose, the only regular fortification in Great Britain or Ireland. Gosport, Portsmouth, and the Common (which is now all turned into streets), may probably contain half as many people as Bristol: and so civil a people I never saw before in any sea-port town in England.

I preached at half an hour after six, in an open part of the Common, adjoining to the new church. The congregation was large and well-behaved; not one scoffer did I see, nor one trifler. In the morning, Tuesday, 10, I went on board an hoy; and in three hours landed at Cowes, in the Isle of Wight; as far exceeding the Isle of Anglesey, both in pleasantness and fruitfulness, as that exceeds the rocks of Scilly.

We rode straight to Newport, the chief town in the isle, and found a little society in tolerable order. Several of them had found peace with God.

At half an hour after six I preached in the market-place, to a numerous congregation: but they were not so serious as those at Portsmouth. Many children made much noise, and many grown persons were talking aloud, almost all the time I was preaching. It was quite otherwise at five in the morning. There was a large congregation again; and every person therein seemed to know this was the word whereby God would judge them in the last day.

In the afternoon, I walked to Carisbrook castle; or rather, the poor remains of it. It stands upon a solid rock on the top of an hill, and commands a beautiful prospect. There is a well in it, cut quite through the rock, said to be seventy-two yards deep; and another in the citadel, near an hundred. They drew up the water by an ass, which they assured us was sixty years old. But all the stately apartments lie in ruins. Only just enough of them is left, to show the chamber where poor King Charles was confined, and the window through which he attempted to escape.

Cornish Smugglers

On Wednesday, 25, the Stewards met at St. Ives, from the western part of Cornwall. The next day I began examining the society; but I was soon obliged to stop short. I found an accursed thing among them; well-nigh one and all bought or sold uncustomed goods. I therefore delayed speaking to any more till I had met them all together. This I did in the evening, and told them plain, either they must put this abomination away, or they would see my face no more. Friday, 27. They severally promised so to do. So I trust this plague is stayed.

Mon. Nov. 12.—I set out in a chaise for Leigh, having delayed my journey as long as I could. I preached at seven, but was extremely cold all the time, the wind coming strong from a door behind, and another on one side; so that my feet felt just as if I had stood in cold water.

Tues. 13.—The chamber wherein I sat, though with a large fire, was much colder than the garden; so that I could not keep myself tolerably warm, even when I was close to the chimney. As we rode home on Wednesday, 14, the wind was high and piercing cold, and blew just in our face, so that the open chaise was no defence, but my feet were quite chilled. When I came home, I had a settled pain in my left breast, a violent cough, and a slow fever; but in a day or two, by following Dr. Fothergill's prescriptions, I found much alteration for the better; and on Sunday, 18, I preached at Spitalfields, and administered the sacrament to a large congregation.

Wesley Writes his Epitaph

Mon. 19.—I retired to Shoreham, and gained strength continually; till about eleven at night, on Wednesday, 21, I was obliged by the cramp to leap out of bed, and continue, for some time, walking up and down the room, though it was a sharp frost. My cough now returned with greater violence, and that by day as well as by night.

Sat. 24.—I rode home, and was pretty well till night; but my cough was then worse than ever. My fever returned at the same time, together with the pain in my left breast; so that I should probably have stayed at home on Sunday, 25, had it not been advertised in the public papers, that I would preach a charity sermon at the chapel, both morning and afternoon. My cough did not interrupt me while I preached in the morning; but it was extremely troublesome while I administered the sacrament. In the afternoon I consulted my friends, whether I should attempt to preach again or no. They thought I should, as it had been advertised. I did so; but very few could hear. My fever increased much while I was preaching: however, I ventured to meet the society; and for near an hour my voice and strength were restored, so that I felt neither pain nor weakness.

Mon. 26.—Dr. F.—— told me plain, I must not stay in town a day longer; adding, "If anything does thee good, it must be the country air, with rest, asses' milk, and riding daily." So (not being able to sit an horse) about noon I took coach for Lewisham.

In the evening (not knowing how it might please God to dispose of me), to prevent vile panegyric, I wrote as follows:

Here lieth the Body

OF

JOHN WESLEY,

A BRAND PLUCKED OUT OF THE BURNING:

WHO DIED OF A CONSUMPTION IN THE FIFTY-FIRST YEAR

OF HIS AGE,

NOT LEAVING, AFTER HIS DEBTS ARE PAID,

TEN POUNDS BEHIND HIM:

PRAYING,

GOD BE MERCIFUL TO ME, AN UNPROFITABLE SERVANT!

He ordered that this, if any, inscription should be placed on his tombstone.

Wesley his own Doctor

Wed. 28.—I found no change for the better, the medicines which had helped me before, now taking no effect. About noon (the time that some of our brethren in London had set apart for joining in prayer) a thought came into my mind to make an experiment. So I ordered some stone brimstone to be powdered, mixed with the white of an egg, and spread on brown paper, which I applied to my side. The pain ceased in five minutes, the fever in half an hour; and from this hour I began to recover strength. The next day I was able to ride, which I continued to do every day till January 1. Nor did the weather hinder me once; it being always tolerably fair (however it was before) between twelve and one o'clock.

Fri. Dec. 14.—Having finished all the books which I designed to insert in the "Christian Library," I broke through the doctor's order, not to write, and began transcribing a journal for the press; and in the evening I went to prayers with the family, without finding any inconvenience.

Thur. 20.—I felt a gradual increase of strength, till I took a decoction of the bark, which I do not find (such is the pecularity of my constitution) will agree with me in any form whatever. This immediately threw me into a purging, which brought me down again a few days, and quite disappointed me in my design of going out on Christmas Day.

1754. Tues. Jan. 1.—I returned once more to London.

On Wednesday, 2, I set out in the machine and the next afternoon came to Chippenham. Here I took a post-chaise, in which I reached Bristol about eight in the evening.

Fri. 4.—I began drinking the water at the Hot Well, having a lodging at a small distance from it; and on Sunday, 6, I began writing Notes on the New Testament; a work which I should scarce ever have attempted, had I not been so ill as not to be able to travel or preach, and yet so well as to be able to read and write.

Mon. 7.—I went on now in a regular method, rising at my hour, and writing from five to nine at night;

except the time of riding, half an hour for each meal, and the hour between five and six in the evening.

Thur. 31.—My wife desiring to pay the last office to her poor dying child, set out for London, and came a few days before he went home, rejoicing and praising God.

Tues. March 19 (Bristol).—Having finished the rough draught, I began transcribing the Notes on the Gospels.

Tues. 26.—I preached for the first time, after an intermission of four months. What reason have I to praise God, that he does not take the word of his truth utterly out of my mouth!

Wesley Retires to Paddington

Mon. April 1.—We set out in the machine, and the next evening reached the Foundery.

Wed. 3.—I settled all the business I could, and the next morning retired to Paddington. Here I spent some weeks in writing; only going to town on Saturday evenings, and leaving it again on Monday morning.

In my hours of walking I read Dr. Calamy's "Abridgment of Mr. Baxter's Life." What a scene is opened here! In spite of all the prejudice of education, I could not but see that the poor Nonconformists had been used without either justice or mercy; and that many of the Protestant Bishops of King Charles had neither more religion, nor humanity, than the Popish Bishops of Queen Mary.

Mon. 29.—I preached at Sadler's Wells, in what was formerly a play-house. I am glad when it pleases God to take possession of what Satan esteemed his own ground. The place, though large, was extremely crowded; and deep attention sat on every face.

Wed. May 22.—Our Conference began; and the spirit of peace and love was in the midst of us. Before we parted, we all willingly signed an agreement, not to act independently on each other : so that the breach lately made has only united us more closely together than ever.

June 2.—(Being Whit Sunday.) I preached at the Foundery; which I had not done before in the evening; still I have not recovered my whole voice or strength; perhaps I never may: but let me use what I have.

Persecuting the Methodists

Mon. Sept. 9.—I preached at Charlton, a village six miles from Taunton, to a large congregation gathered from the towns and country for many miles round. All the farmers here had some time before entered into a joint engagement to turn all out of their service, and give no work to any, who went to hear a Methodist preacher. But there is no counsel against the Lord. One of the chief of them, Mr. G——, was not long after convinced of the truth, and desired those very men to preach at his house. Many of the other confederates came to hear, whom their servants and labourers gladly followed. So the whole device of Satan fell to the ground; and the word of God grew and prevailed.

Wed. October 2.—I walked to Old Sarum, which, in spite of common sense, without house or inhabitants, still sends two Members to the Parliament. It is a large, round hill, encompassed with a broad ditch, which, it seems, has been of a considerable depth. At the top of it is a cornfield; in the midst of which is another round hill, about two hundred yards in diameter, encompassed with a wall, and a deep ditch. Probably before the invention of cannon, this city was impregnable. Troy was ; but now it is vanished away, and nothing left but " the stones of emptiness."

Thur. 3.—I rode to Reading, and preached in the evening. Observing a warm man near the door (which was once of the society), I purposely bowed to him ; but he made no return. During the first prayer he stood, but sat while we sung. In the sermon his countenance changed, and in a little while he turned his face to the wall. He stood at the second hymn, and then kneeled down. As I came out he catched me by the hand, and dismissed me with a hearty blessing.

Fri. 4.—I came to London. On Monday, 7, I retired to a little place near Hackney, formerly a seat of Bishop Bonner's (how are the times changed ?), and still bearing his name. Here I was as in a College.

Twice a day we joined in prayer. The rest of the day (allowing about an hour for meals, and another for walking before dinner and supper) I spent quietly in my study.

Wesley's Prescriptions

1755. Mon. April 7 (Wednesbury).—I was advised to take the Derbyshire road to Manchester. We baited at an house six miles beyond Lichfield. Observing a woman sitting in the kitchen, I asked, " Are you not well ? " and found she had just been taken ill (being on her journey), with all the symptoms of an approaching pleurisy. She was glad to hear of an easy, cheap, and (almost) infallible remedy—an handful of nettles, boiled a few minutes, and applied warm to the side. While I was speaking to her, an elderly man, pretty well dressed, came in. Upon inquiry, he told us he was travelling, as he could, towards his home near Hounslow, in hopes of agreeing with his creditors, to whom he had surren-

dered his all.   But how to get on he knew not, as he
had no money, and had caught a tertian ague.   I hope
a wise Providence directed this wanderer also, that he
might have a remedy for both his maladies.

Mon. 14.—I rode by Manchester (where I preached
about twelve) to Warrington.   At six in the morning,
Tuesday, 15, I preached to a large and serious congregation ; and then went on to Liverpool, one of the
neatest, best-built towns I have seen in England : I think
it is full twice as large as Chester ; most of the streets
are quite straight.   Two thirds of the town, we were
informed, have been added within these forty years.   If
it continue to increase in the same proportion, in forty
years more it will nearly equal Bristol.   The people in
general are the most mild and courteous I ever saw in a
seaport town ; as indeed appears by their friendly behaviour, not only to the Jews and Papists who live
among them, but even to the Methodists (so called).
The preaching-house is a little larger than that at Newcastle.   It was thoroughly filled at seven in the evening ;
and the hearts of the whole congregation seemed to be
moved before the Lord, and before the presence of his
power.

Wesley and the Sunshine

Thur. 24.—We rode in less than four hours the eight
miles (so called) to Newell Hay [from Bolton].   Just as
I began to preach the sun broke out, and shone exceeding hot on the side of my head.   I found, if it continued,
I should not be able to speak long, and lifted up my
heart to God.   In a minute or two it was covered with
clouds, which continued till the service was over.   Let
any who please, call this chance : I call it an answer to
prayer.

Fri. 25.—About ten I preached near Todmorden. The people stood, row above row, on the side of the mountain. They were rough enough in outward appearance; but their hearts were as melting wax.

One can hardly conceive anything more delightful than the vale through which we rode from hence. The river ran through the green meadows on the right. The fruitful hills and woods rose on either hand.

At three in the afternoon I preached at Heptonstall, on the brow of the mountain. The rain began almost as soon as I began to speak. I prayed that, if God saw best, it might be stayed, till I had delivered his word. It was so, and then began again. But we had only a short stage to Ewood.

Tues. May 6.—Our Conference began at Leeds. The point on which we desired all the preachers to speak their minds at large was, " Whether we ought to separate from the Church ? " Whatever was advanced on one side or the other was seriously and calmly considered; and on the third day we were all fully agreed in that general conclusion—that (whether it was lawful or not) it was no ways expedient.

Mon. 12.—We rode (my wife and I) to Northallerton.

Wed. 21.—I preached at Nafferton, near Horsley, about thirteen miles from Newcastle. We rode chiefly on the new western road, which lies on the old Roman wall. Some part of this is still to be seen, as are the remains of most of the towers, which were built a mile distant from each other, quite from sea to sea. But where are the men of renown who built them, and who once made all the land tremble? Crumbled into dust! Gone hence, to be no more seen, till the earth shall give up her dead !

June 2.—We rode to Thirsk, where I met the little society; and then went on to York. The people had been waiting for some time. So I began preaching without delay, and felt no want of strength, though the room was like an oven through the multitude of people.

Sat. 7.—One of the residentiaries sent for Mr. Williamson, who had invited me to preach in his church, and told him, " Sir, I abhor persecution ; but if you let Mr. Wesley preach, it will be the worse for you." He desired it nevertheless; but I declined. Perhaps there is a providence in this also. God will not suffer my little remaining strength to be spent on those who will not hear me but in an honourable way.

The Room Was Like an Oven

Sun. 8.—We were at the minster in the morning, and at our parish-church in the afternoon. The same gentleman preached at both ; but though I saw him at the church, I did not know I had ever seen him before. In the morning he was all life and motion ; in the afternoon he was as quiet as a post. At five in the evening, the rain constrained me to preach in the oven again. The patience of the congregation surprised me. They seemed not to feel the extreme heat, nor to be offended at the close application of those words, " Thou art not far from the kingdom of God."

Mon. 16.—I preached in the evening at Nottingham, and on Thursday afternoon reached London. From a deep sense of the amazing work which God has of late years wrought in England, I preached in the evening on those words (Psalm cxlvii. 20), " He hath not dealt so with any nation " ; no, not even with Scotland or New-England. In both these God has indeed made bare his arm ; yet not in so astonishing a manner as among us.

This must appear to all who impartially consider, 1. The numbers of persons on whom God has wrought: 2. The swiftness of his work in many, both convinced and truly converted in a few days: 3. The depth of it in most of these, changing the heart, as well as the whole conversation: 4. The clearness of it, enabling them boldly to say, "Thou hast loved me; thou hast given thyself for me": 5. The continuance of it.

Tues. 24 (London).—Observing in that valuable book, Mr. Gillies's "Historical Collections," the custom of Christian congregations in all ages to set apart seasons of solemn thanksgivings, I was amazed and ashamed that we had never done this, after all the blessings we had received: and many to whom I mentioned it gladly agreed to set apart a day for that purpose.

"This is no Mazed Man"

Sun. Aug. 31.—At five I preached in Gwennap, to several thousands; but not one of them light or inattentive. After I had done, the storm arose, and the rain poured down, till about four in the morning: then the sky cleared, and many of them that feared God gladly assembled before him.

Mon. Sept. 1.—I preached at Penryn, to abundantly more than the house could contain.

Tues. 2.—We went to Falmouth. The town is not now what it was ten years since: all is quiet from one end to the other. I had thoughts of preaching on the hill near the church; but the violent wind made it impracticable: so I was obliged to stay in our own room. The people could hear in the yard likewise, and the adjoining houses; and all were deeply attentive.

Wed. Sep. 3.—After preaching again, to a congregation who now appeared ready to devour every word, I walked up to Pendennis castle; finely situated on the high point of land which runs out between the bay and the harbour, and commanding both. It might easily be made exceeding strong; but our wooden castles are sufficient.

In the afternoon we rode to Helstone, once turbulent enough, but now quiet as Penryn. I preached at six, on a rising ground, about a musket-shot from the town. Two drunken men strove to interrupt; but one soon walked away: the other leaned on his horse's neck, and fell fast asleep.

About noon, Friday, 5, I called on W. Row, in Breage, in my way to Newlyn. " Twelve years ago," he said, " I was going over Gulval Downs, and I saw many people together; and I asked what was the matter; and they told me a man was going to preach: and I said, ' To be sure it is some mazed man ': but when I saw you, I said, ' Nay, this is no mazed man ': and you preached on God's raising the dry bones; and from that time I could never rest till God was pleased to breathe on me, and raise my dead soul."

Slandering Wesley in the Pulpit

I had given no notice of preaching here; but seeing the poor people flock from every side, I could not send them empty away. So I preached at a small distance from the house; and besought them to consider our " great High Priest, who is passed through into the heavens ": and none opened his mouth; for the lions of Breage too are now changed into lambs. That they were so fierce ten years ago is no wonder; since their wretched minister told them, from the pulpit (seven years before I resigned my fellowship), that " John Wesley was expelled the College for a base child, and

had been quite mazed ever since : that all the Methodists,
at their private societies, put out the lights," &c.; with
abundance more of the same kind.   But a year or two
since, it was observed, he grew thoughtful and melan
choly; and, about nine months ago, he went into his
own necessary house, and hanged himself.

Sat. 6.—In the evening I preached at St. Just.
Except at Gwennap, I have seen no such congregation
in Cornwall.   The sun (nor could we contrive it otherwise) shone full in my face, when I began the hymn :
but just as I ended it, a cloud arose, which covered it
till I had done preaching.   Is anything too small for
the providence of him by whom our very hairs are
numbered ?

Sun. 7.—Last year, a strange letter, written at Penzance, was inserted in the public papers.   To-day I
spoke to the two persons who occasioned that letter.
They are of St. Just parish, sensible men, and no
Methodists.   The name of one is James Tregeer, of the
other, Thomas Sackerly.   I received the account from
James, two or three hours before Thomas came : but
there was no material difference.   In July was twelvemonth, they both said, as they were walking from
St. Just church town toward Sancreet, Thomas, happening to look up, cried out, " James, look, look !   What
is that in the sky ? "   The first appearance, as James
expressed it, was, three large columns of horsemen,
swiftly pressing on, as in a fight, from south-west to
north-east; a broad streak of sky being between each
column.   Sometimes they seemed to run thick together ;
then to thin their ranks.   Afterward they saw a large
fleet of three-mast ships, in full sail toward the Lizard
Point.   This continued above a quarter of an hour :
then, all disappearing, they went on their way.   The

meaning of this, if it was real (which I do not affirm), time only can show.

Extraordinary Coincidence

Sat. 13.—I preached once more at St. Just, on the first stone of their new society-house. In the evening, as we rode to Camborne, John Pearce, of Redruth, was mentioning a remarkable incident: While he lived at Helstone, as their class was meeting one evening, one of them cried, with an uncommon tone, "We will not stay here: we will go to" such an house, which was in a quite different part of the town. They all rose immediately, and went; though neither they nor she knew why. Presently after they were gone, a spark fell into a barrel of gunpowder, which was in the next room, and blew up the house. So did God preserve those who trusted in him, and prevent the blasphemy of the multitude.

Mon. 15.—We walked an hour near the sea-shore [at Cubert], among those amazing caverns, which are full as surprising as Pool's Hole, or any other in the Peak of Derbyshire. Some part of the rock in these natural vaults glitters as bright and ruddy as gold: part is a fine sky-blue; part green; part enamelled, exactly like mother-of-pearl; and a great part, especially near the Holy Well (which bubbles up on the top of a rock, and is famous for curing either scorbutic or scrofulous disorders), is crusted over, wherever the water runs, with an hard, white coat like alabaster.

Tues. 23.—We walked up to Glastonbury Tower, which a gentleman is now repairing. It is the steeple of a church, the foundation of which is still discernible. On the west side of the tower there are niches for images; one of which, as big as the life, is still entire. The hill on which it stands is extremely steep, and of an uncommon height; so that it commands the country on all sides, as well as the Bristol Channel. I was weary enough when we came to Bristol; but I preached till all my complaints were gone; and I had now a little leisure to sit still, and finish the "Notes on the New Testament."

Wed. Nov. 5.—Mr. Whitefield called upon me;— disputings are now no more; we love one another, and join hand in hand to promote the cause of our common Master.

"Macbeth" and Thunder at Drury Lane

Mon. 17.—As we were walking towards Wapping, the rain poured down with such violence, that we were obliged to take shelter till it abated. We then held on to Gravel Lane; in many parts of which the waters were like a river. However, we got on pretty well, till the rain put out the candle in our lantern. We then were obliged to wade through all, till we came to the chapel-yard. Just as we entered it, a little streak of lightning appeared in the south-west. There was likewise a small clap of thunder, and a vehement burst of rain, which rushed so plentifully through our shattered tiles, that the vestry was all in a float. Soon after I began reading prayers, the lightning flamed all round it, and the thunder rolled just over our heads. When it grew louder and louder, perceiving many of the strangers to be much affrighted, I broke off the prayers after the collect, "Lighten our darkness, we beseech thee, O Lord"; and began applying, "The Lord sitteth above the water-flood; the Lord remaineth a king for ever." Presently the lightning, thunder, and rain ceased, and we had a remarkably calm evening.

It was observed, that exactly at this hour, they were

acting " Macbeth " in Drury-lane ; and just as the mock-thunder began, the Lord began to thunder out of heaven. For a while it put them to a stand ; but they soon took courage, and went on. Otherwise it might have been suspected that the fear of God had crept into the very theatre !

Fri. Dec. 12.—As I was returning from Zoar, I came as well as usual to Moorfields ; but there my strength entirely failed, and such a faintness and weariness seized me, that it was with difficulty I got home. I could not but think, how happy it would be (suppose we were ready for the Bridegroom) to sink down and steal away at once, without any of the hurry and pomp of dying ! Yet it is happier still to glorify God in our death, as well as our life.

Tues. 23.—I was in the robe-chamber, adjoining to the House of Lords, when the King put on his robes. His brow was much furrowed with age, and quite clouded with care. And is this all the world can give even to a king ? all the grandeur it can afford ? A blanket of ermine round his shoulders, so heavy and cumbersome he can scarce move under it ! An huge heap of borrowed hair, with a few plates of gold and glittering stones upon his head ! Alas, what a bauble is human greatness ! And even this will not endure.

At Dover Castle

1756. Mon. Jan. 26.—I rode to Canterbury, and preached in the evening to such a congregation as I never saw there before ; in which were abundance of the soldiers, and not a few of their officers.

Wed. 28.—I preached about noon at Dover, to a very serious but small congregation. We afterwards walked up to the castle, on the top of a mountain. It

is an amazing fine situation; and from hence we had a
clear view of that vast piece of the cliff, which a few
days ago divided from the rest, and fell down upon the
beach.

Fri. 30.—In returning to London, I read the life of
the late Czar, Peter the Great. Undoubtedly he was a
soldier, a general, and a statesman, scarce inferior to
any. But why was he called a Christian? What has
Christianity to do either with deep dissimulation or
savage cruelty?

Fri. Feb. 6.—The fast-day was a glorious day: such
as London has scarce seen since the Restoration. Every
church in the city was more than full, and a solemn
seriousness sat on every face. Surely God heareth the
prayer; and there will yet be a lengthening of our tran-
quillity.

Preaching to a Press-gang

Mon. 23.—I paid another visit to Canterbury, but
came in too late to preach.

Tues. 24.—Abundance of soldiers and many officers
came to the preaching. And surely the fear and the
love of God will prepare them either for death or
victory.

Wed. 25.—I dined with Colonel ——, who said,
"No men fight like those who fear God: I had rather
command five hundred such, than any regiment in his
Majesty's army."

Thur. March 11.—I rode to Pill, and preached to a
large and attentive congregation. A great part of them
were seafaring men. In the middle of my discourse, a
press-gang landed from a man-of-war, and came up to
the place: but after they had listened a while, they
went quietly by, and molested nobody.

Mon. 15.—I rode to the Old Passage : but finding we could not pass, we went on to Purton; which we reached about four in the afternoon. But we were no nearer still; for the boatmen lived on the other side, and the wind was so high, we could not possibly make them hear. However, we determined to wait a while ; and in a quarter of an hour they came of their own accord. We reached Coleford before seven ; and found a plain, loving people, who received the word of God with all gladness.

Fri. 19.—I rode over to Howell Harris at Trevecka, though not knowing how to get any further. But he helped us out of our difficulties; offering to send one with us who would show us the way, and bring our horses back : so I then determined to go on to Holyhead, after spending a day or two at Brecknock.

Sat. 20.—It being the day appointed for the Justices and Commissioners to meet, the town was extremely full ; and curiosity (if no better motive) brought most of the gentlemen to the preaching. Such another opportunity could not have been of speaking to all the rich and great of the county : and they all appeared to be serious and attentive. Perhaps one or two may lay it to heart.

Mon. 22.—It continued fair till we came to Builth ; where I preached to the usual congregation. Mr. Phillips then guided us to Royader, about fourteen English miles. It snowed hard behind us and on both sides, but not at all where we were.

Tues. 23.—When we took horse, there was nothing to be seen but a waste of white : the snow covered both hills and vales. As we could see no path, it was not without much difficulty, as well as danger, that we went on. But between seven and eight the sun broke out, and the snow began to melt : so we thought all our difficulty was over; till, about nine, the snow fell faster than ever. In an hour it changed into hail; which, as we rode over the mountains, drove violently in oui face. About twelve this turned into hard rain, followed by an impetuous wind. However, we pushed on through all, and before sunset came to Dolgelly.

Waiting for the Ferry

Here we found everything we wanted except sleep, oi which we were deprived by a company of drunken, roaring sea captains, who kept possession of the room beneath us, till between two and three in the morning: so that we did not take horse till after six; and then we could make no great speed, the frost being exceeding sharp, and much ice in the road. Hence we were not able to reach Tannabull till between eleven and twelve. An honest Welshman here gave us to know (though he spoke no English) that he was just going over the sands. So we hastened on with him, and by that means came in good time to Carnarvon.

Here we passed a quiet and comfortable night, and took horse about six in the morning. Supposing, after we had rode near an hour, that a little house on the other side was the ferry-house, we went down to the water, and called amain: but we could not procure any answer. In the mean time it began to rain hard, though the wind was extremely high. Finding none would come over, we went to a little church which stood near, for shelter.

We had waited about an hour, when a woman and girl came into the church-yard, whom I did not mind, supposing they could speak no English. They were following a sheep, which ran close to us. I then asked, " Is not this Baldon Ferry ? " The girl answered,

" Baldon Ferry! No. The ferry is two miles further."
So we might have called long enough. When we came
to Baldon the wind fell, the sky cleared up, the boat
came over without delay, and soon landed us in Anglesey.
On our way to Holyhead, one met and informed us, the
packet sailed the night before. I said, " Perhaps it may
carry me for all that." So we pushed on, and came
thither in the afternoon. The packet did sail the night
before, and got more than half sea over. But the wind
turning against them and blowing hard, they were glad
to get back this afternoon.

I scarce ever remember so violent a storm as blew
all the night long. The wind continued contrary the
next day.

Irish Honesty

Mon. 29.—We left the harbour about twelve, having
six or seven officers and abundance of passengers on
board. The wind was full west, and there was great
probability of a stormy night. So it was judged best to
put back; but one gentleman making a motion, to try a
little longer, in a short time brought all over to his
opinion. So they agreed to go out, and " look for a
wind."

The wind continued westerly all the night. Nevertheless, in the morning we were within two leagues of
Ireland! Between nine and ten I landed at Howth,
and walked on for Dublin. The congregation in the
evening was such as I never saw here before. I hope
this also is a token for good.

Wed. 31.—In conversing with many, I was surprised
to find that all Ireland is in perfect safety. None here
has any more apprehension of an invasion, than of being
swallowed up in the sea; every one being absolutely

assured, that the French dare not attempt any such thing.

Thur. Apr. 1.—I bought one or two books at Mr. Smith's, on the Blind Quay. I wanted change for a guinea, but he could not give it; so I borrowed some silver of my companion. The next evening a young gentleman came from Mr. Smith's to tell me I had left a guinea on his counter. Such an instance of honesty I have rarely met with, either in Bristol or London.

A Remarkable Premonition Fulfilled

Wed. 28.—I rode to Tullamore; where one of the society, Edward Willis, gave me a very surprising account of himself, he said:

"When I was about twenty years old, I went to Waterford for business. After a few weeks I resolved to leave it; and packed up my things, in order to set out the next morning. This was Sunday; but my landlord pressed me much not to go till the next day. In the afternoon we walked out together, and went into the river. After a while, leaving him near the shore, I struck out into the deep. I soon heard a cry, and, turning, saw him rising and sinking in the channel of the river. I swam back with all speed, and, seeing him sink again, dived down after him. When I was near the bottom, he clasped his arm round my neck, and held me so fast that I could not rise.

"Seeing death before me, all my sins came into my mind, and I faintly called for mercy. In a while my senses went away, and I thought I was in a place full of light and glory, with abundance of people. While I was thus, he who held me died, and I floated up to the top of the water. I then immediately came to myself, and swam to the shore, where several stood who had seen us sink, and said, they never knew such a deliverance before; for I had been under water full twenty minutes. It made me more serious for two or three months. Then I returned to all my sins.

" But in the midst of all, I had a voice following me everywhere, 'When an able minister of the Gospel comes, it will be well with thee!' Some years after I entered into the army: our troop lay at Phillipstown, when Mr. W. came. I was much affected by his preaching; but not so as to leave my sins. The voice followed me still, and when Mr. J. W. came, before I saw him I had an unspeakable conviction that he was the man I looked for: and soon after I found peace with God, and it was well with me indeed."

Preaching in a Loft

Mon. May 10.—I went forward to Clonmell, the pleasantest town, beyond all comparison, which I have yet seen in Ireland. It has four broad, straight streets of well-built houses, which cross each other in the centre of the town. Close to the walls, on the south side, runs a broad, clear river. Beyond this rises a green and fruitful mountain, and hangs over the town. The vale runs many miles both east and west, and is well culti-vated throughout.

I preached at five in a large loft, capable of containing five or six hundred people: but it was not full; many being afraid of its falling, as another did some years before; by which several of the hearers were much hurt, and one so bruised, that she died in a few days.

Tues. 11.—I was at a loss where to preach, the person who owned the loft refusing to let me preach there, or even in the yard below. And the Commanding Officer being asked for the use of the barrack-yard, answered, it was not a proper place. "Not," said he, "that I have any objection to Mr. Wesley. I will hear him, if he preaches under the gallows." It remained to preach in the street: and by this means the congregation was more than doubled. Both the officers and soldiers gave great attention, till a poor man, special drunk, came marching down the street, attended by a Popish mob, with a club in one hand, and a large cleaver in the other, grievously cursing and blaspheming, and swearing he would cut off the preacher's head. It was with difficulty that I restrained the troopers; especially them that were not of the society.

When he came nearer, the mayor stepped out of the congregation, and strove, by good words, to make him quiet; but he could not prevail: on which he went into his house, and returned with his white wand. At the same time he sent for two constables, who presently came with their staves. He charged them not to strike the man, unless he struck first; but this he did immediately, as soon as they came within his reach, and wounded one of them in the wrist. On this, the other knocked him down, which he did three times before he would submit. The mayor then walked before, the constables on either hand, and conducted him to the gaol.

A Terrible Dream

Thur. June 3.—I received a remarkable letter from a clergyman, with whom I had been a day or two before. Part of it ran thus:

"I had the following account from the gentlewoman herself, a person of piety and veracity. She is now the wife of Mr. J—— B——, silversmith, in Cork.

"'About thirty years ago, I was addressed by way of marriage, by Mr. Richard Mercier, then a volunteer in the army.   The young gentleman was quartered at that time in Charleville, where my father lived, who approved of his addresses, and directed me to look upon him as my future husband.   When the regiment left the town, he promised to return in two months, and marry me. From Charleville he went to Dublin; thence to his father's, and from thence to England; where, his father having bought him a Cornetcy of horse, he purchased many ornaments for the wedding; and, returning to Ireland, let us know that he would be at our house in Charleville in a few days.

"'On this the family was busied to prepare for his reception, and the ensuing marriage; when one night, my sister Molly and I being asleep in our bed, I was awakened by the sudden opening of the side-curtain, and, starting up, saw Mr. Mercier standing by the bed-side. He was wrapped up in a loose sheet, and had a napkin folded like a night-cap, on his head.   He looked at me very earnestly, and, lifting up the napkin, which much shaded his face, showed me the left side of his head, all bloody and covered with his brains.   The room mean-time was quite light.   My terror was excessive, which was still increased by his stooping over the bed, and embracing me in his arms.   My cries alarmed the whole family, who came crowding into the room.

"'Upon their entrance, he gently withdrew his arms, and ascended, as it were, through the ceiling.   I continued for some time in strong fits.   When I could speak, I told them what I had seen.   One of them, a day or two after, going to the post-master for letters, found him reading the newspapers, in which was an account, that Cornet Mercier, going into Christ Church belfry, in Dublin, just after the bells had been ringing, and standing under the bells, one of them, which was turned bottom upwards, suddenly turning again, struck one side of his head, and killed him on the spot. On further inquiry, we found he was struck on the left side of his head.' "

Sun. July 4.—In the morning we rode through Tuam, a neat little town, scarce half so large as Islington; nor is the cathedral half so large as Islington church. The old church at Kilconnel, two miles from Aghrim, is abundantly larger. If one may judge by the vast ruins that remain (over all which we walked in the afternoon), it was a far more stately pile of building than any that is now standing in Ireland. Adjoining to it are the ruins of a large monastery; many of the cells and apartments are pretty entire. At the west end of the church lie abundance of skulls, piled one upon another, with innumerable bones round about, scattered as dung upon the earth. O sin, what hast thou done!

The Delights of North Wales

Fri. Aug. 6.—On this and the next day I finished my business in Ireland, so as to be ready to sail at an hour's warning.

Sun. 8.—We were to sail, the wind being fair; but as we were going aboard, it turned full east. I find it of great use to be in suspense: it is an excellent means of breaking our will. May we be ready either to stay longer on this shore, or to lanch into eternity!

On Tuesday evening I preached my farewell sermon. Mr. Walsh did the same in the morning. We then walked to the quay: but it was still a doubt, whether we were to sail or no; Sir T. P. having sent word to the captain of the packet that if the wind was fair, he would go over; and it being his custom to keep the whole ship to himself. But the wind coming to the east, he would not go; so about noon we went on board. In two or three hours we reached the mouth of the harbour. It then fell calm. We had five cabin-passengers, beside Mr. Walsh, Haughton, Morgan, and me. They were all civil, and tolerably serious; the sailors likewise behaved uncommonly well.

Thur. 12.—About eight we began singing on the quarterdeck; which soon drew all our fellow passengers, as well as the captain, with the greatest part of his men. I afterwards gave an exhortation. We then spent some time in prayer. They all kneeled down with us; nor did their seriousness wear off all the day. About nine we landed at Holyhead, after a pleasant passage of twenty-three hours.

Fri. 13.—Having hired horses for Chester, we set out about seven. Before one we reached Bangor, the situation of which is delightful beyond expression. Here we saw a large and handsome cathedral, but no trace of the good old monks of Bangor; so many hundreds of whom fell a sacrifice at once to cruelty and revenge. The country from hence to Penmaen-Mawr is far pleasanter than any garden. Mountains of every shape and size, vales clothed with grass or corn, woods and smaller tufts of trees, were continually varying on the one hand, as was the sea prospect on the other.

Penmaen-Mawr itself rises almost perpendicular to an enormous height from the sea. The road runs along the side of it, so far above the beach, that one could not venture to look down, but that there is a wall built all along, about four foot high. Meantime, the ragged cliff hangs over one's head, as if it would fall every moment. An hour after we had left this awful place, we came to the ancient town of Conway. It is walled round; and the walls are in tolerably good repair. The castle is the noblest ruin I ever saw. It is four-square, and has four large round towers, one at each corner, the inside of which have been stately apartments. One side of the castle is a large church, the windows and arches of which have been curiously wrought. An arm of the sea runs round two sides of the hill on which the castle stands;—once the delight of kings, now overgrown with thorns, and inhabited by doleful birds only.

Wesley's Debt of £1236

Wed. 25.—We rode on to Bristol.

Thur. 26.—About fifty of us being met, the Rules of the Society were read over, and carefully considered one by one; but we did not find any that could be spared. So we all agreed to abide by them all, and to recommend them with our might.

We then largely considered the necessity of keeping in the Church and using the clergy with tenderness; and there was no dissenting voice. God gave us all to be of one mind and of one judgment.

Fri. 27.—The Rules of the Bands were read over and considered, one by one; which, after some verbal alterations, we all agreed to observe and enforce.

Sat. 28.—My brother and I closed the Conference by a solemn declaration of our purpose never to separate from the Church; and all our brethren concurred therein.

Mon. Sep. 6.—I set out in the machine, and on Tuesday evening came to London.

Wednesday and Thursday, I settled my temporal business. It is now about eighteen years since I began writing and printing books; and how much in that time have I gained by printing? Why, on summing up my accounts, I found that on March 1, 1756 (the day I left London last), I had gained by printing and preaching together, a debt of twelve hundred and thirty - six pounds.

Sun. Oct. 10.—I preached to an huge multitude in Moorfields, on, " Why will ye die, O house of Israel ? " It is field-preaching which does the execution still : for usefulness there is none comparable to it.

Wesley on Electricity as a Cure

Tues. Nov. 9.—Having procured an apparatus on purpose, I ordered several persons to be electrified, who were ill of various disorders; some of whom found an immediate, some a gradual, cure. From this time I appointed, first some hours in every week, and afterward an hour in every day, wherein any that desired it, might try the virtue of this surprising medicine. Two or three years after, our patients were so numerous that we were obliged to divide them : so part were electrified in Southwark, part at the Foundery, others near St. Paul's, and the rest near the Seven Dials : the same method we have taken ever since ; and to this day, while hundreds, perhaps thousands, have received unspeakable good, I have not known one man, woman, or child, who has received any hurt thereby : so that when I hear any talk of the danger of being electrified (especially if they are medical men who talk so), I cannot but impute it to great want either of sense or honesty.

1757. Tues. May 31.—I breakfasted at Dumfries, and spent an hour with a poor backslider of London, who had been for some years settled there. We then rode through an uncommonly pleasant country (so widely distant is common report from truth) to Thorny Hill, two or three miles from the Duke of Queens-borough's seat; an ancient and noble pile of building, delightfully situated on the side of a pleasant and fruitful hill. But it gives no pleasure to its owner; for he does not even behold it with his eyes. Surely this is a sore evil under the sun; a man has all things, and enjoys nothing.

We rode afterward partly over and partly between some of the finest mountains, I believe, in Europe; higher than most, if not than any, in England, and clothed with grass to the very top. Soon after four we came to Lead Hill, a little town at the foot of the mountains, wholly inhabited by miners.

In Glasgow Cathedral

Wed. June 1.—We rode on to Glasgow; a mile short of which we met Mr. Gillies, riding out to meet us.

In the evening the tent (so they call a covered pulpit) was placed in the yard of the poor-house, a very large and commodious place. Fronting the pulpit was the infirmary, with most of the patients at or near the windows. Adjoining to this was the hospital for lunatics: several of them gave deep attention. And cannot God give them also the spirit of a sound mind? After sermon, they brought four children to baptize. I was at the kirk in the morning while the minister baptized several immediately after sermon. So I was not at a loss as to their manner of baptizing. I believe this removed much prejudice.

Fri. 3.—At seven the congregation was increased, and earnest attention sat on every face. In the afternoon we walked to the college, and saw the new library, with the collection of pictures. Many of them are by Raphael, Rubens, Vandyke, and other eminent hands; but they have not room to place them to advantage, their whole building being very small.

Sat. 4.—I walked through all parts of the old cathedral, a very large and once beautiful structure; I think, more lofty than that at Canterbury, and nearly the same length and breadth. We then went up the main steeple, which gave us a fine prospect, both of the city and the adjacent country. A more fruitful and better cultivated plain is scarce to be seen in England. Indeed nothing is wanting but more trade (which would naturally bring more people), to make a great part of Scotland no way inferior to the best counties in England.

I was much pleased with the seriousness of the people in the evening; but still I prefer the English congregation. I cannot be reconciled to men sitting at prayer, or covering their heads while they are singing praise to God.

Wesley Sings a Scotch Psalm

Thur. 9.—To-day "Douglas," the play which has made so much noise, was put into my hands. I was astonished to find it is one of the finest tragedies I ever read. What pity, that a few lines were not left out; and that it was ever acted at Edinburgh!

Fri. 10.—I found myself much out of order, till the flux stopped at once, without any medicine. But being still weak, and the sun shining extremely hot, I was afraid I should not be able to go round by Kelso. Vain fear! God took care for this also. The wind, which had been full east for several days, turned this morning full west; and blew just in our face : and about ten the clouds rose, and kept us cool till we came to Kelso.

At six William Coward and I went to the market-house. We stayed some time, and neither man, woman, nor child came near us. At length I began singing a Scotch

psalm, and fifteen or twenty people came within hearing;
but with great circumspection, keeping their distance, as
though they knew not what might follow.   But while I
prayed, their number increased ; so that in a few minutes
there was a pretty large congregation.   I suppose the
chief men of the town were there ; and I spared neither
rich nor poor.   I almost wondered at myself, it not
being usual with me to use so keen and cutting
expressions : and I believe many felt that, for all their
form, they were but heathens still.

Mon. 13.—I proclaimed the love of Christ to sinners,
in the market-place at Morpeth.   Thence we rode to
Placey.   The society of colliers here may be a pattern to
all the societies in England.   No person ever misses his
band or class : they have no jar of any kind among
them ; but with one heart and one mind " provoke one
another to love and to good works."   After preaching I
met the society in a room as warm as any in Georgia :
this, with the scorching heat of the sun, when we rode
on, quite exhausted my strength.   But after we came to
Newcastle I soon recovered, and preached with as much
ease as in the morning.

Thur. 16.—In the evening I preached at Sunderland.
I then met the society, and told them plain, none could
stay with us, unless he would part with all sin ; particularly, robbing the King, selling or buying run goods ;
which I could no more suffer than robbing on the highway. This I enforced on every member the next day.
A few would not promise to refrain : so these I was
forced to cut off.   About two hundred and fifty were of
a better mind.

Wed. 22.—In the evening and the following morning
I preached at Chester-on-the-Strate.   Observing some
very fine, but not very modest pictures, in the parlour

where we supped, I desired my companion, when the company was gone, to put them where they could do no hurt. He piled them on an heap in a corner of the room, and they have not appeared since.

"I Do Indeed Live by Preaching!"

Thur. July 28 (Sheffield).—I received a strange account from Edward Bennet's eldest daughter :

"On Tuesday, the 12th of this month, I told my husband in the morning, 'I desire you will not go into the water to-day, at least, not into the deep water, on the far side of the town ; for I dreamed I saw you there out of your depth, and only your head came up just above the water.' He promised me he would not, and went to work. Soon after four in the afternoon, being at John Hanson's, his partner's house, she was on a sudden extremely sick, so that for some minutes she seemed just ready to expire. Then she was well in a moment. Just at that time, John Hanson, who was an excellent swimmer, persuaded her husband to go into the water on the far side of the town. He objected— the water was deep, and he could not swim ; and being much importuned to go in, stood some time after he was undressed, and then kneeling down, prayed with an earnest and loud voice. When he rose from his knees, John, who was swimming, called him again, and tread-ing the water, said, 'See, it is only breast-high.' He stepped in, and sunk. A man who was near, cutting fern, and had observed him for some time, ran to the bank, and saw his head come up just above the water. The second or third time he rose, he clasped his hands, and cried aloud, 'Lord Jesus, receive my spirit.' Im-mediately he sunk, and rose no more."

One might naturally inquire, What became of John

Hanson? As soon as he saw his partner sink, he swam from him to the other side, put on his clothes, and went straight home.

About noon I preached at Woodseats; in the evening at Sheffield. I do indeed live by preaching!

How quiet is this country now, since the chief persecutors are no more seen! How many of them have been snatched away in an hour when they looked not for it! Some time since, a woman of Thorpe often swore she would wash her hands in the heart's blood of the next preacher that came. But before the next preacher came she was carried to her long home. A little before John Johnson settled at Wentworth, a stout, healthy man, who lived there, told his neighbours, " After May-day we shall have nothing but praying and preaching : but I will make noise enough to stop it." But before May-day he was silent in his grave. A servant of Lord R—— was as bitter as him, and told many lies purposely to make mischief ; but before this was done, his mouth was stopped. He was drowned in one of the fish-ponds.

Wesley at Charterhouse

Mon. Aug. 8 (London).—I took a walk in the Charterhouse. I wondered that all the squares and buildings, and especially the school-boys, looked so little. But this is easily accounted for. I was little myself when I was at school, and measured all about me by myself. Accordingly, the upper boys being then bigger than myself, seemed to me very big and tall ; quite contrary to what they appear now when I am taller and bigger than them. I question if this is not the real ground of the common imagination, that our forefathers, and in general men in past ages, were much larger than now :

an imagination current in the world eighteen hundred years ago. Whereas, in reality, men have been, at least ever since the deluge, very nearly the same as we find them now, both for stature and understanding.

Fri. Sept. 2.—I rode to St. Agnes.

Sun. 4.—I. T. preached at five. I could scarce have believed if I had not heard it, that few men of learning write so correctly as an unlearned tinner speaks extempore. Mr. V. preached two such thundering sermons at church as I have scarce heard these twenty years.

Mon. 5.—I rode on to Illogan; but not to the house where I used to preach: indeed his wife promised Mr. P., before he died, that she would always receive the preachers; but she soon changed her mind. God has just taken her only son, suddenly killed by a pit falling upon him; and on Tuesday last, a young, strong man, riding to his burial, dropped off his horse stone dead. The concurrence of these awful providences added considerably to our congregation.

Sat. 10.—We rode to the Land's End. I know no natural curiosity like this. The vast ragged stones rise on every side, when you are near the point of land, with green turf between as level and smooth as if it were the effect of art. And the rocks which terminate the land are so torn by the sea, that they appear like great heaps of ruins.

Sun. 11.—I preached at St. Just at nine. At one, the congregation in Morva stood on a sloping ground, rank above rank, as in a theatre. Many of them bewailed their want of God; and many tasted how gracious he is.

At five I preached in Newlyn, to an huge multitude; and one only seemed to be offended—a very good sort of woman, who took great pains to get away, crying aloud, "Nay, if going to church and sacrament will not put us to heaven, I know not what will."

Wesley Opposed by Mayor and Minister

Wed. 21.—After spending an hour with a few friends in Truro, I rode forward to Grampound, a mean, inconsiderable, dirty village. However, it is a borough town! Between twelve and one I began preaching in a meadow, to a numerous congregation. While we were singing, I observed a person in black on the far side of the meadow, who said, "Come down; you have no business there." Some boys who were on a wall, taking it for granted that he spoke to them, got down in all haste. I went on, and he walked away. I afterwards understood that he was the minister and the Mayor of Grampound. Soon after two constables came, and said, "Sir, the mayor says you shall not preach within his borough." I answered, "The mayor has no authority to hinder me. But it is a point not worth contesting." So I went about a musket-shot farther, and left the borough to Mr. Mayor's disposal.

Thur. 22.—I rode to Mevagissey, which lies on the south sea, just opposite to Port Isaac on the north. When I was here last, we had no place in the town: I could only preach about half a mile from it. But things are altered now: I preached just over the town, to almost all the inhabitants; and all were still as night. The next evening a drunken man made some noise behind me. But after a few words were spoken to him. he quietly listened to the rest of the discourse.

Sat. 24.—At half-hour after twelve I preached once more, and took my leave of them. All the time I stayed, the wind blew from the sea, so that no boat could stir out. By this means all the fishermen (who are the chief part of the town) had opportunity of hearing.

At six I preached at St. Austle, a neat little town on the side of a fruitful hill.

Sun. 25.—At two I preached in St. Stephen's, near a lone house, on the side of a barren mountain; but neither the house nor the court could contain the people; so we went into a meadow, where all might kneel (which they generally do in Cornwall), as well as stand and hear. And they did hear, and sing, and pray, as for life. I saw none careless or inattentive among them.

Fire at Kingswood School

Mon. Oct. 24.—I preached about noon at Bath, and in the evening at Escot, near Lavington.

Tues. 25.—In my return, a man met me near Hannam, and told me the School house at Kingswood was burned down. I felt not one moment's pain, knowing that God does all things well. When I came thither, I received a fuller account: about eight on Monday evening, two or three boys went into the gallery, up two pair of stairs. One of them heard a strange crackling in the room above. Opening the staircase door, he was beat back by smoke, on which he cried out, " Fire! Murder! Fire!" Mr. Baynes, hearing this, ran immediately down, and brought up a pail of water. But when he went into the room, and saw the blaze, he had not presence of mind to go up to it, but threw the water upon the floor.

Meantime one of the boys rung the bell; another called John Maddern from the next house, who ran up, as did James Burges quickly after, and found the room all in a flame. The deal partitions took fire immediately, which spread to the roof of the house. Plenty of water was now brought; but they could not come nigh the place where it was wanted, the room being so filled with flame and smoke, that none could go into it. At last a long ladder, which lay in the garden, was reared up against the wall of the house. But it was then observed, that one of the sides of it was broke in two, and the other quite rotten. However, John How (a young man, who lived next door) ran up it, with an axe in his hand. But he then found the ladder was so short, that, as he stood on the top of it, he could but just lay one hand over the battlements.

How he got over to the leads none can tell: but he did so, and quickly broke through the roof, on which a vent being made, the smoke and flame issued out as from a furnace: those who were at the foot of the stairs with water, being able to go no further, then went through the smoke to the door of the leads, and poured it down through the tiling. By this means the fire was quickly quenched, having only consumed a part of the partition, with a box of clothes, and a little damaged the roof, and the floor beneath.

In Norfolk and Suffolk

Wed. Nov. 23 (Norwich).—I was shown Dr. Taylor's new meeting-house, perhaps the most elegant one in Europe. It is eight-square, built of the finest brick, with sixteen sash-windows below, as many above, and eight skylights in the dome; which, indeed, are purely ornamental. The inside is finished in the highest taste, and is as clean as any nobleman's saloon. The communion-table is fine mahogany; the very latches of the pew-doors are polished brass. How can it be thought that the old, coarse Gospel should find admission here?

Thur. 24.—A man had spoken to me the last week, as I was going through Thetford, and desired me to preach at Lakenheath, near Mildenhall, in Suffolk: I now purposed so to do, and rode thither from Thetford. One Mr. Evans had lately built a large and convenient preaching house there, at his own expense. It was more than filled at six o'clock many standing at the door. At five in the morning (as uncommon a thing as this was in those parts) the house was nearly filled again with earnest, loving simple people. Several of them came in to Mr. E.'s house afterward, stood a while, and then burst into tears. I promised to call upon them again, and left them much comforted.

1758. Wed. Jan. 4.—I rode to Kingswood, and rejoiced over the school, which is at length what I have so long wished it to be—a blessing to all that are therein, and an honour to the whole body of Methodists.

Another Ninety-mile Journey

Mon. March 6 (London).—I took horse about seven o'clock. The wind being east, I was pleasing myself that we should have it on our back; but in a quarter of an hour it shifted to the north-west, and blew the rain full in our face: and both increased, so that when we came to Finchley Common, it was hard work to sit our horses. The rain continued all the way to Dunstable, where we exchanged the main road for the fields; which, having been just ploughed, were deep enough. However, before three we came to Sundon.

Hence, on Thursday, 9, I rode to Bedford, and found the sermon was not to be preached till Friday. Had I known this in time, I should never have thought of preaching it; having engaged to be at Epworth on Saturday.

Fri. 10.—The congregation at St. Paul's was very large and very attentive.   The judge, immediately after sermon, sent me an invitation to dine with him.   But having no time, I was obliged to send my excuse, and set out between one and two.   The north-east wind was piercing cold, and, blowing exactly in our face, soon brought an heavy shower of snow, then of sleet, and afterwards of hail.   However, we reached Stilton at seven, about thirty miles from Bedford.

Rest was now the more sweet, because both our horses were lame.   However, resolving to reach Epworth at the time appointed, I set out in a post-chaise between four and five in the morning : but the frost made it so bad driving, that my companion came with the lame horses into Stamford as soon as me.   The next stage I went on horseback ; but I was then obliged to leave my mare, and take another post-chaise.   I came to Bawtry about six.   Some from Epworth had come to meet me, but were gone half an hour before I came.   I knew no chaise could go the rest of the road ; so it remained only to hire horses and a guide.

We set out about seven, but I soon found my guide knew no more of the way than myself.   However, we got pretty well to Idlestop, about four miles from Bawtry, where we had just light to discern the river at our side, and the country covered with water.   I had heard that one Richard Wright lived thereabouts, who knew the road over the moor perfectly well.   Hearing one speak (for we could not see him), I called " Who is there ? "   He answered, " Richard Wright."   I soon agreed with him, and he quickly mounted his horse, and rode boldly forward.   The north-east wind blow full in our face ; and I heard them say, " It is very cold ! "   But neither my face, nor hands, nor feet were cold, till between nine and ten we came to Epworth: after travelling more than ninety miles, I was little more tired than when I rose in the morning.

Wesley's Advice to Travellers

Tues. Aug. 1.—The captain with whom we were to sail was in great haste to have our things on board; but I would not send them while the wind was against us. On Wednesday he sent message after message: so in the evening we went down to the ship, near Passage; but there was nothing ready, or near ready for sailing. Hence I learned two or three rules, very needful for those who sail between England and Ireland. 1. Never pay till you set sail: 2. Go not on board till the captain goes on board: 3. Send not your baggage on board till you go yourself.

Thur. 17.—I went to the Bristol cathedral to hear Mr. Handel's "Messiah." I doubt if that congregation was ever so serious at a sermon as they were during this performance. In many parts, especially several of the choruses, it exceeded my expectation.

Mon. Oct. 16.—I rode to Canterbury. As we came into the city, a stone flew out of the pavement and struck my mare upon the leg with such violence that she dropped down at once. I kept my seat, till, in struggling to arise, she fell again, and rolled over me. When she rose I endeavoured to rise too, but found I had no use of my right leg or thigh. But an honest barber came out, lifted me up, and helped me into his shop. Feeling myself very sick, I desired a glass of cold water, which instantly gave me ease.

Fri. 27.—I rode on, through an extremely pleasant and fruitful country, to Colchester. I have seen very few such towns in England. It lies on the ridge of an hill, with other hills on each side which run parallel with it, at a small distance.   The two main streets, one running east and west, the other north and south, are quite straight, the whole length of the town, and full as broad as Cheapside.

I preached at four on St. John's Green, at the side of a high old wall (a place that seemed to be made on purpose), to an extremely attentive audience; and again at eight in the morning, on Saturday, 28, and at four in the afternoon.   In the hours between I took the opportunity of speaking to the members of the society.   In three months here are joined together an hundred and twenty persons.   A few of these know in whom they have believed, and many are sensible of their wants.

Wesley at Norwich and Colchester

Sun. Nov. 5 (Norwich).—We went to St. Peter's church, the Lord's supper being administered there.   I scarce ever remember to have seen a more beautiful parish church: the more so, because its beauty results not from foreign ornaments, but from the very form and structure of it.   It is very large, and of an uncommon height, and the sides are almost all window; so that it has an awful and venerable look, and, at the same time, surprisingly cheerful.

Mon. Dec. 4.—I was desired to step into the little church behind the Mansion House, commonly called St. Stephen's, Walbrook.   It is nothing grand; but neat and elegant beyond expression.   So that I do not wonder at the speech of the famous Italian architect, who met Lord Burlington in Italy: "My Lord, go back and see St. Stephen's in London.   We have not so fine a piece of architecture in Rome."

Fri. 29.—To-day I walked all over the famous

castle (Colchester), perhaps the most ancient building in
England.   A considerable part of it is, without question,
ourteen or fifteen hundred years old.   It was mostly
built with Roman bricks, each of which is about two
inches thick, seven broad, and thirteen or fourteen long.
Seat of ancient kings, British and Roman, once dreaded
far and near!   But what are they now?   Is not "a
living dog better than a dead lion?"   And what is it
wherein they prided themselves, as do the present great
ones of the earth?

> A little pomp, a little sway,
> A sunbeam in a winter's day,
> Is all the great and mighty have
> Between the cradle and the grave!

1759.   Sun. May 6.—I received much comfort at
the old church (Liverpool) in the morning, and at St.
Thomas's in the afternoon.   It was as if both the
sermons had been made for me.   I pity those who can
find no good at church.   But how should they, if
prejudice come between, an effectual bar to the grace of
God?

The Sands of Ravenglass

Sat. **12.**—Setting out early we came to Bottle
about twenty-four measured miles from Fluckborough,
soon after eight, having crossed the Millam Sand, without either guide or difficulty.   Here we were informed
that we could not pass at Ravenglass before one or two
o'clock; whereas, had we gone on (as we afterwards
found), we might have passed immediately.   About
eleven we were directed to a ford, near Manchester Hall,
which they said we might cross at noon.   When we
came thither, they told us we could not cross; so we
sat still till about one: we then found we could have

crossed at noon. However, we reached Whitehaven before night. But I have taken my leave of the sand road. I believe it is ten measured miles shorter than the other; but there are four sands to pass, so far from each other that it is scarce possible to pass them all in a day: especially as you have all the way to do with a generation of liars, who detain all strangers as long as they can, either for their own gain or their neighbours'. I can advise no stranger to go this way; he may go round by Kendal and Keswick, often in less time, always with less expense, and far less trial of his patience.

Useless Doctors

Reflecting to-day on the case of a poor woman who had continual pain in her stomach, I could not but remark the inexcusable negligence of most physicians in cases of this nature. They prescribe drug upon drug, without knowing a jot of the matter concerning the root of the disorder. And without knowing this, they cannot cure, though they can murder, the patient. Whence came this woman's pain? (which she would never have told, had she never been questioned about it)—from fretting for the death of her son. And what availed medicines, while that fretting continued? Why then do not all physicians consider how far bodily disorders are caused or influenced by the mind; and in those cases, which are utterly out of their sphere, call in the assistance of a minister; as ministers, when they find the mind disordered by the body, call in the assistance of a physician? But why are these cases out of their sphere? Because they know not God. It follows, no man can be a thorough physician without being an experienced Christian.

Thur. 17.—I inquired into a signal instance of Providence. When a coal-pit runs far under the ground it is customary here to build a partition wall, nearly from the shaft to within three or four yards of the end, in order to make the air circulate, which then moves down one side of the wall, turns at the end, and then moves briskly up on the other side. In a pit two miles from the town, which ran full four hundred yards under the ground, and had been long neglected, several parts of this wall were fallen down. Four men were sent down to repair it. They were about three hundred yards from the shaft, when the foul air took fire. In a moment it tore down the wall from end to end; and, burning on till it came to the shaft, it then burst and went off like a large cannon.

Fire in a Coal-pit

The men instantly fell on their faces, or they would have been burned to death in a few moments. One of them, who once knew the love of God (Andrew English), began crying aloud for mercy. But in a very short time his breath was stopped. The other three crept on their hands and knees, till two got to the shaft and were drawn up; but one of them died in a few minutes. John M'Combe was drawn up next, burned from head to foot, but rejoicing and praising God. They then went down for Andrew, whom they found senseless: the very circumstance which saved his life. For, losing his senses, he lay flat on the ground, and the greatest part of the fire went over him; whereas, had he gone forward on his hands and knees, he would undoubtedly have been burned to death. But life or death was welcome; for God had restored the light of his countenance.

Mon. 21.—I preached at ten in the market-place at Wigton, and came to Solway Frith, just as the water was fordable. At some times it is so three hours in twelve; at other times, barely one.

After making a short bait at Rothwell, we came to Dumfries before six o'clock. Having time to spare, we took a walk in the churchyard, one of the pleasantest places I ever saw. A single tomb I observed there, which was about an hundred and thirty years old; but the inscription was very hardly legible. So soon do even our sepulchres die! Strange, that men should be so careful about them! But are not many self-condemned therein? They see the folly, while they run into it. So poor Mr. Prior, speaking of his own tomb, has those melancholy words, "For this last piece of human vanity, I bequeath five hundred pounds."

Tues. 22.—We rode through a pleasant country to Thorny Hill, near which is the grand seat of the Duke of Queensborough. How little did the late duke imagine that his son would plough up his park, and let his house run to ruin! But let it go! In a little time the earth itself, and all the works of it, shall be burned up.

Hence we rode through, and over, huge mountains, green to the very top, to Lead Hills; a village containing five hundred families, who have had no minister for these four years. So in Scotland, the poor have not the Gospel preached! Who shall answer for the blood of these men?

Newcastle as a Summer Resort

Mon. June 4.—After preaching (at Alnwick), I rode on to Newcastle. Certainly if I did not believe there was another world, I should spend all my summers here; as I know no place in Great Britain comparable to it for pleasantness. But I seek another country, and therefore am content to be a wanderer upon the earth.

Thur. 21.—I preached at Nafferton at one. As I was riding thence, one stopped me on the road, and said, "Sir, do you not remember. when you was at Prudhoe, two years since, you breakfasted at Thomas Newton's ? I am his sister. You looked upon me as you was going out, and said, 'Be in earnest.' I knew not then what earnestness meant, nor had any thought about it; but the words sunk into my heart, so that I could never rest any more, till I sought and found Christ."

Wesley Likes a Soft Cushion

Fri. 22.——I rode to S——k, and preached to my old congregation of colliers, on, "Why will ye die, O house of Israel?" After preaching, a servant of Mr. —— came and said, "Sir, my master discharges you from preaching any more on his ground; not out of any disrespect to you, but he will stand by the Church." "Simple master Shallow !" as Shakespeare has it: wise wise master rector, his counsellor !

Sat. 23.—I spoke to each of the society in Sunderland. Most of the robbers, commonly called smugglers, have left us; but more than twice the number of honest people are already come in their place ; and if none had come, yet should I not dare to keep those who steal hither from the King or subject.

On Monday and Tuesday evening I preached abroad, near the Keelmen's Hospital, to twice the people we should have had at the house. What marvel the devil does not love field preaching? Neither do I : I love a commodious room, a soft cushion, an handsome pulpit. But where is my zeal, if I do not trample all these under foot, in order to save one more soul?

Wed. July 4 (Hartlepool).—Mr. Jones preached at five, I at eight. Toward the close of the sermon, a queer, dirty, clumsy man, I suppose a country wit, took a deal of pains to disturb the congregation. When I had done, fearing he might hurt those who were gathered about him, I desired two or three of our brethren to go to him, one after the other, and not say much themselves, but let him talk till he was weary. They did so, but without effect, as his fund of ribaldry seemed inexhaustible. W.A. then tried another way. He got into the circle close to him, and listening a while said, " That is pretty ; pray say it over again." " What ! are you deaf ? " " No ; but for the entertainment of the people. Come ; we are all attention." After repeating this twice or thrice, the wag could not stand it ; but, with two or three curses, walked clear off.

Defeating the Press-gang

In the evening I began near Stockton market-place as usual. I had hardly finished the hymn, when I observed the people in great confusion, which was occasioned by a lieutenant of a man-of-war, who had chosen that time to bring his press-gang, and ordered them to take Joseph Jones and William Alwood. Joseph Jones telling him, " Sir, I belong to Mr. Wesley." After a few words, he let him go ; as he did likewise William Alwood, after a few hours, understanding he was a licensed preacher. He likewise seized upon a young man of the town ; but the women rescued nim by main strength. They also broke the lieutenant's head, and so stoned both him and his men, that they ran away with all speed.

Fri. Aug. 3.—I preached at Gainsborough, in Sir Nevil Hickman's great hall. It is full as large as the

Weaver's Hall, in Bristol. At two it was filled with a rude, wild multitude (a few of a better spirit excepted). Yet all but two or three gentlemen were attentive, while I enforced our Lord's words, "What shall it profit a man, if he shall gain the whole world and lose his own soul?" I was walking back through a gaping, staring crowd, when Sir Nevil came and thanked me for my sermon, to the no small amazement of his neighbours, who shrunk back as if they had seen a ghost.

Extraordinary Trances

Mon. 6 (Everton).—I talked largely with Ann Thorn, and two others, who had been several times in trances. What they all agreed in was, 1. That when they went away, as they termed it, it was always at the time they were fullest of the love of God: 2. That it came upon them in a moment, without any previous notice, and took away all their senses and strength: 3. That there were some exceptions : but in general, from that moment, they were in another world, knowing nothing of what was done or said, by all that were round about them.

About five in the afternoon I heard them singing hymns. Soon after, Mr. B. came up, and told me, Alice Miller (fifteen years old) was fallen into a trance. I went down immediately, and found her sitting on a stool, and leaning against the wall, with her eyes open and fixed upward. I made a motion as if going to strike, but they continued immovable. Her face showed an unspeakable mixture of reverence and love, while silent tears stole down her cheeks. Her lips were a little open, and sometimes moved; but not enough to cause any sound.

I do not know whether I ever saw an human face

look so beautiful; sometimes it was covered with a smile, as from joy, mixing with love and reverence; but the tears fell still though not so fast. Her pulse was quite regular. In about half an hour I observed her countenance change into the form of fear, pity, and distress; then she burst into a flood of tears, and cried out, " Dear Lord; they will be damned! They will all be damned!" But in about five minutes her smiles returned, and only love and joy appeared in her face.

About half an hour after six, I observed distress take place again; and soon after she wept bitterly and cried out, " Dear Lord, they will go to hell! The world will go to hell!" Soon after, she said, "Cry aloud! Spare not!" And in a few moments her look was composed again, and spoke a mixture of reverence, joy, and love. Then she said aloud, " Give God the glory." About seven her senses returned. I asked, "Where have you been?"—"I have been with my Saviour." "In heaven, or on earth?"—"I cannot tell; but I was in glory." "Why then did you cry?"—"Not for myself, but for the world; for I saw they were on the brink of hell." "Whom did you desire to give the glory to God?"—"Ministers that cry aloud to the world: else they will be proud; and then God will leave them, and they will lose their own souls."

Wesley Rides 2400 Miles in Seven Months

Tues. 7.—After preaching at four (because of the harvest) I took horse, and rode easily to London. Indeed I wanted a little rest; having rode, in seven months, about four-and-twenty hundred miles.

Mon. 13.—I took a little ride to Croydon, one of the seats of the Archbishops of Canterbury. Was it one of these who ordered, many years ago (for the characters are of old standing), that dreadful inscription to be placed just over the communion-table? "And now, ye priests, this commandment is for you. If ye will not hear, and if ye will not lay it to heart, to give glory unto my name, saith the Lord, I will even send a curse among you, and I will curse your blessings : yea, I have cursed them already, because ye do not lay it to heart. Behold, I will corrupt your seed, and spread dung upon your faces, even the dung of your solemn feasts, and one shall take you away with it."

The Archbishop's palace is an ancient, venerable pile. and the gardens are extremely pleasant. The late Archbishop had improved them at a large expense; but continual illness prevented his enjoying them; till, after four years' constant pain, he was called away—one may hope to the garden of God.

I dined at Mr. B.'s, in Epsom, whose house and gardens lie in what was once a chalk-pit. It is the most elegant spot I ever saw with my eyes; every thing within doors and without, being finished in the most exquisite taste. Surely nothing on earth can be more delightful. O what will the possessor feel, when he cries out,

> Must I then leave thee, paradise? then leave
> These happy shades, and mansions fit for gods?

Thur. 30.—I preached at the Tabernacle in Norwich, to a large, rude, noisy congregation. I took knowledge what manner of teachers they had been accustomed to, and determined to mend them or end them. Accordingly, the next evening, after sermon, I reminded them of two things : the one, that it was not decent to begin talking aloud as soon as service was ended; and hurrying to and fro, as in a bear-garden. The other, that it was a bad custom to gather into knots just after sermon, and turn a place of worship into a coffee-house. I therefore desired, that none would talk under that roof, but go quietly and silently away. And on Sunday, September 2, I had the pleasure to observe, that all went as quietly away, as if they had been accustomed to it for many years.

Sun. Sep. 9.—I met the society at seven; and told them in plain terms, that they were the most ignorant, self-conceited, self-willed, fickle, untractable, disorderly, disjointed society, that I knew in the three kingdoms. And God applied it to their hearts: so that many were profited; but I do not find, that one was offended.

Field-preaching Expedient

Fri. 14.—I returned to London. Saturday, 15. Having left orders for the immediate repairing of West Street chapel, I went to see what they had done, and saw cause to praise God for this also. The main timbers were so rotten, that in many places one might thrust his fingers into them. So that probably, had we delayed till spring, the whole building must have fallen to the ground.

Mon. 17.—I went to Canterbury. Two hundred soldiers, I suppose, and a whole row of officers, attended in the evening. Their number was increased the next evening, and all behaved as men fearing God. Wednesday, 19, I preached at Dover, in the new room, which is just finished. Here also the hearers increase, some of whom are convinced and others comforted daily. Thursday, 20. I strongly applied at Canterbury to the soldiers in particular, " He that hath the Son hath life, and he that hath not the Son of God hath not life."

The next day, in my return to London, I read Mr. Huygens's "Conjectures on the Planetary World." He surprised me. I think he clearly proves that the moon is not habitable: that there are neither

Rivers nor mountains on her spotty globe:

that there is no sea, no water on her surface, nor any atmosphere: and hence he very rationally infers, that "neither are any of the secondary planets inhabited." And who can prove that the primary are? I know the earth is. Of the rest I know nothing.

Sun. 23.—A vast majority of the immense congregation in Moorfields were deeply serious. One such hour might convince any impartial man of the expediency of field-preaching. What building, except St. Paul's church, would contain such a congregation. And if it would, what human voice could have reached them there? By repeated observations I find I can command thrice the number in the open air, that I can under a roof. And who can say the time for field-preaching is over, while, 1. Greater numbers than ever attend: 2. The converting, as well as convincing, power of God is eminently present with them?

Wesley Clothes French Prisoners

Mon. Oct. 1 (Bristol).—All my leisure time, during my stay at Bristol, I employed in finishing the fourth volume of "Discourses"; probably the last which I shall publish.

Mon. 15.—I walked up to Knowle, a mile from Bristol, to see the French prisoners. About eleven hundred of them, we are informed, were confined in that little place, without anything to lie on but a little dirty straw, or anything to cover them but a few foul thin rags, either by day or night, so that they died like rotten sheep. I was much affected, and preached in the evening on (Exodus xxiii. 9), "Thou shalt not oppress a stranger: for ye know the heart of a stranger, seeing ye were strangers in the land of Egypt." Eighteen pounds were contributed immediately, which were made up four-and-twenty the next day. With this we bought linen and woollen cloth, which were made up into shirts, waistcoats, and breeches. Some dozen of stockings were added; all which were carefully distributed, where there was the greatest want. Presently after, the Corporation of Bristol sent a large quantity of mattresses and blankets. And it was not long before contributions were set on foot at London, and in various parts of the kingdom; so that I believe from this time they were pretty well provided with all the necessaries of life.

The Truth about Trances

Sat. Nov. 17. (London).—I spent an hour agreeably and profitably with Lady G—— H——, and Sir C—— H——. It is well a few of the rich and noble are called. O that God would increase their number! But I should rejoice (were it the will of God), if it were done by the ministry of others. If I might choose, I should still (as I have done hitherto) preach the Gospel to the poor.

Fri. 23.—The roads were so extremely slippery, it was with much difficulty we reached Bedford. We had a pretty large congregation; but the stench from the swine under the room was scarce supportable. Was ever a preaching-place over a hog-sty before? Surely they love the Gospel, who come to hear it in such a place.

Sun. 25.—In the afternoon God was eminently present with us, though rather to comfort than convince.

But I observed a remarkable difference, since I was here (Everton) before, as to the manner of the work. None now were in trances, none cried out, none fell down or were convulsed: only some trembled exceedingly, a low murmur was heard, and many were refreshed with the multitude of peace.

The danger was, to regard extraordinary circumstances too much, such as outcries, convulsions, visions, trances; as if these were essential to the inward work, so that it could not go on without them. Perhaps the danger is, to regard them too little; to condemn them altogether; to imagine they had nothing of God in them, and were a hindrance to his work. Whereas the truth is, 1. God suddenly and strongly convinced many that they were lost sinners; the natural consequence whereof were sudden outcries and strong bodily convulsions: 2. To strengthen and encourage them that believed, and to make his work more apparent, he favoured several of them with divine dreams, others with trances and visions: 3. In some of these instances, after a time, nature mixed with grace: 4. Satan likewise mimicked this work of God in order to discredit the whole work: and yet it is not wise to give up this part any more than to give up the whole. At first, it was, doubtless, wholly from God. It is partly so at this day; and he will enable us to discern how far, in every case, the work is pure, and where it mixes or degenerates.

Wed. 28.—I returned to London; and on Thursday, 29, the day appointed for the general thanksgiving, I preached again in the chapel near the Seven Dials, both morning and afternoon. I believed the oldest man in England has not seen a thanksgiving-day so observed before. It had the solemnity of the General Fast. All the shops were shut up: the people in the streets appeared, one and all, with an air of seriousness : the prayers, lessons, and whole public service, were admirably suited to the occasion. The prayer for our enemies, in particular, was extremely striking : perhaps it is the first instance of the kind in Europe. There was no noise, hurry, bonfires, fireworks in the evening ; and no public diversions. This is indeed a Christian holiday, a "rejoicing unto the Lord." The next day came the news that Sir Edward Hawke had dispersed the French fleet.

Sun. Dec. 9.—I had, for the first time, a love-feast for the whole society. Wednesday, 12. I began reading over the Greek Testament and the notes, with my brother and several others ; carefully comparing the translation with the original, and correcting or enlarging the notes as we saw occasion.

The same day I spent part of the afternoon in the British Museum. There is a large library, a great number of curious manuscripts, many uncommon monuments of antiquity, and the whole collection of shells, butterflies, beetles, grasshoppers, &c., which the indefatigable Sir Hans Sloane, with such vast expense and labour, procured in a life of fourscore years.

Wesley and the Irish Question

1760. Wed. Jan. 16.—One came to me, as she said, with a message from the Lord, to tell me, I was laying up treasures on earth, taking my ease, and minding only my eating and drinking. I told her, God knew me better ; and if he had sent her, he would have sent her with a more proper message.

Mon. April 21.—In riding to Rosmead, I read Sir John Davis's " Historical Relations concerning Ireland." None who reads these can wonder, that, fruitful as it is, it was always so thinly inhabited; for he makes it plain, 1. That murder was never capital among the native Irish; the murderer only paid a small fine to the Chief of his sept. 2. When the English settled here, still the Irish had no benefit of the English laws. They could not so much as sue an Englishman. So the English beat, plundered, yea, murdered them, at pleasure. Hence, 3. Arose continual wars between them, for three hundred and fifty years together; and hereby both the English and Irish natives were kept few, as well as poor.

4. When they were multiplied during a peace of forty years, from 1600 to 1641, the general massacre, with the ensuing war, again thinned their numbers; not so few as a million of men, women, and children, being destroyed in four years' time. 5. Great numbers have ever since, year by year, left the land merely for want of employment. 6. The gentry are continually driving away hundreds, yea, thousands, of them that remain, by throwing such quantities of arable land into pasture, which leaves them neither business nor food. This it is that now dispeoples many parts of Ireland, of Connaught in particular, which, it is supposed, has scarce half the inhabitants at this day which it had fourscore years ago.

Attack on Wesley's Hat

Tues. June 10.—I rode to Drumersnave, a village delightfully situated.

At noon William Ley, James Glasbrook, and I rode to Carrick-upon-Shannon. In less than an hour, an Esquire and Justice of the peace came down with a drum, and what mob he could gather. I went into the garden with the congregation, while he was making a

speech to his followers in the street. He then attacked
William Ley (who stood at the door), being armed with
an halbert and long sword; and ran at him with
the halbert, but missing his thrust, he then struck at him,
and broke it short upon his wrist. Having made his
way through the house to the other door, he was at a
full stop. James Glasbrook held it fast on the other
side.

While he was endeavouring to force it open, one told
him I was preaching in the garden. On this he quitted
the door in haste, ran round the house, and with part
of his retinue, climbed over the wall into the garden;
and with a whole volley of oaths and curses declared,
"You shall not preach here to-day." I told him, " Sir,
I do not intend it ; for I have preached already." This
made him ready to tear the ground. Finding he was
not to be reasoned with, I went into the house. Soon
after he revenged himself on James Glasbook (by breaking
the truncheon of his halbert on his arm), and on my hat,
which he beat and kicked most valiantly ; but a gentleman rescued it out of his hands, and we rode quietly
out of the town.

Wed. Sept. 10.—When I came to St. Ives, I was
determined to preach abroad ; but the wind was so
high, I could not stand where I had intended. But we
found a little inclosure near it, one end of which was
native rock, rising ten or twelve feet perpendicular, from
which the ground fell with an easy descent. A jetting
out of the rock, about four feet from the ground, gave
me a very convenient pulpit. Here well nigh the whole
town, high and low, rich and poor, assembled together.
Nor was there a word to be heard, or a smile seen, from
one end of the congregation to the other. It was just
the same the three following evenings. Indeed I was

afraid on Saturday, that the roaring of the sea, raised
by the north wind, would have prevented their hearing.
But God gave me so clear and strong a voice, that I
believe scarce one word was lost.

Sun. 14.—At eight I chose a large ground, the sloping
side of a meadow, where the congregation stood, row
above row, so that all might see as well as hear.   It was
a beautiful sight.   Every one seemed to take to himself
what was spoken.   I believe every backslider in the
town was there.   And surely God was there, to " heal
their backslidings."

I began at Zennor, as soon as the Church service
ended : I suppose scarce six persons went away.

At five I went once more into the ground at St. Ives,
and found such a congregation as I think was never seen
in a place before (Gwennap excepted) in this county.
Some of the chief of the town were now not in the
skirts, but in the thickest of the people.   The clear sky,
the setting sun, the smooth, still water, all agreed with
the state of the audience.

"A Kind of Waterspout"

Wed. 17.—The room at St. Just was quite full at
five, and God gave us a parting blessing.   At noon I
preached on the cliff near Penzance, where no one now
gives an uncivil word.   Here I procured an account,
from an eye-witness, of what happened the twenty-seventh
of last month.   A round pillar, narrowest at bottom, of
a whitish colour, rose out of the sea near Mousehole,
and reached the clouds.   One who was riding over the
strand from Marazion to Penzance saw it stand for a
short space, and then move swiftly toward her, till the
skirt of it touching her, the horse threw her and ran
away.   It had a strong sulphurous smell.   It dragged

with it abundance of sand and pebbles from the shore; and then went over the land, carrying with it corn, furze, or whatever it found in its way. It was doubtless a kind of water-spout; but a water-spout on land, I believe, is seldom seen.

Fri. 19.—I rode to Illogan. We had heavy rain before I began, but scarce any while I was preaching. I learned several other particulars here concerning the water-spout. It was seen near Mousehole an hour before sunset. About sunset it began travelling over the land, tearing up all the furze and shrubs it met. Near an hour after sunset it passed (at the rate of four or five miles an hour) across Mr. Harris's fields, in Camborne, sweeping the ground as it went, about twenty yards in diameter at bottom, and broader and broader up to the clouds. It made a noise like thunder, took up eighteen stacks of corn, with a large hay-stack and the stones whereon it stood, scattered them abroad (but it was quite dry), and then passed over the cliff into the sea.

Sat. 20.—In the evening I took my old stand in the main street in Redruth. A multitude of people, rich and poor, calmly attended. So is the roughest become one of the quietest towns in England.

A Tinner's Story

Sun. 21.—I preached in the same place at eight. Mr. C——, of St. Cubert, preached at the church both morning and afternoon, and strongly confirmed what I had spoken. At one, the day being mild and calm, we had the largest congregation of all. But it rained all the time I was preaching at Gwennap. We concluded the day with a love-feast, at which James Roberts, a tinner of St. Ives, related how God had dealt with his soul.

He was one of the first in society in St. Ives, but soon relapsed into his old sin, drunkenness, and wallowed in it for two years, during which time he headed the mob who pulled down the preaching-house. Not long after, he was standing with his partner at Edward May's shop when the preacher went by. His partner said, "I will tell him I am a Methodist." "Nay," said Edward, "your speech will bewray you." James felt the word as a sword, thinking in himself, "So does my speech now bewray me!" He turned and hastened home, fancying he heard the devil stepping after him all the way. For forty hours he never closed his eyes, nor tasted either meat or drink. He was then at his wit's end, and went to the window, looking to drop into hell instantly, when he heard those words, "I will be merciful to thy unrighteousness, thy sins and iniquities will I remember no more." All his load was gone; and he has now for many years walked worthy of the Gospel.

Wed. Oct. 22.—Being informed that some neighbouring gentlemen had declared they would apprehend the next preacher who came to Pensford, I rode over to give them the meeting; but none appeared. The house was more than filled with deeply attentive hearers. It seems the time is come at length for the word of God to take root here also.

Fri. 24.—I visited the French prisoners at Knowle, and found many of them almost naked again. In hopes of provoking others to jealousy, I made another collection for them, and ordered the money to be laid out in linen and waistcoats, which were given to those that were most in want.

Sat. 25.—King George was gathered to his fathers. When will England have a better Prince?

Many of us agreed to observe Friday, 31, as a day of fasting and prayer for the blessing of God upon our nation, and in particular on his present Majesty. We met at five, at nine, at one, and at half-past eight. I expected to be a little tired, but was more lively after twelve at night than I was at six in the morning.

Wesley Writes to the "London Chronicle"

1761. Jan. Fri. 2.—I wrote the following letter:

"To the Editor of the London Chronicle.

"Sir,—Of all the seats of woe on this side hell, few, I suppose, exceed or even equal Newgate. If any region of horror could exceed it a few years ago, Newgate in Bristol did; so great was the filth, the stench, the misery, and wickedness, which shocked all who had a spark of humanity left.

How was I surprised then, when I was there a few weeks ago! 1. Every part of it, above stairs and below, even the pit, wherein the felons are confined at night, is as clean and sweet as a gentleman's house; it being now a rule, that every prisoner wash and clean his apartment throughly twice a week. 2. Here is no fighting or brawling. If any thinks himself ill-used, the cause is immediately referred to the keeper, who hears the contending parties face to face, and decides the affair at once. 3. The usual grounds of quarrelling are removed. For it is very rarely that any one cheats or wrongs another, as being sure, if any thing of this kind is discovered, to be committed to a closer confinement.

4. Here is no drunkenness suffered, however advantageous it might be to the keeper, as well as the tapster. 5. Nor any whoredom; the women prisoners

being narrowly observed, and kept separate from the men: nor is any woman of the town now admitted, no, not at any price. 6. All possible care is taken to prevent idleness: those who are willing to work at their callings are provided with tools and materials, partly by the keeper, who gives them credit at a very moderate profit; partly by the alms occasionally given, which are divided with the utmost prudence and impartiality. Accordingly, at this time, among others, a shoemaker, a tailor, a brazier, and a coach-maker are working at their several trades.

7. Only on the Lord's day they neither work nor play, but dress themselves as clean as they can, to attend the public service in the chapel, at which every person under the roof is present. None is excused, unless sick; in which case he is provided, *gratis*, both with advice and medicines. 8. And in order to assist them in things of the greatest concern (besides a sermon every Sunday and Thursday), they have a large Bible chained on one side of the chapel, which any of the prisoners may read. By the blessing of God on these regulations the prison now has a new face: nothing offends either the eye or ear; and the whole has the appearance of a quiet, serious family. And does not the keeper of Newgate deserve to be remembered full as well as the Man of Ross? May the Lord remember him in that day! Meantime, will no one follow his example? I am, Sir,

> " Your humble servant,
>
> " John Wesley."

Sat. March 14.—I rode (from Birmingham) to Wednesbury. Sunday, 15. I made a shift to preach within at eight in the morning; but in the afternoon I knew not what to do, having a pain in my side, and a sore throat. However, I resolved to speak as long as I could. I stood at one end of the house, and the people (supposed to be eight or ten thousand) in the field adjoining. I spoke from, " I count all things but loss, for the excellency of the knowledge of Christ Jesus my Lord." When I had done speaking, my complaints were gone.

Mon. 16.—I intended to rest two or three days ; but being pressed to visit Shrewsbury, and having no other time, I rode over to-day, though upon a miserable beast. When I came, my head ached as well as my side. I found the door of the place where I was to preach surrounded by a numerous mob. But they seemed met, only to starve. Yet part of them came in ; almost all that did (a large number) behaved quietly and seriously.

Preaching in the Inn Yard

Tues. 17.—At five the congregation was large, and appeared not a little affected. The difficulty now was, how to get back. For I could not ride the horse on which I came. But this too was provided for. We met in the street with one who lent me his horse, which was so easy that I grew better and better till I came to Wolverhampton. None had yet preached abroad in this furious town ; but I was resolved, with God's help, to make a trial, and ordered a table to be set in the inn-yard. Such a number of wild men I have seldom seen ; but they gave me no disturbance, either while I preached, or when I afterwards walked through the midst of them.

About five I preached to a far larger congregation at Dudley, and all as quiet as at London. The scene is changed, since the dirt and stones of this town were flying about me on every side.

Sat. May 2 (Aberdeen).—In the afternoon I sent to the Principal and Regent to desire leave to preach in the College Close. This was readily granted; but as it began to rain, I was desired to go into the hall. I suppose this is full an hundred feet long, and seated all around. The congregation was large, notwithstanding the rain; and full as large at five in the morning.

Wesley Preaches at Aberdeen

Mon. 4.—About noon I took a walk to the King's College, in Old Aberdeen. It has three sides of a square, handsomely built, not unlike Queen's College in Oxford. Going up to see the hall, we found a large company of ladies, with several gentlemen. They looked, and spoke to one another, after which one of the gentlemen took courage and came to me. He said, " We came last night to the College Close, but could not hear, and should be extremely obliged if you would give us a short discourse here." I knew not what God might have to do; and so began without delay, on, " God was in Christ, reconciling the world unto Himself.' I believe the word was not lost: it fell as dew on the tender grass.

In the afternoon I was walking in the library of the Marischal College, when the Principal, and the Divinity Professor, came to me; and the latter invited me to his lodgings, where I spent an hour very agreeably. In the evening, the eagerness of the people made them ready to trample each other under foot. It was some time before they were still enough to hear; but then they devoured every word. After preaching, Sir Archibald Grant (whom business had called to town) sent and desired to speak to me. I could not then, but promised to wait upon him, with God's leave in my return to Edinburgh.

Tues. 5.—I accepted the Principal's invitation, and
spent an hour with him at his house. I observed no
stiffness at all, but the easy good breeding of a man of
sense and learning.   I suppose both he and all the
Professors, with some of the magistrates, attended in
the evening.   I set all the windows open ; but the hall,
notwithstanding, was as hot as a bagnio.

Wed. 6.—At half-hour after six I stood in the College
Close, and proclaimed Christ crucified.   My voice was so
strengthened that all could hear ; and all were earnestly
attentive.

Wesley's Criticism of Edinburgh

Mon. 11.—I took my leave of Edinburgh for the
present. The situation of the city, on a hill shelving
down on both sides, as well as to the east, with the
stately castle upon a craggy rock on the west, is inexpressibly fine.   And the main street, so broad and finely
paved, with the lofty houses on either hand (many of
them seven or eight stories high), is far beyond any in
Great Britain. But how can it be suffered, that all
manner of filth should still be thrown even into this
street continually ?   Where are the magistracy, the
gentry, the nobility of the land ?   Have they no concern
for the honour of their nation ?   How long shall the
capital city of Scotland, yea, and the chief street of it,
stink worse than a common sewer ?   Will no lover of
his country, or of decency and common sense, find a
remedy for this ?

Holyrood House, at the entrance of Edinburgh, the
ancient palace of the Scottish Kings, is a noble structure.
It was rebuilt and furnished by King Charles the Second.
One side of it is a picture-gallery, wherein are pictures
of all the Scottish Kings, and an original one of the

celebrated Queen Mary: it is scarce possible for any
who looks at this to think her such a monster as some
have painted her; nor indeed for any who considers the
circumstances of her death, equal to that of an ancient
martyr.

A Busy Week

Mon. June 15.—I rode to Durham, having appointed
to preach there at noon. The meadow, near the river side,
was quite convenient, and the small rain neither disturbed
me nor the congregation. In the afternoon I rode to
Hartlepool; but I had much ado to preach; my strength
was gone as well as my voice; and, indeed, they
generally go together. Three days in a week I can
preach thrice a day without hurting myself; but I had
now far exceeded this, besides meeting classes and
exhorting the societies. I was obliged to lie down good
part of Tuesday: however, in the afternoon I preached
at Cherington, and in the evening at Hartlepool again,
though not without difficulty. Wednesday, 17. I rode
to Stockton, where, a little before the time of preaching,
my voice and strength were restored at once. The next
evening it began to rain just as I began to preach; but
it was suspended till the service was over: it then rained
again till eight in the morning.

Fri. 19.—It was hard work to ride eight miles (so
called) in two hours and a half; the rain beating upon
us, and the by-road being exceeding slippery. But we
forgot all this when we came to the Grange; so greatly
was God present with His people. Thence we rode to
Darlington. Here we were under a difficulty again:
not half the people could come in, and the rain forbade
my preaching without. But at one (the hour of preaching) the rain stopped and did not begin again till past

two; so the people stood very conveniently in the yard; and many did not care to go away. When I went in, they crowded to the door and windows, and stayed till I took horse. At seven I preached at Yarm, and desired one of our brethren to take my place in the morning.

Wesley and Impositions

Sun. 21.—I rode to Osmotherley, where the minister read prayers seriously, and preached an useful sermon. After service I began in the church-yard : I believe many were wounded and many comforted. After dinner I called on Mr. Adams, who first invited me to Osmotherley. He was reading the strange account of the two missionaries who have lately made such a figure—in the newspapers. I suppose the whole account is just such another gross imposition upon the public as the man's gathering the people together to see him go into the quart bottle. " Men seven hundred years old ! " And why not seven yards high ? He that can believe it, let him believe it.

Mon. 22.—I spoke, one by one, to the society at Hutton Rudby. At eleven I preached once more, though in great weakness of body, and met the stewards of all the societies. I then rode to Stokesley, and, having examined the little society, went on for Guisborough. The sun was burning hot; but, in a quarter of an hour, a cloud interposed, and he troubled us no more. I was desired by a gentlemen of the town to preach in the market-place; and there a table was placed for me, but it was in a bad neighbourhood; for there was so vehement a stench of stinking fish, as was ready to suffocate me, and the people roared like the waves of the sea; but the voice of the Lord was mightier; and in a few minutes the whole multitude was still, and seriously attended while I proclaimed "Jesus Christ, made of God unto us wisdom, and righteousness, and sanctification, and redemption."

Tues. 23.—I began about five, near the same place, and had a great part of the same audience; yet they were not the same. The change might easily be read in their countenance. When we took horse, and just faced the sun, it was hard work for man and beast; but about eight the wind shifted, and blowing in our face, kept us cool till we came to Whitby.

In the evening I preached on the top of the hill, to which you ascend by an hundred ninety and one steps. The congregation was exceeding large, and ninety-nine in an hundred were attentive. When I began, the sun shone full in my face; but he soon clouded, and shone no more till I had done.

Wed. 24.—I walked round the old Abbey, which, both with regard to its size (being, I judge, an hundred yards long), and the workmanship of it, is one of the finest, if not the finest, ruin in the kingdom. Hence we rode to Robin Hood's Bay, where I preached at six in the Lower Street, near the quay. In the midst of the sermon a large cat, frighted out of a chamber, leaped down upon a woman's head, and ran over the heads or shoulders of many more; but none of them moved or cried out, any more than if it had been a butterfly.

Thur. 25.—I had a pleasant ride to Scarborough, the wind tempering the heat of the sun. I had designed to preach abroad in the evening; but the thunder, lightning, and rain prevented: however, I stood on a balcony, and several hundreds of people stood below: and, notwithstanding the heavy rain, would not stir till I concluded.

Fri. July 3.—We returned to York, where I was desired to call upon a poor prisoner in the castle. I had formerly occasion to take notice of an hideous monster, called a Chancery Bill; I now saw the fellow to it, called a Declaration. The plain fact was this: Some time since a man who lived near Yarm assisted others in running some brandy. His share was near four pounds. After he had wholly left off that bad work, and was following his own business, that of a weaver, he was arrested, and sent to York gaol; and, not long after, comes down a Declaration, "that Jac. Wh—— had landed a vessel laded with brandy and Geneva, at the port of London, and sold them there, whereby he was indebted to his Majesty five hundred and seventy-seven pounds and upwards." And to tell this worthy story, the lawyer takes up thirteen or fourteen sheets of treble stamped paper.

A Monster Called a Declaration

O England, England! will this reproach never be rolled away from thee? Is there any thing like this to be found, either among Papists, Turks, or heathens? In the name of truth, justice, mercy, and common sense, I ask, 1. Why do men lie for lying sake? Is it only to keep their hands in? What need else, of saying it was the port of London, when every one knew the brandy was landed above three hundred miles from thence? What a monstrous contempt of truth does this show, or rather hatred to it! 2. Where is the justice of swelling four pounds into five hundred and seventy-seven? 3. Where is the common sense of taking up fourteen sheets to tell a story that may be told in ten lines? 4. Where is the mercy of thus grinding the face of the poor? thus sucking the blood of a poor, beggared prisoner? Would not this be execrable villainy, if the paper and writing together were only sixpence a sheet, when they have stripped him already of his little all, and not left him fourteen groats in the world?

Sun. 5.—Believing one hindrance of the work of God in York, was the neglect of field-preaching, I preached this morning at eight, in an open place, near the city walls. Abundance of people ran together, most of whom were deeply attentive. One or two only were angry, and threw a few stones; but it was labour lost; for none regarded them.

Sun. 12.—I had appointed to be at Haworth; but the church would not near contain the people who came from all sides: however, Mr. Grimshaw had provided for this by fixing a scaffold on the outside of one of the windows, through which I went after prayers, and the people likewise all went out into the church-yard. The afternoon congregation was larger still. What has God wrought in the midst of those rough mountains!

Some Impudent Women

Mon. 13.—About five I preached at Paddiham, another place eminent for all manner of wickedness. The multitude of people obliged me to stand in the yard of the preaching-house. Over against me, at a little distance, sat some of the most impudent women I ever saw: yet I am not sure that God did not reach their hearts; for

They roar'd, and would have blush'd, if capable of shame.

Fri. 24.—About one I preached at Bramley, where Jonas Rushford, about fourteen years old, gave me the following relation:

"About this time last year I was desired by two of our neighbours to go with them to Mr. Crowther's at

Skipton, who would not speak to them, about a man that had been missing twenty days, but bid them bring a boy twelve or thirteen years old. When we came in, he stood reading a book.

Seen in a Looking-glass

"He put me into a bed, with a looking-glass in my hand, and covered me all over. Then he asked me whom I had a mind to see ; and I said, ' My mother.' I presently saw her with a lock of wool in her hand, standing just in the place, and the clothes she was in, as she told me afterwards. Then he bid me look again for the man that was missing, who was one of our neighbours. And I looked and saw him riding towards Idle, but he was very drunk ; and he stopped at the alehouse and drank two pints more, and he pulled out a guinea to change. Two men stood by, a big man and a little man ; and they went on before him, and got two hedge-stakes ; and when he came up, on Windle Common, at the top of the hill, they pulled him off his horse, and killed him, and threw him into a coal-pit. And I saw it all as plain as if I was close to them. And if I saw the men, I should know them again.

"We went back to Bradford that night ; and the next day I went with our neighbours and showed them the spot where he was killed, and the pit he was thrown into ; and a man went down and brought him up. And it was as I had told them ; his handkerchief was tied about his mouth, and fastened behind his neck."

Is it improbable only, or flatly impossible, when all the circumstances are considered, that this should all be pure fiction ? They that can believe this, may believe a man's getting into a bottle.

Mon. July 27.—I preached at Staincross about eleven; about five, at Barley Hall; the next morning, at Sheffield. In the afternoon I rode on to Matlock Bath. The valley which reaches from the town to the bath is pleasant beyond expression. In the bottom of this runs a little river, close to which a mountain rises, almost perpendicular, to an enormous height, part covered with green, part with ragged and naked rocks. On the other side, the mountain rises gradually with tufts of trees here and there. The brow on both sides is fringed with trees, which seem to answer each other.

Wesley at Matlock Bath and Boston

Many of our friends were come from various parts. At six I preached standing under the hollow of a rock, on one side of a small plain; on the other side of which was a tall mountain. There were many well-dressed hearers, this being the high season; and all of them behaved well. But as I walked back, a gentleman-like man asked me, "Why do you talk thus of faith? Stuff, nonsense!" Upon inquiry, I found he was an eminent Deist. What, has the plague crept into the Peak of Derbyshire?

Thur. Aug. 13.—I took a walk through Boston. I think it is not much smaller than Leeds; but, in general, it is far better built. The church is indeed a fine building. It is larger, loftier, nay, and rather more lightsome, than even St. Peter's at Norwich: and the steeple is, I suppose, the highest tower in England, nor less remarkable for the architecture than the height.

Sat. Nov. 14.—I spent an hour with a little company near Grosvenor Square. For many years this has been the darkest, driest spot, of all in or near

London. But God has now watered the barren wilderness, and it is become a fruitful field.

Preaching at Deptford, Welling, and Sevenoaks, in my way, on Thursday, December 3, I came to Shoreham. There I read the celebrated " Life of St. Katherine, of Genoa." Mr. Lesley calls one " a devil of a saint": I am sure this was a fool of a saint ; that is, if it was not the folly of her historian, who has aggrandised her into a mere idiot. Indeed we seldom find a saint of God's making, sainted by the Bishop of Rome.

Fri. 25 (London).—We began, as usual, at four. A few days since, one who lived in known sin, finding heavy conviction, broke away, and ran out, she knew not whither. She met one who offered her a shilling a week to come and take care of her child. She went gladly. The woman's husband, hearing her stir between three and four, began cursing and swearing bitterly. His wife said, " I wish thou wouldest go with her, and see if anything will do thee good." He did so. In the first hymn God broke his heart ; and he was in tears all the rest of the service. How soon did God recompense this poor woman for taking the stranger in !

Preaching by Moonlight

1762. Mon. Jan. 4.—After preaching to a large congregation at Wrestlingworth, we rode on to Harston. I never preached a whole sermon by moonlight before. However, it was a solemn season ; a season of holy mourning to some ; to others, of joy unspeakable.

Mon. March 29.—I preached about twelve in the new room at Chepstow. One of the congregation was a neighbouring clergyman, who lived in the same staircase with me at Christ Church, and was then far more serious than me. Blessed be God, who has looked upon me at last! Now let me redeem the time!

In the afternoon we had such a storm of hail as I scarce ever saw in my life. The roads likewise were so extremely bad that we did not reach Hereford till past eight. Having been well battered both by hail, rain, and wind, I got to bed as soon as I could, but was waked many times by the clattering of the curtains. In the morning I found the casement wide open; but I was never the worse. I took horse at six, with William Crane and Francis Walker. The wind was piercing cold, and we had many showers of snow and rain; but the worst was, part of the road was scarce passable; so that at Church Stretton, one of our horses lay down and would go no farther. However, William Crane and I pushed on, and before seven reached Shrewsbury.

A large company quickly gathered together: many of them were wild enough; but the far greater part were calm and attentive, and came again at five in the morning.

Some Rough Journeys

Wed. 31.—Having been invited to preach at Wem, Mrs. Glynne desired she might take me thither in a post-chaise; but in little more than an hour we were fast enough: however, the horses pulled till the traces broke. I should then have walked on had I been alone, though the mud was deep, and the snow drove impetuously; but I could not leave my friend; so I waited patiently till the man had made shift to mend the traces; and the horses pulled amain; so that with much ado, not long after the time appointed, I came to Wem.

I came: but the person who invited me was gone; gone out of town at four in the morning; and I could find no one who seemed either to expect or desire my company. I inquired after the place where Mr. Mather preached; but it was filled with hemp. It remained only to go into the market-house: but neither any man, woman, nor child cared to follow us; the north wind roared so loud on every side, and poured in from every quarter. However, before I had done singing, two or three crept in; and after them, two or three hundred; and the power of God was so present among them, that I believe many forgot the storm.

The wind grew still higher in the afternoon, so that it was difficult to sit our horses; and it blew full in our face, but could not prevent our reaching Chester in the evening. Though the warning was short, the room was full; and full of serious, earnest hearers, many of whom expressed a longing desire of the whole salvation of God. Here I rested on Thursday.

Friday, April 2. I rode to Parkgate, and found several ships; but the wind was contrary. I preached at five in the small house they have just built; and the hearers were remarkably serious. I gave notice of preaching at five in the morning. But at half-hour after four one brought us word that the wind was come fair, and Captain Jordan would sail in less than an hour. We were soon in the ship, wherein we found about three-score passengers. The sun shone bright, the wind was moderate, the sea smooth, and we wanted nothing but room to stir ourselves; the cabin being filled with hops, so that we could not get into it but by climbing over them on our hands and knees. In the afternoon we were abreast of Holyhead. But the scene was quickly changed: the wind rose higher and higher, and by seven o'clock blew a storm. The sea broke over us continually, and sometimes covered the ship, which both pitched and rolled in an uncommon manner. So I was informed; for, being a little sick, I lay down at six, and slept, with little intermission, till near six in the morning. We were then near Dublin Bay, where we went into a boat, which carried us to Dunleary. There we met with a chaise just ready, in which we went to Dublin.

Remarkable Speaking Statue

Mon. April 26.—In the evening I preached to a large congregation in the market-house at Lurgan. I now embraced the opportunity which I had long desired, of talking with Mr. Miller, the contriver of that statue which was in Lurgan when I was there before. It was the figure of an old man, standing in a case, with a curtain drawn before him, over against a clock which stood on the other side of the room. Every time the clock struck, he opened the door with one hand, drew back the curtain with the other, turned his head, as if looking round on the company, and then said with a clear, loud, articulate voice, " Past one, two, three," and so on. But so many came to see this (the like of which all allowed was not to be seen in Europe) that Mr. Miller was in danger of being ruined, not having time to attend his own business ; so, as none offered to purchase it, or to reward him for his pains, he took the whole machine in pieces; nor has he any thought of ever making any thing of the kind again.

Wed. 28.—In the morning I rode to Monaghan. The commotions in Munster having now alarmed all Ireland, we had hardly alighted, when some wise persons informed the Provost there were three strange sort of men come to the King's Arms. So the Provost with his officers came without delay, to secure the north from so imminent a danger. I was just come out, when I was required to return into the house. The Provost asked me many questions, and perhaps the affair might have turned serious, had I not had two letters with me, which I had lately received; one from the Bishop of London-derry, the other from the Earl of Moira. Upon reading these, he excused himself for the trouble he had given, and wished me a good journey.

Between six and seven I preached at Coot Hill, and in the morning rode on to Enniskillin. After riding round and round, we came in the evening to a lone house called Carrick-a-beg. It lay in the midst of horrid mountains; and had no very promising appearance. However, it afforded corn for our horses, and potatoes for ourselves. So we made an hearty supper, called in as many as pleased of the family to prayers, and, though we had no fastening either for our doors or our windows, slept in peace.

Wesley and the Oatmeal Sellers

Mon. May 3 (Sligo).—In the evening a company of players began acting in the upper part of the market-house, just as we began singing in the lower. The case of these is remarkable. The Presbyterians for a long time had their public worship here; but when the strollers came to town, they were turned out; and from that time had no public worship at all. On Tuesday evening the lower part too was occupied by buyers and sellers of oatmeal; but as soon as I began, the people quitted their sacks, and listened to business of greater importance.

Sun. 16.—I had observed to the society last week

that I had not seen one congregation ever in Ireland behave so ill at church as that at Athlone, laughing, and staring about during the whole service. I had added, " This is your fault; for if you had attended the church, as you ought to have done, your presence and example would not have failed to influence the whole congregation." And so it appeared; I saw not one to-day, either laughing, talking, or staring about; but a remarkable seriousness was spread from the one end of the church to the other.

The Irish Whiteboys

Mon. 24.—I went with two friends, to see one of the greatest natural wonders in Ireland,—Mount Eagle, vulgarly called Crow Patrick. The foot of it is fourteen miles from Castlebar. There we left our horses, and procured a guide. It was just twelve when we alighted; the sun was burning hot, and we had not a breath of wind. Part of the ascent was a good deal steeper than an ordinary pair of stairs. About two we gained the top, which is an oval, grassy plain, about an hundred and fifty yards in length, and seventy or eighty in breadth. The upper part of the mountain much resembles the Peak of Teneriffe. I think it cannot rise much less than a mile perpendicular from the plain below. There is an immense prospect on one side toward the sea, and on the other over the land. But as most of it is waste and uncultivated, the prospect is not very pleasing.

Mon. June 14.—I rode to Cork. Here I procured an exact account of the late commotions. About the beginning of December last, a few men met by night near Nenagh, in the county of Limerick, and threw down the fences of some commons, which had been lately

inclosed.   Near the same time the others met in the
county of Tipperary, of Waterford, and of Cork.   As
no one offered to suppress or hinder them, they increased
in number continually, and called themselves Whiteboys, wearing white cockades, and white linen frocks.
In February, there were five or six parties of them, two
or three hundred men in each, who moved up and down,
chiefly in the night; but for what end, did not appear.
Only they levelled a few fences, dug up some grounds,
and hamstrung some cattle, perhaps fifty or sixty in all.

One body of them came into Cloheen, of about five
hundred foot, and two hundred horse.   They moved as
exactly as regular troops, and appeared to be thoroughly
disciplined.   They now sent letters to several gentlemen,
threatening to pull down their houses.   They compelled
every one they met to take an oath to be true to Queen
Sive (whatever that meant) and the Whiteboys; not to
reveal their secrets; and to join them when called upon.
It was supposed, eight or ten thousand were now
actually risen, many of them well armed; and that a far
greater number were ready to rise whenever they should
be called upon.   Those who refused to swear, they
threatened to bury alive.   Two or three they did bury
up to the neck, and left them; where they must quickly
have perished, had they not been found in time by some
travelling by.   At length, toward Easter, a body of
troops, chiefly light horse, were sent against them.
Many were apprehended and committed to gaol; the
rest of them disappeared.   This is the plain, naked fact,
which has been so variously represented.

Whitewashing Kilkenny Marble

Sat. July 10.—We rode to Kilkenny, one of the
pleasantest and the most ancient cities in the kingdom;

and not inferior to any at all in wickedness, or in hatred to this way. I was therefore glad of a permission to preach in the Town Hall; where a small, serious company attended in the evening. Sunday, 11. I went to the cathedral; one of the best built which I have seen in Ireland. The pillars are all of black marble; but the late Bishop ordered them to be white-washed! Indeed, marble is so plentiful near this town, that the very streets are paved with it.

Mon. 12.—I went to Dunmore Cave, three or four miles from Kilkenny. It is full as remarkable as Poole's Hole, or any other in the Peak. The opening is round, parallel to the horizon, and seventy or eighty yards across. In the midst of this, there is a kind of arch, twenty or thirty feet high. By this you enter into the first cave, nearly round, and forty or fifty feet in diameter. It is encompassed with spar-stones, just like those on the sides of Poole's Hole. On one side of the cave is a narrow passage, which goes under the rock two or three hundred yards; on the other, an hollow, which no one has ever been able to find an end of. I suppose this hole too, as well as many others, was formed by the waters of the deluge, retreating into the great abyss, with which probably it communicates.

Mon. 26.—In some respects the work of God in Dublin was more remarkable than even that in London. 1. It is far greater, in proportion to the time, and to the number of people. That society had above seven-and-twenty hundred members; this not a fifth part of the number. Six months after the flame broke out there, we had about thirty witnesses of the great salvation. In Dublin there were about forty in less than four months. 2. The work was more pure. In all this time, while they were mildly and tenderly treated, there were none of them headstrong or unadvisable; none that were wiser than their teachers; none who dreamed of being immortal or infallible, or incapable of temptation: in short, no whimsical or enthusiastic persons: all were calm and sober-minded.

Wesley in Cornwall

Friday, Aug. 27.—I set out for the west; and having preached at Shepton and Middlesey in the way, came on Saturday to Exeter. When I began the service there, the congregation (beside ourselves) were two women, and one man. Before I had done, the room was about half full. This comes of omitting field-preaching.

Sun. 29.—I preached at eight on Southernay Green, to an extremely quiet congregation. At the cathedral we had an useful sermon, and the whole service was performed with great seriousness and decency. Such an organ I never saw or heard before, so large, beautiful, and so finely toned; and the music of " Glory be to God in the highest," I think exceeded the " Messiah " itself. I was well pleased to partake of the Lord's supper with my old opponent, Bishop Lavington. O may we sit down together in the kingdom of our Father!

At five I went to Southernay Green again, and found a multitude of people; but a lewd, profane, drunken vagabond had so stirred up many of the baser sort, that there was much noise, hurry, and confusion. While I was preaching, several things were thrown, and much pains taken to overturn the table; and after I concluded, many endeavoured to throw me down, but I walked through the midst, and left them.

Saturday, Sept. 4.—After preaching in Grampound, I rode on to Truro. I almost expected there would be some disturbance, as it was market-day, and I stood in the street at a small distance from the market. But all was quiet. Indeed both persecution and popular tumult seem to be forgotten in Cornwall.

Sun. 5.—As I was enforcing, in the same place, those solemn words, "God forbid that I should glory, save in the cross of our Lord Jesus Christ," a poor man began to make some tumult; but many cried out "Constables, take him away." They did so, and the hurry was over. At one I preached in the main street at Redruth, where rich and poor were equally attentive. The wind was so high at five, that I could not stand in the usual place at Gwennap. But at a small distance was a hollow, capable of containing many thousand people. I stood on one side of this amphitheatre toward the top, with the people beneath and on all sides, and enlarged on those words in the Gospel for the day (Luke x. 23, 24), "Blessed are the eyes which see the things that ye see, and which hear the things that ye hear."

Wed. 15.—The more I converse with the believers in Cornwall, the more I am convinced that they have sustained great loss for want of hearing the doctrine of Christian perfection clearly and strongly enforced. I see, wherever this is not done, the believers grow dead and cold. Nor can this be prevented, but by keeping up in them an hourly expectation of being perfected in love. I say an hourly expectation; for to expect it at death, or some time hence, is much the same as not expecting it at all.

That detestable practice of cheating the King (smuggling) is no more found in our societies. And since that accursed thing has been put away, the work of God has everywhere increased.

Mon. October 25.—I preached at one, in the shell of the new house at Shepton Mallet. In digging the foundation they found a quarry of stone, which was more than sufficient for the house.

Thur. 28.—One who had adorned the Gospel in life and in death, having desired that I should preach her funeral sermon, I went with a few friends to the house, and sang before the body to the room. I did this the rather, to show my approbation of that solemn custom, and to encourage others to follow it. As we walked, our company swiftly increased, so that we had a very numerous congregation at the room. And who can tell, but some of these may bless God from it to all eternity?

Wesley's Day of Pentecost

Many years ago my brother frequently said, "Your day of Pentecost is not fully come; but I doubt not it will; and you will then hear of persons sanctified, as frequently as you do now of persons justified." Any unprejudiced reader may observe, that it was now fully come. And accordingly we did hear of persons sanctified, in London, and most other parts of England, and in Dublin, and many other parts of Ireland, as frequently as of persons justified; although instances of the latter were far more frequent than they had been for twenty years before. That many of these did not retain the gift of God, is no proof that it was not given them. That many do retain it to this day, is matter of praise and thanksgiving. And many of them are gone to him whom they loved, praising him with their latest breath; just in the spirit of Ann Steed, the first witness in Bristol of the great salvation; who, being worn out with sickness and racking pain, after she had commended to God all that were round her, lifted up her eyes, cried aloud, " Glory! Hallelujah !" and died.

Wesley in Aberdeen Again

1763. Mon. May 16.—Setting out a month later than usual, I judged it needful to make the more haste; so I took post-chaises, and by that means easily reached Newcastle, on Wednesday, 18. Thence I went on at leisure, and came to Edinburgh, on Saturday, 21. The next day I had the satisfaction of spending a little time with Mr. Whitefield. Humanly speaking, he is worn out; but we have to do with him who hath all power in heaven and earth.

Mon. 23.—I rode to Forfar, and on Tuesday, 24, rode on to Aberdeen.

Wed. 25.—I inquired into the state of things here. Surely never was there a more open door. The four ministers of Aberdeen, the minister of the adjoining town, and the three ministers of Old-Aberdeen, hitherto seem to have no dislike, but rather to wish us " good luck in the name of the Lord." Most of the town's people as yet seem to wish us well; so that there is no open opposition of any kind. O what spirit ought a preacher to be of, that he may be able to bear all this sunshine !

About noon I went to Gordon's Hospital, built near the town for poor children. It is an exceeding handsome building, and (what is not common) kept exceeding clean. The gardens are pleasant, well laid out, and in extremely good order; but the old bachelor who founded it, has expressly provided that no woman should ever be there.

At seven, the evening being fair and mild, I preached to a multitude of people, in the College Close, on, " Stand

in the ways and see, and ask for the old paths." But
the next evening, the weather being raw and cold, I
preached in the College Hall. What an amazing willing-
ness to hear runs through this whole kingdom ! There
want only a few zealous, active labourers, who desire
nothing but God; and they might soon carry the Gospel
through all this country, even as high as the Orkneys.

Plain Dealing in Scotland

Fri. 27.—I set out for Edinburgh again. About one
I preached at Brechin. All were deeply attentive.
Perhaps a few may not be forgetful hearers. Afterwards
we rode on to Broughty Castle, two or three miles below
Dundee. We were in hopes of passing the river here,
though we could not at the town; but we found our
horses could not pass till eleven or twelve at night.
So we judged it would be best, to go over ourselves and
leave them behind. In a little time we procured a kind
of a boat, about half as long as a London wherry, and
three or four feet broad. Soon after we had put off, I
perceived it leaked on all sides, nor had we anything
to lade out the water. When we came toward the
middle of the river, which was three miles over, the
wind being high, and the water rough, our boatmen
seemed a little surprised; but we encouraged them to
pull away, and in less than half an hour we landed safe.
Our horses were brought after us; and the next day we
rode on to Kinghorn-ferry, and had a pleasant passage
to Leith.

Sun. 29.—I preached at seven in the High School
yard, Edinburgh. It being the time of the General
Assembly, which drew together, not the ministers only,
but abundance of the nobility and gentry, many of both
sorts were present; but abundantly more at five in the

afternoon. I spake as plain as ever I did in my life. But I never knew any in Scotland offended at plain dealing. In this respect the North Britons are a pattern to all mankind.

Tues. June 7.—There is something remarkable in the manner wherein God revived his work in these parts. A few months ago the generality of people in this circuit were exceeding lifeless. Samuel Meggot, perceiving this, advised the society at Barnard Castle to observe every Friday with fasting and prayer. The very first Friday they met together, God broke in upon them in a wonderful manner; and his work has been increasing among them ever since. The neighbouring societies heard of this, agreed to follow the same rule, and soon experienced the same blessing. Is not the neglect of this plain duty (I mean fasting, ranked by our Lord with almsgiving and prayer) one general occasion of deadness among Christians? Can any one willingly neglect it, and be guiltless?

The Drunkard's Magnificat

Thur. 16.—At five in the evening I preached at Dewsbury, and on Friday, 17, reached Manchester. Here I received a particular account of a remarkable incident: An eminent drunkard of Congleton used to divert himself, whenever there was preaching there, by standing over against the house, cursing and swearing at the preacher. One evening he had a fancy to step in, and hear what the man had to say. He did so: but it made him so uneasy that he could not sleep all night. In the morning he was more uneasy still; he walked in the fields, but all in vain, till it came in his mind to go to one of his merry companions, who was always ready to abuse the Methodists. He told him how he

was, and asked what he should do. " Do ! " said
Samuel, " go and join the society. I will; for I was
never so uneasy in my life." They did so without
delay. But presently David cried out, " I am sorry I
joined; for I shall get drunk again, and they will turn
me out." However, he stood firm for four days ; on the
fifth, he was persuaded by the old companions to " take
one pint," and then another, and another, till one of
them said, " See, here is a Methodist drunk ! "

David started up, and knocked him over, chair and
all. He then drove the rest out of the house, caught
up the landlady, carried her out, threw her into the
kennel; went back to the house, broke down the door,
threw it into the street, and then ran into the fields, tore
his hair, and rolled up and down on the ground. In a
day or two was a love-feast ; he stole in, getting behind,
that none might see him. While Mr. Furze was at
prayer, he was seized with a dreadful agony, both of body
and mind. This caused many to wrestle with God for
him. In a while he sprung up on his feet, stretched
out his hands, and cried aloud, " All my sins are forgiven ! " At the same instant, one on the other side of
the room cried out, " Jesus is mine ! And he has taken
away all my sins." This was Samuel H. David burst
through the people, caught him in his arms, and said,
"Come, let us sing the Virgin Mary's song; I never
could sing it before. ' My soul doth magnify the Lord,
and my spirit doth rejoice in God my Saviour.' " And
their following behaviour plainly showed the reality of
their profession.

Mon. 20.—I preached at Maxfield about noon. As
I had not been well, and was not quite recovered, our
brethren insisted on sending me in a chaise to Burslem,
Between four and five I quitted the chaise, and took my

horse. Presently after, hearing a cry, I looked back, and saw the chaise upside down (the wheel having violently struck against a stone), and well nigh dashed in pieces. About seven I preached to a large congregation at Burslem; these poor potters, four years ago, were as wild and ignorant as any of the colliers in Kingswood. Lord, thou hast power over thy own clay!

Wesley Praises Wales

Sat. Aug. 20 (Brecknock).—We took horse at four, and rode through one of the pleasantest countries in the world. When we came to Trecastle, we had rode fifty miles in Monmouthshire and Brecknockshire; and I will be bold to say, all England does not afford such a line of fifty miles' length, for fields, meadows, woods, brooks, and gently-rising mountains, fruitful to the very top. Carmarthenshire, into which we came soon after, has at least as fruitful a soil; but it is not so pleasant, because it has fewer mountains, though abundance of brooks and rivers. About five I preached on the green at Carmarthen to a large number of deeply attentive people. Here two gentlemen from Pembroke met me, with whom we rode to St. Clare, intending to lodge there; but the inn was quite full: so we concluded to try for Larn, though we knew not the way, and it was now quite dark. Just then came up an honest man who was riding thither, and we willingly bore him company.

Thur. 25.—I was more convinced than ever that the preaching like an Apostle, without joining together those that are awakened, and training them up in the ways of God, is only begetting children for the murderer. How much preaching has there been for these twenty years all over Pembrokeshire! But no regular societies, no discipline, no order or connection ; and the consequence is, that nine in ten of the once-awakened are now faster asleep than ever.

Fri. 26.—We designed to take horse at four (from Haverfordwest), but the rain poured down, so that one could scarce look out. About six, however, we set out, and rode through heavy rain to St. Clare. Having then little hopes of crossing the sands, we determined to go round by Carmarthen ; but the hostler told us we might save several miles, by going to Llansteffan's Ferry. We came thither about noon, where a good woman informed us the boat was aground, and would not pass till the evening : so we judged it best to go by Carmarthen still. But when we had rode three or four miles, I recollected that I had heard speak of a ford, which would save us some miles' riding. We inquired of an old man, who soon mounted his horse, showed us the way, and rode through the river before us.

Soon after my mare dropped a shoe, which occasioned so much loss of time, that we could not ride the sands, but were obliged to go round, through a miserable road to Llanellos. To mend the matter, our guide lost his way, both before we came to Llanellos and after ; so that it was as much as we could do to reach Bocher Ferry a little after sunset. Knowing it was impossible then to reach Penreese, as we designed, we went on straight to Swansea.

Methodists and their Wealth

Sat. Sept. 17 (Bristol).—I preached on the green at Bedminster. I am apt to think many of the hearers scarce ever heard a Methodist before, or perhaps any other preacher. What but field-preaching could reach these poor sinners? And are not their souls also precious in the sight of God?

Sun. 18.—I preached in the morning in Princess Street, to a numerous congregation. Two or three gentleman, so-called, laughed at first; but in a few minutes they were as serious as the rest. On Monday evening I gave our brethren a solemn caution, not to "love the world, neither the things of the world." This will be their grand danger: as they are industrious and frugal, they must needs increase in goods. This appears already: in London, Bristol, and most other trading towns, those who are in business have increased in substance seven-fold, some of them twenty, yea, an hundred-fold. What need, then, have these of the strongest warnings, lest they be entangled therein, and perish!

Fri. 23.—I preached at Bath. Riding home we saw a coffin, carrying into St. George's church, with many children attending it. When we came near, we found they were our own children, attending the corpse of one of their school-fellows, who had died of the small-pox; and God thereby touched many of their hearts in a manner they never knew before.

Mon. 26.—I preached to the prisoners in Newgate, and in the afternoon rode over to Kingswood, where I had a solemn watch-night, and an opportunity of speaking closely to the children. One is dead, two recovered, seven are ill still; and the hearts of all are like melting wax.

Sat. October 1.—I returned to London, and found our house in ruins, great part of it being taken down, in order to a thorough repair. But as much remained as I wanted: six foot square suffices me by day or by night.

Thur. Dec. 22.—I spent a little time in a visit

to Mr. M——; twenty years ago a zealous and useful
magistrate, now a picture of human nature in disgrace ;
feeble in body and mind ; slow of speech and of understanding.   Lord, let me not live to be useless !

1764. Mon. Jan. 16.—I rode to High Wycombe,
and preached to a more numerous and serious congregation than ever I saw there before.   Shall there be yet
another day of visitation to this careless people ?

A large number was present at five in the morning :
but my face and gums were so swelled I could hardly
speak.   After I took horse, they grew worse and worse,
till it began to rain.   I was then persuaded to put on
an oil-case hood, which (the wind being very high) kept
rubbing continually on my cheek, till both pain and
swelling were gone.

A Difficult Crossing

Between twelve and one we crossed Ensham Ferry.
The water was like a sea on both sides.   I asked the
ferryman, "Can we ride the causeway ? "   He said,
"Yes, sir; if you keep in the middle."   But this was
the difficulty, as the whole causeway was covered with
water to a considerable depth.   And this in many parts
ran over the causeway with the swiftness and violence of
a sluice.   Once my mare lost both her fore feet, but she
gave a spring, and recovered the causeway : otherwise
we must have taken a swim ; for the water on either
side was ten or twelve feet deep.   However, after one or
two more plunges more, we got through, and came safe
to Whitney.

Mon. Feb. 6.—I opened the new chapel at Wapping.

Thur. 16.—I once more took a serious walk through
the tombs in Westminster Abbey.   What heaps of un-
meaning stone and marble !   But there was one tomb

which showed common sense; that beautiful figure of Mr. Nightingale endeavouring to screen his lovely wife from Death. Here indeed the marble seems to speak, and the statues appear only not alive.

Fri. 24—I returned to London. Wednesday, 29. I heard "Judith," an oratorio, performed at the Lock. Some parts of it are exceedingly fine ; but there are two things in all modern pieces of music, which I could never reconcile to common sense. One is, singing the same words ten times over; the other, singing different words by different persons, at one and the same time. And this, in the most solemn addresses to God, whether by way of prayer or of thanksgiving. This can never be defended by all the musicians in Europe, till reas n is quite out of date.

Wesley at Birmingham, Walsall, and Derby

Wed. March 21.—We had an exceeding large con gregation at Birmingham, in what was formerly the playhouse. Happy would it be, if all the playhouses in the kingdom were converted to so good an use. After service the mob gathered, and threw some dirt and stones at those who were going out. But it is probable they will soon be calmed, as some of them are in gaol already. A few endeavoured to make a disturbance the next evening during the preaching ; but it was lost labour ; the congregation would not be diverted from taking earnest heed to the things that were spoken.

Fri. 23.—I rode to Dudley, formerly a den of lions, but now as quiet as Bristol. They had just finished their preaching-house, which was thoroughly filled. I saw no trifler ; but many in tears.

Mon. 26.—I was desired to preach at Walsal. James Jones was alarmed at the motion, apprehending there would be much disturbance.   However, I determined to make the trial.   Coming into the house, I met with a token for good.   A woman was telling her neighbour why she came : " I had a desire," said she, " to hear this man ; yet I durst not, because I heard so much ill of him ; but this morning I dreamed I was praying earnestly, and I heard a voice, saying, ' See the eighth verse of the first chapter of St. John.'   I waked, and got my Bible, and read, ' He was not that Light, but was sent to bear witness of that Light.'   I got up, and came away with all my heart."

The house not being capable of containing the people, about seven I began preaching abroad ; and there was no opposer, no, nor a trifler to be seen.   All present were earnestly attentive.   How is Walsal changed !   How has God either tamed the wild beasts, or chained them up !

Tues. 27.—We rode to Derby.   Mr. Dobinson believed it would be best for me to preach in the market-place, as there seemed to be a general inclination in the town, even among people of fashion, to hear me.   He had mentioned it to the mayor, who said he did not apprehend there would be the least disturbance ; but if there should be any thing of the kind, he would take care to suppress it.   A multitude of people were gathered at five, and were pretty quiet till I had named my text.   Then " the beasts of the people " lifted up their voice, hallooing and shouting on every side.   Finding it impossible to be heard, I walked softly away.   An innumerable retinue followed me ; but only a few pebble-stones were thrown, and no one hurt at all.   Most of the rabble followed quite to Mr. D——'s house ; but it seems, without any malice prepense ; for they stood stock-still about an hour, and then quietly went away.

Sat. 31 (Rotherham).—An odd circumstance occurred during the morning preaching. It was well, only serious persons were present. An ass walked gravely in at the gate, came up to the door of the house, lifted up his head, and stood stock-still, in a posture of deep attention. Might not "the dumb beast reprove" many who have far less decency, and not much more understanding?

"No Law for Methodists"

At noon I preached (the room being too small to contain the people) in a yard, near the bridge, in Doncaster. The wind was high and exceeding sharp, and blew all the time on the side of my head. In the afternoon I was seized with a sore throat, almost as soon as I came to Epworth; however, I preached, though with some difficulty; but afterward I could hardly speak. Being better the next day, Sunday, April 1, I preached about one at Westwood Side, and soon after four, in the market-place at Epworth, to a numerous congregation. At first, indeed, but few could hear; but the more I spoke, the more my voice was strengthened, till toward the close, all my pain and weakness were gone, and all could hear distinctly.

Mon. April 2.—I had a day of rest. Tuesday, 3, I preached, about nine, at Scotter, a town six or seven miles east of Epworth, where a sudden flame is broke out, many being convinced of sin almost at once, and many justified. But there were many adversaries stirred up by a bad man, who told them, "There is no law for Methodists." Hence continual riots followed; till, after a while, an upright magistrate took the cause in hand, and so managed both the rioters and him who set them at work, that they have been quiet as lambs ever since.

Thur. 5.—About eleven I preached at Elsham. The two persons who are the most zealous and active here are the steward and gardener of a gentleman, whom the minister persuaded to turn them off unless they would leave " this way." He gave them a week to consider of it ; at the end of which they calmly answered, " Sir, we choose rather to want bread here, than to want 'a drop of water' hereafter." He replied, " Then follow your own conscience, so you do my business as well as formerly."

Fri. 6.—I preached at Ferry at nine in the morning, and in the evening ; and, about noon, in Sir N. H.'s hall, at Gainsborough. Almost as soon as I began to speak, a cock began to crow over my head; but he was quickly dislodged, and the whole congregation, rich and poor, were quiet and attentive.

Wesley Unhorsed

Sun. 8.—I set out for Misterton, though the common road was impassable, being all under water; but we found a way to ride round. I preached at eight, and I saw not one inattentive hearer. In our return, my mare rushing violently through a gate, struck my heel against the gate-post, and left me behind her in an instant, laid on my back at full length. She stood still till I rose and mounted again; and neither of us was hurt at all.

Tues. 10.—The wind abating, we took boat at Barton, with two such brutes as I have seldom seen. Their blasphemy, and stupid gross obscenity, were beyond all I ever heard. We first spoke to them mildly; but it had no effect. At length we were constrained to rebuke them sharply ; and they kept themselves tolerably within bounds, till we landed at Hull. I preached at five, two hours sooner than was expected ; by this means we had tolerable room for the greatest part of them that came ; and I believe not many of them came in vain.

Mon. 16.—At six I began preaching in the street at Thirsk. The congregation was exceeding large. Just as I named my text, " What is a man profited, if he shall gain the whole world and lose his own soul ? " a man on horseback, who had stopped to see what was the matter, changed colour and trembled. Probably he might have resolved to save his soul, had not his drunken companion dragged him away.

Wesley on Holy Island

Mon. May 21.—I took my leave of Newcastle; and about noon preached in the market-place at Morpeth. A few of the hearers were a little ludicrous at first; but their mirth was quickly spoiled. In the evening I preached in the Court-house at Alnwick, where I rested the next day. Wednesday, 23. I rode over the sands to Holy Island, once the famous seat of a Bishop ; now the residence of a few poor families, who live chiefly by fishing. At one side of the town are the ruins of a cathedral, with an adjoining monastery. It appears to have been a lofty and elegant building, the middle aisle being almost entire. I preached in what was once the market-place, to almost all the inhabitants of the island, and distributed some little books among them, for which they were exceeding thankful. In the evening I preached at Berwick-upon-Tweed ; the next evening at Dunbar ; and on Friday, 25, about ten, at Haddington, in Provost D.'s yard, to a very elegant congregation. But I expect little good will be done here ; for we begin at the wrong end : religion must not go from the greatest to the least, or the power would appear to be of men.

In the evening I preached at Musselborough; and the next, on the Calton Hill at Edinburgh. It being the time of the General Assembly, many of the Ministers were there. The wind was high and sharp, and blew away a few delicate ones. But most of the congregation did not stir till I had concluded.

Sun. 27.—At seven I preached in the High School yard, on the other side of the city. The morning was extremely cold. In the evening it blew a storm. However, having appointed to be on the Calton Hill, I began there, to an huge congregation. At first, the wind was a little troublesome; but I soon forgot it. And so did the people for an hour and a half, in which I fully delivered my own soul.

Wesley at the General Assembly

Mon. 28.—I spent some hours at the General Assembly, composed of about an hundred and fifty ministers. I was surprised to find 1. That any one was admitted, even lads, twelve or fourteen years old: 2. That the chief speakers were lawyers, six or seven on one side only: 3. That a single question took up the whole time, which, when I went away, seemed to be as far from a conclusion as ever, namely, " Shall Mr. Lindsay be removed to Kilmarnock parish or not?" The argument for it was, " He has a large family, and this living is twice as good as his own." The argument against it was, " The people are resolved not to hear him, and will leave the kirk if he comes." If then the real point in view had been, as their law directs, " the greater good of the Church," instead of taking up five hours, the debate might have been determined in five minutes.

On Monday and Tuesday I spoke to the members of

the society severally.   Thursday, 31.   I rode to Dundee, and, about half an hour after six, preached on the side of a meadow near the town.   Poor and rich attended. Indeed, there is seldom fear of wanting a congregation in Scotland.   But the misfortune is, they know everything : so they learn nothing.

At Inverness

Thur. June 7.—I rode over to Sir Archibald Grant's, twelve computed miles from Aberdeen.   It is surprising to see how the country between is improved even within these three years.   On every side the wild, dreary moors are ploughed up, and covered with rising corn.   All the ground near Sir Archibald's, in particular, is as well cultivated as most in England.   About seven I preached. The kirk was pretty well filled, though upon short notice.   Certainly this is a nation " swift to hear, and slow to speak," though not " slow to wrath."

Sun. 10.—About eight we reached Inverness.   I could not preach abroad, because of the rain ; nor could I hear of any convenient room ; so that I was afraid my coming hither would be in vain, all ways seemed to be blocked up.   At ten I went to the kirk.   After service, Mr. Fraser, one of the ministers, invited us to dinner, and then to drink tea.   As we were drinking tea, he asked at what hour I would please to preach.   I said, " At half-hour past five."   The high kirk was filled in a very short time ; and I have seldom found greater liberty of spirit.   The other minister came afterwards to our inn, and showed the most cordial affection.   Were it only for this day, I should not have regretted the riding an hundred miles.

Mon. 11.—A gentleman who lives three miles from the town invited me to his house, assuring me the

minister of his parish would be glad if I would make use
of his kirk; but time would not permit, as I had appointed to be at Aberdeen on Wednesday. All I could
do was, to preach once more at Inverness. I think the
church was fuller now than before; and I could not
but observe the remarkable behaviour of the whole
congregation after service. Neither man, woman, nor
child spoke one word all the way down the main
street. Indeed the seriousness of the people is the
less surprising, when it is considered, that, for at least
an hundred years, this town has had such a succes-
sion of pious ministers as very few in Great Britain
have known.

After Edinburgh, Glasgow, and Aberdeen, I think
Inverness is the largest town I have seen in Scotland.
The main streets are broad and straight; the houses
mostly old, but not very bad, nor very good. It stands
in a pleasant and fruitful country, and has all things
needful for life and godliness. The people in general
speak remarkably good English, and are of a friendly
courteous behaviour.

A Sermon and Congregation to Order

About eleven we took horse. While we were dining
at Nairn, the inn-keeper said, " Sir, the gentlemen of
the town have read the little book you gave me on
Saturday, and would be glad if you would please to
give them a sermon." Upon my consenting, the bell
was immediately rung, and the congregation was quickly
in the kirk. O what a difference is there between South
and North Britain! Every one here at least loves to
hear the word of God; and none takes it into his head
to speak one uncivil word to any, for endeavouring to
save their souls.

Doubting whether Mr. Grant was come home, Mr. Kershaw called at the Grange Green, near Forres, while I rode forward.   Mr. Grant soon called me back.   I have seldom seen a more agreeable place.   The house is an old castle, which stands on a little hill, with a delightful prospect all four ways ; and the hospitable master has left nothing undone to make it still more agreeable.   He showed us all his improvements, which are very considerable in every branch of husbandry.   In his gardens many things were more forward than at Aberdeen, yea, or Newcastle.   And how is it, that none but one Highland gentleman has discovered that we have a tree in Britain, as easily raised as an ash ; the wood of which is of full as fine a red as mahogany, namely, the laburnum ?   I defy any mahogany to exceed the chairs which he has lately made of this.

Tues. 12.—We rode through the pleasant and fertile county of Murray to Elgin.   I never suspected before that there was any such country as this near an hundred and fifty miles beyond Edinburgh ; a country which is supposed to have generally six weeks more sunshine in a year than any part of Great Britain.

At Elgin are the ruins of a noble cathedral ; the largest that I remember to have seen in the kingdom.   We rode thence to the Spey, the most rapid river, next the Rhine, that I ever saw.   Though the water was not breast-high to our horses, they could very hardly keep their feet. We dined at Keith, and rode on to Strathbogie, much improved by the linen-manufacture.   All the country from Fochabers to Strathbogie has little houses scattered up and down ; and not only the valleys, but the mountains themselves, are improved with the utmost care. There want only more trees to make them more pleasant than most of the mountains in England.   The whole family at our inn, eleven or twelve in number, gladly joined with us in prayer at night. Indeed, so they did at every inn where we lodged ; for among all the sins they have imported from England, the Scots have not yet learned, at least not the common people, to scoff at sacred things.

Wed. 13.—We reached Aberdeen about one. Between six and seven, both this evening and the next I preached in the shell of the new house, and found it a time of much consolation. Friday, 15. We set out early, and came to Dundee just as the boat was going off. We designed to lodge at the house on the other side ; but could not get either meat, drink, or good words ; so we were constrained to ride on to Cupar. After travelling near ninety miles, I found no weariness at all; neither were our horses hurt. Thou, O Lord, dost save both man and beast !

Wesley and a Scotch Communion

Sat. 16.—We had a ready passage at Kinghorn, and in the evening I preached on the Calton Hill, to a very large congregation ; but a still larger assembled at seven on Sunday morning in the High School yard. Being afterwards informed that the Lord's supper was to be administered in the west kirk, I knew not what to do ; but at length I judged it best to embrace the opportunity, though I did not admire the manner of administration. After the usual morning service, the minister enumerated several sorts of sinners, whom he forbade to approach. Two long tables were set on the sides of one aisle, covered with table-cloths. On each side of them a bench was placed for the people. Each table held four or five and thirty.

Three ministers sat at the top, behind a cross-table ;

one of whom made a long exhortation, closed with the words of our Lord ; and, then, breaking the bread, gave it to him who sat on each side him.   A piece of bread was then given to him who sat first on each of the four benches.   He broke off a little piece, and gave the bread to the next; so it went on, the deacons giving more when wanted.   A cup was then given to the first person on each bench, and so by one to another.   The minister continued his exhortation all the time they were receiving ; then four verses of the twenty-second Psalm were sung, while new persons sat down at the tables.   A second minister then prayed, consecrated, and exhorted.   I was informed the service usually lasted till five in the evening.   How much more simple, as well as more solemn, is the service of the Church of England !

The evening congregation on the hill was far the largest I have seen in the kingdom; and the most deeply affected.   Many were in tears ; more seemed cut to the heart.   Surely this time will not soon be forgotten. Will it not appear in the annals of eternity?

Wesley's Likes and Dislikes

Mon. July 2.—I gave a fair hearing to two of our brethren who had proved bankrupts. Such we immediately exclude from our society, unless it plainly appears not to be their own fault.   Both these were in a prosperous way till they fell into that wretched trade of bill-broking, wherein no man continues long without being wholly ruined.   By this means, not being sufficiently accurate in their accounts, they ran back without being sensible of it.   Yet it was quite clear that I—— R—— is an honest man ; I would hope the same concerning the other.

Tues. 3 (Leeds).—I was reflecting on an odd circumstance, which I cannot account for. I never relish a
tune at first hearing, not till I have almost learned to
sing it; and as I learn it more perfectly, I gradually
lose my relish for it. I observe something similar in
poetry ; yea, in all the objects of imagination. I seldom
relish verses at first hearing; till I have heard them
over and over, they give me no pleasure ; and they give
me next to none when I have heard them a few times
more, so as to be quite familiar. Just so a face or a
picture, which does not strike me at first, becomes more
pleasing as I grow more acquainted with it ; but only
to a certain point : for when I am too much acquainted,
it is no longer pleasing. O, how imperfectly do we
understand even the machine which we carry about
us !

Thur. 5.—I had the comfort of leaving our brethren
at Leeds united in peace and love. About one I
preached in a meadow at Wakefield. At first the sun
was inconvenient ; but it was not many minutes before
that inconvenience was removed by the clouds coming
between. We had not only a larger, but a far more
attentive, congregation than ever was seen here before.
One, indeed, a kind of gentleman, was walking away
with great unconcern, when I spoke aloud. " Does
Gallio care for none of these things ? But where will
you go, with the wrath of God on your head, and the
curse of God on your back ? " He stopped short,
stood still, and went no farther till the sermon was
ended.

Sat. 14.—In the evening I preached at Liverpool;
and the next day, Sunday, 15, the house was full
enough. Many of the rich and fashionable were there,
and behaved with decency. Indeed, I have always

observed more courtesy and humanity at Liverpool than at most sea-ports in England.

She Thought, "I Laugh Prettily."

Mon. 16.—In the evening the house was fuller, if possible, than the night before. I preached on the "one thing needful"; and the rich behaved as seriously as the poor. Only one young gentlewoman (I heard) laughed much. Poor thing! Doubtless she thought, "I laugh prettily."

Fri. 20.—At noon we made the same shift at Congleton as when I was here last. I stood in the window, having put as many women as it would contain into the house. The rest, with the men, stood below in the meadow, and many of the townsmen wild enough. I have scarce found such enlargement of heart since I came from Newcastle. The brutes resisted long, but were at length overcome; not above five or six excepted. Surely man shall not long have the upper hand; God will get unto himself the victory.

It rained all the day till seven in the evening, when I began preaching at Burslem. Even the poor potters here are a more civilised people than the better sort (so called) at Congleton. A few stood with their hats on; but none spoke a word, or offered to make the least disturbance.

Sat. 21.—I rode to Bilbrook, near Wolverhampton, and preached between two and three. Thence we went on to Madeley, an exceeding pleasant village, encompassed with trees and hills. It was a great comfort to me to converse once more with a Methodist of the old stamp, denying himself, taking up his cross, and resolved to be "altogether a Christian."

Sun. 22.—At ten Mr. Fletcher read prayers, and I

preached on those words in the gospel, "I am the good Shepherd : the good Shepherd layeth down his life for the sheep." The church would nothing near contain the congregation ; but a window near the pulpit being taken down, those who could not come in stood in the churchyard, and I believe all could hear. The congregation, they said, used to be much smaller in the afternoon than in the morning ; but I could not discern the least difference, either in number or seriousness.

I found employment enough for the intermediate hours, in praying with various companies who hung about the house, insatiably hungering and thirsting after the good word.

An Exhausting Day

Wed. 25.—I took horse a little after four, and, about two, preached in the market-place at Llanidloes, two or three and forty miles from Shrewsbury. At three we rode forward through the mountains to the Fountain-head. I was for lodging there ; but Mr. B—— being quite unwilling, we mounted again about seven. After having rode an hour, we found we were quite out of the way, having been wrong directed at setting out. We were then told to ride over some grounds ; but our path soon ended in the edge of a bog : however, we got through to a little house, where an honest man, instantly mounting his horse, galloped before us, up hill and down, till he brought us into a road, which, he said, led straight to Roes-fair.

We rode on, till another met us, and said, "No ; this is the way to Aberystwith. If you go to Roes-fair, you must turn back, and ride down to yonder bridge." The master of a little house near the bridge then directed us to the next village, where we inquired again (it being past nine), and were once more set exactly wrong. Having wandered an hour upon the mountains, through rocks, and bogs, and precipices, we, with abundance of difficulty, got back to the little house near the bridge. It was in vain to think of rest there, it being full of drunken, roaring miners; besides that, there was but one bed in the house, and neither grass, nor hay, nor corn, to be had. So we hired one of them to walk with us to Roes-fair, though he was miserably drunk, till, by falling all his length in a purling stream, he came tolerably to his senses. Between eleven and twelve we came to the inn; but neither here could we get any hay.

When we were in bed, the good hostler and miner thought good to mount our beasts. I believe it was not long before we rose that they put them into the stable. But the mule was cut in several places, and my mare was bleeding like a pig, from a wound behind, two inches deep, made, it seemed, by a stroke with a pitch-fork. What to do we could not tell, till I remembered, I had a letter for one Mr. Nathaniel Williams, whom, upon inquiry, I found to live but a mile off. We walked thither, and found "an Israelite indeed," who gladly received both man and beast.

After I had got a little rest, Mr. W. desired me to give an exhortation to a few of his neighbours. None was more struck therewith than one of his own family, who before cared for none of these things. He sent a servant with us after dinner to Tregarron, from whence we had a plain road to Lampeter.

Fri. 27.—We rode through a lovely vale, and over pleasant and fruitful hills, to Carmarthen. Thence, after a short bait, we went on to Pembroke, and came before I was expected; so I rested that night, having not quite recovered my journey from Shrewsbury to Roes-fair.

Sun. 29.—The minister of St. Mary's sent me word he was very willing I should preach in his church : but, before service began, the mayor sent to forbid it ; so he preached a very useful sermon himself.   The mayor's behaviour so disgusted many of the gentry, that they resolved to hear where they could ; and accordingly flocked together in the evening from all parts of the town : and perhaps the taking up this cross may profit them more than my sermon in the church would have done.

Seven Hours on Horseback

Mon. 30.—I rode to Haverfordwest : but no notice had been given, nor did any in the town know of my coming.   However, after a short time, I walked up toward the castle, and began singing an hymn.   The people presently ran together from all quarters.   They have curiosity at least; and some, I cannot doubt, were moved by a nobler principle.   Were zealous and active labourers here, what an harvest might there be, even in this corner of the land!   We returned through heavy rain to Pembroke.

Tues. 31.   We set out for Glamorganshire, and rode up and down steep and stony mountains, for about five hours, to Larn.   Having procured a pretty ready passage there, we went on to Lansteffan Ferry, where we were in some danger of being swallowed up in the mud before we could reach the water.   Between one and two we reached Kidwelly, having been more than seven hours on horseback, in which time we could have rode round by Carmarthen with more ease both to man and beast.

I have, therefore, taken my leave of these ferries ;

considering we save no time by crossing them (not even when we have a ready passage), and so have all the trouble, danger, and expense, clear gains. I wonder that any man of common sense, who has once made the experiment, should ever ride from Pembroke to Swansea any other way than by Carmarthen.

The Ride from Pembroke to Swansea

An honest man at Kidwelly told us there was no difficulty in riding the sands; so we rode on. In ten minutes one overtook us who used to guide persons over them; and it was well he did, or, in all probability, we had been swallowed up. The whole sands are at least ten miles over, with many streams of quicksands intermixed. But our guide was thoroughly acquainted with them, and with the road on the other side. By his help, between five and six, we came well tired to Oxwych in Gower.

I had sent two persons on Sunday, that they might be there early on Monday, and so sent notice of my coming all over the country : but they came to Oxwych scarce a quarter of an hour before me; so that the poor people had no notice at all : nor was there any to take us in; the person with whom the preacher used to lodge being three miles out of town. After I had stayed a while in the street (for there was no public-house), a poor woman gave me house room. Having had nothing since breakfast, I was very willing to eat or drink; but she simply told me, she had nothing in the house but a dram of gin. However, I afterwards procured a dish of tea at another house, and was much refreshed. About seven I preached to a little company, and again in the morning. They were all attention; so that even for the sake of this handful of people I did not regret my labour.

Sun. November 4.—I proposed to the leaders, the

assisting the Society for the Reformation of Manners with regard to their heavy debt. One of them asked, " Ought we not to pay our own debt first ? " After some consultations, it was agreed to attempt it. The general debt of the society in London occasioned chiefly by repairing the Foundery and chapels, and by building at Wapping and Snowsfields, was about nine hundred pounds. This I laid before the society in the evening, and desired them all to set their shoulders to the work, either by a present contribution, or by subscribing what they could pay, on the 1st of January, February or March.

Mon. 5 (London).—My scraps of time this week I employed in setting down my present thoughts upon a single life, which indeed, are just the same they have been these thirty years ; and the same they must be, unless I give up my Bible.

Wesley's Experiments with Lions

Mon. Dec. 31.—I thought it would be worth while to make an odd experiment. Remembering how surprisingly fond of music the lion at Edinburgh was, I determined to try whether this was the case with all animals of the same kind. I accordingly went to the Tower with one who plays on the German flute. He began playing near four or five lions ; only one of these (the rest not seeming to regard it at all) rose up, came to the front of his den, and seemed to be all attention. Meantime, a tiger in the same den started up, leaped over the lion's back, turned and ran under his belly, leaped over him again, and so to and fro incessantly. Can we account for this by any principle of mechanism ? Can we account for it at all?

1765. Tues. January 1.—This week I wrote an

answer to a warm letter, published in the "London Magazine," the author whereof is much displeased that I presume to doubt of the modern astronomy. I cannot help it. Nay, the more I consider, the more my doubts increase : so that, at present, I doubt whether any man on earth knows either the distance or magnitude, I will not say of a fixed star, but of Saturn, or Jupiter ; yea, of the sun or moon.

Sun. 20.—I employed all my leisure hours this week in revising my letters and papers. Abundance of them I committed to the flames. Perhaps some of the rest may see the light when I am gone.

Breakfast with Mr. Whitefield

Mon. October 21.—I went in the coach from Bristol to Salisbury, and on Thursday, 24, came to London.

Mon. 28.—I breakfasted with Mr. Whitefield, who seemed to be an old, old man, being fairly worn out in his Master's service, though he has hardly seen fifty years, and yet it pleases God that I, who am now in my sixty-third year, find no disorder, no weakness, no decay, no difference from what I was at five-and-twenty ; only that I have fewer teeth, and more grey hairs.

Sun. November 24.—I preached on those words in the lesson for the day, " The Lord our righteousness." I said not one thing which I have not said, at least, fifty times within this twelvemonth ; yet it appeared to many entirely new, who much importuned me to print my sermon, supposing it would stop the mouths of all gainsayers. Alas, for their simplicity ! In spite of all I can print, say, or do, will not those who seek occasion of offence find occasion ?

Tues. December 3.—I rode to Dover, and found a little company more united together than they have been for many years. Whilst several of them continued to rob the King, we seemed to be ploughing upon the sand; but since they have cut off the right hand, the word of God sinks deep into their hearts.

Thur. 5.—I rode back to Feversham. Here I was quickly informed that the mob and the magistrates had agreed together to drive Methodism, so called, out of the town. After preaching, I told them what we had been constrained to do by the magistrate at Rolvenden; who perhaps would have been richer, by some hundred pounds, had he never meddled with the Methodists; concluding, "Since we have both God and the law on our side, if we can have peace by fair means, we had much rather; we should be exceeding glad; but if not, we will have peace."

Wed. 18.—Riding through the Borough, all my mare's feet flew up, and she fell with my leg under her. A gentleman, stepping out, lifted me up, and helped me into his shop. I was exceeding sick, but was presently relieved by a little hartshorn and water. After resting a few minutes, I took a coach; but when I was cold, found myself much worse; being bruised on my right arm, my breast, my knee, leg, and ankle, which swelled exceedingly. However, I went on to Shoreham; where by applying treacle twice a day, all the soreness was removed, and I recovered some strength, so as to be able to walk a little on plain ground. The word of God does at length bear fruit here also, and Mr. P. is comforted over all his trouble. Saturday, 21. Being not yet able to ride, I returned in a chariot to London.

Sun. 22.—I was ill able to go through the service at West Street; but God provided for this also. Mr.

Greaves, being just ordained, came straight to the chapel, and gave me the assistance I wanted.

Thur. 26.—I should have been glad of a few days' rest, but it could not be at this busy season. However, being electrified morning and evening, my lameness mended, though but slowly.

1766. Fri. Jan. 31.—Mr. Whitefield called upon me. He breathes nothing but peace and love. Bigotry cannot stand before him, but hides its head wherever he comes.

Two Deeds

Wed. February 5 (London).—One called upon me who had been cheated out of a large fortune, and was now perishing for want of bread. I had a desire to clothe him, and send him back to his own country; but was short of money. However, I appointed him to call again in an hour. He did so; but before he came, one from whom I expected nothing less, put twenty guineas into my hand; so I ordered him to be clothed from head to foot, and sent him straight away to Dublin.

Mon. April 7.—I preached at Warrington, about noon, to a large congregation, rich and poor, learned and unlearned. I never spoke more plain; nor have I ever seen a congregation listen with more attention. Thence I rode to Liverpool, and thoroughly regulated the society, which had great need of it. Wednesday, 9. I took much pains with a sensible woman who had taken several imprudent steps. But it was labour lost—neither argument nor persuasion made the least impression. O, what power less than almighty can convince a thorough paced enthusiast!

Thur. 10.—I looked over the wonderful deed which was lately made here; on which I observed, 1. It takes

Painted at the age of 63 by Nathaniel Hone, R. A.
(*National Portrait Gallery*)
JOHN WESLEY (1703-1791)

up three large skins of parchment, and so could not cost less than six guineas ; whereas our own deed, transcribed by a friend, would not have cost six shillings. 2. It is verbose beyond all sense and reason ; and withal so ambiguously worded, that one passage only might find matter for a suit of ten or twelve years in Chancery. 3. It everywhere calls the house a meeting-house, a name which I particularly object to. 4. It leaves no power either to the assistant or me, so much as to place or displace a steward. 5. Neither I, nor all the Conference, have power to send the same preacher two years together. To crown all, 6. If a preacher is not appointed at the Conference, the trustees and the congregation are to choose one by most votes ! And can any one wonder I dislike this deed, which tears the Methodist discipline up by the roots ?

Is it not strange, that any who have the least regard either for me or our discipline, should scruple to alter this uncouth deed ?

Wesley Covered with Mud

Tues. June 24.—Before eight we reached Dumfries, and after a short bait pushed on in hopes of reaching Solway-frith before the sea was come in. Designing to call at an inn by the frith side, we inquired the way, and were directed to leave the main road, and go straight to the house which we saw before us. In ten minutes Duncan Wright was embogged ; however, the horse plunged on, and got through. I was inclined to turn back : but Duncan telling me I needed only go a little to the left, I did so, and sunk at once to my horse's shoulders. He sprung up twice, and twice sunk again, each time deeper than before. At the third plunge he threw me on one side, and we both made shift to scramble out. I was covered with fine, soft mud, from my feet to the crown of my head; yet, blessed be God, not hurt at all. But we could not cross till between seven and eight o'clock. An honest man crossed with us, who went two miles out of his way to guide us over the sands to Skilburness; where we found a little, clean house, and passed a comfortable night.

Sat. July 19.—I took a view of Beverley minster, such a parish church as has scarce its fellow in England. It is a most beautiful as well as stately building, both within and without, and is kept more nicely clean than any cathedral which I have seen in the kingdom; but where will it be when the earth is burned up, and the elements melt with fervent heat? About one I preached at Pocklington (though my strength was much exhausted), and in the evening at York.

Sun. 27.—As Baildon church would not near contain the congregation, after the prayers were ended, I came out into the church-yard, both morning and afternoon. The wind was extremely high, and blew in my face all the time; yet, I believe, all the people could hear. At Bradford there was so huge a multitude, and the rain so damped my voice, that many in the skirts of the congregation could not hear distinctly. They have just built a preaching-house, fifty-four feet square, the largest octagon we have in England; and it is the first of the kind where the roof is built with common sense, rising only a third of its breadth; yet it is as firm as any in England; nor does it at all hurt the walls. Why then does any roof rise higher? Only through want of skill, or want of honesty, in the builder.

Tues. 29.—In the evening I preached near the preaching-house at Paddiham, and strongly insisted on communion with God, as the only religion that would

avail us. At the close of the sermon came Mr. M.
His long, white beard showed that his present disorder
was of some continuance. In all other respects, he was
quite sensible; but he told me, with much concern,
" You can have no place in heaven without—a beard !
Therefore, I beg, let yours grow immediately."

Wesley Secures Justice for Methodists

Sat. Aug. 30.—We rode to Stallbridge, long the
seat of war, by a senseless, insolent mob, encouraged by
their betters, so called to outrage their quiet neighbours.
For what? Why, they were mad : they were Methodists.
So, to bring them to their senses, they would beat their
brains out. They broke their windows, leaving not one
whole pane with glass, spoiled their goods, and assaulted
their persons with dirt, and rotten eggs, and stones, whenever they appeared in the street. But no magistrate,
though they applied to several, would show them either
mercy or justice. At length they wrote to me. I
ordered a lawyer to write to the rioters. He did so ;
but they set him at naught. We then moved the Court
of King's Bench. By various artifices, they got the
trial put off, from one assizes to another, for eighteen
months. But it fell so much the heavier on themselves,
when they were found guilty ; and, from that time,
finding there is law for Methodists, they have suffered
them to be at peace.

I preached near the main street, without the least
disturbance, to a large and attentive congregation.
Thence we rode on to Axminster, but were throughly wet
before we came thither. The rain obliged me to preach
within at six ; but at seven on Sunday morning, I cried
in the market-place, " The kingdom of God is at hand ;
repent ye, and believe the Gospel."

In the evening I preached in the street at Ashburton. Many behaved with decency; but the rest, with such stupid rudeness as I have not seen, for a long time, in any part of England.

Mon. September 1.—I came to Plymouth Dock, where, after heavy storms, there is now a calm. The house, notwithstanding the new galleries, were extremely crowded in the evening. I strongly exhorted the back-sliders to return to God; and I believe many received "the word of exhortation."

Tues. 2.—Being invited to preach in the Tabernacle at Plymouth, I began about two in the afternoon. In the evening I was offered the use of Mr. Whitefield's room at the dock; but, large as it is, it would not contain the congregation. At the close of the sermon, a large stone was thrown in at one of the windows, which came just behind me, and fell at my feet, the best place that could have been found. So no one was hurt or frightened, not many knowing anything of the matter.

Gwennap's Famous Amphitheatre

Sun. 7.—At eight I preached in Mousehole, a large village south-west from Newlyn. Thence I went to Buryan church, and, as soon as the service was ended, preached near the church-yard, to a numerous congregation. Just after I began, I saw a gentleman before me, shaking his whip, and vehemently striving to say something. But he was abundantly too warm to say anything intelligibly. So, after walking a while to and fro, he wisely took horse, and rode away.

Fri. 12.—I rode to St. Hilary, and in the evening preached near the new house on, " Awake, thou that sleepest." In returning to my lodging, it being dark, my horse was just stepping into a tin-pit, when an honest man caught him by the bridle, and turned his head the other way.

Sun. 14.—I preached in St. Agnes at eight. The congregation in Redruth, at one, was the largest I ever had seen there; but small, compared to that which assembled at five, in the natural amphitheatre at Gwennap; far the finest I know in the kingdom. It is a round, green hollow, gently shelving down, about fifty feet deep; but I suppose it is two hundred across one way, and near three hundred the other. I believe there were full twenty thousand people; and, the evening being calm, all could hear.

Mon. 15.—I preached at Cubert, and next morning rode on to St. Columb. Being desired to break the ice here, I began preaching, without delay, in a gentleman's yard adjoining to the main street. I chose this, as neither too public nor too private. I fear the greater part of the audience understood full little of what they heard. However, they behaved with seriousness and good manners.

Hence I rode to Port-Isaac, now one of the liveliest places in Cornwall. The weather being uncertain, I preached near the house. But there was no rain while I preached, except the gracious rain which God sent upon his inheritance.

Here Mr. Buckingham met me, who, for fear of offending the bishop, broke off all commerce with the Methodists. He had no sooner done this, than the bishop rewarded him by turning him out of his curacy; which, had he continued to walk in Christian simplicity, he would probably have had to this day.

Wed. 17.—I twice stopped a violent bleeding from a cut, by applying a brier-leaf. The room at Launceston

would not near contain the congregation in the evening
to whom I strongly applied the case of the impotent
man at the pool of Bethesda. Many were much
affected: but, O, how few are willing to be made
whole!

Wesley on a Country Life

Mon. Nov. 3.—I rode to Brentford from London,
where all was quiet, both in the congregation and the
society. Tuesday, 4. I preached at Brentford, Batter-
sea, Deptford, and Welling, and examined the several
societies. Wednesday, 5. I rode by Shoreham to
Sevenoaks. In the little journeys which I have lately
taken, I have thought much on the huge encomiums
which have been for many ages bestowed on a country
life. How have all the learned world cried out,

> O fortunati nimium, sua si bona norint,
> Agricolæ!

But, after all, what a flat contradiction is this to
universal experience! See that little house, under the
wood, by the river side! There is rural life in perfection. How happy then is the farmer that lives there?
Let us take a detail of his happiness. He rises with, or
before, the sun, calls his servants, looks to his swine
and cows, then to his stables and barns. He sees to the
ploughing and sowing his ground, in winter or in spring.
In summer and autumn he hurries and sweats among
his mowers and reapers. And where is his happiness in
the meantime? Which of these employments do we
envy? Or do we envy the delicate repast that
succeeds, which the poet so languishes for?—

> O quando faba, Pythagoræ cognata, simulque
> Uncta satis pingui ponentur oluscula lardo!

' O the happiness of eating beans well greased with fat
bacon !   Nay, and cabbage too ! "—Was Horace in his
senses when he talked thus, or the servile herd of his
imitators ?   Our eyes and ears may convince us there
is not a less happy body of men in all England than the
country farmers.   In general their life is supremely
dull ; and it is usually unhappy too.   For of all people
in the kingdom they are most discontented ; seldom
satisfied either with God or man.

Wesley and the Character of a Methodist

1767.   Thur. March 5.—I at length obliged Dr. D. by
entering into the lists with him.   The letter I wrote
(though not published till two or three weeks after) was
as follows :

> " *To the Editor of Lloyd's Evening Post.*

" Sir,—Many times the publisher of the ' Christian
Magazine ' has attacked me without fear or wit ; and
hereby he has convinced his impartial readers of one
thing at least—that (as the vulgar say) his fingers itch to
be at me ; that he has a passionate desire to measure
swords with me.   But I have other work upon my
hands : I can employ the short remainder of my life to
better purpose.

" The occasion of his late attack is this : Five or six
and thirty years ago, I much admired the character of a
perfect Christian drawn by Clemens Alexandrinus.
Five or six and twenty years ago, a thought came into
my mind, of drawing such a character myself, only in a
more scriptural manner, and mostly in the very words
of Scripture : this I entitled, ' The Character of a
Methodist,' believing that curiosity would incite more
persons to read it, and also that some prejudice might

thereby be removed from candid men. But that none might imagine I intended a panegyric either on myself or my friends, I guarded against this in the very title-page, saying, both in the name of myself and them, 'Not as though I had already attained, either were already perfect.' To the same effect I speak in the conclusion, 'These are the same principles and practices of our sect; these are the marks of a true Methodist'; that is, a true Christian, as I immediately after explain myself: 'by these alone do those who are in derision so called desire to be distinguished from other men.' (P. 11.) 'By these marks do we labour to distinguish ourselves from those whose minds or lives are not according to the Gospel of Christ.' (P. 12.)

"Upon this Rusticulus, or Dr. Dodd, says, 'A Methodist, according to Mr. Wesley, is one who is perfect, and sinneth not in thought, word, or deed.'

"Sir, have me excused. This is not 'according to Mr. Wesley.' I have told all the world I am not perfect; and yet you allow me to be a Methodist. I tell you flat, I have not attained the character I draw. Will you pin it upon me in spite of my teeth?

"'But Mr. Wesley says, the other Methodists have.' I say no such thing. What I say, after having given a scriptural account of a perfect Christian, is this: 'By these marks the Methodists desire to be distinguished from other men; by these we labour to distinguish ourselves.' And do not you yourself desire and labour after the very same thing?

"But you insist, 'Mr. Wesley affirms the Methodists' (that is, all Methodists) 'to be perfectly holy and righteous.' Where do I affirm this? Not in the tract before us. In the front of this I affirm just the contrary; and that I affirm it anywhere else is more than I know. Be pleased, sir, to point out the place: till this is done, all you add (bitterly enough) is mere *brutum fulmen;* and the Methodists (so called) may still declare (without any impeachment of their sincerity), that they do not come to the holy table 'trusting in their own righteousness, but in God's manifold and great mercies.' I am, Sir,

"Yours, &c.,

"JOHN WESLEY."

The Sexton's Strange Apparition

Sat. Aug. 1.—Before I left Glasgow I heard so strange an account, that I desired to hear it from the person himself. He was a sexton, and yet for many years had little troubled himself about religion. I set down his words, and leave every man to form his own judgment upon them: "Sixteen weeks ago, I was walking, an hour before sunset, behind the high-kirk; and, looking on one side, I saw one close to me, who looked in my face, and asked me how I did. I answered, 'Pretty well.' He said, 'You have had many troubles; but how have you improved them?' He then told me all that ever I did; yea, and the thoughts that had been in my heart; adding, 'Be ready for my second coming': and he was gone I knew not how. I trembled all over, and had no strength in me; but sunk down to the ground. From that time I groaned continually under the load of sin, till at the Lord's supper it was all taken away."

Fri. Sep. 25.—I was desired to preach at Freshford; but the people durst not come to the house, because of the small-pox, of which Joseph Allen, "an Israelite indeed," had died the day before. So they placed a table near the church-yard. But I had no sooner begun to speak, than the bells began to ring, by the procurement of a neighbouring gentleman. However, it was labour lost; for my voice prevailed, and the people heard me distinctly : nay, a person extremely deaf, who had not been able to hear a sermon for several years, told his neighbours, with great joy, that he had heard and understood all, from the beginning to the end.

Queer Houses at Sheerness

Mon. Nov. 23.—I went to Canterbury. Here I met with the Life of Mahomet, wrote, I suppose, by the Count de Boulanvilliers. Whoever the author is, he is a very pert, shallow, self-conceited coxcomb, remarkable for nothing but his immense assurance and thorough contempt of Christianity. And the book is a dull, ill-digested romance, supported by no authorities at all; whereas Dean Prideaux (a writer of ten times his sense) cites his authorities for every thing he advances.

In the afternoon I rode to Dover; but the gentleman I was to lodge with was gone a long journey. He went to bed well, but was dead in the morning : such a vapour is life! At six I preached; but the house would by no means contain the congregation. Most of the officers of the garrison were there. I have not found so much life here for some years.

Sun. Dec. 13.—To-day I found a little soreness on the edge of my tongue, which the next day spread to my gums, then to my lips, which inflamed, swelled, and, the skin bursting, bled considerably. Afterward, the roof of my mouth was extremely sore, so that I could chew nothing. To this was added a continual spitting. I knew a little rest would cure all. But this was not to be had; for I had appointed to be at Sheerness on

Wednesday, the 16th. Accordingly, I took horse between five and six, and came thither between five and six in the evening.

At half an hour after six, I began reading prayers (the governor of the fort having given me the use of the chapel), and afterwards preached, though not without difficulty, to a large and serious congregation. The next evening it was considerably increased, so that the chapel was as hot as an oven. In coming out, the air, being exceeding sharp, quite took away my voice, so that I knew not how I should be able the next day to read prayers or preach to so large a congregation. But in the afternoon the governor cut the knot, sending word, I must preach in the chapel no more. A room being offered, which held full as many people as I was able to preach to, we had a comfortable hour; and many seemed resolved to " seek the Lord while he may be found."

Such a town as many of these live in is scarce to be found again in England. In the dock adjoining to the fort there are six old men-of-war. These are divided into small tenements, forty, fifty, or sixty in a ship, with little chimneys and windows; and each of these contains a family. In one of them, where we called, a man and his wife, and six little children lived. And yet all the ship was sweet and tolerably clean; sweeter than most sailing ships I have been in. Saturday, 19. I returned to London.

Wesley in the Marshalsea Prison

1768. Sat. Jan. 2.—I called on a poor man in the Marshalsea, whose case appeared to be uncommon. He is by birth a Dutchman, a chymist by profession. Being but half-employed at home, he was advised to come to

London, where he doubted not of having full employment. He was recommended to a countryman of his to lodge, who after six weeks arrested him for much more than he owed, and hurried him away to prison, having a wife near her time, without money, friend, or a word of English to speak. I wrote the case to Mr. T——, who immediately gave fifteen pounds; by means of which, with a little addition, he was set at liberty, and put in a way of living. But I never saw him since: and reason good; for he could now live without me.

Mon. 4.—At my leisure hours this week, I read Dr. Priestley's ingenious book on Electricity. He seems to have accurately collected and well digested all that is known on that curious subject. But how little is that all! Indeed the use of it we know; at least, in some good degree. We know it is a thousand medicines in one: in particular, that it is the most efficacious medicine in nervous disorders of every kind, which has ever yet been discovered. But if we aim at theory, we know nothing. We are soon

Lost and bewilder'd in the fruitless search.

Mon. 11.—This week I spent my scraps of time in reading Mr. Wodrow's "History of the Sufferings of the Church of Scotland." It would transcend belief, but that the vouchers are too authentic to admit of any exception. O what a blessed Governor was that good-natured man, so called, King Charles the Second! Bloody Queen Mary was a lamb, a mere dove, in comparison of him!

Mon. Feb. 8.—I met with a surprising poem, entitled, "Choheleth; or, the Preacher." It is a paraphrase, in tolerable verse, on the Book of Ecclesiastes. I really think the author of it (a Turkey Merchant)

understands both the difficult expressions, and the connexion of the whole, better than any other either ancient
or modern writer whom I have seen.   He was at Lisbon
during the great earthquake, just then sitting in his night-
gown and slippers.   Before he could dress himself, part
of the house he was in fell, and blocked him up.   By
this means his life was saved ; for all who had run out
were dashed in pieces by the falling houses.

Wesley Travels North

Mon. March 14.—I set out on my northern journey,
and preached at Stroud in the evening.   Tuesday, 15.
About noon I preached at Painswick, and in the evening
at Gloucester.   The mob here was for a considerable
time both noisy and mischievous.   But an honest magistrate, taking the matter in hand, quickly tamed the
beasts of the people.   So may any magistrate, if he will ;
so that wherever a mob continues any time, all they do
is to be imputed not so much to the rabble as to the
justices.

Wed. 16.—About nine I preached at Cheltenham—a
quiet, comfortable place ; though it would not have been
so, if either the rector or the Anabaptist minister could
have prevented it.   Both these have blown the trumpet
with their might ; but the people had no ears to hear.
In the afternoon I preached at Upton, and then rode on
to Worcester.   But the difficulty was, where to preach.
No room was large enough to contain the people ; and
it was too cold for them to stand abroad.   At length we
went to a friend's, near the town, whose barn was larger
than many churches.   Here a numerous congregation
soon assembled ; and again at five, and at ten in the
morning.   Nothing is wanting here but a commodious
house : and will not God provide this also ?

Fri. 18.—The vicar of Pebworth had given notice in the church on Sunday, that I was to preach there on Friday. But the squire of the parish said, " It is contrary to the canons " (wise squire !), "and it shall not be." So I preached about a mile from it, at Broadmarston, by the side of Mr. Eden's house. The congregation was exceeding large, and remarkably attentive. In the morning, the chapel (so it anciently was) was well filled at five. The simplicity and earnestness of the people promise a glorious harvest.

Sat. 19.—We rode to Birmingham. The tumults which subsisted here so many years are now wholly suppressed by a resolute magistrate. After preaching, I was pleased to see a venerable monument of antiquity, George Bridgins, in the one hundred and seventh year of his age. He can still walk to the preaching, and retains his senses and understanding tolerably well. But what a dream will even a life of a hundred years appear to him the moment he awakes in eternity !

Preaching in a North Wind

Sun. 20.—About one I preached on West-Bromwich heath ; in the evening, near the preaching-house in Wednesbury. The north wind cut like a razor ; but the congregation, as well as me, had something else to think of.

Tues. 22.—I read over a small book, " Poems, by Miss Whately," a farmer's daughter. She had little advantage from education, but an astonishing genius. Some of her elegies I think quite equal to Mr. Gray's. If she had had proper helps for a few years, I question whether she would not have excelled any female poet that ever yet appeared in England.

Wed. 30.—I rode to a little town called New Mills, in the High-peak ot Derbyshire. I preached at noon in their large new chapel, which (in consideration that preaching-houses have need of air) has a casement in every window, three inches square! That is the custom of the country!

Wesley Instructs Parents

In the evening and the following morning I brought strange things to the ears of many in Manchester, concerning the government of their families, and the education of their children. But some still made that very silly answer, " O, he has no children of his own ! " Neither had St. Paul, nor (that we know) any of the Apostles. What then ? Were they therefore unable to instruct parents ? Not so. They were able to instruct every one that had a soul to be saved.

Wed. April 6.—About eleven I preached at Wigan, in a place near the middle of the town, which I suppose was formerly a playhouse. It was very full, and very warm. Most of the congregation were wild as wild might be; yet none made the least disturbance. Afterwards, as I walked down the street, they stared sufficiently ; but none said an uncivil word.

In the evening we had a huge congregation at Liverpool ; but some pretty, gay, fluttering things did not behave with so much good manners as the mob at Wigan. The congregations in general were quite well-behaved, as well as large, both morning and evening; and I found the society both more numerous and more lively than ever it was before.

Mon. 11.—I rode to Bolton; on Wednesday, to Kendal. Seceders and mongrel Methodists have so surfeited the people here, that there is small prospect of doing good : however, I once more " cast " my " bread upon the waters," and left the event to God.

Thur. 14.—I rode on, through continued rain, to Ambleside. It cleared up before we came to Keswick, and we set out thence in a fair day; but on the mountains the storm met us again, which beat on us so impetuously, that our horses could scarce turn their faces against it. However, we made shift to reach Cockermouth ; but there was no room for preaching, the town being in an uproar through the election for Members of Parliament; so, after drying ourselves, we thought it best to go on to Whitehaven.

Wesley and Mary Queen of Scots

Tues. 26.—I came to Aberdeen.

Here I found a society truly alive, knit together in peace and love. The congregations were large both morning and evening, and, as usual, deeply attentive. But a company of strolling players, who have at length found place here also, stole away the gay part of the hearers. Poor Scotland ! Poor Aberdeen ! This only was wanting to make them as completely irreligious as England.

Fri. 29.—I read over an extremely sensible book, but one that surprised me much : it is " An inquiry into the Proofs of the Charges commonly advanced against Mary Queen of Scots." By means of original papers, he has made it more clear than one would imagine it possible at this distance : 1. That she was altogether innocent of the murder of Lord Darnley, and no way privy to it: 2. That she married Lord Bothwell (then near seventy years old, herself but four-and-twenty) from the pressing instance of the nobility in a body, who at the same time assured her he was innocent of the King's murder:

3. That Murray, Morton, and Lethington, themselves contrived that murder, in order to charge it upon her; as well as forged those vile letters and sonnets which they palmed upon the world for hers.

"But how then can we account for the quite contrary story, which has been almost universally received?" Most easily. It was penned and published in French, English, and Latin (by Queen Elizabeth's order), by George Buchanan, who was secretary to Lord Murray, and in Queen Elizabeth's pay; so he was sure to throw dirt enough. Nor was she at liberty to answer for herself. "But what then was Queen Elizabeth?" As just and merciful as Nero, and as good a Christian as Mahomet.

Sun. May 1.—I preached at seven in the new room; in the afternoon at the College kirk, in Old Aberdeen. At six, knowing our house could not contain the congregation, I preached in the castle gate, on the paved stones. A large number of people were all attention; but there were many rude, stupid creatures round about them, who knew as little of reason as of religion: I never saw such brutes in Scotland before. One of them threw a potato, which fell on my arm: I turned to them; and some were ashamed.

Wesley at Scoon and Holyrood

Mon. 2.—I set out early from Aberdeen, and about noon preached in Brechin. After sermon, the provost desired to see me, and said, " Sir, my son had epileptic fits from his infancy: Dr. Ogylvie prescribed for him many times, and at length told me he could do no more. I desired Mr. Blair last Monday to speak to you. On Tuesday morning my son said to his mother, he had just been dreaming that his fits were gone, and he was

perfectly well.   Soon after I gave him the drops you
advised : he is perfectly well, and has not had one fit
since."

Thur. 5.—We rode through the pleasant and fruitful
Carse of Gowry, a plain, fifteen or sixteen miles long,
between the river Tay and the mountains, very thick
inhabited, to Perth.   In the afternoon we walked over
to the royal palace at Scoon.   It is a large old house,
delightfully situated, but swiftly running to ruin.   Yet
there are a few good pictures, and some fine tapestry
left, in what they call the Queen's and the King's
chambers.   And what is far more curious, there is a
bed and a set of hangings in the (once) royal apartment,
which was wrought by poor Queen Mary, while she was
imprisoned in the Castle of Lochlevin.   It is some of
the finest needlework I ever saw, and plainly shows
both her exquisite skill and unwearied industry.

Sat. 14.—I walked once more through Holyrood
House, a noble pile of building ; but the greatest
part of it left to itself, and so (like the palace at Scone)
swiftly running to ruin.   The tapestry is dirty, and
quite faded ; the fine ceilings dropping down ; and
many of the pictures in the gallery torn or cut through.
This was the work of good General Hawley's soldiers
(like General, like men !), who, after running away from
the Scots at Falkirk, revenged themselves on the harmless canvas !

Sun. 15.—At eight I preached in the High School
yard ; and I believe not a few of the hearers were cut to
the heart.   Between twelve and one a far larger congregation assembled on the Castle Hill ; and I believe
my voice commanded them all, while I opened and
enforced those awful words, " I saw the dead, small and
great, stand before God."   In the evening our house

was sufficiently crowded, even with the rich and honourable. " Who hath warned " these " to flee from the wrath to come ? " O may they at length awake and " arise from the dead ! "

Wesley's Old Schoolfellow

Wed. June 1.—Many of the militia were present at Barnard Castle in the evening, and behaved with decency. I was well pleased to lodge at a gentleman's, an old schoolfellow, half a mile from the town. What a dream are the fifty or sixty years that have slipped away since we were at the Charterhouse !

Thur. 2.—I preached, at noon, at a farmer's house, near Brough, in Westmoreland. The sun was hot enough, but some shady trees covered both me and most of the congregation. A little bird perched on one of them, and sung, without intermission, from the beginning of the service unto the end. Many of the people came from far ; but I believe none of them regretted their labour.

Fri. 3.—In running down one of the mountains yesterday, I had got a sprain in my thigh : it was rather worse to-day ; but as I rode to Barnard Castle, the sun shone so hot upon it, that, before I came to the town, it was quite well. In the evening the commanding officer gave orders there should be no exercise, that all the Durham militia (what a contrast !) might be at liberty to attend the preaching. Accordingly, we had a little army of officers as well as soldiers ; and all behaved well. A large number of them were present at five in the morning.

Tues. 7.—I went down by water to South Shields, and preached at noon, to far more than could hear. We went, after dinner, to Tynemouth Castle, a magnificent heap of ruins. Within the walls are the remains of a very large church, which seems to have been of exquisite workmanship; and the stones are joined by so strong a cement, that, but for Cromwell's cannon, they might have stood a thousand years.

Wesley's Wife Ill

Sun. Aug. 14.—Hearing my wife was dangerously ill, I took chaise immediately and reached the Foundery before one in the morning. Finding the fever was turned, and the danger over, about two I set out again, and in the afternoon came (not at all tired) to Bristol.

Wed. Sept. 7 (Penzance).—After the early preaching, the select society met; such a company of lively believers, full of faith and love, as I never found in this county before. This, and the three following days, I preached at as many places as I could, though I was at first in doubt, whether I could preach eight days together, mostly in the open air, three or four times a day. But my strength was as my work: I hardly felt any weariness, first or last.

Sun. 11.—About nine I preached at St. Agnes, and again between one and two. At first I took my old stand at Gwennap, in the natural amphitheatre. I suppose no human voice could have commanded such an audience on plain ground; but the ground rising all round gave me such an advantage, that I believe all could hear distinctly.

Mon. 12.—I preached about noon at Callistick, and in the evening at Kerley. It rained all the time; but that did not divert the attention of a large congregation. At noon, Tuesday, 13, I preached in Truro, and in the evening at Mevagissey. It was a season of solemn joy; I have not often found the like. Surely God's thoughts are not as our thoughts! **Can any** good be done at Mevagissey?

Fri. 16.—I rode, through heavy rain, to Polperro. Here the room over which we were to lodge being filled with pilchards and conger-eels, the perfume was too potent for me; so that I was not sorry when one of our friends invited me to lodge at her house. Soon after I began to preach, heavy rain began; yet none went away till the whole service was ended.

Sat. 17.—When we came to Crimble Passage, we were at a full stop. The boatmen told us the storm was so high, that it was not possible to pass: however, at length we persuaded them to venture out; and we did not ship one sea till we got over.

Sun. 18.—Our room at the Dock contained the morning congregation tolerably well. Between one and two I began preaching on the quay in Plymouth. Notwithstanding the rain, abundance of people stood to hear. But one silly man talked without ceasing, till I desired the people to open to the right and left, and let me look him in the face. They did so. He pulled off his hat, and quietly went away.

Wesley and Seaport Towns

Wed. Nov. 30.—I rode to Dover, and came in just before a violent storm began. It did not hinder the people. Many were obliged to go away after the house was filled. What a desire to hear runs through all the seaport towns wherever we come! Surely God is besieging this nation, and attacking it at all the entrances!

Wed. Dec. 14.—I saw the Westminster scholars act the "Adelphi" of Terence; an entertainment not unworthy of a Christian. O how do these Heathens shame us!

Their very comedies contain both excellent sense, the liveliest pictures of men and manner, and so fine strokes of genuine morality, as are seldom found in the writings of Christians.

1769.   Mon. Jan. 9.—I spent a comfortable and profitable hour with Mr. Whitefield, in calling to mind the former times, and the manner wherein God prepared us for a work which it had not then entered into our hearts to conceive.

Fri. Feb. 17 (Yarmouth).—I abridged Dr. Watts's pretty "Treatise on the Passions." His hundred and seventy-seven pages will make a useful tract of four-and-twenty. Why do persons who treat the same subjects with me, write so much larger books? Of many reasons, is not this the chief—we do not write with the same view? Their principal end is to get money; my only one, to do good.

Mon. 27 (London.)—I had one more agreeable conversation with my old friend and fellow labourer, George Whitefield. His soul appeared to be vigorous still, but his body was sinking apace ; and unless God interposes, he must soon finish his labours

Wesley's Land-Shark

Thur. March 30 (Dublin).—I was summoned to the Court of Conscience by a poor creature who fed my horses three or four times while I was on board. For this service he demanded ten shillings. I gave him half a crown. When I informed the Court of this, he was sharply reproved. Let all beware of these land-sharks on our sea-coasts !—My scraps of time this week I employed in reading the account of Commodore Byron. I never before read of any who endured such hardships, and survived them. Sure no novel in the world can be more affecting, or more surprising, than this history.

Wed. April 19 (Armagh).—We took horse about ten, being desired to call at Kinnard (ten or eleven miles out of the way), where a little society had been lately formed, who were much alive to God. At the town-end, I was met by a messenger from Arch-deacon C——e, who desired I would take a bed with him; and soon after by another, who told me the Arch-deacon desired I would alight at his door. I did so; and found an old friend whom I had not seen for four or five and thirty years.

Wesley Opens a New Church

He received me with the most cordial affection; and, after a time, said, "We have been building a new church, which my neighbours expected me to open; but if you please to do it, it will be as well." Hearing the bell, the people flocked together from all parts of the town, and "received the word with all readiness of mind." I saw the hand of God was in this, for the strengthening of this loving people.

Hence we rode through a pleasant country to Charle-mount, where I preached to a very large and serious congregation, near the fort, which has a ditch round it, with some face of a fortification; and probably (according to custom) costs the Government a thousand a year, for not three farthings' service!

Thur. 20. — I went on to Castle - caulfield, and preached on the green adjoining to the castle, to a plain, serious people, who still retain all their earnestness and simplicity. Thence I rode to Cookstown; a town consisting of one street about a mile long, running directly through a bog. I preached to most of the inhabitants of the town : and so the next day, morning and evening. Many "received the word with gladness," Perhaps they will not all be stony-ground hearers.

We took the new road to Dungiven. But it was hard work.

> Nigh founder'd, on we fared.
> Treading the crude consistence.

We were near five hours going fourteen miles, partly on horseback, partly on foot. We had, as usual, a full house at Londonderry in the evening, and again at eight on Sunday morning. In the afternoon we had a brilliant congregation. But such a sight gives me no great pleasure ; as I have very little hope of doing them good : only " with God all things are possible."

Both this evening and the next I spoke exceeding plain to the members of the society. In no other place in Ireland has more pains been taken by the most able of our preachers. And to how little purpose ! Bands they have none : four-and-forty persons in society ! The greater part of these heartless and cold. The audience in general dead as stones. However, we are to deliver our message ; and let our Lord do as seemeth him good.

A Forsaken Beauty

Thur. May 25.—I rode to Bandon. In the evening we were obliged to be in the house ; but the next, Friday, 26, I stood in the main street, and cried to a numerous congregation, " Fear God, and keep his commandments ; for this is the whole of man." Afterwards I visited one that a year or two ago was in high life, an eminent beauty, adored by her husband, admired and caressed by some of the first men in the nation. She was now without husband, without friend, without fortune, confined to her bed, in constant pain, and in black despair, believing herself forsaken of God, and possessed by a legion of devils! Yet I found great liberty in praying for her, and a strong hope that she will die in peace.

Tues. June 27.—[From a letter "to a pious and sensible woman"] "By Christian perfection, I mean, 1. Loving God with all our heart. Do you object to this? I mean, 2. A heart and life all devoted to God. Do you desire less? I mean, 3. Regaining the whole image of God. What objection to this? I mean, 4. Having all the mind that was in Christ. Is this going too far? I mean, 5. Walking uniformly as Christ walked. And this surely no Christian will object to. If any one means anything more or any-thing else by perfection, I have no concern with it. But if this is wrong, yet what need of this heat about it, this violence, I had almost said, fury of opposition, carried so far as even not to lay out anything with this man, or that woman, who professes it?"

Mon. July 3.—I rode to Coolylough (where was the quarterly meeting), and preached at eleven, and in the evening. While we were singing, I was surprised to see the horses from all parts of the ground gathering about us. Is it true then that horses, as well as lions and tigers, have an ear for music?

Sun. 30.—At five I preached at Leeds; and on Monday, 31, prepared all things for the ensuing Confer-ence. Tuesday, August 1, it began; and a more loving one we never had. On Thursday I mentioned the case of our brethren at New York, who had built the first Methodist preaching-house in America, and were in great want of money and much more of preachers. Two of our preachers, Richard Boardman and Joseph Pillmoor, willingly offered themselves for the service;

by whom we determined to send them fifty pounds, as a token of our brotherly love.

Wesley at the Countess of Huntingdon's

Wed. Aug. 23.—I went on to Trevecka. Here we found a concourse of people from all parts, come to celebrate the Countess of Huntingdon's birth-day, and the anniversary of her school, which was opened on the twenty-fourth of August, last year. I preached in the evening, to as many as her chapel could well contain; which is extremely neat, or rather, elegant; as is the dining-room, the school, and all the house. About nine Howell Harris desired me to give a short exhortation to his family. I did so; and then went back to my Lady's and laid me down in peace.

Thur. 24.—I administered the Lord's supper to the family. At ten the public service began. Mr. Fletcher preached an exceeding lively sermon in the court, the chapel being far too small. After him, Mr. William Williams preached in Welsh, till between one and two o'clock. At two we dined. Meantime, a large number of people had baskets of bread and meat carried to them in the court. At three I took my turn there, then Mr. Fletcher, and, about five, the congregation was dismissed. Between seven and eight the love-feast began, at which I believe many were comforted. In the evening several of us retired into the neighbouring wood, which is exceeding pleasantly laid out in walks; one of which leads to a little mount, raised in the midst of a meadow, that commands a delightful prospect. This is Howell Harris's work, who has likewise greatly enlarged and beautified his house; so that, with the gardens, orchards, walks, and pieces of water that surround it, it is a kind of little paradise.

LADY HUNTINGDON

Fri. 25.—We rode through a lovely country to Chep-stow. I had designed to go straight on, but yielded to the importunity of our friends to stay and preach in the evening. Meantime, I took a walk through Mr. Morris's woods. There is scarce anything like them in the kingdom. They stand on the top, and down the side, of a steep mountain, hanging in a semicircular form over the river. Through these woods abundance of serpen-tine walks are cut, wherein many seats and alcoves are placed; most of which command a surprising prospect of rocks and fields on the other side of the river. And must all these be burned up? What will become of us then, if we set our hearts upon them?

The Gentleman with Rotten Eggs

Fri. Sept. 8.—I preached about nine at Taunton, and then rode on to Bridgewater.

This afternoon I went to the top of Brent Hill: I know not, I ever before saw such a prospect. West-ward, one may see to the mouth of the Bristol Channel; and the three other ways, as far as the eye can reach. And most of the land which you see is well cultivated, well wooded, and well watered: so that the globe of earth, in its present condition, can hardly afford a more pleasing scene.

Tues. 19.—Between twelve and one, I preached at Freshford; and on White's Hill, near Bradford, in the evening. By this means many had an opportunity of hearing, who would not have come to the room. I had designed to preach there again the next evening; but a gentleman in the town desired me to preach at his door. The beasts of the people were tolerably quiet till I had nearly finished my sermon. They then lifted up their voice, especially one, called a gentleman, who had filled his pocket with rotten eggs : but, a young man coming unawares, clapped his hands on each side, and mashed them all at once. In an instant he was perfume all over; though it was not so sweet as balsam.

Tues. Oct. 24.—I preached at Alston, in a large malt-room, where one side of my head was very warm, through the crowd of people, the other very cold, having an open window at my ear. Between six and seven I preached at Northampton; and it was an awful season.

This evening there was such an aurora borealis as I never saw before : the colours, both the white, the flame-colour, and the scarlet, were so exceeding strong and beautiful. But they were awful too : so that abundance of people were frighted into many good resolutions.

Wesley on Geology and Rousseau

Tues. Dec. 26.—I read the letters from our preachers in America, informing us that God had begun a glorious work there; that both in New York and Philadelphia multitudes flock to hear, and behave with the deepest seriousness; and that the society in each place already contains above an hundred members.

Friday, 29, we observed as a day of fasting and prayer, partly on account of the confused state of public affairs, partly as preparatory to the solemn engagement which we were about to renew.

1770. Mon. Jan. 1.—About eighteen hundred of us met together; it was a most solemn season. As we did openly "avouch the Lord to be our God, so did He avouch us to be His people."

Wed. 17.—In a little journey, which I took into Bedfordshire, I finished Dr. Burnet's "Theory of the Earth." He is doubtless one of the first-rate writers, both as to sense and style; his language is remarkably clear, unaffected, nervous, and elegant. And as to his theory, none can deny that it is ingenious, and consistent with itself. And it is highly probable, 1. That the earth arose out of the chaos in some such manner as he describes: 2. That the antediluvian earth was without high or abrupt mountains, and without sea, being one uniform crust, enclosing the great abyss: 3. That the flood was caused by the breaking of this crust, and its sinking into the abyss of waters: and 4. That the present state of the earth, both internal and external, shows it to be the ruins of the former earth. This is the substance of his two former books, and thus far I can go with him.

I have no objection to the substance of his third book upon the general conflagration, but think it one of the noblest tracts which is extant in our language. And I do not much object to the fourth, concerning the new heavens and the new earth. The substance of it is highly probable.

Sat. Feb. 3, and at my leisure moments on several of the following days, I read with much expectation a celebrated book—Rousseau upon Education. But how was I disappointed! Sure a more consummate coxcomb never saw the sun! How amazingly full of himself! Whatever he speaks, he pronounces as an oracle. But many of his oracles are as palpably false, as that "young children never love old people." No! Do they never love grandfathers and grandmother? Frequently more than they do their own parents. Indeed, they love all that love them, and that with more warmth and sincerity than when they come to riper years.

But I object to his temper, more than to his judgment: he is a mere misanthorpe; a cynic all over. So indeed is his brother-infidel, Voltaire; and well nigh as great a coxcomb. But he hides both his doggedness and vanity a little better; whereas here it stares us in the face continually.

As to his book, it is whimsical to the last degree; grounded neither upon reason nor experience. To cite particular passages would be endless; but any one may observe concerning the whole, the advices which are good are trite and common, only disguised under new expressions. And those which are new, which are really his own, are lighter than vanity itself. Such discoveries I always expect from those who are too wise to believe their Bibles.

Swedenborg an Entertaining Madman

Wed. 28.—I sat down to read and seriously consider some of the writing of Baron Swedenborg. I began with huge prejudice in his favour, knowing him to be a pious man, one of a strong understanding, of much learning, and one who thoroughly believed himself. But I could not hold out long. Any one of his visions puts his real character out of doubt. He is one of the most ingenious, lively, entertaining madmen, that ever set pen to paper. But his waking dreams are so wild, so far remote both from Scripture and common sense, that one might as easily swallow the stories of "Tom Thumb," or "Jack the Giant-Killer."

Mon. March 5.—I came to Newbury, where I had been much importuned to preach. But where? The Dissenters would not permit me to preach in their meeting-house. Some were then desirous to hire the old playhouse; but the good mayor would not suffer it to be so profaned! So I made use of a workshop—a large, commodious place. But it would by no means contain the congregation.   All that could hear behaved well; and I was in hopes God would have a people in this place also.   The next evening I preached at Bristol, and spent the rest of the week there.

Wesley and his Horses

Wed. 21.—In the following days I went on slowly, through Staffordshire and Cheshire, to Manchester.   In this journey, as well as in many others, I observed a mistake that almost universally prevails; and I desire all travellers to take good notice of it, which may save them both from trouble and danger.   Near thirty years ago, I was thinking, " How is it that no horse ever stumbles while I am reading? "   (History, poetry, and philosophy I commonly read on horseback, having other employment at other times.)   No account can possibly be given but this: because then I throw the reins on his neck.   I then set myself to observe; and I aver, that in riding above an hundred thousand miles, I scarce ever remember any horse (except two, that would fall head over heels any way) to fall, or make a considerable stumble   while I rode with a slack rein. To fancy, therefore, that a tight rein prevents stumbling is a capital blunder.   I have repeated the trial more frequently than most men in the kingdom can do.   A slack rein will prevent stumbling if anything will.   But in some horses nothing can.

Wed. April 25.—Taking horse at five, we rode to Dunkeld, the first considerable town in the Highlands. We were agreeably surprised: a pleasanter situation cannot be easily imagined.   Afterwards we went some miles on a smooth, delightful road, hanging over the river Tay; and then went on, winding through the mountains, to the Castle of Blair.   The mountains, for the next twenty miles, were much higher, and covered with snow. In the evening we came to Dalwhinny, the dearest inn I have met with in North Britain. In the morning we were informed, so much snow had fallen in the night, that we could get no farther. And indeed, three young women, attempting to cross the mountain to Blair, were swallowed up in the snow. However, we resolved, with God's help, to go as far as we could. But, about noon, we were at a full stop: the snow, driving together on the top of the mountain, had quite blocked up the road. We dismounted, and, striking out of the road warily, sometimes to the left, sometimes to the right, with many stumbles, but no hurt, we got on to Dalmagarry, and before sunset, to Inverness.

Fri. 27.—I breakfasted with the senior minister, Mr. M'Kenzie, a pious and friendly man. At six in the evening I began preaching in the church, and with very uncommon liberty of spirit. At seven in the morning I preached in the library, a large commodious room; but it would not contain the congregation; many were constrained to go away. Afterwards I rode over to Fort George, a very regular fortification, capable of containing four thousand men. As I was just taking horse, the commanding officer sent word, I was welcome to preach. But it was a little too late: I had then but just time to ride back to Inverness.

Wesley at Nairn, Elgin, and Aberdeen

Mon. 30.—We set out in a fine morning. A little before we reached Nairn, we were met by a messenger from the minister, Mr. Dunbar; who desired, I would breakfast with him, and give them a sermon in his church. Afterwards we hastened to Elgin, through a pleasant and well-cultivated country. When we set out from hence, the rain began, and poured down till we came to the Spey, the most impetuous river I ever saw. Finding the large boat was in no haste to move, I stepped into a small one, just going off. It whirled us over the stream almost in a minute. I waited at the inn at Fochabers (dark and dirty enough in all reason), till our friends overtook me with the horses. The outside of the inn at Keith was of the same hue, and promised us no great things. But we were agreeably disappointed. We found plenty of everything, and so dried ourselves at leisure.

Sun. May 6.—I preached in the college kirk at Old Aberdeen, to a very serious (though mostly genteel) congregation. In the evening I preached at our own room, and early in the morning took my leave of this loving people. We came to Montrose about noon. I had designed to preach there; but found no notice had been given. However, I went down to the green, and sung a hymn. People presently flocked from all parts, and God gave me great freedom of speech; so that I hope we did not meet in vain.

At seven in the evening I preached at Arbroath, properly Aberbrothwick. The whole town seems moved: the congregation was the largest I have seen since we left Inverness; and the society, though but of nine months' standing, is the largest in the kingdom, next that of Aberdeen.

Tues. 8.—I took a view of the small remains of the abbey. I know nothing like it in all North Britain. I paced it, and found it an hundred yards long. The breadth is proportionable. Part of the west end, which is still standing, shows it was full as high as Westminster Abbey. The south end of the cross aisle likewise is standing, near the top of which is a large circular window.

The zealous Reformers, they told us, burnt this down. God deliver us from reforming mobs!

I have seen no town in Scotland which increases so fast, or which is built with so much common sense, as this. Two entire new streets, and part of a third, have been built within these two years. They run parallel with each other, and have a row of gardens between them. So that every house has a garden; and thus both health and convenience are consulted.

Where Are the Highlands?

Mon. 14.—After ten years' inquiry, I have learned what are the Highlands of Scotland. Some told me, " The Highlands begin when you cross the Tay "; others, "when you cross the North Esk "; and others, " when you cross the river Spey ": but all of them missed the mark. For the truth of the matter is, the Highlands are bounded by no river at all, but by carns, or heaps of stones laid in a row, south-west and north-east, from sea to sea. These formerly divided the kingdom of the Picts from that of the Caledonians, which included all the country north of the carns; several whereof are still remaining. It takes in Argyleshire, most of Perthshire, Murrayshire, with all the north-west counties. This is called the Highlands, because a considerable part of it (though not the whole) is mountainous. But it is not more mountainous than North Wales, nor than many parts of England and Ireland; nor do I believe it has any mountain higher than Snowdon Hill, or the Skiddaw in Cumberland. Talking Erse, therefore, is not the thing that distinguishes these from the Lowlands. Neither is this or that river; both the Tay, the Esk, and the Spey running through the Highlands, not south of them.

Fri. 18.—We rode over to the Earl of Haddington's seat, finely situated between two woods. The house is exceeding large and pleasant, commanding a wide prospect both ways : and the Earl is cutting walks through the woods, smoothing the ground, and much enlarging and beautifying his garden. Yet he is to die ! In the evening, I trust God broke some of the stony hearts of Dunbar. A little increase here is in the society likewise ; and all the members walk unblamably.

Wesley and the Turnpikes

Fri. June 15.—I was agreeably surprised to find the whole road from Thirsk to Stokesley, which used to be extremely bad, better than most turnpikes. The gentlemen had exerted themselves, and raised money enough to mend it effectually. So they have done for several hundred miles in Scotland, and throughout all Connaught in Ireland ; and so they undoubtedly might do throughout all England, without saddling the poor people with the vile imposition of turnpikes for ever.

In the afternoon we come to Whitby. Having preached thrice a day for five days, I was willing to preach in the house ; but notice had been given of my preaching in the market-place ; so I began at six, to a large congregation most of them deeply attentive.

Sun. 17.—We had a poor sermon at church. However, I went again in the afternoon, remembering the words of Mr. Philip Henry, " If the preacher does not know his duty, I bless God that I know mine."

Thur. 28.—I can hardly believe that I am this day entered into the sixty-eighth year of my age. How marvellous are the ways of God ! How has He kept me even from a child ! From ten to thirteen or fourteen, I had little but bread to eat, and not great plenty of that.

I believe this was so far from hurting me, that it laid the foundation of lasting health. When I grew up, in consequence of reading Dr. Cheyne, I chose to eat sparingly, and drink water. This was another great means of continuing my health, till I was about seven-and-twenty. I then began spitting of blood, which continued several years. A warm climate cured this. I was afterwards brought to the brink of death by a fever; but it left me healthier than before. Eleven years after, I was in the third stage of a consumption; in three months it pleased God to remove this also. Since that time I have known neither pain nor sickness, and am now healthier than I was forty years ago. This hath God wrought!

Wesley in St. Albans Abbey

Mon. July 30.—I preached at Bingham, ten miles from Nottingham. I really admired the exquisite stupidity of the people. They gaped and stared while I was speaking of death and judgment, as if they had never heard of such things before. And they were not helped by two surly, ill-mannered clergymen, who seemed to be just as wise as themselves. The congregation at Houghton in the evening was more noble, behaving with the utmost decency.

Tues. 31.—At nine I preached in the market-place at Loughborough, to almost as large a congregation as at Nottingham, and equally attentive. Thence I rode to Markfield. Notwithstanding the harvest, the church was quickly filled. And great was our rejoicing in our great High Priest, through whom we "came boldly to the throne of grace." In the evening I preached in the Castle Yard at Leicester, to a multitude of awakened and unawakened. One feeble attempt was made to disturb them : a man was sent to cry fresh salmon at a little distance; but he might as well have spared the pains, for none took the least notice of him.

Wed. Aug. 1.—I rode to Northampton. It being still extremely hot, I determined not to be cooped up, but took my stand on the side of the common, and cried aloud to a large multitude of rich and poor, "Acquaint thyself now with him, and be at peace."

Thur. 2.—Some friends from London met us at St. Albans. Before dinner we took a walk in the abbey, one of the most ancient buildings in the kingdom, near a thousand years old; and one of the largest, being five hundred and sixty feet in length (considerably more than Westminster Abbey), and broad and high in proportion. Near the east end is the tomb and vault of good Duke Humphrey. Some now living remember since his body was entire. But after the coffin was opened, so many were curious to taste the liquor in which it was preserved, that in a little time the corpse was left bare, and then soon mouldered away. A few bones are now all that remain. How little is the spirit concerned at this!

Wesley and the Druid Monuments

Tues. 21.—I rode on to Tiverton, and thence through Launceston, Camelford, Port Isaac, Cubert, St. Agnes, and Redruth, to St. Ives. Here God has made all our enemies to be at peace with us, so that I might have preached in any part of the town. But I rather chose a meadow, where such as would might sit down, either on the grass or on the hedges—so the Cornish term their broad stone walls, which are usually covered with grass. Here I enforced, "Fear God, and keep His commandments; for this is the whole of man."

Sat. Sept. 1.—I took a walk to the top of that celebrated hill, Carn Brae. Here are many monuments of remote antiquity, scarce to be found in any other part of Europe: Druid altars of enormous size, being only huge rocks, strangely suspended one upon the other; and rock-basins, hollowed on the surface of the rock, it is supposed, to contain the holy water. It is probable these are at least coeval with Pompey's theatre, if not with the pyramids of Egypt. And what are they the better for this? Of what consequence is it either to the dead or the living, whether they have withstood the wastes of time for three thousand or three hundred years?

Congregation of 20,000

Sun. 2.—At five in the evening I preached in the natural amphitheatre at Gwennap. The people covered a circle of near fourscore yards diameter, and could not be fewer than twenty thousand. Yet, upon inquiry, I found they could all hear distinctly, it being a calm, still evening.

After visiting Medros, Plymouth, and Collumpton, I came on Friday, 7, to Taunton. Presently, after preaching, I took horse. The rain obliged us to make haste; but in a while the saddle came over his neck, and then turned under his belly. I had then only to throw myself off, or I must have fallen under him. I was a little bruised, but soon mounted again, and rode to Lympsham, and the next day to Bristol.

Sun. 9.—My voice was weak when I preached at Princes Street in the morning. It was stronger at two in the afternoon, while I was preaching under the sycamore tree in Kingswood; and strongest of all at five in the evening, when we assembled near King's Square in Bristol.

Thur. Oct. 11.—About eleven I preached at Winchester, to a genteel and yet serious congregation. I was a little tired before I came to Portsmouth, but the congregation soon made me forget my weariness. Indeed the people in general here are more noble than most in the south of England. They receive the word of God " with all readiness of mind," and showed civility, at least, to all that preach it.

Fire at Portsmouth Dock

Fri. 12.—I walked round the Dock, much larger than any in England. The late fire began in a place where no one comes, just at low water, and at a time when all were fast asleep. So that none can doubt its being done by design. It spread with such amazing violence, among tow, and cordage, and dry wood, that none could come near without the utmost danger. Nor was anything expected, but the whole dock would be consumed, if not the town also. But this God would not permit. It stopped on one side, close to the commissioner's house ; and just as it was seizing the town on the other side, the wind changed and drove it back. Afterwards the fury of it was checked, by water, by sand, and by pulling down some buildings. And yet it was full five weeks before it was wholly put out.

Wesley Preaches Whitefield's Funeral Sermon

Sat. Nov. 10.—I returned to London, and had the melancholy news of Mr. Whitefield's death confirmed by his executors, who desired me to preach his funeral sermon on Sunday, the 18th. In order to write this, I retired to Lewisham on Monday ; and on Sunday following, went to the chapel in Tottenham Court Road. An immense multitude was gathered together from all corners of the town. I was at first afraid that a great part of the congregation would not be able to hear; but it pleased God so to strengthen my voice, that even those at the door heard distinctly. It was an awful season : all were still as night; most appeared to be deeply affected ; and an impression was made on many, which one would hope will not speedily be effaced.

The time appointed for my beginning at the Tabernacle was half-hour after five ; but it was quite filled at three, so I began at four. At first the noise was exceeding great ; but it ceased when I began to speak ; and my voice was again so strengthened that all who were within could hear, unless an accidental noise hindered here or there for a few moments. O that all may hear the voice of him with whom are the issues of life and death ; and who so loudly, by this unexpected stroke, calls all his children to love one another !

Fri. 23.——Being desired by the trustees of the tabernacle at Greenwich to preach Mr. Whitefield's funeral sermon there, I went over to-day for that purpose ; but neither would this house contain the congregation. Those who could not get in made some noise at first, but in a little while all were silent. Here, likewise, I trust God has given a blow to that bigotry which had prevailed for many years.

Mon. Dec. 3.—— I took a little journey into Kent. In the evening I preached at Chatham, in the new house, which was sufficiently crowded with attentive hearers.

Tues. 4.——I preached at Canterbury.

Wed. 5.——We went to Dover, where, with some difficulty, we climbed to the top of Shakespeare's cliff. It is exceeding high, and commands a vast prospect both by sea and land ; but it is nothing so terrible in itself as it is in his description. I preached to a very serious congregation in the evening as well as in the morning. The same, likewise, we observed at Canterbury; so that I hope to see good days here also.

Fri. 7.—I preached in Feversham at nine, and in the evening at Chatham. So we go through water and fire! And all is well, so we are doing or suffering the will of our Lord!

Wesley's Wife Leaves Him

Wed. 19.—About noon I preached at Dorking. The hearers were many, and seemed all attention. About an hundred attended at Ryegate in the evening, and between twenty and thirty in the morning; dull indeed as stones.

1771. Wed. Jan. 2.—I preached in the evening, at Deptford, a kind of funeral sermon for Mr. Whitefield. In every place I wish to show all possible respect to the memory of that great and good man.

Wed. 23.—For what cause I know not to this day, ——[Wesley's wife] set out for Newcastle, purposing "never to return." *Non eam reliqui: non dimisi: non revocabo*—[I did not desert her: I did not send her away: I will not recall her].

Fri. 25.—I revised and transcribed my will, declaring as simply, as plainly, and as briefly as I could, nothing more nor nothing else, but "what I would have done with the worldly goods which I leave behind me."

Thur. Feb. 14.—I went through both the upper and lower rooms of the London workhouse. It contains about an hundred children, who are in as good order as any private family. And the whole house is as clean, from top to bottom, as any gentleman's needs be. And why is not every workhouse in London, yea, through the kingdom, in the same order? Purely for want either of sense, or of honesty and activity, in them that superintend it.

Mon. 25.—I showed a friend, coming out of the country, the tombs in Westminster Abbey. The two with which I still think none of the others worthy to be compared are that of Mrs. Nightingale, and that of the Admiral rising out of his tomb at the resurrection. But the vile flattery inscribed on many of them reminded me of that just reflection :

> If on the sculptured marble you rely,
> Pity that worth like his should ever die.
> If credit to the real life you give,
> Pity a wretch like him should ever live !

The Earl of Desmond's Castle

Wed. May 22 (Ireland).—After preaching at Balligarane, I rode to Ashkayton. There are no ruins, I believe, in the kingdom of Ireland, to be compared to these. The old Earl of Desmond's Castle is very large, and has been exceeding strong. Not far from this, and formerly communicating with it by a gallery, is his great hall, or banqueting room. The walls are still firm and entire; and these with the fine carvings of the window-frames (all of polished marble), give some idea of what it was once. Its last master lived like a prince for many years, and rebelled over and over against Queen Elizabeth. After his last rebellion, his army being totally routed, he fled into the woods with two or three hundred men. But the pursuit was so hot, that these were soon scattered from him, and he crept alone into a small cabin. He was sitting there, when a soldier came in and struck him. He rose and said, "I am the Earl of Desmond." The wretch, rejoicing that he had found so great a prize, cut off his head at once. Queen Elizabeth and King

James allowed a pension to his relict for many years. I have seen a striking picture of her, in her widow's weeds, said to be taken when she was an hundred and forty years old.

At a small distance from the castle stands the old abbey, the finest ruin of the kind in the kingdom. Not only the walls of the church, and many of the apartments, but the whole cloisters are entire. They are built of black marble exquisitely polished, and vaulted over with the same. So that they are as firm now as when they were built, perhaps seven or eight hundred years ago; and, if not purposely destroyed (as most of the ancient buildings in Ireland have been), may last these thousand years. But add these to the years they have stood already, and what is it to eternity? A moment!

Mon. June 24.—This day I entered the sixty-ninth year of my age. I am still a wonder to myself. My voice and strength are the same as at nine-and-twenty This also hath God wrought.

Wesley in Winchester Cathedral

Tues. Oct. 1.—I went on to Salisbury. Wednesday, 2. I preached at Whitchurch; Thursday, 3, at Winchester. I now found time to take a view of the cathedral. Here the sight of that bad Cardinal's tomb, whom the sculptor has placed in a posture of prayer, brought to my mind those fine lines of Shakespeare, which he put into the mouth of King Henry the Sixth:

> Lord Cardinal,
> If thou hast any hope of Heaven's grace,
> Give us a sign. He dies, and makes no sign.

On Thursday and Friday evening I preached at Portsmouth Common. Saturday, 5. I set out at two. About ten some of our London friends met me at

Cobham, with whom I took a walk in the neighbouring gardens, inexpressibly pleasant, through the variety of hills and dales, and the admirable contrivance of the whole. And now, after spending his life in bringing it to perfection, the grey-headed owner advertises it to be sold! Is there anything under the sun that can satisfy a spirit made for God?

Wed. 16.—I preached at South-Lye. Here it was that I preached my first sermon, six-and-forty years ago. One man was in my present audience who heard it. Most of the rest are gone to their long home.

Wed. 30.—I walked over to Winchelsea from Rye, said to have been once a large city, with abundance of trade and of inhabitants, the sea washing the foot of the hill on which it stands. The situation is exceeding bold, the hill being high and steep on all sides. But the town is shrunk almost into nothing, and the seven churches into half an one. I preached at eleven in the new square, to a considerable number of serious people; and at Rye in the evening, where were many that are " not far from the kingdom of God."

Tues. Nov. 5.—In our way to Bury we called at Felsham, near which is the seat of the late Mr. Reynolds. The house is, I think, the best contrived and the most beautiful I ever saw. It has four fronts, and five rooms on a floor, elegantly, though not sumptuously, furnished. At a small distance stands a delightful grove. On every side of this, the poor, rich man, who had no hope beyond the grave, placed seats, to enjoy life as long as he could. But being resolved none of his family should be " put into the ground," he built a structure in the midst of the grove, vaulted above and beneath, with niches for coffins, strong enough to stand for ages. In one of these he had soon the satisfaction of laying the remains of his only child ; and, two years after, those of his wife. After two years more, in the year 1759, having eat, and drank, and forgotten God, for eighty-four years, he went himself to give an account of his stewardship.

Wesley at Windsor Park

Fri. 29.—We viewed the improvements of that active and useful man, the late Duke of Cumberland. The most remarkable work is the triangular tower which he built on the edge of Windsor Park. It is surrounded with shrubberies and woods, having some straight, some serpentine, walks in them, and commands a beautiful prospect all three ways : a very extensive one to the south-west. In the lower part is an alcove, which must be extremely pleasant in a summer evening. There is a little circular projection at each corner, one of which is filled by a geometrical staircase : the other two contain little apartments, one of which is a study. I was agreeably surprised to find many of the books not only religious, but admirably well chosen. Perhaps the great man spent many hours here, with only him that seeth in secret ; and who can say how deep that change went, which was so discernible in the latter part of his life ?

Hence we went to Mr. Bateman's house, the oddest I ever saw with my eyes. Everything breathes antiquity ; scarce a bedstead is to be seen that is not an hundred and fifty years old ; and everything is quite out of the common way : he scorns to have anything like his neighbours. For six hours, I suppose, these elegant oddities would much delight a curious man ; but after six months they would probably give him no more pleasure than a collection of feathers.

Mon. Dec. 16.—I rode to Dorking, where were many

people; but none were cut to the heart. Tuesday, 17. I went on to Ryegate-place. In King Henry the Fourth's time, this was an eminent monastery. At the dissolution of monasteries, it fell into the hands of the great spoiler, Henry the Eighth. Queen Elizabeth, pleased with the situation, chose it for one of her palaces. The gentleman who possesses it now has entirely changed the form of it; pulling down whole piles of ancient building, and greatly altering what remains. Yet, after all that is taken away, it still looks more like a palace than a private house. The staircase is of the same model with that at Hampton-court: one would scarce know which is the original. The chimney-piece in the hall is probably one of the most curious pieces of wood-work now in the kingdom. But how long? How many of its once bustling inhabitants are already under the earth! And how little a time will it be before the house itself, yea, the earth shall be burned up!

Sat. 21.—I met an old friend, James Hutton, whom I had not seen for five-and-twenty years. I felt this made no difference; my heart was quite open; his seemed to be the same; and we conversed just as we did in 1738, when we met in Fetter Lane.

Monday, 23, and so all the following days, when I was not particularly engaged, I spent an hour in the morning with our preachers, as I used to do with my pupils at Oxford. Wednesday, 25. I preached early at the Foundery; morning and afternoon, at the chapel. In returning thence at night, a coach ran full against my chaise, and broke one of the shafts and the traces in pieces. I was thankful that this was all; that neither man nor beast received the least hurt.

Mon. 30.—At my brother's request, I sat again for

my picture.   This melancholy employment always reminds me of that natural reflection—

> Behold, what frailty we in man may see!
> His shadow is less given to change than he.

1772. Tues. Jan. 14.—I spent an agreeable hour with Dr. S——, the oldest acquaintance I now have.   He is the greatest genius in little things that ever fell under my notice.   Almost everything about him is of his own invention, either in whole or in part.   Even his fire-screen, his lamps of various sorts, his ink-horn, his very save-all.   I really believe, were he seriously to set about it, he could invent the best mouse-trap that ever was in the world.

Wesley as Art Critic

Thur. 16.—I set out for Luton.   The snow lay so deep on the road, that it was not without much difficulty, and some danger, we at last reached the town.   I was offered the use of the church: the frost was exceeding sharp, and the glass was taken out of the windows. However, for the sake of the people, I accepted the offer, though I might just as well have preached in the open air.   I suppose four times as many people were present, as would have been at the room; and about an hundred in the morning.   So I did not repent of my journey through the snow.

Fri. Feb. 7.—I called on a friend at Hampton Court, who went with me through the house.   It struck me more than anything of the kind I have seen in England, more than Blenheim House itself.   One great difference is, everything there appears designedly grand and splendid; here everything is quite, as it were, natural, and one thinks it cannot be otherwise.   If the expression may be allowed, there is a kind of stiffness runs through

the one, and an easiness through the other.   Of pictures
I do not pretend to be a judge; but there is one, by
Paul Rubens, which particularly struck me, both with
the design and the execution of it.   It is Zacharias and
Elizabeth, with John the Baptist, two or three years old,
coming to visit Mary, and our Lord sitting upon her
knee.   The passions are surprisingly expressed, even in
the children; but I could not see either the decency or
common sense of painting them stark naked: nothing
can defend or excuse this: it is shockingly absurd, even
an Indian being the judge.   I allow, a man who paints
thus may have a good hand, but certainly no brains.

Wesley on "A Sentimental Journey"

Tues. 11.—I casually took a volume of what is called,
"A Sentimental Journey through France and Italy."
Sentimental! what is that? It is not English: he
might as well say, Continental. It is not sense. It
conveys no determinate idea; yet one fool makes
many. And this nonsensical word (who would believe
it ?) is become a fashionable one! However, the book
agrees full well with the title ; for one is as queer as the
other. For oddity, uncouthness, and unlikeness to
all the world beside, I suppose, the writer is without a
rival.

Wed. 12.—In returning, I read a very different book,
published by an honest Quaker, on that execrable sum
of all villanies, commonly called the Slave Trade. I
read of nothing like it in the heathen world, whether
ancient or modern: and it infinitely exceeds, in every
instance of barbarity, whatever Christian slaves suffer in
Mahometan countries.

Fri. 14.—I began to execute a design, which had
long been in my thoughts, to print as accurate an

edition of my works, as a bookseller would do. Surely I ought to be as exact for God's sake, as he would be for money.

Mon. 17.—One gave me a very remarkable relation : A gay young woman lately came up to London. Curiosity led her to hear a sermon, which cut her to the heart. One standing by, observed how she was affected, and took occasion to talk with her. She lamented that she should hear no more such sermons, as she was to go into the country the next day ; but begged her new acquaintance to write to her there, which she promised to do. In the country her convictions so increased, that she resolved to put an end to her own life. With this design she was going up stairs, when her father caled her, and gave her a letter from London. It was from her new acquaintance, who told her, " Christ is just ready to receive you : now is the day of salvation." She cried out, " It is, it is ! Christ is mine ! " and was filled with joy unspeakable. She begged her father to give her pen, ink, and paper, that she might answer her friend immediately. She told her what God had done for her soul, and added, " We have no time to lose ! The Lord is at hand !   Now, even now, we are stepping into eternity." She directed her letter, dropped down, and died.

Wesley and the Boarding-school

Fri. 21.—I met several of my friends, who had begun a subscription to prevent my riding on horseback ; which I cannot do quite so well, since a hurt which I got some months ago. If they continue it, well ; if not, I shall have strength according to my need.

Mon. April 6 (Manchester).—In the afternoon I drank tea at Am. O. But how was I shocked !   The

children that used to cling about me, and drink in every
word, had been at a boarding-school. There they had
unlearned all religion, and even seriousness; and had
learned pride, vanity, affectation, and whatever could
guard them against the knowledge and love of God.
Methodist parents, who would send your girls headlong
to hell, send them to a fashionable boarding-school!

Tues. 14.—I set out for Carlisle. A great part of
the road was miserably bad. However, we reached it
in the afternoon, and found a small company of plain,
loving people. The place where they had appointed me
to preach was out of the gate; yet it was tolerably
filled with attentive hearers. Afterwards, inquiring for
the Glasgow road, I found it was not much round to go
by Edinburgh; so I chose that road, and went five
miles forward this evening, to one of our friends' houses.
Here we had an hearty welcome, under a lowly roof,
with sweet and quiet rest.

Wed. 15.—Though it was a lone house, we had a
large congregation at five in the morning. Afterwards
we rode for upwards of twenty miles, through a most
delightful country; the fruitful mountains rising on
either hand, and the clear stream running beneath.
In the afternoon we had a furious storm of rain and
snow: however, we reached Selkirk safe. Here I
observed a little piece of stateliness which was quite
new to me: the maid came in, and said, "Sir, the lord
of the stable waits to know if he should feed your
horses." We call him ostler in England. After supper
all the family seemed glad to join with us in prayer.

Thur. 16.—We went on through the mountains,
covered with snow, to Edinburgh.

Sat. 18.—I set out for Glasgow. One would rather
have imagined it was the middle of January than the

middle of April. The snow covered the mountains on either hand, and the frost was exceeding sharp; so I preached within, both this evening and on Sunday morning. But in the evening the multitude constrained me to stand in the street. My text was, "What God has cleansed, that call not thou common." Hence I took occasion to fall upon their miserable bigotry for opinions and modes of worship. Many seemed to be not a little convinced; but how long will the impression continue ?

Wesley at Greenock and Glasgow

Mon. 20.—I went on to Greenock, a sea-port town, twenty miles west of Glasgow. It is built very much like Plymouth Dock, and has a safe and spacious harbour. The trade and inhabitants, and consequently the houses, are increasing swiftly; and so is cursing, swearing, drunkenness, Sabbath-breaking, and all manner of wickedness. Our room is about thrice as large as that at Glasgow; but it would not near contain the congregation. I spoke exceeding plain, and not without hope that we may see some fruit, even among this hardhearted generation.

Tues. 21.—The house was very full in the morning; and they showed an excellent spirit; for after I had spoke a few words on the head, every one stood up at the singing. In the afternoon I preached at Port-Glasgow, a large town, two miles east of Greenock. Many gay people were there, careless enough; but the greater part seemed to hear with understanding. In the evening I preached at Greenock; and God gave them a loud call, whether they will hear or whether they will forbear.

Wed. 22.—About eight I preached once more in the

Masons' Lodge, at Port-Glasgow. The house was crowded
greatly ; and I suppose all the gentry of the town were
part of the congregation. Resolving not to shoot over
their heads, as I had done the day before, I spoke
strongly of death and judgment, heaven and hell. This
they seemed to comprehend ; and there was no more
laughing among them, or talking with each other ; but
all were quietly and deeply attentive.

In the evening, when I began at Glasgow, the congregation being but small, I chose a subject fit for
experienced Christians ; but soon after, a heap of fine
gay people came in : yet I could not decently break off
what I was about, though they gaped and stared abundantly. I could only give a short exhortation in the
close, more suited to their capacity.

Wesley Receives the Freedom of Perth

Tues. 28 (Dunkeld).—We walked through the Duke
of Athol's gardens, in which was one thing I never saw
before—a summer-house in the middle of a green-
house, by means of which one might in the depth of
winter enjoy the warmth of May, and sit surrounded
with greens and flowers on every side.

In the evening I preached once more at Perth, to a
large and serious congregation. Afterwards they did
me an honour I never thought of—presented me with
the freedom of the city.

In my way to Perth, I read over the first volume of
Dr. Robertson's " History of Charles the Fifth." I
know not when I have been so disappointed. It might
as well be called the History of Alexander the Great.
Here is a quarto volume of eight or ten shillings' price,
containing dry, verbose dissertations on feudal government, the substance of all which might be comprised in

half a sheet of paper ! But " Charles the Fifth ! " Where
is Charles the Fifth ?

Leave off thy reflections, and give us thy tale !

Wed. 29.—I went on to Brechin, and preached in
the town-hall to a congregation of all sorts, Seceders,
Glassites, Nonjurors, and what not ?   O what excuse have
ministers in Scotland for not declaring the whole counsel
of God, where the bulk of the people not only endure,
but love plain dealing !

Friday and Saturday.—I rested at Aberdeen.

Sun. May 3.—I went in the morning to the English
church. Here, likewise, I could not but admire
the exemplary decency of the congregation. This was
the more remarkable, because so miserable a reader
I never heard before. Listening with all attention, I
understood but one single word, Balak, in the first
lesson; and one more, begat, was all I could possibly
distinguish in the second. Is there no man of spirit
belonging to this congregation ?   Why is such a
burlesque upon public worship suffered ?   Would it
not be far better to pay this gentleman for doing
nothing, than for doing mischief; for bringing a scandal
upon religion ?

About three I preached at the College kirk in the Old
Town to a large congregation, rich and poor; at six, in
our own house, on the narrow way. I spoke exceeding
plain, both this evening and the next; yet none were
offended. What encouragement has every preacher in
this country, " by manifestation of the truth," to " commend " himself " to every man's conscience in the sight
of God ! "

Tues. 5.—In the evening I preached in the new
house at Arbroath (properly Aberbrotheck). In this

town there is a change indeed! It was wicked to a proverb; remarkable for Sabbath-breaking, cursing, swearing, drunkenness, and a general contempt of religion. But it is not so now. Open wickedness disappears; no oaths are heard, no drunkenness seen in the streets. And many have not only ceased from evil, and learned to do well, but are witnesses of the inward kingdom of God, " righteousness, peace, and joy in the Holy Ghost."

Wed. 6.—The magistrates here also did me the honour of presenting me with the freedom of their corporation. I value it as a token of their respect, though I shall hardly make any farther use of it.

Wesley Visits the Bass Rock

Wed. 20—In the evening I preached at Dunbar. Thursday, 21. I went to the Bass, seven miles from it, which, in the horrid reign of Charles the Second, was the prison of those venerable men who suffered the loss of all things for a good conscience. It is a high rock surrounded by the sea, two or three miles in circumference, and about two miles from the shore. The strong east wind made the water so rough, that the boat could hardly live: and when we came to the only landing-place (the other sides being quite perpendicular), it was with much difficulty that we got up, climbing on our hands and knees. The castle, as one may judge by what remains, was utterly inaccessible. The walls of the chapel, and of the Governor's house, are tolerably entire. The garden walls are still seen near the top of the rock, with the well in the midst of it. And round the walls there are spots of grass, that feed eighteen or twenty sheep.

But the proper natives of the island are Solund-geese,

a bird about the size of a Muscovy duck, which breed
by thousands, from generation to generation, on the
sides of the rock.   It is peculiar to these, that they lay
but one egg, which they do not sit upon at all, but keep
it under one foot (as we saw with our eyes), till it is
hatched.   How many prayers did the holy men confined
here offer up, in that evil day !   And how many thanksgivings should we return, for all the liberty, civil and
religious, which we enjoy !

At our return, we walked over the ruins of Tantallon
Castle, once the seat of the great Earls of Douglas.   The
front walls (it was four square) are still standing, and by
their vast height and huge thickness, give us a little idea
of what it once was.   Such is human greatness !

Fri. 22.—We took a view of the famous Roman
camp, lying on a mountain, two or three miles from
the town.   It is encompassed with two broad and deep
ditches, and is not easy of approach on any side.   Here
lay General Lesley with his army, while Cromwell was
starving below.   He had no way to escape; but the
enthusiastic fury of the Scots delivered him.   When
they marched into the valley to swallow him up, he
mowed them down like grass.

Sat. 23.—I went on to Alnwick, and preached in the
town hall.   What a difference between an English and a
Scotch congregation !   These judge themselves rather
than the preacher; and their aim is, not only to know,
but to love and obey.

Through the Dales

Mon. June 1.—I began a little tour through the
Dales.   About nine, I preached at Kiphill; at one, at
Wolsingham.   Here we began to trace the revival of the
work of God; and here began the horrid mountains we

had to climb over. However, before six, we reached Barnard Castle. I preached at the end of the preaching-house, to a large congregation of established Christians. At five in the morning, the house was near full of persons ripe for the height and depth of the Gospel.

Tues. 2.—We rode to New-Orygan in Teesdale. The people were deeply attentive; but, I think, not deeply affected. From the top of the next enormous mountain, we had a view of Weardale. It is a lovely prospect. The green gently rising meadows and fields, on both sides of the little river, clear as crystal, were sprinkled over with innumerable little houses; three in four of which (if not nine in ten) are sprung up since the Methodists came hither. Since that time, the beasts are turned into men, and the wilderness into a fruitful field.

Thur. 4.—At five I took my leave of this blessed people. I was a little surprised, in looking attentively upon them, to observe so many beautiful faces as I never saw before in one congregation; many of the children in particular, twelve or fourteen of whom (chiefly boys) sat full in my view. But I allow, much more might be owing to grace than nature, to the heaven within, that shone outward.

Field-preaching as Wesley's Cross

Fri. Aug. 21.—I preached again about eight, and then rode back to Harford. After dinner we hasted to the Passage; but the watermen were not in haste to fetch us over; so I sat down on a convenient stone, and finished the little tract I had in hand. However, I got to Pembroke in time, and preached in the town hall, where we had a solemn and comfortable opportunity.

Sun. Sept. 6.—I preached on the quay, at Kingswood, and near King's Square. To this day field-preaching is a cross to me. But I know my commission, and see no other way of " preaching the Gospel to every creature."

Wed. Oct. 14.—A book was given me to write on, " The Works of Mr. Thomson," of whose poetical abilities I had always had a very low opinion ; but looking into one of his tragedies, " Edward and Eleonora," I was agreeably surprised. The sentiments are just and noble ; the diction strong, smooth, and elegant ; and the plot conducted with the utmost art, and wrought off in a most surprising manner. It is quite his masterpiece, and I really think might vie with any modern performance of the kind.

Good or Bad Spirits?

Sat. 31.—A young man of good sense, and an unblamable character, gave me a strange account of what (he said) had happened to himself, and three other persons in the same house. As I knew they all feared God, I thought the matter deserved a farther examination. So in the afternoon I talked largely with them all. The sum of their account was this :

" Near two years ago, Martin S—— and William J—— saw, in a dream, two or three times repeated to each of them, a person who told them there was a large treasure hid in such a spot, three miles from Norwich, consisting of money and plate, buried in a chest, between six and eight feet deep. They did not much regard this, till each of them, when they were broad awake, saw an elderly man and woman standing by their bedside, who told them the same thing, and bade them go and dig it up, between eight and twelve at night. Soon after, they went ; but, being afraid, took a third man with them. They began digging at eight, and after they had dug six feet, saw the top of a coffer, or chest. But presently it sunk down into the earth; and there appeared over the place a large globe of bright fire, which, after some time, rose higher and higher, till it was quite out of sight. Not long after, the man and woman appeared again, and said, 'You spoiled all, by bringing that man with you.' From this time, both they and Sarah and Mary J——, who live in the same house with them, have heard, several times in a week, delightful music, for a quarter of an hour at a time. They often hear it before those persons appear; often when they do not appear." They asked me whether they were good or bad spirits; but I could not resolve them.

A Remarkable Dream

Tues. Nov. 17.—One was relating a remarkable story, which I thought worthy to be remembered. Two years ago, a gentleman of large fortune in Kent dreamed that he was walking through the churchyard, and saw a new monument with the following inscription:

Here lies the Body

OF

SAMUEL SAVAGE, ESQ.,

WHO DEPARTED THIS LIFE ON SEPTEMBER —, 1772, AGED —

He told his friends in the morning, and was much affected: but the impression soon wore off. But on that day he did depart; and a stone was erected with that very inscription.

A gentlewoman present added a relation equally surprising, which she received from the person's own mouth:

"Mrs. B——, when about fourteen years of age, being at a boarding-school, a mile or two from her father's, dreamed she was on the top of the church-steeple, when a man came up, and threw her down to the roof of the church. Yet she seemed not much hurt, till he came to her again, and threw her to the bottom. She thought she looked hard at him, and said, 'Now you have hurt me sadly, but I shall hurt you worse'; and waked. A week after, she was to go to her father's. She set out early in the morning. At the entrance of a little wood, she stopped, and doubted whether she should not go round, instead of through it. But, knowing no reason, she went straight through, till she came to the other side. Just as she was going over the style, a man pulled her back by the hair. She immediately knew it was the same man whom she had seen in her dream. She fell on her knees, and begged him, 'For God's sake, do not hurt me any more.' He put his hands round her neck, and squeezed her so, that she instantly lost her senses. He then stripped her, carried her a little way, and threw her into a ditch.

"Meantime, her father's servant coming to the school, and hearing she was gone without him, walked back. Coming to the style, he heard several groans, and, looking about, saw many drops of blood. He traced them to the ditch, whence the groans came. He lifted her up, not knowing her at all, as her face was covered with blood, carried her to a neighbouring house, and running to the village, quickly brought a surgeon. She was just alive; but her throat was much hurt, so that she could not speak at all.

"Just then a young man of the village was missing. Search being made, he was apprehended in an alehouse two miles off. He had all her clothes with him in a

bag, which, he said, he found. It was three months
before she was able to go abroad. He was arraigned at
the Assizes. She knew him perfectly, and swore to the
man. He was condemned, and soon after executed."

Wed. Dec. 2.—I preached at the new preaching-
house, in the parish of Bromley. In speaking severally
to the members of the society, I was surprised at the
openness and artlessness of the people. Such I should
never have expected to find within ten miles of London.

Wesley's Letters and Friends

1773. Fri. Jan. 1.—We (as usual) solemnly renewed
our covenant with God.

Mon. 4.—I began revising my letters and papers.
One of them was wrote above an hundred and fifty years
ago (in 1619), I suppose, by my grandfather's father, to
her he was to marry in a few days. Several were wrote
by my brothers and me when at school, many while we
were at the University; abundantly testifying (if it be
worth knowing) what was our aim from our youth up.

Thur. 7.—I called where a child was dying of the
smallpox, and rescued her from death and the doctors,
who were giving her saffron, &c., to drive them out!
Can any one be so ignorant still?

We observed Friday 8, as a day of fasting and
prayer, on account of the general want of trade and
scarcity of provisions. The next week I made an end
of revising my letters; and from those I had both wrote
and received, I could not but make one remark—that
for above these forty years, of all the friends who were
once the most closely united, and afterwards separated
from me, every one had separated himself! He left me,
not I him. And from both mine and their own letters,
the steps whereby they did this are clear and undeniable.

Wed. Feb. 24.—A very remarkable paragraph was published in one of the Edinburgh papers :

" We learn from the Rosses, in the county of Donegal, in Ireland, that a Danish man-of-war, called the *North Crown*, commanded by the Baron D'Ulfeld, arrived off those islands, from a voyage of discovery towards the Pole.   They sailed from Bornholme, in Norway, the 1st of June 1769, with stores for eighteen months, and some able astronomers, landscape-painters, and every apparatus suitable to the design ; and steering N. by E. half E., for thirty-seven days, with a fair wind and open sea, discovered a large rocky island, which having doubled, they proceeded W.N.W., till the 17th of September, when they found themselves in a strong current, between two high lands, seemingly about ten leagues distant, which carried them at a prodigious rate for three days when, to their great joy, they saw the main land of America, that lies between the most westerly part of the settlements on Hudson's River and California. Here they anchored in a fine cove, and found abundance of wild deer and buffaloes, with which they victualled ; and sailing southward, in three months got into the Pacific Ocean, and returned by the Straits of Le Maine and the West India Islands.   They have brought many curiosities, particularly a prodigious bird, called a contor, or contose, above six feet in height, of the eagle kind, whose wings, expanded, measure twenty-two feet four inches.   After bartering some skins with the country people, for meal, rum, and other necessaries, they sailed for Bremen, to wait the thaw, previous to their return to Copenhagen.

" February 24, 1773."

If this account is true, one would hope not only the

King of Denmark will avail himself of so important a discovery.

I came to Liverpool on Saturday, March 20.

Mon. 22.—The captain was in haste to get my chaise on board. About eleven we went on board ourselves : and before one, we ran on a sand bank. So, the ship being fast, we went ashore again.

Tues. 23.—We embarked again on board the *Freemason*, with six other cabin-passengers, four gentlemen, and two gentlewomen, one of whom was daily afraid of falling in labour. This gave me several opportunities of talking closely and of praying with her and her companion. We did not come abreast of Holyhead till Thursday morning. We had then a strong gale, and a rolling sea. Most of the passengers were sick enough, but it did not affect me at all. In the evening the gentlemen desired I would pray with them ; so we concluded the day in a solemn and comfortable manner.

Wesley and his Chaise

Fri. 26.—We landed at Dunleary, and hired a coach to Dublin.

On Monday and Tuesday I examined the society, a little lessened, but now well united together. I was a little surprised to find the Commissioners of the Customs would not permit my chaise to be landed, because, they said, the captain of a packet-boat had no right to bring over goods. Poor pretence ! However, I was more obliged to them than I then knew ; for had it come on shore, it would have been utterly spoiled.

Mon. April 5.—Having hired such a chaise as I could, I drove to Edinderry.

Mon. 12.—I preached at Ballinasloe and Aghrim.

Tues. 13.—As I went into Eyre Court, the street was

full of people, who gave us a loud huzza when we passed through the market-place. I preached in the open air, to a multitude of people, all civil, and most of them serious. A great awakening has been in this town lately; and many of the most notorious and profligate sinners are entirely changed, and are happy witnesses of the gospel salvation.

Incidents in Ireland

Wed. 21.—Some applied to the Quakers at Enniscorthy, for the use of their meeting-house. They refused: so I stood at Hugh M'Laughlin's door, and both those within and without could hear. I was in doubt which way to take from hence, one of my chaise-horses being much tired; till a gentleman of Ballyrane, near Wexford, told me, if I would preach at his house the next evening, he would meet me on the road with a fresh horse. So I complied, though it was some miles out of the way. Accordingly, he met us on Thurday 22, six or seven miles from Enniscorthy. But we found his mare would not draw at all: so we were forced to go on as we could. I preached in the evening at Ballyrane, to a deeply serious congregation. Early in the morning we set out, and, at two in the afternoon, came to Ballibac-ferry.

A troop of sailors ran down to the shore, to see the chaise put into the boat. I was walking at a small distance, when I heard them cry out, " Avast ! Avast ! The coach is overset into the river." I thought, " However, it is well my bags are on shore ; so my papers are not spoiled." In less than an hour they fished up the chaise, and got it safe into the boat. As it would not hold us all, I got in myself, leaving the horses to come after. At half-hour after three I came to Passage.

Finding no post-chaise could be had, and having no
time to spare, I walked on (six or seven miles) to Waterford, and began preaching without delay, on, " My yoke
is easy, and my burden is light."

Sun. 25.—Word being brought me that the Mayor
was willing I should preach in the bowling-green, I went
thither in the evening.   An huge multitude was quickly
gathered together.   I preached on, " I saw the dead,
small and great, stand before God."   Some attempted
to disturb, but without success ; the bulk of the congregation being deeply attentive.   But as I was drawing to
a conclusion, some of the Papists set on their work in
earnest.   They knocked down John Christian, with two
or three more, who endeavoured to quiet them; and
then began to roar like the waves of the sea; but
hitherto could they come, and no farther.   Some gentlemen, who stood near me, rushed into the midst of them ;
and, after bestowing some heavy blows, seized the ring-
leader, and delivered him to the constable ; and one of
them undertook to conduct me home.   So few received
any hurt, but the rioters themselves ; which, I trust, will
make them more peaceable for the time to come.

A Neglected School

Thur. May 13.—We went on, through a most dreary
country, to Galway ; where, at the late survey, there
were twenty thousand Papists, and five hundred Protestants.   But which of them are Christians, have the
mind that was in Christ, and walk as He walked ?   And
without this, how little does it avail, whether they are
called Protestants or Papists !   At six I preached in the
court-house, to a large congregation, who all behaved well.

Fri. 14.—In the evening I preached at Ballinrobe ;
and on Saturday went on to Castlebar.   Entering the

town, I was struck with the sight of the Charter-school;
—no gate to the courtyard, a large chasm in the wall,
heaps of rubbish before the house-door, broken windows
in abundance ; the whole a picture of slothfulness, nasti-
ness, and desolation !

I did not dream there were any inhabitants, till, the
next day, I saw about forty boys and girls walking from
church. As I was just behind them, I could not but
observe, 1. That there was neither master nor mistress,
though, it seems, they were both well : 2. That both
boys and girls were completely dirty : 3. That none of
them seemed to have any garters on, their stockings
hanging about their heels : 4. That in the heels, even of
many of the girls' stockings, were holes larger than a
crown-piece. I gave a plain account of these things to
the trustees of the Charter-school in Dublin : whether
they are altered or no, I cannot tell.

Mobbed by Masons

Mon. 24.—About noon I preached at Tonnylommon.
One of my horses having a shoe loose, I borrowed
Mr. Watson's horse, and left him with the chaise.
When we came near Enniskillen, I desired two only to
ride with me, and the rest of our friends to keep at a
distance. Some masons were at work on the first
bridge, who gave us some coarse words. We had
abundance more as we rode through the town ; but
many soldiers being in the street, and taking knowledge
of me in a respectful manner, the mob shrunk back.
An hour after Mr. Watson came in the chaise. Before
he came to the bridge many ran together, and began to
throw whatever came next to hand. The bridge itself
they had blocked up with large stones, so that a carriage
could not pass ; but an old man cried out, " Is this the

way you use strangers ? " and rolled away the stones. The mob quickly rewarded him by plastering him over with mortar from head to foot. They then fell upon the carriage, which they cut with stones in several places, and well nigh covered with dirt and mortar. From one end of the town to the other, the stones flew thick about the coachman's head. Some of them were two or three pounds' weight, which they threw with all their might. If but one of them had struck him, it would have effectually prevented him from driving any farther ; and, then, doubtless, they would have given an account of the chaise and horses.

I preached at Sydore in the evening and morning, and then set out for Roosky. The road lay not far from Enniskillen. When we came pretty near the town, both men and women saluted us, first with bad words, and then with dirt and stones. My horses soon left them behind ; but not till they had broke one of the windows, the glass of which came pouring in upon me ; but did me no further hurt.

About an hour after, John Smith came to Enniskillen. The masons on the bridge preparing for battle, he was afraid his horse would leap with him into the river; and therefore chose to alight. Immediately they poured in upon him a whole shower of dirt and stones. However, he made his way through the town, though pretty much daubed and bruised.

Wed. 26.—We set out at half-hour past two, and reached Omagh a little before eleven. Finding I could not reach Ding-bridge by two o'clock in the chaise, I rode forward with all the speed I could; but the horse dropping a shoe, I was so retarded that I did not reach the place till between three and four. I found the minister and the people waiting; but the church would not near contain them ; so I preached near it to a mixed multitude of rich and poor, Churchmen, Papists, and Presbyterians. I was a little weary and faint when I came, the sun having shone exceeding hot; but the number and behaviour of the congregation made me forget my own weariness.

Having a good horse, I rode to the place where I was to lodge (two miles off) in about an hour. After tea they told me another congregation was waiting : so I began preaching without delay ; and warned them of the madness which was spreading among them, namely, leaving the church. Most of them, I believe, will take the advice; I hope all that are of our society.

Wesley at Derry and Armagh

Thur. 27.—I went on to Londonderry. Friday, 28. I was invited to see the bishop's palace (a grand and beautiful structure), and his garden, newly laid, and exceeding pleasant. Here I innocently gave some offence to the gardener, by mentioning the English of a Greek word. But he set us right, warmly assuring us that the English name of the flower is not Crane's bill, but Geranium !

Sat. 29.—We walked out to one of the pleasantest spots which I have seen in the kingdom. It is a garden laid out on the steep side of an hill; one shady walk of which, in particular, commands all the vale and the hill beyond. The owner finished his walks—and died.

Sat. June 5. Armagh.—I walked over the fine improvements which the Primate has made near his lodge. The ground is hardly two miles round ; but it is laid out to the best advantage. Part is garden, part meadow, part planted with shrubs or trees of various kinds. The house is built of fine white stone, and is fit for a nobleman. He intends to carry away a bog which lies behind it, and have a large piece of water in its place. He intends also to improve the town greatly, and to execute many other grand designs; I doubt too many even for a Primate of Ireland, that is above seventy years old!

The Speaking Statue Again

Mon. 14.—After preaching at Lurgan, I inquired of Mr. Miller, whether he had any thoughts of perfecting his speaking statue, which had so long lain by. He said he had altered his design; that he intended, if he had life and health, to make two, which would not only speak, but sing hymns alternately with an articulate voice; that he had made a trial, and it answered well. But he could not tell when he should finish it, as he had much business of other kinds, and could only give his leisure hours to this. How amazing is it that no man of fortune enables him to give all his time to the work!

I preached in the evening at Lisburn. All the time I could spare here was taken up by poor patients. I generally asked, "What remedies have you used?" and was not a little surprised. What has fashion to do with physic? Why (in Ireland, at least), almost as much as with head-dress. Blisters, for any thing or nothing, were all the fashion when I was in Ireland last. Now the grand fashionable medicine for twenty diseases (who would imagine it?) is mercury sublimate! Why is it not an halter, or a pistol? They would cure a little more speedily.

Tues. 15.—When I came to Belfast, I learned the real cause of the late insurrections in this neighbour-hood. Lord Donegal, the proprietor of almost the

whole country, came hither to give his tenants new
leases.   But when they came, they found two merchants
of the town had taken their farms over their heads; so
that multitudes of them, with their wives and children,
were turned out to the wide world.   It is no wonder
that, as their lives were now bitter to them, they
should fly out as they did.   It is rather a wonder that
they did not go much farther.   And if they had, who
would have been most in fault?   Those who were
without home, without money, without food for themselves and families? or those who drove them to this
extremity?

The Earthquake at Madeley

Mon. July 5.—About eleven we crossed Dublin-bar,
and were at Hoy-lake the next afternoon.   This was
the first night I ever lay awake in my life, though I was
at ease in body and mind.   I believe few can say this:
in seventy years I never lost one night's sleep!

I went, by moderate stages, from Liverpool to
Madeley; where I arrived on Friday, 9.   The next
morning we went to see the effects of the late earthquake:
such it undoubtedly was.   On Monday, 27, at four in
the morning, a rumbling noise was heard, accompanied
with sudden gusts of wind, and wavings of the ground.
Presently the earthquake followed, which only shook the
farmer's house, and removed it entire about a yard; but
carried the barn about fifteen yards, and then swallowed
it up in a vast chasm; tore the ground into numberless
chasms, large and small; in the large, threw up mounts,
fifteen or twenty feet high: carried an hedge, with two
oaks, above forty feet, and left them in their natural posi-
tion.   It then moved under the bed of the river; which,
making more resistance, received a ruder shock, being

shattered in pieces, and heaved up about thirty feet from its foundations. By throwing this, and many oaks, into its channel, the Severn was quite stopped up, and constrained to flow backward, till, with incredible fury, it wrought itself a new channel. Such a scene of desolation I never saw. Will none tremble when God thus terribly shakes the earth?

Mon. Aug. 16.—In the evening I preached at St. Austle; Tuesday, 17, in the coinage-hall at Truro; at six, in the main street at Helstone. How changed is this town, since a Methodist preacher could not ride through it without hazard of his life!

A Man of Seventy Preaches to 30,000 People

Sat. 21.—I preached in Illogan and at Redruth; Sunday, 22, in St. Agnes church-town, at eight; about one at Redruth; and at five, in the amphitheatre at Gwennap. The people both filled it, and covered the ground round about, to a considerable distance. So that, supposing the space to be fourscore yards square, and to contain five persons in a square yard, there must be above two and thirty thousand people; the largest assembly I ever preached to. Yet I found, upon inquiry, all could hear, even to the skirts of the congregation! Perhaps the first time that a man of seventy had been heard by thirty thousand persons at once!

Mon. Sept. 13.—My cold remaining, I was ill able to speak. In the evening I was much worse, my palate and throat being greatly inflamed. However, I preached as I could; but I could then go no farther. I could swallow neither liquids nor solids, and the windpipe seemed nearly closed. I lay down at my usual time, but the defluxion of rheum was so uninterrupted,

that I slept not a minute till near three in the morning.
On the following nine days I grew better.

Sun. 19.—I thought myself able to speak to the
congregation, which I did for half an hour; but afterwards I found a pain in my left side and in my shoulder
by turns, exactly as I did at Canterbury twenty years
before. In the morning I could scarce lift my hand to
my head; but, after being electrified, I was much better;
so that I preached with tolerable ease in the evening;
and the next evening read the letters, though my voice
was weak. From this time I slowly recovered my voice
and my strength; and on Sunday preached without any
trouble.

Mon. Oct. 4.—I went, by Shepton-mallet, to Shaftes-
bury, and on Tuesday to Salisbury. Wednesday, 6.
Taking chaise at two in the morning, in the evening I
came well to London. The rest of the week I made
what inquiry I could into the state of my accounts.
Some confusion had arisen from the sudden death of
my book-keeper; but it was less than might have been
expected.

A Monster Elm

Monday, 11, and the following days, I took a little
tour through Bedfordshire and Northamptonshire. Between Northampton and Towcester we met with a great
natural curiosity, the largest elm I ever saw; it was
twenty-eight feet in circumference; six feet more than
that which was some years ago in Magdalen-college walks
at Oxford.

1774. Mon. Jan. 24.—I was desired by Mrs. Wright,
of New-York, to let her take my effigy in wax-work. She
has that of Mr. Whitefield and many others; but none
of them, I think, comes up to a well-drawn picture.

Fri. May 20.—I rode over to Mr. Fraser's, at Monedie, whose mother-in-law was to be buried that day. O what a difference is there between the English and the Scotch method of burial! The English does honour to human nature; and even to the poor remains, that were once a temple of the Holy Ghost! But when I see in Scotland a coffin put into the earth, and covered up without a word spoken, it reminds me of what was spoken concerning Jehoiakim, "He shall be buried with the burial of an ass!"

Wesley Arrested in Edinburgh

Wed. June 1.—I went to Edinburgh, and the next day examined the society one by one. I was agreeably surprised. They have fairly profited since I was here last. Such a number of persons having sound Christian experience I never found in this society before. I preached in the evening to a very elegant congregation, and yet with great enlargement of heart.

Sat. 4.—I found uncommon liberty at Edinburgh in applying Ezekiel's vision of the dry bones. As I was walking home, two men followed me, one of whom said, "Sir, you are my prisoner. I have a warrant from the Sheriff to carry you to the Tolbooth." At first I thought he jested; but finding the thing was serious, I desired one or two of our friends to go up with me. When we were safe lodged in a house adjoining to the Tolbooth, I desired the officer to let me see his warrant. I found the prosecutor was one George Sutherland, once a member of the society. He had deposed, "That Hugh Saunderson, one of John Wesley's preachers, had taken from his wife one hundred pounds in money, and upwards of thirty pounds in goods; and had, besides that, terrified her into madness; so that, through the want of her help, and the loss of business, he was damaged five hundred pounds."

Before the Sheriff, Archibald Cockburn, Esq., he had deposed, " That the said John Wesley and Hugh Saunderson, to evade her pursuit, were preparing to fly the country; and therefore he desired his warrant to search for, seize, and incarcerate them in the Tolbooth, till they should find security for their appearance." To this request the Sheriff had assented, and given his warrant for that purpose.

But why does he incarcerate John Wesley? Nothing is laid against him, less or more. Hugh Saunderson preaches in connexion with him. What then? Was not the Sheriff strangely overseen?

Mr. Sutherland furiously insisted that the officer should carry us to the Tolbooth without delay. However, he waited till two or three of our friends came, and gave a bond for our appearance on the 24th instant. Mr. S. did appear, the cause was heard, and the prosecutor fined one thousand pounds.

Wesley's Terrible Ride

Sun. 5.—About eight I preached at Ormiston, twelve miles from Edinburgh. The house being small, I stood in the street, and proclaimed " the grace of our Lord Jesus Christ." The congregation behaved with the utmost decency. So did that on the Castle-hill in Edinburgh, at noon; though I strongly insisted, that God "now commandeth all men everywhere to repent." In the evening the house was thoroughly filled; and many seemed deeply affected. I do not wonder that Satan, had it been in his power, would have had me otherwise employed this day.

Mon. 20.—About nine I set out from Sunderland for Horsley, with Mr. Hopper and Mr. Smith. I took Mrs.

Smith and her two little girls, in the chaise with me. About two miles from the town, just on the brow of the hill, on a sudden both the horses set out, without any visible cause, and flew down the hill, like an arrow out of a bow. In a minute John fell off the coach-box. The horses then went on full speed, sometimes to the edge of the ditch on the right, sometimes on the left. A cart came up against them: they avoided it as exactly as if the man had been on the box. A narrow bridge was at the foot of the hill. They went directly over the middle of it. They ran up the next hill with the same speed; many persons meeting us, but getting out of the way. Near the top of the hill was a gate, which led into a farmer's yard. It stood open. They turned short, and run through it, without touching the gate on one side, or the post on the other.

I thought, "However, the gate which is on the other side of the yard, and is shut, will stop them": but they rushed through it, as if it had been a cobweb, and galloped on through the corn-field. The little girls cried out, "Grandpapa, save us!" I told them, "Nothing will hurt you: do not be afraid"; feeling no more fear or care (blessed be God!) than if I had been sitting in my study. The horses ran on, till they came to the edge of a steep precipice. Just then Mr. Smith, who could not overtake us before, galloped in between. They stopped in a moment. Had they gone on ever so little, he and we must have gone down together!

I am persuaded both evil and good angels had a large share in this transaction: how large we do not know now; but we shall know hereafter.

Tues. 28.—This being my birth-day, the first day of my seventy-second year, I was considering, How is this, that I find just the same strength as I did thirty years

ago ? That my sight is considerably better now, and my
nerves firmer, than they were then ? That I have none
of the infirmities of old age, and have lost several I had
in my youth ? The grand cause is, the good pleasure of
God, who doeth whatsoever pleaseth Him. The chief
means are : 1. My constantly rising at four, for about
fifty years. 2. My generally preaching at five in the
morning ; one of the most healthy exercises in the world.
3. My never travelling less, by sea or land, than four
thousand five hundred miles in a year.

A Collier's Remarkable Escape

Sat. July 30.—I went to Madeley ; and in the evening
preached under a sycamore-tree, in Madeley-wood, to a
large congregation, good part of them colliers, who
drank in every word. Surely never were places more
alike, than Madeley-wood, Gateshead-fell, and Kingswood.

Sun. 31.—The church could not contain the congregation, either morning or afternoon ; but in the evening I
preached to a still larger congregation at Broseley ; and
equally attentive. I now learned the particulars of a
remarkable story, which I had heard imperfectly before :
—Some time since, one of the colliers here, coming
home at night, dropped into a coal-pit, twenty-four yards
deep. He called aloud for help, but none heard all that
night, and all the following day. The second night,
being weak and faint, he fell asleep, and dreamed that
his wife, who had been some time dead, came to him,
and greatly comforted him. In the morning, a gentleman going a hunting, an hare started up just before the
hounds, ran straight to the mouth of the pit, and was
gone ; no man could tell how. The hunters searched
all round the pit, till they heard a voice from the bottom

They quickly procured proper help, and drew up the man unhurt.

Tues. Aug. 2.—I preached at ten in the town-hall at Evesham, and rode on to Broadmarston.

Thur. 4.—I crossed over to Tewkesbury, and preached at noon in a meadow near the town, under a tall oak. I went thence to Cheltenham. As it was the high season for drinking the waters, the town was full of gentry : so I preached near the market-place in the evening, to the largest congregation that was even seen there. Some of the footmen at first made a little disturbance; but I turned to them, and they stood reproved.

Sat. 6.—I walked from Newport to Berkeley-castle. It is a beautiful, though very ancient, building ; and every part of it kept in good repair, except the lumber-room and the chapel ; the latter of which, having been of no use for many years, is now dirty enough. I particularly admired the fine situation, and the garden on the top of the house. In one corner of the castle is the room where poor Richard II. was murdered. His effigy is still preserved, said to be taken before his death. If he was like this, he had an open, manly countenance, though with a cast of melancholy. In the afternoon we went on to Bristol.

Wesley at Corfe Castle

Mon. Oct. 10.—I preached at Salisbury; and on Tuesday, 11, set out for the Isle of Purbeck. When we came to Corfe-castle, the evening being quite calm and mild, I preached in a meadow near the town, to a deeply attentive congregation, gathered from all parts of the island.

Wed. 12.—I preached to a large congregation at five, who seemed quite athirst for instruction. Afterwards we took a walk over the remains of the castle, so bravely defended in the last century, against all the power of the Parliament forces, by the widow of the Lord Chief Justice Banks. It is one of the noblest ruins I ever saw : the walls are of an immense thickness, defying even the assaults of time, and were formerly surrounded by a deep ditch. The house, which stands in the middle, on the very top of the rock, has been a magnificent structure. Some time since the proprietor fitted up some rooms on the south-west side of this, and laid out a little garden, commanding a large prospect, pleasant beyond description. For a while he was greatly delighted with it : but the eye was not satisfied with seeing. It grew familiar ; it pleased no more ; and is now run all to ruin. No wonder : what can delight always, but the knowledge and love of God ?

A Methodist Isaac Newton

Monday, 31, and the following days, I visited the societies near London. Friday, November 4. In the afternoon John Downes (who had preached with us many years) was saying, " I feel such a love to the people at West-street, that I could be content to die with them. I do not find myself very well; but I must be with them this evening." He went thither, and began preaching, on, " Come unto me, ye that are weary and heavy-laden." After speaking ten or twelve minutes, he sunk down and spake no more, till his spirit returned to God.

I suppose he was by nature full as great a genius as Sir Isaac Newton. I will mention but two or three instances of it :—When he was at school, learning Algebra, he came one day to his master, and said, " Sir, I can prove this proposition a better way than it is proved in the book."

His master thought it could not be; but upon trial, acknowledged it to be so. Some time after, his father sent him to Newcastle with a clock, which was to be mended. He observed the clockmaker's tools, and the manner how he took it in pieces, and put it together again; and when he came home, first made himself tools, and then made a clock, which went as true as any in the town. I suppose such strength of genius as this has scarce been known in Europe before.

Another proof of it was this :—Thirty years ago, while I was shaving, he was whittling the top of a stick : I asked, " What are you doing ? " He answered, " I am taking your face, which I intend to engrave on a copper-plate." Accordingly, without any instruction, he first made himself tools, and then engraved the plate. The second picture which he engraved, was that which was prefixed to the " Notes upon the New Testament." Such another instance, I suppose, not all England, or perhaps Europe, can produce.

For several months past, he had far deeper communion with God, than ever he had had in his life; and for some days he had been frequently saying, " I am so happy, that I scarce know how to live. I enjoy such fellowship with God, as I thought could not be had on this side heaven." And having now finished his course of fifty-two years, after a long conflict with pain, sickness, and poverty, he gloriously rested from his labours, and entered into the joy of his Lord.

Sun. 13.—After a day of much labour, at my usual time (half-hour past nine), I lay down to rest. I told my servants, " I must rise at three, the Norwich coach setting out at four." Hearing one of them knock, though sooner than I expected, I rose and dressed myself; but afterwards, looking at my watch, I found it was but half-hour past ten. While I was considering what to do, I heard a confused sound of many voices below : and looking out at the window towards the yard, I saw it was as light as day. Meantime, many large flakes of fire were continually flying about the house ; all the upper part of which was built of wood, which was near as dry as tinder. A large deal-yard, at a very small distance from us, was all in a light fire ; from which the north-west wind drove the flames directly · upon the Foundery ; and there was no possibility of help, for no water could be found. Perceiving I could be of no use, I took my Diary and my papers, and retired to a friend's house. I had no fear ; committing the matter into God's hands, and knowing He would do whatever was best. Immediately the wind turned about from north-west to south-east ; and our pump supplied the engines with abundance of water ; so that in a little more than two hours, all the danger was over.

Wesley in the Fens

Tues. 22.—I took a solemn and affectionate leave of the society at Norwich. About twelve we took coach. About eight, Wednesday, 23, Mr. Dancer met me with a chaise, and carried me to Ely. O what want of common sense ! Water covered the high-road for a mile and a half. I asked, "How must foot-people come to the town ?" "Why, they must wade through !"

About two I preached in a house well filled with plain, loving people. I then took a walk to the cathedral, one of the most beautiful I have seen. The western tower is exceeding grand ; and the nave of an amazing height. Hence we went through a fruitful and pleasant country, though surrounded with fens, to Sutton. Here many people had lately been stirred up : they had prepared a large barn. At six o'clock it was well filled; and it seemed as if God sent a message to every soul.

Fri. 25.—I set out between eight and nine in a one-horse chaise, the wind being high and cold enough. Much snow lay on the ground, and much fell as we crept along over the fen-banks.

Honest Mr. Tubbs would needs walk and lead the horse through water and mud up to his mid-leg, smiling and saying, "We fen-men do not mind a little dirt." When we had gone about four miles, the road would not admit of a chaise. So I borrowed a horse, and rode forward ; but not far, for all the grounds were under water. Here therefore I procured a boat, full twice as large as a kneading-trough. I was at one end, and a boy at the other, who paddled me safe to Erith. There Miss L—— waited for me with another chaise, which brought me to It. Ives.

No Methodist, I was told, had preached in this town : so I thought it high time to begin; and about one I preached to a very well-dressed, and yet well-behaved congregation. Thence my new friend (how long will she be such ?) carried me to Godmanchester, near Huntingdon. A large barn was ready, in which Mr. Berridge and Mr. Venn used to preach. And though the weather was still severe, it was well filled with deeply attentive people.

Sat. 26.—I set out early, and in the evening reached London.

1775. Wed. Feb. 22.—I had an opportunity of seeing Mr. Gordon's curious garden at Mile-end, the like of which I suppose is hardly to be found in England, if in Europe. One thing in particular I learned here, the real nature of the tea-tree. I was informed, 1. That the green and the bohea are of quite different species. 2,

That the bohea is much tenderer than the green. 3.
That the green is an evergreen; and bears, not only in
the open air, but in the frost, perfectly well. 4. That
the herb of Paraguay likewise bears the frost, and is a
species of tea. 5. And I observed that they are all
species of bay or laurel. The leaf of green tea is both
of the colour, shape, and size of a bay leaf: that of
bohea is smaller, softer, and of a darker colour. So is
the herb of Paraguay; which is of a dirty green, and no
larger than our common red sage.

Wesley's Coach Upset

Sun. Aug. 6.—At one I proclaimed the glorious
Gospel to the usual congregation at Birstal, and in the
evening at Leeds. Then, judging it needful to pay a
short visit to our brethren at London, I took the stage-
coach, with five of my friends, about eight o'clock.
Before nine, a gentleman in a single-horse chaise struck
his wheel against one of ours. Instantly the weight of
the men at top overset the coach; otherwise, ten times
the shock would not have moved it; but neither the
coachman, nor the men at top, nor any within, were
hurt at all. On Tuesday, in the afternoon, we were met
at Hatfield by many of our friends, who conducted us
safe to London.

Monday, October 30, and the following days, I visited
the little societies in the neighbourhood of London.

Saturday, November 11. I made some additions to the
" Calm Address to our American Colonies." Need any
one ask from what motive this was wrote? Let him
look round : England is in a flame! a flame of malice
and rage against the King, and almost all that are in
authority under him. I labour to put out this flame
Ought not every true patriot to do the same?

hireling writers on either side judge of me by themselves, that I cannot help.

Sun. 12.—I was desired to preach, in Bethnal-green church, a charity sermon for the widows and orphans of the soldiers that were killed in America. Knowing how many would seek occasion of offence, I wrote down my sermon. I dined with Sir John Hawkins and three other gentlemen that are in commission for the peace ; and was agreeably surprised at a very serious conversation, kept up during the whole time I stayed.

Wesley and the American War

Mon. 27.—I set out for Norwich. That evening I preached at Colchester; Tuesday, at Norwich; Wednesday, at Yarmouth.

About this time I published the following letter in Lloyd's " Evening Post : "—

" Sir,—I have been seriously asked, ' From what motive did you publish your *Calm Address to the American Colonies ?* '

" I seriously answer, Not to get money. Had that been my motive, I should have swelled it into a shilling pamphlet, and have entered it at Stationers' Hall.

" Not to get preferment for myself, or my brother's children. I am a little too old to gape after it for myself : and if my brother or I sought it for them, we have only to show them to the world.

" Not to please any man living, high or low. I know mankind too well. I know they that love you for political service, love you less than their dinner ; and they that hate you, hate you worse than the devil.

" Least of all did I write with a view to inflame any : just the contrary. I contributed my mite toward putting out the flame which rages all over the land. This I have

more opportunity of observing than any other man in
England. I see with pain to what an height this already
rises, in every part of the nation. And I see many
pouring oil into the flame, by crying out, 'How unjustly,
how cruelly, the King is using the poor Americans; who
are only contending for their liberty, and for their legal
privileges !'

"Now there is no possible way to put out this flame,
or hinder its rising higher and higher, but to show that
the Americans are not used either cruelly or unjustly;
that they are not injured at all, seeing they are not
contending for liberty (this they had, even in its full
extent, both civil and religious); neither for any legal
privileges; for they enjoy all that their charters grant.
But what they contend for is, the illegal privilege of
being exempt from parliamentary taxation. A privilege
this, which no charter ever gave to any American colony
yet; which no charter can give, unless it be confirmed
both by King, Lords, and Commons; which, in fact,
our colonies never had; which they never claimed till
the present reign : and probably they would not have
claimed it now, had they not been incited thereto by
letters from England. One of these was read, according
to the desire of the writer, not only at the continental
Congress, but likewise in many congregations throughout
the Combined Provinces. It advised them to seize upon
all the King's officers; and exhorted them, 'Stand
valiantly, only for six months, and in that time there
will be such commotions in England that you may have
your own terms.'

"This being the real state of the question, without
any colouring or aggravation, what impartial man can
either blame the King, or commend the Americans?

"With this view, to quench the fire, by laying the

blame where it was due, the 'Calm Address' was written.

> "Sir, I am,
>> "Your humble servant,
>>> "JOHN WESLEY."

Preaching from the Stocks

1776. January 1.—About eighteen hundred of us met together in London, in order to renew our covenant with God; and it was, as usual, a very solemn opportunity.

Sun. 14. As I was going to West-street chapel, one of the chaise-springs suddenly snapped asunder; but the horses instantly stopping, I stepped out without the least inconvenience.

At all my vacant hours in this and the following week, I endeavoured to finish the "Concise History of England." I am sensible it must give offence, as in many parts I am quite singular; particularly with regard to those injured characters, Richard III. and Mary Queen of Scots. But I must speak as I think; although still waiting for, and willing to receive, better information.

Tues. April 30.—In the evening I preached in a kind of square, at Colne, to a multitude of people, all drinking in the word. I scarce ever saw a congregation wherein men, women, and children stood in such a posture: and this in the town wherein, thirty years ago, no Methodist could show his head! The first that preached here was John Jane, who was innocently riding through the town, when the zealous mob pulled him off his horse, and put him in the stocks. He seized the opportunity and vehemently exhorted them "to flee from the wrath to come."

Wed. May 1.—I set out early, and the next afternoon

reached Whitehaven; and my chaise-horses were no worse for travelling near a hundred and ten miles in two days.

In travelling through Berkshire, Oxfordshire, Bristol, Gloucestershire, Worcestershire, Warwickshire, Stafford-shire, Cheshire, Lancashire, Yorkshire,Westmoreland, and Cumberland, I diligently made two inquiries: the first was, concerning the increase or decrease of the people; the second, concerning the increase or decrease of trade. As to the latter, it is, within these two last years, amazingly increased; in several branches in such a manner as has not been known in the memory of man : such is the fruit of the entire civil and religious liberty which all England now enjoys ! And as to the former, not only in every city and large town, but in every village and hamlet, there is no decrease, but a very large and swift increase. One sign of this is the swarms of little children which we see in every place. Which, then, shall we most admire, the ignorance or confidence of those that affirm population decreases in England ? I doubt not but it increases full as fast here as in any province of North-America.

"A Very Extraordinary Genius"

Mon. 6.—After preaching at Cockermouth and Wigton, I went on to Carlisle, and preached to a very serious congregation. Here I saw a very extraordinary genius, a man blind from four years of age, who could wind worsted, weave flowered plush on an engine and loom of his own making; who wove his own name in plush, and made his own clothes, and his own tools of every sort. Some years ago, being shut up in the organ-loft at church, he felt every part of it, and afterwards made an organ for himself, which, judges say, is an exceeding good one.

He then taught himself to play upon it psalm-tunes, anthems, voluntaries, or anything which he heard. I heard him play several tunes with great accuracy, and a complex voluntary : I suppose all Europe can hardly produce such another instance. His name is Joseph Strong. But what is he the better for all this, if he is still "without God in the world?"

Fri. 17.—I reached Aberdeen in good time. Saturday, 18. I read over Dr. Johnson's "Tour to the Western Isles." It is a very curious book, wrote with admirable sense, and, I think, great fidelity ; although, in some respects, he is thought to bear hard on the nation, which I am satisfied he never intended.

Mon. 20.—I preached about eleven at Old-Meldrum, but could not reach Banff till near seven in the evening. I went directly to the Parade, and proclaimed to a listening multitude "the grace of our Lord Jesus Christ." All behaved well but a few gentry, whom I rebuked openly, and they stood corrected.

Neat and Elegant Banff

Banff is one of the neatest and most elegant towns that I have seen in Scotland. It is pleasantly situated on the side of a hill, sloping from the sea, though close to it ; so that it is sufficiently sheltered from the sharpest winds. The streets are straight and broad. I believe it may be esteemed the fifth, if not the fourth, town in the kingdom. The county, quite from Banff to Keith, is the best peopled of any I have seen in Scotland. This is chiefly, if not entirely, owing to the late Earl of Findlater. He was indefatigable in doing good, took pains to procure industrious men from all parts, and to provide such little settlements for them as enabled them to live with comfort.

About noon I preached at the New-mills, nine miles from Banff, to a large congregation of plain, simple people. As we rode in the afternoon the heat overcame me, so that I was weary and faint before we came to Keith; but I no sooner stood up in the market-place than I forgot my weariness; such were the seriousness and attention of the whole congregation, though as numerous as that at Banff. Mr. Gordon, the Minister of the parish, invited me to supper, and told me his kirk was at my service. A little society is formed here already; and is in a fair way of increasing. But they were just now in danger of losing their preaching-house, the owner being determined to sell it. I saw but one way to secure it for them, which was to buy it myself. So (who would have thought it?) I bought an estate, consisting of two houses, a yard, a garden, with three acres of good land. But he told me flat, " Sir, I will take no less for it than sixteen pounds ten shillings, to be paid, part now, part at Michaelmas, and the residue next May."

A Town of Beggars

Here Mr. Gordon showed me a great curiosity. Near the top of the opposite hill a new town is built, containing, I suppose, a hundred houses, which is a town of beggars. This, he informed me, was the professed, regular occupation of all the inhabitants. Early in spring they all go out, and spread themselves over the kingdom; and in autumn they return, and do what is requisite for their wives and children.

Mon. 27.—I paid a visit to St. Andrews, once the largest city in the kingdom. It was eight times as large as it is now, and a place of very great trade : but the sea rushing from the north-east, gradually destroyed the harbour and trade together: in consequence of which whole streets (that were) are now meadows and gardens. Three broad, straight, handsome streets remain, all pointing at the old cathedral; which, by the ruins, appears to have been above three hundred feet long, and proportionately broad and high : so that it seems to have exceeded York Minster, and to have at least equalled any cathedral in England.   Another church, afterwards used in its stead, bears date 1124.   A steeple, standing near the cathedral, is thought to have stood thirteen hundred years.

Wesley Criticises the Scotch Universities

What is left of St. Leonard's college is only a heap of ruins.   Two colleges remain.   One of them has a tolerable square ; but all the windows are broke, like those of a brothel.   We were informed, the students do this before they leave the college.   Where are their blessed Governors in the mean time?   Are they all fast asleep?   The other college is a mean building, but has a handsome library newly erected.   In the two colleges, we learned, were about seventy students ; near the same number as at Old-Aberdeen.   Those at New-Aberdeen are not more numerous : neither those at Glasgow.   In Edinburgh, I suppose, there are a hundred.   So four Universities contain three hundred and ten students !   These all come to their several colleges in November, and return home in May !   So they may study five months in the year, and lounge all the rest !   O where was the common sense of those who instituted such colleges? In the English colleges, every one may reside all the year, as all my pupils did ; and I should have thought myself little better than a highwayman, if I had not lectured them every day in the year but Sundays.

Fri. June 28.—I am seventy-three years old, and far

abler to preach than I was at three-and-twenty. What natural means has God used to produce so wonderful an effect? 1. Continual exercise and change of air, by travelling above four thousand miles in a year: 2. Constant rising at four: 3. The ability, if ever I want, to sleep immediately: 4. The never losing a night's sleep in my life: 5. Two violent fevers and two deep consumptions. These, it is true, were rough medicines: but they were of admirable service; causing my flesh to come again as the flesh of a little child. May I add, lastly, evenness of temper? I feel and grieve; but, by the grace of God, I fret at nothing. But still " the help that is done upon earth, He doeth it himself." And this He doeth in answer to many prayers.

Smuggling in Cornwall

Sat. Aug. 17.—We found Mr. Hoskins, at Cubert (Cornwall), alive; but just tottering over the grave. I preached in the evening, on 2 Cor. v. 1–4; probably the last sermon he will hear from me. I was afterwards inquiring, if that scandal of Cornwall, the plundering of wrecked vessels, still subsisted. He said, " As much as ever; only the Methodists will have nothing to do with it. But three months since a vessel was wrecked on the south coast, and the tinners presently seized on all the goods; and even broke in pieces a new coach which was on board, and carried every scrap of it away." But is there no way to prevent this shameful breach of all the laws both of religion and humanity: Indeed there is. The gentry of Cornwall may totally prevent it whenever they please. Let them only see that the laws be strictly executed upon the next plunderers; and after an example is made of ten of these, the next wreck will be unmolested. Nay, there is a milder way. Let them only agree together to discharge any tinner or labourer that is concerned in the plundering of a wreck, and advertise his name, that no Cornish gentleman may employ him any more; and neither tinner nor labourer will any more be concerned in that bad work.

Sun. 18.—The passage through the sands being bad for a chaise, I rode on horseback to St. Agnes, where the rain constrained me to preach in the house. As we rode back to Redruth, it poured down amain, and found its way through all our clothes. I was tired when I came in; but after sleeping a quarter of an hour, all my weariness was gone.

In Bethnal Green Hamlet

1777. Wed. Jan. 1.—We met, as usual, to renew our covenant with God. It was a solemn season, wherein many found His power present to heal, and were enabled to urge their way with strength renewed.

Thur. 2.—I began expounding, in order, the book of Ecclesiastes. I never before had so clear a sight either of the meaning or the beauties of it. Neither did I imagine that the several parts of it were in so exquisite a manner connected together; all tending to prove that grand truth—that there is no happiness out of God.

Wed. 15.—I began visiting those of our society who lived in Bethnal-green hamlet. Many of them I found in such poverty as few can conceive without seeing it. O why do not all the rich that fear God constantly visit the poor! Can they spend part of their spare-time better? Certainly not. So they will find in that day when " every man shall receive his own reward according to his own labour."

Such another scene I saw the next day, in visiting

another part of the society. I have not found any such distress, no, not in the prison of Newgate. One poor man was just creeping out of his sick-bed, to his ragged wife and three little children ; who were more than half naked, and the very picture of famine; when one bringing in a loaf of bread, they all ran, seized upon it, and tore it in pieces in an instant. Who would not rejoice that there is another world ?

City Road Chapel Begun

Monday, April 21, was the day appointed for laying the foundation of the new chapel. The rain befriended us much, by keeping away thousands who purposed to be there. But there were still such multitudes, that it was with great difficulty I got through them, to lay the first stone. Upon this was a plate of brass (covered with another stone), on which was engraved, " This was laid by Mr. John Wesley, on April 1, 1777." Probably this will be seen no more, by any human eye; but will remain there, till the earth and the works thereof are burned up.

Sun. 27.—The sun breaking out, I snatched the opportunity of preaching to many thousands in Moorfields. All were still as night, while I showed how " the Son of God was manifested to destroy the works of the devil."

Wed. May 14.—At eleven I preached at Pocklington, with an eye to the death of that lovely woman, Mrs. Cross. A gay young gentleman, with a young lady, stepped in, stayed five minutes, and went out again, with as easy an unconcern as if they had been listening to a ballad-singer. I mentioned to the congregation the deep folly and ignorance implied in such behaviour. These pretty fools never thought that for this very opportunity they are to give an account before men and angels !

In the evening I preached at York. I would gladly have rested the next day, feeling my breast much out of order. But notice having been given of my preaching at Tadcaster, I set out at nine in the morning. About ten the chaise broke down. I borrowed a horse; but as he was none of the easiest, in riding three miles I was so thoroughly electrified, that the pain in my breast was quite cured. I preached in the evening at York; on Friday took the diligence ; and on Saturday afternoon came to London.

Wesley in the Isle of Man

Fri. 30.—I went on to Whitehaven, where I found a little vessel waiting for me. After preaching in the evening, I went on board about eight o'clock, and before eight in the morning landed at Douglas, in the Isle of Man

Douglas exceedingly resembles Newlyn in Cornwall; both in its situation, form, and buildings; only it is much larger, and has a few houses equal to most in Penzance. As soon as we landed, I was challenged by Mr. Booth, who had seen me in Ireland, and whose brother has been for many years a member of the society in Coolylough. A chaise was provided to carry me to Castletown. I was greatly surprised at the country. All the way from Douglas to Castletown it is as pleasant and as well cultivated as most parts of England, with many gentlemen's seats. Castletown a good deal resembles Galway; only it is not so large. At six I preached near the castle, I believe, to all the inhabitants of the town. Two or three gay young women showed they knew nothing about religion ; all the rest were deeply serious.

Sun. June 1.—At six I preached in our own room; and, to my surprise, saw all the gentlewomen there. Young as well as old were now deeply affected, and would fain have had me stayed, were it but an hour or two; but I was forced to hasten away, in order to be at Peeltown before the service began.

Mr. Corbett said, he would gladly have asked me to preach, but that the Bishop had forbidden him; who had also forbidden all his Clergy to admit any Methodist Preacher to the Lord's supper. But is any Clergyman obliged, either in law or conscience, to obey such a prohibition? By no means. The will even of the King does not bind any English subject, unless it be seconded by an express law. How much less the will of a Bishop? "But did not you take an oath to obey him?" No, nor any Clergyman in the three kingdoms. This is a mere vulgar error. Shame that it should prevail almost universally.

As it rained, I retired after service into a large malt-house. Most of the congregation followed, and devoured the word. It being fair in the afternoon, the whole congregation stopped in the church-yard; and the word of God was with power. It was a happy opportunity.

The Manx Men

Mon. 2.—The greater part of them were present at five in the morning. A more loving, simple-hearted people than this I never saw. And no wonder; for they have but six Papists, and no Dissenters, in the island. It is supposed to contain near thirty thousand people, remarkably courteous and humane. Ever since smuggling was suppressed, they diligently cultivate their land: and they have a large herring fishery, so that the country improves daily.

The old castle at Peel (as well as the cathedral built within it) is only a heap of ruins. It was very large, and exceeding strong, with many brass guns; but they are now removed to England.

I set out for Douglas in the one-horse chaise, Mrs. Smyth riding with me. In about an hour, in spite of all I could do, the headstrong horse ran the wheel against a large stone: the chaise overset in a moment; but we fell so gently on smooth grass, that neither of us was hurt at all. In the evening I preached at Douglas, to near as large a congregation as that at Peel, but not near so serious. Before ten we went on board, and about twelve on Tuesday, 3, landed at Whitehaven. I preached at five in the afternoon; and hastening to Cockermouth, found a large congregation waiting in the castle-yard. Between nine and ten o'clock I took chaise; and about ten on Wednesday, 4, reached Settle. In the evening I preached near the market-place, and all but two or three gentlefolks were seriously attentive. Thursday, 5. About noon I came to Otley.

"Taught by a Chaise Boy"

Mon. July 21.—Having been much pressed to preach at Jatterson, a colliery, six or seven miles from Pembroke, I began soon after seven. The house was presently filled, and all the space about the doors and windows; and the poor people drank in every word. I had finished my sermon, when a gentleman, violently pressing in, bade the people get home and mind their business. As he used some bad words, my driver spake to him. He fiercely said, "Do you think I need to be taught by a chaise-boy?" The lad replying, "Really, Sir, I do think so," the conversation ended.

Tues. Aug. 5.—Our yearly Conference began. I

now particularly inquired (as that report had been spread far and wide) of every assistant, " Have you reason to believe, from your own observation, that the Methodists are a fallen people ?   Is there a decay or an increase in the work of God where you have been ?   Are the societies in general more dead, or more alive to God, than they were some years ago ? "   The almost universal answer was, " If we must ' know them by their fruits,' there is no decay in the work of God among the people in general.   The societies are not dead to God : they are as much alive as they have been for many years. And we look on this report as a mere device of Satan, to make our hands hang down."

Are the Methodists a Fallen People ?

" But how can this question be decided ? "   You, and you, can judge no farther than you see.   You cannot judge of one part by another ; of the people of London, suppose, by those of Bristol.   And none but myself has an opportunity of seeing them throughout the three kingdoms.

But to come to a short issue.   In most places, the Methodists are still a poor despised people, labouring under reproach, and many inconveniences ; therefore, wherever the power of God is not, they decrease.   By this, then, you may form a sure judgment.   Do the Methodists in general decrease in number ?   Then they decrease in grace ; they are a fallen, or, at least, a falling people.   But they do not decrease in number ; they continually increase ; therefore, they are not a fallen people.

The Conference concluded on Friday, as it began, in much love.

Wesley Starts a Magazine

Mon. Nov. 14.—Having been many times desired, for near forty years, to publish a magazine, I at length complied ; and now began to collect materials for it. If it once begin, I incline to think it will not end but with my life.

Wed. Dec. 17.—Just at this time there was a combination among many of the post-chaise drivers on the Bath road, especially those that drove in the night, to deliver their passengers into each other's hands. One driver stopped at the spot they had appointed, where another waited to attack the chaise. In consequence of this many were robbed ; but I had a good Protector still. I have travelled all roads, by day and by night, for these forty years, and never was interrupted yet.

1778. Friday, Jan. 27, was the day appointed for the national fast ; and it was observed with due solemnity. All shops were shut up ; all was quiet in the streets ; all places of public worship were crowded ; no food was served up in the King's house till five o'clock in the evening. Thus far, at least, we acknowledge God may direct our paths.

Sun. June 28.—I am this day seventy-five years old ; and I do not find myself, blessed be God, any weaker than I was at five-and-twenty. This also hath God wrought !

Wesley Discusses Old Sermons

Tues. Sept. 1.—I went to Tiverton. I was musing here on what I heard a good man say long since— " Once in seven years I burn all my sermons ; for it is a shame if I cannot write better sermons now than I could seven years ago." Whatever others can do, I really cannot. I cannot write a better sermon on the Good Steward, than I did seven years ago: I cannot write a better on the Great Assize, than I did twenty years ago: I cannot write a better on the Use of Money, than I did near thirty years ago: nay, I know not that I can write a better on the Circumcision of the Heart, than I did five-and-forty years ago. Perhaps, indeed, I may have read five or six hundred books more than I had then, and may know a little more history, or natural philosophy, than I did: but I am not sensible that this has made any essential addition to my knowledge in divinity. Forty years ago I knew and preached every Christian doctrine which I preach now.

Among the Ruins

Thur. 3.—About noon I preached at Cathanger, about eight miles from Taunton. It was an exceeding large house, built (as the inscription over the gate testifies) in the year 1555, by Sergeant Walsh, who had then eight thousand pounds a year; perhaps more than equal to twenty thousand now. But the once famous family is now forgotten; the estate is mouldered almost into nothing; and three quarters of the magnificent buildings lie level with the dust. I preached in the great hall, like that of Lincoln College, to a very serious congregation.

In the evening I preached at South-Petherton, once a place of renown, and the capital of a Saxon kingdom; as is vouched by a palace of King Ina still remaining, and a very large and ancient church. I suppose the last blow given to it was by Judge Jefferies, who, after Monmouth's rebellion, hanged so many of the inhabitants, and drove so many away, that it is never likely to lift up its head again.

City Road Chapel Opened

Sunday, November 1, was the day appointed for opening the new chapel in the City-road. It is perfectly neat, but not fine; and contains far more people than the Foundery: I believe, together with the morning chapel, as many as the Tabernacle. Many were afraid that the multitudes, crowding from all parts, would have occasioned much disturbance. But they were happily disappointed: there was none at all: all was quietness decency, and order. I preached on part of Solomon's Prayer at the Dedication of the Temple; and both in the morning and afternoon (when I preached on the hundred forty and four thousand standing with the Lamb on Mount Zion), God was eminently present in the midst of the congregation.

Mon. 2.—I went to Chatham, and preached in the evening to a lively, loving congregation. Tuesday, 3. I went by water to Sheerness. Our room being far too small for the people that attended, I sent to the Governor to desire (what had been allowed me before) the use of the chapel. He refused me (uncivilly enough), affecting to doubt whether I was in orders! So I preached to as many as it would contain in our own room.

Wed. 4.—I took a view of the old church at Minster, once a spacious and elegant building. It stands pleasantly on the top of a hill, and commands all the country round. We went from thence to Queensborough, which contains above fifty houses, and sends two members to Parliament. Surely the whole Isle of Sheppey is now but a shadow of what it was once.

Thur. 5.—I returned to Chatham, and the following morning set out on the stage-coach for London. At the end of Stroud, I chose to walk up the hill, leaving the

WESLEY'S CHAPEL, CITY ROAD

coach to follow me. But it was in no great haste: it did not overtake me till I had walked above five miles. I cared not if it had been ten: the more I walk, the sounder I sleep.

Sun. 15.—Having promised to preach in the evening at St. Antholine's church, I had desired one to have a coach ready at the door, when the service at the new chapel was ended. But he had forgot; so that, after preaching and meeting the society, I was obliged to walk as fast as I could to the church. The people were so wedged together, that it was with difficulty I got in. The church was extremely hot; but this I soon forgot; for it pleased God to send a gracious rain upon his inheritance.

Sun. 29.—I was desired to preach a charity sermon in St. Luke's church, Old-street. I doubt whether it was ever so crowded before; and the fear of God seemed to possess the whole audience. In the afternoon I preached at the new chapel; and at seven, in St. Margaret's, Rood-lane; full as much crowded as St. Luke's. Is then the scandal of the cross ceased?

Wesley goes North

1779. Mon. Mar. 15.—I began my tour through England and Scotland; the lovely weather continuing, such as the oldest man alive has not seen before, for January, February, and half of March. In the evening I preached at Stroud, the next morning at Gloucester, designing to preach in Stanley at two, and at Tewkesbury in the evening: but the minister of Gratton (near Stanley) sending me word, I was welcome to the use of his church, I ordered notice to be given, that the service would begin there at six o'clock. Stanley chapel was thoroughly filled at two. It is eighteen years since I was there before; so that many of those whom I saw here then were now grey-headed; and many were gone to Abraham's bosom.   May we follow them as they did Christ !

Thur. 25.—I preached in the new house which Mr. Fletcher has built in Madeley-wood.   The people here exactly resemble those at Kingswood; only they are more simple and teachable.   But for want of discipline, the immense pains which he has taken with them has not done the good which might have been expected.

I preached at Shrewsbury in the evening, and on Friday, 26, about noon, in the assembly-room at Broseley. It was well we were in the shade; for the sun shone as hot as it usually does at midsummer.   We walked from thence to Coalbrook-dale, and took a view of the bridge which is shortly to be thrown over the Severn.   It is one arch, a hundred feet broad, fifty-two high, and eighteen wide; all of cast-iron, weighing many hundred tons.   I doubt whether the Colossus at Rhodes weighed much more.

Thur. April 15.—I went to Halifax, where a little thing had lately occasioned great disturbance.   An angel blowing a trumpet was placed on the sounding-board over the pulpit.   Many were vehemently against this; others as vehemently for it : but a total end was soon put to the contest; for the angel vanished away.   The congregations, morning and evening, were very large; and the work of God seems to increase in depth as well as extent.

Sun. May 2.—Dr. Kershaw, the vicar of Leeds, desired me to assist him at the sacrament.   It was a solemn season.   We were ten clergymen, and seven or eight hundred communicants.   Mr. Atkinson desired

me to preach in the afternoon.   Such a congregation
had been seldom seen there; but I preached to a much
larger in our own house at five; and I found no want of
strength.

Mon. June 28.—I preached in the new preaching-
house, at Robin-Hood's-bay, and then went on to Scarborough.   Tuesday, 29, I spent agreeably and profitably
with my old friends; and in my way to Bridlington,
Wednesday, 30, took a view of Flamborough-head.   It
is an huge rock, rising perpendicular from the sea to an
immense height, which gives shelter to an innumerable
multitude of sea-fowl of various kinds.   I preached in
the evening at Bridlington, and afterwards heard a very
uncommon instance of paternal affection :—A gentleman
of the town had a favourite daughter, whom he set up in
a milliner's shop.   Some time after she had a concern
for her soul, and believed it her duty to enter into the
society.   Upon this her good father forbad her his
house ; demanding all the money he had laid out; and
required her instantly to sell all her goods, in order to
make the payment !

Wesley Attended by Felons

Wed. July 21.—When I came to Coventry, I found
notice had been given for my preaching in the park ;
but the heavy rain prevented.   I sent to the Mayor,
desiring the use of the town-hall.   He refused ; but the
same day gave the use of it to a dancing-master.   I
then went to the women's market.   Many soon gathered
together, and listened with all seriousness.   I preached
there again the next morning, Thursday, 22, and again
in the evening.   Then I took coach for London.   I
was nobly attended : behind the coach were ten convicted felons, loudly blaspheming and rattling their

chains; by my side sat a man with a loaded blunderbuss, and another upon the coach.

Sun. 25.—Both the chapels were full enough. On Monday, I retired to Lewisham to write.

Tues. August 3. Our Conference began; which continued and ended in peace and love. Sunday, 8. I was at West-street in the morning, and at the new chapel in the evening, when I took a solemn leave of the affectionate congregation. This was the last night which I spent at the Foundery. What hath God wrought there in one-and-forty years!

Fri. August 13 (Monmouth).—As I was going down a steep pair of stairs, my foot slipped, and I fell down several steps. Falling on the edge of one of them, it broke the case of an almanack, which was in my pocket, all to pieces. The edge of another stair met my right buckle, and snapped the steel chape of it in two; but I was not hurt. So doth our good Master give his angels charge over us! In the evening I preached at Brecknock.

"Make your Will before you Sleep"

Thurs. Sept. 23.—In the evening one sat behind me in the pulpit at Bristol, who was one of our first masters at Kingswood. A little after he left the school he likewise left the society. Riches then flowed in upon him; with which, having no relations, Mr. Spencer designed to do much good—after his death. "But God said unto him, Thou fool!" Two hours after he died intestate, and left all his money to—be scrambled for!

Reader, if you have not done it already, make your will before you sleep!

Wed. Oct. 6.—At eleven I preached in Winchester, where there are four thousand five hundred French prisoners. I was glad to find they have plenty of wholesome food ; and are treated, in all respects, with great humanity.

In the evening I preached at Portsmouth-common. Thursday, 7. I took a view of the camp adjoining to the town, and wondered to find it as clean and as neat as a gentleman's garden. But there was no chaplain. The English soldiers of this age have nothing to do with God !

Fri. 8.—We took chaise, as usual, at two, and about eleven came to Cobham. Having a little leisure, I thought I could not employ it better than in taking a walk through the gardens. They are said to take up four hundred acres, and are admirably well laid out. They far exceed the celebrated gardens at Stow.

This night I lodged in the new house at London. How many more nights have I to spend there ?

1780. Sun. Jan. 23.—In the evening I retired to Lewisham, to prepare matter (who would believe it) for a monthly magazine. Friday, February 4, being the national fast, I preached first at the new chapel, and then at St. Peter's Cornhill. What a difference in the congregation ! Yet out of these stones God can raise up children to Abraham.

Wesley at the German Settlement

Mon. April 17.—I left Leeds in one of the roughest mornings I have ever seen. We had rain, hail, snow, and wind, in abundance. About nine I preached at Bramley ; between one and two at Pudsey. Afterwards I walked to Fulneck, the German settlement. Mr. Moore showed us the house, chapel, hall, lodging-rooms, the apartments of the widows, the single men, and single women. He showed us likewise the workshops of various

kinds, with the shops for grocery, drapery, mercery, hard-
ware, &c., with which, as well as with bread from their
bakehouse, they furnish the adjacent country. I see not
what but the mighty power of God can hinder them from
acquiring millions; as they, 1. Buy all materials with
ready money at the best hand; 2. Have above a hundred young men, above fifty young women, many widows,
and above a hundred married persons; all of whom are
employed from morning to night, without any intermission, in various kinds of manufactures, not for journey-
men's wages, but for no wages at all, save a little very
plain food and raiment: as they have. 3. A quick sale
for all their goods, and sell them all for ready money.
But can they lay up treasure on earth, and at the same
time lay up treasure in heaven?

Sat. May 20.—I took one more walk through Holy-
rood-house, the mansion of ancient kings. But how
melancholy an appearance does it make now! The
stately rooms are dirty as stables; the colours of the
tapestry are quite faded; several of the pictures are cut
and defaced. The roof of the royal chapel is fallen in;
and the bones of James the Fifth, and the once beautiful
Lord Darnley, are scattered about like those of sheep or
oxen. Such is human greatness! Is not "a living dog
better than a dead lion?"

Sun. 21.—The rain hindered me from preaching at
noon upon the Castle-hill. In the evening the house
was well filled, and I was enabled to speak strong words.
But I am not a preacher for the people of Edinburgh.

Tues. 23.—A gentleman took me to see Roslyn-
castle, eight miles from Edinburgh. It is now all in
ruins, only a small dwelling-house is built on one part of
it. The situation of it is exceeeding fine, on the side of
a steep mountain, hanging over a river, from which

another mountain rises, equally steep, and clothed with wood. At a little distance is the chapel, which is in perfect preservation, both within and without. I should never have thought it had belonged to any one less than a sovereign prince ! the inside being far more elegantly wrought with variety of Scripture histories in stone-work, than I believe can be found again in Scotland; perhaps not in all England.

The Bishop of Durham's Tapestry

Wed. 31.—I went to Mr. Parker's, at Shincliff, near Durham. The congregation being far too large to get into the house, I stood near his door. It seemed as if the whole village were ready to receive the truth in the love thereof. Perhaps their earnestness may provoke the people of Durham to jealousy.

In the afternoon we took a view of the castle at Durham, the residence of the bishop. The situation is wonderfully fine, surrounded by the river, and commanding all the country ; and many of the apartments are large and stately; but the furniture is mean beyond imagination ! I know not where I have seen such in a gentleman's house, or a man of five hundred a year, except that of the Lord Lieutenant in Dublin. In the largest chambers, the tapestry is quite faded ; beside that, it is coarse and ill-judged. Take but one instance :—In Jacob's vision you see, on the one side, a little paltry ladder, and an angel climbing it, in the attitude of a chimney-sweeper; and on the other side Jacob staring at him, from under a large silver-laced hat.

Mon. June 5 (York).—An arch news-writer published a paragraph to-day, probably designed for wit, concerning the large pension which the famous Wesley received for defending the king. This so increased the congregation in the evening, that scores were obliged to go away. And God applied that word to many hearts, " I will not destroy the city for ten's sake ? "

Mon. 12.—About eleven I preached at Newton-upon-Trent, to a large and very genteel congregation. Thence we went to Newark : but our friends were divided as to the place where I should preach. At length they found a convenient place, covered on three sides, and on the fourth open to the street. It contained two or three thousand people well, who appeared to hear as for life. Only one big man, exceeding drunk, was very noisy and turbulent, till his wife seized him by the collar, gave him two or three hearty boxes on the ear, and dragged him away like a calf. But, at length, he got out of her hands, crept in among the people, and stood as quiet as a lamb.

Wesley on " Boston Stump "

Fri. 16.—We went on to Boston, the largest town in the county, except Lincoln. From the top of the steeple (which I suppose is by far the highest tower in the kingdom) we had a view not only of all the town, but of all the adjacent country. Formerly this town was in the fens ; but the fens are vanished away : great part of them is turned into pasture, and part into arable land. At six the house contained the congregation, all of whom behaved in the most decent manner.

Wed. 28.—I went to Sheffield : but the house was not ready ; so I preached in the square.

I can hardly think I am entered this day into the seventy-eighth year of my age. By the blessing of God, I am just the same as when I entered the twenty-eighth. This hath God wrought, chiefly by my constant exercise, my rising early, and preaching morning and evening.

Mon. Sept. 11.—As I drew near Bath, I wondered what had drawn such a multitude of people together, till I learnt, that one of the members for the city had given an ox to be roasted whole. But their sport was sadly interrupted by heavy rain, which sent them home faster than they came; many of whom dropped in at our chapel, where I suppose they never had been before.

Wesley at Sevenoaks

Mon. Oct. 16.—I went to Tunbridge-wells, and preached to a serious congregation, on Rev. xx. 12. Tuesday, 17. I came back to Sevenoaks, and in the afternoon walked over to the Duke of Dorset's seat. The park is the pleasantest I ever saw; the trees are so elegantly disposed. The house, which is at least two hundred years old, is immensely large. It consists of two squares, considerably bigger than the two quad-rangles in Lincoln college. I believe we were shown above thirty rooms, beside the hall, the chapels, and three galleries.

The pictures are innumerable; I think, four times as many as in the castle at Blenheim. Into one of the galleries opens the king's bedchamber, ornamented above all the rest. The bed-curtains are cloth-of-gold; and so richly wrought, that it requires some strength to draw them. The tables, the chairs, the frames of the looking-glasses, are all plated over with silver. The tapestry, representing the whole history of Nebuchadnezzar, is as fresh as if newly woven. But the bed-curtains are exceed-ing dirty, and look more like copper than gold. The silver on the tables, chairs, and glass, looks as dull as lead. And, to complete all, King Nebuchadnezzar among the beasts, together with his eagle's claws, has a large crown upon his head, and is clothed in scarlet and gold.

Wesley Visits Lord George in the Tower

Sat. Dec. 16 (London).—Having a second message from Lord George Gordon, earnestly desiring to see me, I wrote a line to Lord Stormont, who, on Monday, 18, sent me a warrant to see him. On Tuesday, 19, I spent an hour with him, at his apartment in the Tower. Our conversation turned upon Popery and religion. He seemed to be well acquainted with the Bible; and had abundance of other books, enough to furnish a study. I was agreeably surprised to find he did not complain of any person or thing; and cannot but hope, his confinement will take a right turn, and prove a lasting blessing to him.

Fri. 22.—At the desire of some of my friends, I accompanied them to the British Museum. What an immense field is here for curiosity to range in! One large room is filled from top to bottom with things brought from Otaheite; two or three more with things dug out of the ruins of Herculaneum! Seven huge apartments are filled with curious books; five with manuscripts; two with fossils of all sorts, and the rest with various animals. But what account will a man give to the Judge of quick and dead for a life spent in collecting all these?

Sun. 24.—Desiring to make the most of this solemn day, I preached early in the morning at the new chapel; at ten and four I preached at West-street; and in the evening met the society at each end of the town.

Fri. 29.—I saw the indictment of the Grand Jury against Lord George Gordon. I stood aghast! What a shocking insult upon truth and common sense! But it is the usual form. The more is the shame. Why will not the Parliament remove this scandal from our nation?

Sat. 30.—Waking between one and two in the morning, I observed a bright light shine upon the chapel. I easily concluded there was a fire near; probably in the adjoining timber-yard. If so, I knew it would soon lay us in ashes. I first called all the family to prayer; then going out, we found the fire about a hundred yards off, and had broke out while the wind was south. But a sailor cried out, " Avast! Avast! the wind is turned in a moment!" So it did, to the west, while we were at prayer, and so drove the flame from us. We then thankfully returned, and I rested well the residue of the night.

1781. Thur. Jan. 25.—I spent an agreeable hour at a concert of my nephews. But I was a little out of my element among lords and ladies. I love plain music and plain company best.

A Rough Voyage

Mon. April 9.—Desiring to be in Ireland as soon as possible, I hastened to Liverpool, and found a ship ready to sail; but the wind was contrary, till on Thursday morning, the captain came in haste, and told us, the wind was come quite fair. So Mr. Floyd, Snowden, Joseph Bradford, and I, with two of our sisters, went on board. But scarce were we out at sea, when the wind turned quite foul, and rose higher and higher. In an hour I was so affected, as I had not been for forty years before. For two days I could not swallow the quantity of a pea of anything solid, and very little of any liquid. I was bruised and sore from head to foot, and ill able to turn me on the bed.

All Friday, the storm increasing, the sea of consequence was rougher and rougher. Early on Saturday morning, the hatches were closed, which, together with the violent motion, made our horses so turbulent, that I was afraid we must have killed them, lest they should damage the ship. Mrs. S. now crept to me, threw her arms over me, and said, "O Sir, we will die together!" We had by this time three feet water in the hold, though it was an exceeding light vessel. Meantime we were furiously driving on a lee-shore; and when the captain cried, "Helm-a-lee," she would not obey the helm. I called our brethren to prayers; and we found free access to the throne of grace. Soon after we got, I know not how, into Holyhead harbour, after being sufficiently buffeted by the winds and waves for two days and two nights.

The more I considered, the more I was convinced, it was not the will of God I should go to Ireland at this time. So we went into the stage-coach without delay, and the next evening came to Chester.

I now considered in what place I could spend a few days to the greatest advantage. I soon thought of the Isle of Man, and those parts of Wales which I could not well see in my ordinary course. I judged it would be best to begin with the latter. So, after a day or two's rest, on Wednesday, 18, I set out for Brecon, purposing to take Whitchurch (where I had not been for many years) and Shrewsbury in my way. At noon I preached in Whitchurch, to a numerous and very serious audience; in the evening at Shrewsbury; where, seeing the earnestness of the people, I agreed to stay another day.

Not knowing the best way from hence to Brecon, I thought well to go round by Worcester. I took Broseley in my way, and thereby had a view of the iron bridge over the Severn: I suppose the first and the only one in Europe. It will not soon be imitated.

Tues. May 1.—I rode to St. David's, seventeen measured miles from Haverford. I was surprised to find all the land, for the last nine or ten miles, so fruitful and well cultivated. What a difference is there between the westermost parts of England, and the westermost parts of Wales ! the former (the west of Cornwall), so barren and wild ; the latter, so fruitful and well-improved. But the town itself is a melancholy spectacle. I saw but one tolerable good house in it. The rest were miserable huts indeed. I do not remember so mean a town even in Ireland. The cathedral has been a large and stately fabric, far superior to any other in Wales. But a great part of it is fallen down already ; and the rest is hastening into ruin : one blessed fruit (among many) of bishops residing at a distance from their see. Here are the tombs and effigies of many ancient worthies : Owen Tudor in particular. But the zealous Cromwellians broke off their noses, hands, and feet; and defaced them as much as possible. But what had the Tudors done to them ? Why, they were progenitors of Kings.

In the Isle of Man

Wed. 30.—I embarked on board the packet-boat, for the Isle of Man. We had a dead calm for many hours : however, we landed at Douglas on Friday morning. Both the preachers met me here, and gave me a comfortable account of the still increasing work of God.

Before dinner, we took a walk in a garden near the town, wherein any of the inhabitants of it may walk. It is wonderfully pleasant ; yet not so pleasant as the gardens of the Nunnery (so it is still called), which are not far from it. These are delightfully laid out, and yield to few places of the size in England.

At six I preached in the market-place, to a large

congregation; all of whom, except a few children, and two or three giddy young women, were seriously attentive.

Sat. June 2. — I rode to Castleton, through a pleasant and (now) well-cultivated country. At six I preached in the market-place, to most of the inhabitants of the town, on, " One thing is needful." I believe the word carried conviction into the hearts of nearly all that heard it. Afterwards I walked to the house of one of our English friends, about two miles from the town. All the day I observed, wherever I was, one circumstance that surprised me:—In England we generally hear the birds singing, morning and evening; but here thrushes and various other kinds of birds, were singing all day long. They did not intermit, even during the noon-day heat, where they had a few trees to shade them.

Preaching at Peel

June 3.—(Being Whitsunday.) I preached in the market-place again about nine, to a still larger congregation than before, on, "I am not ashamed of the Gospel of Christ." How few of the genteel hearers could say so! About four in the afternoon, I preached at Barewle, on the mountains, to a larger congregation than that in the morning. The rain began soon after I began preaching; but ceased in a few minutes. I preached on, "They were all filled with the Holy Ghost"; and showed in what sense this belongs to us and to our children.

Between six and seven I preached on the sea-shore at Peel, to the largest congregation I have seen in the island; even the society nearly filled the house. I soon found what spirit they were of. Hardly in England (unless perhaps at Bolton) have I found so plain, so earnest, so simple a people.

Mon. 4.—We had such a congregation at five, as

might have been expected on a Sunday evening. We then rode through and over the mountains to Beer-garrow; where I enforced, on an artless, loving congregation, "If any man thirst, let him come unto me and drink." A few miles from thence, we came to Bishop's-court, where good Bishop Wilson resided near threescore years. There is something venerable, though not magnificent, in the ancient palace; and it is undoubtedly situated in one of the pleasantest spots of the whole island.

Tues. 5.—In the afternoon we rode through a pleasant and fruitful country to Ramsay, about as large as Peel, and more regularly built. The rain was again suspended while I preached to well nigh all the town; but I saw no inattentive hearers.

An Ideal Circuit

Wed. 6.—This morning we rode through the most woody, and far the pleasantest, part of the island; —a range of fruitful land, lying at the foot of the mountains, from Ramsay, through Sulby, to Kirk-michael. Here we stopped to look at the plain tomb-stones of those two good men, Bishop Wilson and Bishop Hildesley; whose remains are deposited, side by side, at the east end of the church. We had scarce reached Peel before the rain increased; but here the preaching-house contained all that could come. Afterwards, Mr. Crook desired me to meet the singers. I was agreeably surprised. I have not heard better singing either at Bristol or London. Many, both men and women, have admirable voices; and they sing with good judgment. Who would have expected this in the Isle of Man?

Thur. 7.—I met our little body of Preachers. They were two-and-twenty in all. I never saw in England so

many stout, well-looking Preachers together. If their
spirit be answerable to their look, I know not what can
stand before them. In the afternoon I rode over to
Dawby, and preached to a very large and very serious
congregation.

Fri. 8.—Having now visited the island round, east,
south, north, and west, I was thoroughly convinced that
we have no such circuit as this, either in England, Scotland, or Ireland. It is shut up from the world; and,
having little trade, is visited by scarce any strangers.
Here are no Papists, no Dissenters of any kind, no Cal-
vinists, no disputers. Here is no opposition, either from
the Governor (a mild, humane man), from the bishop
(a good man), or from the bulk of the clergy. One or
two of them did oppose for a time; but they seem now
to understand better. So that we have now rather too
little, than too much reproach; the scandal of the cross
being, for the present, ceased. The natives are a plain,
artless, simple people; unpolished, that is, unpolluted;
few of them are rich or genteel; the far greater part
moderately poor; and most of the strangers that settle
among them are men that have seen affliction. The
Local Preachers are men of faith and love, knit together
in one mind and one judgment. They speak either Manx
or English, and follow a regular plan, which the assistant
gives them monthly.

The isle is supposed to have thirty thousand inhabitants. Allowing half of them to be adults, and our
societies to contain one or two and twenty hundred
members, what a fair proportion is this! What has been
seen like this, in any part either of Great Britain or
Ireland?

Sat. 9.—We would willingly have set sail; but the
strong north-east wind prevented us. Monday, 11. It

being moderate, we put to sea : but it soon died away into a calm; so I had time to read over and consider Dr. Johnson's "Tour through Scotland." I had heard that he was severe upon the whole nation; but I could find nothing of it. He simply mentions (but without any bitterness) what he approved or disapproved: and many of the reflections are extremely judicious; some of them very affecting.

Tues. 12.—Having several passengers on board, I offered to give them a sermon; which they willingly accepted. And all behaved with the utmost decency, while I showed "His commandments are not grievous." Soon after, a little breeze sprung up, which, early in the morning, brought us to Whitehaven.

Thur. 28.—I preached at eleven in the main street at Selby, to a large and quiet congregation; and in the evening at Thorne. This day I entered my seventy-ninth year; and, by the grace of God, I feel no more of the infirmities of old age, than I did at twenty-nine. Friday, 29. I preached at Crowle and at Epworth. I have now preached thrice a day for seven days following; but it is just the same as if it had been but once.

"A Low, Soft, Solemn Sound"

1782. March 29.—(Being Good Friday.) I came to Macclesfield just time enough to assist Mr. Simpson in the laborious service of the day. I preached for him morning and afternoon; and we administered the sacrament to about thirteen hundred persons. While we were administering, I heard a low, soft, solemn sound, just like that of an Æolian harp. It continued five or six minutes, and so affected many, that they could not refrain from tears. It then gradually died away. Strange that no other organist (that I know) should think of this. In the evening I preached at our room. Here was that harmony which art cannot imitate.

Tues. May 14.—Some years ago four factories for spinning and weaving were set up at Epworth. In these a large number of young women, and boys and girls, were employed. The whole conversation of these was profane and loose to the last degree. But some of these stumbling in at the prayer-meeting were suddenly cut to the heart. These never rested till they had gained their companions. The whole scene was changed. In three of the factories, no more lewdness or profaneness were found; for God had put a new song in their mouth, and blasphemies were turned to praise. Those three I visited to day, and found religion had taken deep root in them. No trifling word was heard among them, and they watch over each other in love. I found it exceeding good to be there, and we rejoiced together in the God of our salvation.

Fri. 31.—As I lodged with Lady Maxwell at Saughton-hall (a good old mansion-house, three miles from Edinburgh), she desired me to give a short discourse to a few of her poor neighbours. I did so, at four in the afternoon, on the story of Dives and Lazarus. About seven I preached in our house at Edinburgh, and fully delivered my own soul.

Sat. June 1.—I spent a little time with forty poor children, whom Lady Maxwell keeps at school. They are swiftly brought forward in reading and writing, and learn the principles of religion. But I observe in them all the love of finery. Be they ever so poor, they must have a scrap of finery. Many of them have not a shoe to their foot: but the girl in rags is not without her ruffles.

Sun. 2.—Mr. Collins intended to have preached on

the Castle-hill at twelve o'clock; but the dull minister kept us in the kirk till past one. At six the house was well filled: and I did not shun to declare the whole counsel of God. I almost wonder at myself. I seldom speak anywhere so roughly as in Scotland. And yet most of the people hear and hear, and are just what they were before.

Wesley Enters His 80th Year

Sat. 15 (Kelso).—As I was coming down stairs, the carpet slipped from under my feet, which, I know not how, turned me round, and pitched me back, with my head foremost, for six or seven stairs. It was impossible to recover myself till I came to the bottom. My head rebounded once or twice from the edge of the stone stairs. But it felt to me exactly as if I had fallen on a cushion or a pillow. Dr. Douglas ran out, sufficiently affrighted. But he needed not. For I rose as well as ever; having received no damage, but the loss of a little skin from one or two of my fingers. Doth not God give his angels charge over us, to keep us in all our ways?

Wed. 26.—I preached at Thirsk; Thursday, 27, at York. Friday, 28. I entered into my eightieth year; but, blessed be God, my time is not "labour and sorrow." I find no more pain or bodily infirmities than at five-and-twenty. This I still impute, 1. To the power of God, fitting me for what He calls me to. 2. To my still travelling four or five thousand miles a year. 3. To my sleeping, night or day, whenever I want it. 4. To my rising at a set hour. And, 5. To my constant preaching, particularly in the morning.

Sat. July 6.—I came to Birmingham, and preached once more in the old, dreary preaching-house.

Sun. 7.—I opened the new house at eight, and it contained the people well: but not in the evening; many were then constrained to go away. In the middle of the sermon, a huge noise was heard, caused by the breaking of a bench on which some people stood. None of them was hurt; yet it occasioned a general panic at first: but in a few minutes all was quiet.

Sun. 14.—I heard a sermon in the old church, at Birmingham, which the preacher uttered with great vehemence against these " hairbrained, itinerant enthusiasts." But he totally missed his mark; having not the least conception of the persons whom he undertook to describe.

No Repose for Wesley

Wed. 17.—I went on to Leicester; Thursday, 18, to Northampton; and Friday, 19, to Hinxworth, in Hertfordshire. Adjoining to Miss Harvey's house is a pleasant garden; and she has made a shady walk round the neighbouring meadows. How gladly could I repose awhile here! But repose is not for me in this world. In the evening many of the villagers flocked together, so that her great hall was well filled. I would fain hope, some of them received the seed in good ground, and will bring forth fruit with patience.

Sat. 20.—We reached London. All the following week the congregations were uncommonly large. Wednesday, 24. My brother and I paid our last visit to Lewisham, and spent a few pensive hours with the relict of our good friend, Mr. Blackwell. We took one more walk round the garden and meadow, which he took so much pains to improve. Upwards of forty years this has been my place of retirement, when I could spare two or three days from London.

Tues. Aug. 13.—Being obliged to leave London a little sooner than I intended, I concluded the conference to-day; and desired all our brethren to observe it as day of solemn thanksgiving. At three in the afterno I took coach. About one on Wednesday morning we were informed that three highwaymen were on the road before us, and had robbed all the coaches that had passed, some of them within an hour or two. I felt no uneasiness on the account, knowing that God would take care of us: and he did so; for, before we came to the spot, all the highwaymen were taken; so we went on unmolested, and early in the afternoon came safe to Bristol.

Thur. 15.—I set out for the west; preached at Taunton in the evening; Friday noon, at Collumpton; and in the evening, at Exeter.

A Christian Bishop's Furniture

Sun. 18.—I was much pleased with the decent behaviour of the whole congregation at the cathedral; as also with the solemn music at the post-communion, one of the finest compositions I ever heard. The bishop inviting me to dinner, I could not but observe, 1. The lovely situation of the palace, covered with trees, and as rural and retired as if it was quite in the country. 2. The plainness of the furniture, not costly or showy, but just fit for a Christian bishop. 3. The dinner sufficient, but not redundant; plain and good, but not delicate. 4. The propriety of the company—five clergymen and four of the aldermen; and, 5. The genuine, unaffected courtesy of the bishop, who, I hope, will be a blessing to his whole diocese.

We set out early in the morning, Monday, 19, and in the afternoon came to Plymouth. I preached in the evening, and at five and twelve on Tuesday, purposing to preach in the square at the Dock in the evening; but the rain prevented. However, I did so on Wednesday evening. A little before I concluded, the commanding officer came into the square with his regiment; but he immediately stopped the drums, and drew up all his men in order on the high side of the square. They were all still as night; nor did any of them stir, till I had pronounced the blessing.

"The Tide is now Turned"

1783. Wed. Jan. 1.—May I begin to live to-day! Sunday, 5. We met to renew our covenant with God. We never meet on this occasion without a blessing; but I do not know that we had ever so large a congregation before.

Sun. 19.—I preached at St. Thomas's church in the afternoon, and at St. Swithin's in the evening. The tide is now turned; so that I have more invitations to preach in churches than I can accept of.

Fri. Feb. 21.—At our yearly meeting for that purpose, we examined our yearly accounts, and found the money (just answering the expense) was upwards of three thousand pounds a year. But that is nothing to me: what I receive of it yearly, is neither more nor less than thirty pounds.

Sun. June 1.—I was refreshed by the very sight of the congregation at the new chapel (London). Monday, 2, and the following days, I employed in settling my business, and preparing for my little excursion. Wednesday, 11. I took coach with Mr. Brackenbury, Broadbent, and Whitfield; and in the evening we reached Harwich. I went immediately to Dr. Jones, who received me in the most affectionate manner. About nine in the morning we sailed, and at nine on Friday, 13, landed at Helvoetsluys.

Wesley Visits Holland

Here we hired a coach for Briel, but were forced to hire a waggon also, to carry a box which one of us could have carried on his shoulders. At Briel we took a boat to Rotterdam. We had not been long there, when Mr. Bennet, a bookseller, who had invited me to his house, called upon me. But as Mr. Loyal, the minister of the Scotch congregation, had invited me, he gave up his claim, and went with us to Mr. Loyal's. I found a friendly, sensible, hospitable, and, I am persuaded, a pious man. We took a walk together round the town, all as clean as a gentleman's parlour. Many of the houses are as high as those in the main street at Edinburgh; and the canals, running through the chief streets, make them convenient, as well as pleasant; bringing the merchants' goods up to their doors. Stately trees grow on all their banks. The whole town is encompassed with a double row of elms; so that one may walk all round it in the shade.

Sat. 14.—I had much conversation with the two English ministers, sensible, well-bred, serious men. These, as well as Mr. Loyal, were very willing I should preach in their churches; but they thought it would be best for me to preach in the Episcopal church. By our conversing freely together, many prejudices were removed, and all our hearts seemed to be united together.

In the evening we again took a walk round the town, and I observed, 1. Many of the houses are higher than most in Edinburgh. It is true they have not so many stories; but each story is far loftier. 2. The streets, the outside and inside of their houses in every part, doors, windows, well-staircases, furniture, even floors, are kept so nicely clean that you cannot find a speck of dirt. 3. There is such a grandeur and elegance in the fronts of the large houses, as I never saw elsewhere; and such a profusion of marble within, particularly in their lower floors and staircases, as I wonder other nations do not imitate. 4. The women and children (which I least of all expected) were in general the most beautiful I ever saw. They were surprisingly fair, and had an inexpressible air of innocence in their countenance. 5. This was wonderfully set off by their dress, which was *simplex munditiis*, plain and neat in the highest degree. 6. It has lately been observed, that growing vegetables greatly resist putridity: so there is an use in their numerous rows of trees which was not thought of at first. The elms balance the canals, preventing the putrefaction which those otherwise might produce.

The Reverent Dutch

One little circumstance I observed, which I suppose is peculiar to Holland: to most chamber-windows a looking-glass is placed on the outside of the sash, so as to show the whole street, with all the passengers. There is something very pleasing in these moving pictures. Are they found in no other country?

Sun. 15.—The Episcopal church is not quite so large as the chapel in West-street. It is very elegant both without and within. The service began at half-past nine. Such a congregation had not often been there before. I preached on, "God created man in his own image." The people seemed, "all but their attention, dead." In the afternoon the church was so filled as (they informed me) it had not been for these fifty years. I preached on, "God hath given us eternal life; and this life is in his

Son." I believe God applied it to many hearts. Were it only for this hour, I am glad I came to Holland.

One thing which I peculiarly observed was this, and the same in all the churches in Holland : at coming in, no one looks on the right or the left hand, or bows or courtesies to any one; but all go straight forward to their seats, as if no other person was in the place. During the service, none turns his head on either side, or looks at anything but his book or the minister ; and in going out, none take notice of any one, but all go straight forward till they are in the open air.

After church an English gentleman invited me to his country-house, not half a mile from the town. I scarce ever saw so pretty a place. The garden before the house was in three partitions, each quite different from the others. The house lay between this and another garden (nothing like any of the others), from which you looked through a beautiful summer-house, washed by a small stream, into rich pastures filled with cattle. We sat under an arbour of stately trees, between the front and the back gardens. Here were four such children (I suppose seven, six, five, and three years old) as I never saw before in one family ; such inexpressible beauty and innocence shone together !

In the evening I attended the service of the great Dutch church, as large as most of our cathedrals. The organ (like those in all the Dutch churches) was elegantly painted and gilded; and the tunes that were sung were very lively, and yet solemn.

Mon. 16.—We set out in a track-skuit for the Hague. By the way we saw a curiosity ; the gallows near the canal, surrounded with a knot of beautiful trees ; so the dying man will have one pleasant prospect here, whatever befalls him hereafter ! At eleven we came to Delft, a large, handsome town, where we spent an hour at a merchant's house, who, as well as his wife, a very agreeable woman, seemed both to fear and to love God. Afterwards we saw the great church; I think nearly, if not quite, as long as York Minster. It is exceedingly light and elegant within, and every part is kept exquisitely clean. The tomb of William the First is much admired; particularly his statue, which has more life than one would think could be expressed in brass.

The Beautiful Hague

When we came to the Hague, though we had heard much of it, we were not disappointed. It is, indeed, beautiful beyond expression. Many of the houses are exceeding grand, and are finely intermixed with water and wood; yet are not too close, but so as to be sufficiently ventilated by the air.

Being invited to tea by Madam de Vassenaar (one of the first quality in the Hague), I waited upon her in the afternoon. She received us with that easy openness and affability which is almost peculiar to Christians and persons of quality. Soon after came ten or twelve ladies more, who seemed to be of her own rank (though dressed quite plain), and two most agreeable gentlemen; one of whom, I afterwards understood, was a colonel in the Prince's Guards. After tea I expounded the three first verses of the thirteenth of the first Epistle to the Corinthians. Captain M. interpreted, sentence by sentence. I then prayed, and Colonel V. after me. I believe this hour was well employed.

Tues. 17.—As we walked over the Place we saw the Swiss Guards at their exercise. They are a fine body of men, taller, I suppose, than any English regiment; and they all wear large black whiskers, which they take care to keep as black as their boots. Afterwards we saw the gardens at the Old Palace, beautifully laid out, with a large piece of water in the middle, and a canal at each end: the open walks in it are pleasant, but the shady serpentine walks are far pleasanter.

We dined at Mrs. L——'s, in such a family as I have seldom seen. Her mother, upwards of seventy, seemed to be continually rejoicing in God her Saviour: the daughter breathes the same spirit; and her grandchildren, three little girls and a boy, seem to be all love. I have not seen four such children together in all England. A gentleman coming in after dinner, I found a particular desire to pray for him. In a little while he melted into tears, as indeed did most of the company.

Wed. 18. In the afternoon Madam de Vassenaar invited us to a meeting at a neighbouring lady's house. I expounded Gal. vi. 14, and Mr. M. interpreted as before.

At Leyden and Amsterdam

Thurs. 19.—We took boat at seven. Mrs. L. and one of her relations, being unwilling to part so soon, bore us company to Leyden; a large and populous town, but not so pleasant as Rotterdam. In the afternoon we went on to Haerlem, where a plain, good man and his wife received us in a most affectionate manner. At six we took boat again. As it was filled from end to end, I was afraid we should not have a very pleasant journey. After Mr. Ferguson had told the people who we were, we made a slight excuse, and sung an hymn. They were all attention. We then talked a little, by means of our interpreter, and desired that any of them who pleased would sing. Four persons did so; and sung well. After a while we sung again: so did one or two of them; and all our hearts were strangely knit together, so that when we came to Amsterdam they dismissed us with abundance of blessings.

Fri. 20.—We breakfasted at Mr. Ferguson's, near the heart of the city. At eleven we drank coffee (the custom in Holland) at Mr. J——'s, a merchant, whose dining-room is covered, both walls and ceiling, with the most beautiful paintings. He and his lady walked with us in the afternoon to the Stadt-house; perhaps the grandest buildings of the kind in Europe. The great hall is a noble room indeed, near as large as that of Christ-church in Oxford. But I have neither time nor inclination to describe particularly this amazing structure.

The Warmly Affectionate Dutch

Sun. 22.—I went to the new church, so called still, though four or five hundred years old. It is larger, higher, and better illuminated than most of our cathedrals. The screen that divides the church from the choir is of polished brass, and shines like gold. I understood the Psalms that were sung, and the text well, and a little of the sermon ; which Mr. De H. delivered with great earnestness. At two I began the service at the English church, an elegant building, about the size of West-street chapel. Only it has no galleries ; nor have any of the churches in Holland. I preached on Isaiah lv. 6, 7 ; and I am persuaded many received the truth in the love thereof.

After dinner Mrs. J—— took me in a coach to the Mere, and thence round the country to Zeeburg. I never saw such a country before : I suppose there is no such summer country in Europe. From Amsterdam to Mere is all a train of the most delightful gardens. Turning upon the left, you then open upon the Texel, which spreads into a sea. Zeeburg itself is a little house built on the edge of it, which commands both a land and a sea prospect. What is wanting to make the inhabitants happy, but the knowledge and love of God ?

Wed. 25.—We took boat for Haerlem. The great church here is a noble structure, equalled by few cathedrals in England, either in length, breadth, or height: the organ is the largest I ever saw, and is said to be the finest in Europe. Hence we went to Mr. Van Ka——'s, whose wife was convinced of sin and justified by reading Mr. Whitefield's sermons.

Here we were as at home. Before dinner we took a walk in Haerlem Wood. It adjoins to the town, and is cut out in many shady walks; with lovely vistas shooting out every way. The walk from the Hague to Scheveling is pleasant; those near Amsterdam more so; but these exceed them all.

We returned in the afternoon to Amsterdam; and in the evening took leave of as many of our friends as we could. How entirely were we mistaken in the Hollanders, supposing them to be of a cold, phlegmatic, unfriendly temper ! I have not met with a more warmly affectionate people in all Europe ! no, not in Ireland !

Wesley at Utrecht

Thur. 26.—Our friends having largely provided us with wine and fruits for our little journey, we took boat in a lovely morning for Utrecht.

Utrecht has much the look of an English town. The streets are broad, and have many noble houses. In quietness and stillness it much resembles Oxford. The country all round is like a garden: and the people I conversed with are not only civil and hospitable, but friendly and affectionate, even as those at Amsterdam.

Mon. 30.—We hired a coach for Rotterdam, at half a crown per head. We dined at Gouda, at Mr Van Flooten's, minister of the town, who received us with all possible kindness. Before dinner we went into the church, famous for its painted windows; but we had not time to survey a tenth part of them: we could only observe, in general, that the colours were exceeding lively, and the figures exactly proportioned. In the evening we reached once more the hospitable house of Mr. Loyal, at Rotterdam.

Tues. July 1.—I called on as many as I could of my friends, and we parted with much affection. We then hired a yacht, which brought us to Helvoetsluys about eleven the next day. At two we went on board; but the wind turning against us, we did not reach Harwich till about nine on Friday morning. After a little rest, we procured a carriage, and reached London about eleven at night.

Two Hours With Dr. Johnson

I can by no means regret either the trouble or expense which attended this little journey. It opened me a way into, as it were, a new world; where the land, the buildings, the people, the customs, were all such as I had never seen before. But as those with whom I conversed were of the same spirit with my friends in England, I was as much at home in Utrecht and Amsterdam, as in Bristol and London.

Sun. 6.—We rejoiced to meet once more with our English friends in the new chapel; who were refreshed with the account of the gracious work which God is working in Holland also.

Thur. Dec. 18.—I spent two hours with that great man, Dr. Johnson, who is sinking into the grave by a gentle decay.

JOHN WESLEY AND DR. JOHNSON

JOHN WESLEY VISITS LORD GEORGE GORDON
IN THE TOWER

Mon. April 5.—I was surprised, when I came to Chester, to find that there also morning preaching was quite left off, for this worthy reason : " Because the people will not come, or, at least, not in the winter." If so, the Methodists are a fallen people. Here is proof. They have " lost their first love " : and they never will or can recover it, till they " do the first works."

Wesley and Early Rising

As soon as I set foot in Georgia, I began preaching at five in the morning ; and every communicant, that is, every serious person in the town, constantly attended throughout the year : I mean, every morning, winter and summer, unless in the case of sickness. They did so till I left the province. In the year 1738, when God began his great work in England, I began preaching at the same hour, winter and summer, and never wanted a congregation. If they will not attend now, they have lost their zeal ; and then, it cannot be denied, they are a fallen people.

And, in the mean time, we are labouring to secure the preaching-houses to the next generation ! In the name of God, let us, if possible, secure the present generation from drawing back to perdition ! Let all the preachers that are still alive to God join together as one man, fast and pray, lift up their voice as a trumpet, be instant, in season, out of season, to convince them they are fallen ; and exhort them instantly to repent, and " do the first works " : this in particular—rising in the morning, without which neither their souls nor bodies can long remain in health.

Mon. 19.—I went on to Ambleside ; where, as I was sitting down to supper, I was informed, notice had been given of my preaching, and that the congregation was waiting.   I would not disappoint them ; but preached immediately on salvation by faith.   Among them were a gentleman and his wife, who gave me a remarkable relation.

Remarkable Escape from Prison

She said she had often heard her mother relate, what an intimate acquaintance had told her, that her husband was concerned in the Rebellion of 1745.   He was tried at Carlisle, and found guilty.   The evening before he was to die, sitting and musing in her chair, she fell fast asleep.   She dreamed, one came to her, and said, " Go to such a part of the wall, and among the loose stones you will find a key, which you must carry to your husband."   She waked ; but, thinking it a common dream, paid no attention to it.   Presently she fell asleep again, and dreamed the very same dream. She started up, put on her cloak and hat, and went to that part of the wall, and among the loose stones found a key.   Having, with some difficulty, procured admission into the gaol, she gave this to her husband.   It opened the door of his cell, as well as the lock of the prison door.   So at midnight he escaped for life.

The Banks of the Spey

Sat. May 8.—We reached the banks of the Spey.   I suppose there are few such rivers in Europe.   The rapidity of it exceeds even that of the Rhine : and it was now much swelled with melting snow.   However, we made shift to get over before ten ; and about twelve reached Elgin.   Here I was received by a daughter of good Mr. Plenderleith, late of Edinburgh; with whom, having spent an agreeable hour, I hastened toward Forres: but we were soon at full stop again; the river Findhorn also was so swollen, that we were afraid the ford was not passable.   However, having a good guide, we passed it without much difficulty.   I found Sir Lodowick Grant almost worn out. Never was a visit more seasonable.   By free and friendly conversation his spirits were so raised, that I am in hopes it will lengthen his life.

Sun. 9.—I preached to a small company at noon, on, "His commandments are not grievous." As I was concluding, Colonel Grant and his lady came in: for whose sake I began again, and lectured, as they call it, on the former part of the fifteenth chapter of St. Luke. We had a larger company in the afternoon, to whom I preached on "judgment to come."   And this subject seemed to affect them most.

Twelve and a Half Miles in Heavy Rain

Mon. 10.—I set out for Inverness.   I had sent Mr. M'Allum before, on George Whitfield's horse, to give notice of my coming. Hereby I was obliged to take both George and Mrs. M'Allum with me in my chaise.   To ease the horses, we walked forward from Nairn, ordering Richard to follow us, as soon as they were fed: he did so, but there were two roads.   So, as we took one, and he the other, we walked about twelve miles and a half of the way, through heavy rain.   We then found Richard waiting for us at a little ale-house, and drove on to Inverness.   But, blessed be God, I was no more tired than when I set out from Nairn.   I preached at seven to a far larger congregation than I had seen here since I preached in the kirk.   And surely the labour was not in vain: for God sent a message to many hearts.

Tues. 11.—Notwithstanding the long discontinuance of morning preaching, we had a large congregation at five. I breakfasted at the first house I was invited to at Inverness, where good Mr. M'Kenzie then lived. His three daughters live in it now ; one of whom inherits all the spirit of her father. In the afternoon we took a walk over the bridge, into one of the pleasantest countries I have seen. It runs along by the side of the clear river, and is well-cultivated and well-wooded. And here first we heard abundance of birds, welcoming the return of spring. The congregation was larger this evening than the last: and great part of them attended in the morning. We had then a solemn parting, as we could hardly expect to meet again in the present world.

Incidents in Scotland

Tues. 18.—I preached at Dundee. Wednesday, 19. I crossed over the pleasant and fertile county of Fife, to Melval-house, the grand and beautiful seat of Lord Leven. He was not at home, being gone to Edinburgh, as the King's Commissioner ; but the Countess was, with two of her daughters, and both her sons-in-law. At their desire, I preached in the evening, on, "It is appointed unto man once to die"; and I believe God made the application.

Thur. 20.—It blew a storm; nevertheless, with some difficulty, we crossed the Queen's-ferry.

Sat. 22 (Edinburgh).—A famous actress, just come down from London (which, for the honour of Scotland, is just during the sitting of the Assembly), stole away a great part of our congregation to-night. How much wiser are these Scots than their forefathers !

Sun. 23.—I went in the morning to the Tolbooth kirk; in the afternoon, to the old Episcopal chapel. But they have lost their glorying : they talked, the moment service was done, as if they had been in London.   In the evening the Octagon was well filled; and I applied, with all possible plainness, "God is a Spirit; and they that worship him must worship him in spirit and in truth."

Wesley at 81

Mon. June 28 (Epworth).—To-day I entered on my eighty-second year, and found myself just as strong to labour, and as fit for any exercise of body or mind, as I was forty years ago.   I do not impute this to second causes, but to the Sovereign Lord of all.   It is He who bids the sun of life stand still, so long as it pleaseth him.

I am as strong at eighty-one, as I was at twenty-one; but abundantly more healthy, being a stranger to the head-ache, tooth-ache, and other bodily disorders which attended me in my youth.   We can only say, "The Lord reigneth ! "   While we live, let us live to him !

In the afternoon I went to Gainsborough, and willingly accepted the offer of Mr. Dean's chapel.   The audience was large and seemed much affected : possibly some good may be done even at Gainsborough!   Tuesday, 29.   I preached in the street at Scotter, to a large and deeply attentive congregation.   It was a solemn and comfortable season.   In the evening I read prayers and preached in Owstone church; and again in the morning. Wednesday, 30.   In the evening I preached at Epworth. In the residue of the week, I preached morning and evening in several of the neighbouring towns.

Wed. Aug. 18.—I went to Admiral Vaughan's, at Tracoon, one of the pleasantest seats in Great Britain. The house is embosomed in lofty woods, and does not appear till you drop down upon it.   The Admiral governs his family, as he did in his ship, with the utmost punctuality. The bell rings, and all attend without delay, whether at meals, or at morning and evening prayer. I preached at seven, on Phil. iii. 8; and spent the evening in serious conversation.

Tues. 31.—Dr. Coke, Mr. Whatcoat, and Mr. Vasey, came down from London, in order to embark for America.

Wed. Sep. 1.—Being now clear in my own mind, I took a step which I had long weighed in my mind, and appointed Mr. Whatcoat and Mr. Vasey to go and serve the desolate sheep in America. Thursday, 2. I added to them three more; which, I verily believe, will be much to the glory of God.

Sun. 12.—Dr. Coke read prayers, and I preached, in the new room. Afterward I hastened to Kingswood, and preached under the shade of that double row of trees which I planted about forty years ago. How little did any one then think that they would answer such an intention! The sun shone as hot as it used to do even in Georgia; but his rays could not pierce our canopy; and our Lord, meantime, shone upon many souls, and refreshed them that were weary.

Burglary at Wesley's House

Sat. Nov. 20 (London).—At three in the morning two or three men broke into our house, through the kitchen window. Thence they came up into the parlour, and broke open Mr. Moore's bureau, where they found two or three pounds: the night before I had prevented his leaving there seventy pounds, which he had just received. They next broke open the cupboard, and took away some silver spoons. Just at this time the alarum, which Mr. Moore, by mistake, had set for half-past three (instead of four), went off, as it usually did, with a thundering noise. At this the thieves ran away with all speed; though their work was not half done; and the whole damage which we sustained scarce amounted to six pounds.

Sun. Dec. 26.—I preached the condemned criminals' sermon in Newgate. Forty-seven were under sentence of death. While they were coming in, there was something very awful in the clink of their chains. But no sound was heard, either from them or the crowded audience, after the text was named, "There is joy in heaven over one sinner that repenteth, more than over ninety and nine just persons, that need not repentance." The power of the Lord was eminently present, and most of the prisoners were in tears. A few days after, twenty of them died at once, five of whom died in peace. I could not but greatly approve of the spirit and behaviour of Mr. Villette, the Ordinary; and I rejoiced to hear that it was the same on all similar occasions.

Wesley at 81 Begs £200

Fri. 31.—We had a solemn watch-night, and ushered in the new year with the voice of praise and thanksgiving.

1785. Sat. Jan. 1.—Whether this be the last or no, may it be the best year of my life! Sunday, 2. A larger number of people were present this evening at the renewal of our covenant with God, than was ever seen before on the occasion.

Tues. 4.—At this season we usually distribute coals and bread among the poor of the society. But I now considered, they wanted clothes, as well as food. So on this, and the four following days I walked through the town, and begged two hundred pounds, in order to

clothe them that needed it most.   But it was hard work
as most of the streets were filled with melting snow,
which often lay ankle deep; so that my feet were
steeped in snow water nearly from morning till evening:
I held it out pretty well till Saturday evening; but I
was laid up with a violent flux, which increased every
hour, till, at six in the morning, Dr. Whitehead called
upon me.   His first draught made me quite easy; and
three or four more perfected the cure.   If he lives some
years, I expect he will be one of the most eminent physicians in Europe.

I supposed my journeys this winter had been over
but I could not decline one more.   Monday, 17. I set
out for poor Colchester, to encourage the little flock.
They had exceeding little of this world's goods, but
most of them had a better portion.   Tuesday, 18. I went
on to Mistleythorn, a village near Manningtree.   Some
time since, one of the shipwrights of Deptford-yard, being
sent hither to superintend the building of some men-of-
war, began to read sermons on a Sunday evening in his
own house.   Afterwards he exhorted them a little,
and then formed a little society.   Some time after, he
begged one of our preachers to come over and help
them.   I now found a lively society, and one of the
most elegant congregations I had seen for many years.
Yet they seemed as willing to be instructed, as if they
had lived in Kingswood.   Wednesday, 19. I returned
to Colchester; and on Thursday, 20, preached to a
lovely congregation at Purfleet, and the next morning
returned to London.

Sun. 23.—I preached morning and afternoon at West-
street, and in the evening in the chapel at Knightsbridge:
I think it will be the last time; for I know not that
I have ever seen a worse-behaved congregation.

Tues. 25.—I spent two or three hours in the House of Lords. I had frequently heard that this was the most venerable assembly in England. But how was I disappointed ! What is a lord, but a sinner, born to die !

Fifty Years Growth of Methodism

Thurs. March 24 (Worcester).—I was now considering how strangely the grain of mustard-seed, planted about fifty years ago, has grown up. It has spread through all Great Britain and Ireland ; the Isle of Wight, and the Isle of Man ; then to America, from the Leeward Islands, through the whole continent, into Canada and Newfoundland. And the societies, in all these parts, walk by one rule, knowing religion is holy tempers ; and striving to worship God, not in form only, but likewise " in spirit and in truth."

Tues. June 28.—By the good providence of God, I finished the eighty-second year of my age. Is anything too hard for God ? It is now eleven years since I have felt any such thing as weariness : many times I speak till my voice fails, and I can speak no longer ; frequently I walk till my strength fails, and I can walk no farther ; yet even then I feel no sensation of weariness, but am perfectly easy from head to foot. I dare not impute this to natural causes : it is the will of God.

Tues. Aug. 9.—I crossed over to the Isle of Wight. Here also the work of God prospers : we had a comfortable time at Newport, where is a very teachable, though uncommonly elegant, congregation. Wednesday, 10. We took a walk to the poor remains of Carisbrook-castle. It seems to have been once exceeding strong, standing on a steep ascent. But even what little of it is left is now swiftly running to ruin. The window, indeed, through which King Charles attempted to make his escape, is still in being; and brought to my mind that whole train of occurrences, wherein the hand of God was so eminently seen.

Thur. 25.—About nine I preached at Mousehole, where there is now one of the liveliest societies in Cornwall. Hence we went to the Land's-end, in order to which we clambered down the rocks, to the very edge of the water; and I cannot think but the sea has gained some hundred yards since I was here forty years ago.

Wesley Visits the House of Lords

1786. Mon. Jan. 9.—At leisure hours this week, I read the Life of Sir William Penn, a wise and good man. But I was much surprised at what he relates concerning his first wife; who lived, I suppose, fifty years, and said a little before her death, "I bless God, I never did anything wrong in my life!" Was she then ever convinced of sin? And if not, could she be saved on any other footing than a heathen?

Tues. 24.—I was desired to go and hear the King deliver his speech in the House of Lords. But how agreeably was I surprised! He pronounced every word with exact propriety. I much doubt whether there be any other king in Europe, that is so just and natural a speaker.

Wed. June 28.—I entered into the eighty-third year of my age. I am a wonder to myself. It is now twelve years since I have felt any such sensation as weariness. I am never tired (such is the goodness of God!) either with writing, preaching, or travelling. One natural cause undoubtedly is, my continual exercise and change of air. How the latter contributes to health I know not; but certainly it does.

*   *   *

The remainder of this Journal was not published in Wesley's lifetime and was not revised by him. The MS. was "so ill written as to be scarcely legible."

.   ,   .   .

Tues. Sept. 26.—Reached London. I now applied myself in earnest to the writing of Mr. Fletcher's Life, having procured the best materials I could. To this I dedicated all the time I could spare, till November, from five in the morning till eight at night. These are my studying hours; I cannot write longer in a day without hurting my eyes.

Wesley Visits Hatfield House

Mon. Oct. 2.—I went to Chatham, and had much comfort with the loving, serious congregation in the evening, as well as at five in the morning. Tuesday, 3. We then ran down, with a fair, pleasant wind, to Sheerness. The preaching-house here is now finished, but by means never heard of. The building was undertaken a few months since, by a little handful of men, without any probable means of finishing it. But God so moved the hearts of the people in the dock, that even those who do not pretend to any religion, carpenters, shipwrights, labourers, ran up, at all their vacant hours, and worked with all their might, without any pay. By this means a large square house was soon elegantly finished, both within and without; and it is the neatest building, next to the new chapel in London, of any in the south of England.

Thurs. 19.—I returned to London. In this journey I had a full sight of Lord Salisbury's seat, at Hatfield. The park is delightful. Both the fronts of the house are very handsome, though antique. The hall, the assembly-room, and the gallery are grand and beautiful. The chapel is extremely pretty ; but the furniture in general (excepting the pictures, many of which are originals) is just such as I should expect in a gentleman's house of five hundred a year.

Sat. Dec. 23.—By great importunity I was induced (having little hope of doing good) to visit two of the felons in Newgate, who lay under sentence of death. They appeared serious; but I can lay little stress on appearances of this kind. However, I wrote in their behalf to a great man ; and perhaps it was in consequence of this that they had a reprieve.

Sun. 24.—I was desired to preach at the Old Jewry. But the church was cold, and so was the congregation. We had a congregation of another kind the next day, Christmas-day, at four in the morning, as well as five in the evening at the new chapel, and at West-street chapel about noon.

Wesley's Threat to Deptford

1787. Mon. Jan. 1.—We began the service at four in the morning, to an unusually large congregation. We had another comfortable opportunity at the new chapel at the usual hour, and a third in the evening at West-street. Tuesday, 2. I went over to Deptford ; but it seemed, I was got into a den of lions. Most of the leading men of the society were mad for separating from the Church. I endeavoured to reason with them, but in vain : they had neither good sense nor even good manners left. At length, after meeting the whole society, I told them, "If you are resolved, you may have your service in church-hours ; but, remember, from that time you will see my face no more." This struck deep ; and from that hour I have heard no more of separating from the Church !

Monday, 8, and the four following days, I went a begging for the poor. I hoped to be able to provide food and raiment for those of the society who were in pressing want, yet had no weekly allowance : these were about two hundred : but I was much disappointed. Six or seven, indeed, of our brethren, gave ten pounds apiece. If forty or fifty had done this, I could have carried my design into execution. However, much good was done with two hundred pounds, and many sorrowful hearts made glad.

Wesley Visits the Irish Parliament House

Wed. July 4.—I spent an hour at the New-Dargle, a gentleman's seat four or five miles from Dublin. I have not seen so beautiful a place in the kingdom. It equals the Leasowes in Warwickshire ; and it greatly exceeds them in situation ; all the walks lying on the side of a mountain, which commands all Dublin-bay, as well as an extensive and finely variegated land-prospect. A little river runs through it, which occasions two cascades, at a small distance from each other. Although many places may exceed this in grandeur, I believe none can exceed it in beauty.

Afterwards I saw the Parliament-house. The House of Lords far exceeds that at Westminster ; and the Lord-Lieutenant's throne as far exceeds that miserable throne (so called) of the King in the English House of Lords. The House of Commons is a noble room indeed. It is an octagon, wainscoted round with Irish oak, which shames all mahogany, and galleried all round for the convenience of the ladies. The Speaker's chair is far more grand than the throne of the Lord-Lieutenant. But what surprised me above all, were the kitchens of the House, and the large apparatus for good eating. Tables were placed from one end of a large hall to the other; which, it seems, while the Parliament sits, are daily covered with meat at four or five o'clock, for the accommodation of the Members.

Wed. 11.—At five I took an affectionate leave of this loving (Irish) people; and, having finished all my business here, in the afternoon I went down with my friends, having taken the whole ship, and went on board the Prince of Wales, one of the Parkgate packets. At seven we sailed with a fair, moderate wind. Between nine and ten I lay down, as usual, and slept till near four, when I was waked by an uncommon noise, and found the ship lay beating upon a large rock, about a league from Holyhead. The captain, who had not long lain down, leaped up; and, running upon the deck, when he saw how the ship lay, cried out, "Your lives may be saved, but I am undone!" Yet no sailor swore, and no woman cried out. We immediately went to prayer; and presently the ship, I know not how, shot off the rock, and pursued her way, without any more damage than the wounding a few of her outside planks. About three in the afternoon we came safe to Parkgate; and in the evening went on to Chester.

A Visit to the Channel Islands

Mon. Aug. 13.—We set out from Yarmouth with a fair wind; but it soon turned against us, and blew so hard that in the afternoon we were glad to put in at Swanage.

Tues. 14.—Sailing on, with a fair wind, we fully expected to reach Guernsey in the afternoon; but the wind turning contrary, and blowing hard, we found it would be impossible. We then judged it best to put in at the Isle of Alderney; but we were very near being shipwrecked in the bay. When we were in the middle of the rocks, with the sea rippling all round us, the wind totally failed. Had this continued, we must have struck upon one or other of the rocks; so we went to prayer, and the wind sprung up instantly. About sunset we landed; and, though we had five beds in the same room, slept in peace.

About eight I went down to a convenient spot on the beach, and began giving out a hymn. A woman and two little children joined us immediately. Before the hymn was ended, we had a tolerable congregation; all of whom behaved well: part, indeed, continued at forty or fifty yards' distance; but they were all quiet and attentive.

"A Little Circumstance"

It happened (to speak in the vulgar phrase) that three or four who sailed with us from England, a gentleman, with his wife and sister, were near relations of the Governor. He came to us this morning, and, when I went into the room, behaved with the utmost courtesy. This little circumstance may remove prejudice, and make a more open way for the Gospel.

Soon after we set sail, and, after a very pleasant passage, through little islands on either hand, we came to the venerable castle, standing on a rock, about a quarter of a mile from Guernsey. The isle itself makes a beautiful appearance, spreading as a crescent to the right and left; about seven miles long, and five broad; part high land, and part low. The town itself is boldly situated, rising higher and higher from the water. The first thing I observed in it was, very narrow streets, and exceeding high houses. But we quickly went on to Mr. De Jersey's, hardly a mile from the town. Here I found a most cordial welcome, both from the master of the house, and all his family.   I preached at seven, in a large room, to as deeply serious a congregation as I ever saw.

Thur. 16.—I had a very serious congregation at five, in a large room of Mr. De Jersey's house.   His gardens and orchards are of a vast extent, and wonderfully pleasant; and I know no nobleman in Great Britain that has such variety of the most excellent fruit; which he is every year increasing, either from France or other parts of the Continent.   What quantity of fruit he has, you may conjecture from one sort only :—this summer he gathered fifty pounds of strawberries daily, for six weeks together.

In the evening I preached at the other end of the town, in our own preaching-house.   So many people squeezed in (though not near all who came), that it was as hot as a stove.   But this none seemed to regard; for the word of God was sharper than a two-edged sword.

At the Governor's House

Fri. 17.—I waited upon the Governor, and spent half an hour very agreeably.   In the afternoon we took a walk upon the pier, the largest and finest I ever saw. The town is swiftly increasing; new houses starting up on every side.

In the evening I did not attempt to go into the house, but stood near it, in the yard, surrounded with tall, shady trees, and proclaimed to a large congregation, "God is a Spirit; and they that worship him must worship him in spirit and in truth."   I believe many were cut to the heart this hour, and some not a little comforted.

Sat. 18.—Dr. Coke and I dined at the Governor's.   I was well pleased to find other company.   We conversed seriously for upwards of an hour, with a sensible, well-bred, agreeable man.   In the evening I preached to the largest congregation I have seen here.

Sun. 19.—Joseph Bradford preached at six in the morning, at Montplaisir les Terres, to a numerous congregation. I preached at half an hour past eight, and the house contained the congregation. At ten I went to the French church, where there was a large and well-behaved congregation. At five we had the largest congregation of all.

"Because I have Lived so Many Years"·

Mon. 20.—We embarked between three and four in the morning, in a very small, inconvenient sloop, and not a swift sailer; so that we were seven hours in sailing what is called seven leagues. About eleven we landed at St. Helier, and went straight to Mr. Brackenbury's house. It stands very pleasantly, near the end of the town; and has a large, convenient garden, with a lovely range of fruitful hills, which rise at a small distance from it. I preached in the evening to an exceeding serious congregation, on Matt. iii. ult.: and almost as many were present at five in the morning; whom I exhorted to go on to perfection.

Tues. 21.—We took a walk to one of our friends in the country. Near his house stood what they call the college. It is a free school, designed to train up children for the university; exceeding finely situated, in a quiet recess, surrounded by tall woods. Not far from it stands, on the top of a high hill (I suppose a Roman mount), an old chapel, believed to be the first Christian church which was built in the island. From hence we had a view of the whole island, the pleasantest I ever saw; as far superior to the Isle of Wight as that is to the Isle of Man. The little hills, almost covered with large trees, are inexpressibly beautiful: it seems they are to be equalled in the Isle of Guernsey. In the evening I was obliged to preach abroad, on, "Now is the day of salvation." I think a blessing seldom fails to attend that subject.

Wed. 22.—In the evening, the room not containing the people, I was obliged to stand in the yard. I preached on Rom. iii. 22, 23 ; and spoke exceeding plain : even the gentry heard with deep attention. How little does God turn to his own glory ! Probably many of these flock together, because I have lived so many years. And perhaps even this may be the means of their living for ever.

Detained by Contrary Winds

Mon. 27.—Captain Cabot, the master of a Guernsey sloop, called upon us early in the morning, and told us, if we chose to go that way, he would set out between five and six. But the wind being quite contrary, we judged it best to wait a little longer. In the evening, being appointed to preach at seven, I was obliged to preach within. We were extremely crowded ; but the power of God was so manifested while I declared, " We preach Jesus Christ, and him crucified," that we soon forgot the heat, and were glad of being detained a little longer than we intended.

I thought when I left Southampton, to have been there again as this day ; but God's thoughts were not as my thoughts. Here we are shut up in Jersey ; for how long we cannot tell. But it is all well ; for thou, Lord, hast done it.

Tues. 28.—Being still detained by contrary winds, I preached at six in the evening to a larger congregation than ever, in the assembly-room. It conveniently contains five or six hundred people. Most of the gentry were present ; and I believe felt that God was there in an uncommon degree. Being still detained, I preached there again the next evening, to a larger congregation than ever. I now judged, I had fully delivered my own soul : and in the morning, the wind serving for Guernsey, and not for Southampton, I returned thither not unwillingly; since it was not by my choice, but by the clear providence of God : for in the afternoon I was offered the use of the assembly-room ; a spacious chamber in the market-place, which would contain thrice as many as our former room. I willingly accepted the offer, and preached at six to such a congregation as I had not seen here before; and the word seemed to sink deep into their hearts. I trust it will not return empty.

Tues. Sept. 4.—The storm continued, so that we could not stir. I took a walk to-day, through what is called the New-ground, where the gentry are accustomed to walk in the evening. Both the upper ground, which is as level as a bowling-green, and the lower, which is planted with rows of trees, are wonderfully beautiful. In the evening I fully delivered my own soul, by showing what it is to build upon a rock. But still we could not sail; the wind being quite contrary, as well as exceeding high.

Sails for Penzance

It was the same on Wednesday. In the afternoon we drank tea at a friend's, who was mentioning a captain just come from France, that proposed to sail in the morning for Penzance; for which the wind would serve, though not for Southampton. In this we plainly saw the hand of God ; so we agreed with him immediately; and in the morning, Thursday, 6, went on board with a fair, moderate wind; but we had but just entered the ship when the wind died away. We cried to God for help ; and it presently sprung up, exactly fair, and it did not cease till it brought us into Penzance bay.

Sat. Dec. 22.—I yielded to the importunity of a painter, and sat an hour and a half, in all, for my picture. I think it was the best that was ever taken; but what is the picture of a man above fourscore?

Wesley on His Old Age

Sat. March 1.—(Being Leap-year.) I considered, what difference do I find by an increase of years? I find, 1. Less activity; I walk slower, particularly up-hill: 2. My memory is not so quick: 3. I cannot read so quick by candle-light. But I bless God, that all my other powers of body and mind remain just as they were.

Sat. April 19.—We went on to Bolton, where I preached in the evening in one of the most elegant houses in the kingdom, and to one of the liveliest congregations. And this I must avow, there is not such a set of singers in any of the Methodist congregations in the three kingdoms. There cannot be; for we have near a hundred such trebles, boys and girls, selected out of our Sunday-schools, and accurately taught, as are not found together in any chapel, cathedral, or music-room within the four seas. Besides, the spirit with which they all sing, and the beauty of many of them, so suits the melody, that I defy any to exceed it; except the singing of angels in our Father's house.

Sun. 20.—At eight, and at one, the house was thoroughly filled. About three I met between nine hundred and a thousand of the children belonging to our Sunday-schools. I never saw such a sight before. They were all exactly clean, as well as plain, in their apparel. All were serious and well-behaved. Many, both boys and girls, had as beautiful faces as, I believe, England or Europe can afford. When they all sung together, and none of them out of tune, the melody was beyond that of any theatre; and, what is the best of all, many of them truly fear God, and some rejoice in his salvation. These are a pattern to all the town. Their usual diversion is to visit the poor that are sick (sometimes six, or eight, or ten together), to exhort, comfort, and pray with them. Frequently ten or more of them get together to sing and pray by themselves; sometimes thirty or forty; and are so earnestly engaged, alternately singing, praying and crying, that they know not how to part. You children that hear this, why should not you go and do likewise? Is not God here as well as at Bolton? Let God arise and maintain his own cause, even " out of the mouths of babes and sucklings ! "

Wesley's Reasons for His Long Life

Sat. June 28.—I this day enter on my eighty-fifth year : and what cause have I to praise God, as for a thousand spiritual blessings, so for bodily blessings also ! How little have I suffered yet by " the rush of numerous years ! " It is true, I am not so agile as I was in times past. I do not run or walk so fast as I did; my sight is a little decayed; my left eye is grown dim, and hardly serves me to read; I have daily some pain in the ball of my right eye, as also in my right temple (occasioned by a blow received some months since), and in my right shoulder and arm, which I impute partly to a sprain, and partly to the rheumatism.

I find likewise some decay in my memory, with regard to names and things lately past; but not at all with regard to what I have read or heard twenty, forty, or sixty years ago; neither do I find any decay in my hearing, smell, taste, or appetite (though I want but a third part of the food I did once); nor do I feel any such thing as weariness, either in travelling or preaching : and I am not conscious of any decay in writing sermons; which I do as readily, and I believe as correctly, as ever.

To what cause can I impute this, that I am as I am? First, doubtless, to the power of God, fitting me for the work to which I am called, as long as he pleases to continue me therein; and, next, subordinately to this, to the prayers of his children.

May we not impute it as inferior means,

1. To my constant exercise and change of air?

2. To my never having lost a night's sleep, sick or well, at land or at sea, since I was born?

3. To my having sleep at command; so that whenever I feel myself almost worn out, I call it, and it comes, day or night?

4. To my having constantly, for above sixty years, risen at four in the morning?

5. To my constant preaching at five in the morning, for above fifty years?

6. To my having had so little pain in my life; and so little sorrow, or anxious care?

Even now, though I find pain daily in my eye, or temple, or arm; yet it is never violent, and seldom lasts many minutes at a time.

Whether or not this is sent to give me warning that I am shortly to quit this tabernacle, I do not know; but be it one way or the other, I have only to say,

> My remnant of days
> I spend to his praise
> Who died the whole world to redeem:
> Be they many or few,
> My days are his due,
> And they all are devoted to Him!

I preached in the morning on Psalm xc. 12; in the evening on Acts xiii. 40, 41; and endeavoured to improve the hours between to the best advantage.

Sun. 29.—At eight I preached at Misterton, as usual; about one to a numerous congregation at Newby, near Haxey; and about four at my old stand in Epworth market-place, to the great congregation.

Sun. July 6.—I came to Epworth before the church service began; and was glad to observe the seriousness with which Mr. Gibson read prayers, and preached a plain useful sermon; but was sorry to see scarce twenty communicants, half of whom came on my account. I was informed likewise, that scarce fifty persons used to attend the Sunday service. What can be done to remedy this sore evil?

"What is to be Done?"

I fain would prevent the members here from leaving the Church; but I cannot do it. As Mr. G. is not a pious man, but rather an enemy to piety, who frequently preaches against the truth, and those that hold and love it, I cannot with all my influence persuade them either to hear him, or to attend the sacrament administered by him. If I cannot carry this point even while I live, who then can do it when I die? And the case of Epworth is the case of every church where the minister neither loves nor preach the Gospel. The Methodists will not attend his ministrations. What then is to be done?

At four I preached in the market-place, on Rom. vi. 23; and vehemently exhorted the listening multitude to choose the better part.

Mon. 7.—Having taken leave of this affectionate people, probably for the last time, I went over to Finningley; and preached at eleven, on that verse in the second lesson, Luke xix. 42. After dinner we walked over Mr. H.'s domain, the like to which I never saw in so small a compass. It contains a rabit-warren, deer, swans, pheasants in abundance, besides a fish-pond and an elegant garden. Variety indeed! But is there no danger that such a multitude of things should divert the mind from the " one thing needful ? "

An Important Conference

I preached at the new chapel (London) every evening during the conference, which continued nine days, beginning on Tuesday, July 29, and ending on Wednesday, August 6 : and we found the time little enough ; being obliged to pass over many things very briefly, which deserved a fuller consideration.

Sun. Aug. 3.—I preached at the new chaapel, so filled as it scarce ever was before, both morning and evening.

Mon. 4. At five we had a good evening congregation ; and I believe many felt the power of the word ; or, rather, of God, speaking therein.

One of the most important points considered at this conference, was that of leaving the Church. The sum of a long conversation was, 1. That, in a course of fifty years, we had neither premeditately nor willingly varied from it in one article either of doctrine or discipline. 2. That we were not yet conscious of varying from it in any point of doctrine. 3. That we have in a course of years, out of necessity, not choice, slowly and warily varied in some points of discipline, by preaching in the fields, by extemporary prayer, by employing lay preachers, bv forming and regulating societies, and by holding yearly conferences. But we did none of these things till we were convinced we could no longer omit them, but at the peril of our souls.

Wed. 6.—Our conference ended, as it began, in great peace. We kept this day as a fast, meeting at five, nine, and one, for prayer; and concluding the day with a solemn watch-night.

The three following days I retired, revised my papers, and finished all the work I had to do in London.

Sun. 10. I was engaged in a very unpleasing work; the discharge of an old servant. She had been my housekeeper at West-street for many years, and was one of the best housekeepers I had had there; but her husband was so notorious a drunkard, that I could not keep them in the house any longer. She received her dismission in an excellent spirit, praying God to bless us all.

I preached in the morning at West-street to a large congregation, but to a far larger at the new chapel in the evening. It seems the people in general do not expect that I shall remain among them a great while after my brother; and that, therefore, they are willing to hear while they can. In the evening we set out in the mail coach, and early in the morning got to Portsmouth.

Sat. Sept. 6.—I walked over to Mr. Henderson's, at Hannam, and thence to Bristol. But my friends, more kind than wise, would scarce suffer it. It seemed so sad a thing to walk five or six miles! I am ashamed, that a Methodist preacher, in tolerable health, should make any difficulty of this.

"The Gentle Steps of Age"

Mon. Dec. 15.—In the evening I preached at Miss Teulon's school in Highgate. I think it was the coldest night I ever remember. The house we were in stood on the edge of the hill, and the east wind set full in the window. I counted eleven, twelve, one, and was then obliged to dress, the cramp growing more and more violent. But in the morning, not only the cramp was gone, but likewise the lameness which used to follow it.

About this time I was reflecting on the gentle steps whereby age steals upon us. Take only one instance. Four years ago my sight was as good as it was at five-and-twenty. I then began to observe that I did not see things quite so clear with my left eye as with my right; all objects appeared a little browner to that eye. I began next to find some difficulty in reading a small print by candle-light. A year after, I found it in reading such a print by day-light. In winter, 1786, I could not well read our four-shilling hymn-book, unless with a large candle; the next year I could not read letters, if wrote with a small or bad hand. Last winter a pearl appeared on my left eye, the sight of which grew exceeding dim. The right eye seems unaltered; only I am a great deal nearer sighted than ever I was. Thus are "those that look out at the windows darkened"; one of the marks of old age. But I bless God, "the grasshopper is" not "a burden." I am still capable of travelling, and my memory is much the same as ever it was; and so, I think, is my understanding.

Wesley Sits to Romney

1789. Thur. Jan. 1.—If this is to be the last year of my life, according to some of those prophecies, I hope it will be the best. I am not careful about it, but heartily receive the advice of the angel in Milton,—

"How well is thine: how long permit to Heaven."

Mon. 5.—At the earnest desire of Mrs. T——, I once more sat for my picture. Mr. Romney is a painter indeed. He struck off an exact likeness at once; and did more in one hour than Sir Joshua did in ten.

Fri. 9.—I left no money to any one in my will, because I had none. But now considering, that, when-

ever I am removed, money will soon arise by the sale
of books, I added a few legacies by a codicil, to be paid
as soon as may be.   But I would fain do a little good
while I live; for who can tell what will come after
him?

Tues. 13.—I spent a day or two with my good old
friends at Newington.   Thursday, 15. I retired to
Camberwell, and carried on my Journal, probably as
far as I shall live to write it.

Tues. 20.—I retired in order to finish my year's
accounts.   If possible, I must be a better economist;
for instead of having anything beforehand, I am now
considerably in debt: but this I do not like.   I would
fain settle even my accounts before I die.

Wesley Explains Methodism

Sunday, March 1, was a solemn day indeed.   The
new chapel was sufficiently crowded both morning and
afternoon; and few that expected a parting blessing,
were disappointed of their hope.   At seven in the
evening I took the mail-coach; and having three of our
brethren, we spent a comfortable night, partly in sound
sleep, and partly in singing praise to God.   It will now
quickly be seen whether they who prophesied some time
since, that I should not outlive this month, be sent of
God or not.   One way or the other, it is my care to be
always ready.

April 12 (Dublin).—(Being Easter-day.) We had a
solemn assembly indeed; many hundred communicants
in the morning; and in the afternoon far more hearers
than our room would contain, though it is now considerably enlarged.   Afterwards I met the society, and
explained to them at large the original design of the
Methodists, namely, not to be a distinct party, but to

stir up all parties, Christians or heathens, to worship
God in spirit and in truth ; but the Church of England in
particular ; to which they belonged from the beginning.
With this view I have uniformly gone on for fifty years,
never varying from the doctrine of the Church at all ;
nor from her discipline, of choice, but of necessity : so,
in a course of years, necessity was laid upon me (as I
have proved elsewhere), 1. To preach in the open air.
2. To pray extempore. 3. To form societies. 4. To
accept of the assistance of lay preachers : and, in a few
other instances, to use such means as occurred, to
prevent or remove evils that we either felt or feared.

Wesley Describes Himself at Eighty-five

Sun. June 28.—In the conclusion of the morning
service, we had a remarkable blessing : and the same in
the evening, moving the whole congregation as the heart
of one man.

This day I enter on my eighty-sixth year. I now
find I grow old : 1. My sight is decayed ; so that I
cannot read a small print, unless in a strong light. 2.
My strength is decayed ; so that I walk much slower
than I did some years since. 3. My memory of names,
whether of persons or places, is decayed ; till I stop a
little to recollect them. What I should be afraid of, is,
if I took thought for the morrow, that my body should
weigh down my mind ; and create either stubbornness,
by the decrease of my understanding ; or peevishness,
by the increase of bodily infirmities : but Thou shalt
answer for me, O Lord my God.

Sat. Aug. 8.—I settled all my temporal business, and,
in particular, chose a new person to prepare the Arminian
Magazine ; being obliged, however unwillingly, to drop
Mr. O——, for only these two reasons : 1. The errata

Painted in 1789 by William Hamilton, R. A.
(*The original is now in National Portrait Gallery*)
REV. JOHN WESLEY, A. M.

are unsufferable; I have borne them for these twelve years, but can bear them no longer. 2. Several pieces are inserted without my knowledge, both in prose and verse. I must try whether these things cannot be amended for the short residue of my life.

"How Is the Tide Turned"

Mon. 17.—In the afternoon, as we could not pass by the common road, we procured leave to drive round by some fields, and got to Falmouth in good time. The last time I was here, about forty years ago, I was taken prisoner by an immense mob, gaping and roaring like lions: but how is the tide turned! High and low now lined the street, from one end of the town to the other, out of stark love and kindness, gaping and staring as if the King were going by. In the evening I preached on the smooth top of the hill, at a small distance from the sea, to the largest congregation I have ever seen in Cornwall, except in or near Redruth. And such a time I have not known before, since I returned from Ireland. God moved wonderfully on the hearts of the people, who all seemed to know the day of their visitation.

Wed. 19.—I preached at noon in the high street in Helstone, to the largest and most serious congregation which I ever remember to have seen there. Thursday, 20. I went on to St. Just, and preached in the evening to a lovely congregation, many of whom have not left their first love. Friday, 21. About eleven I preached Newlyn, and in the evening at Penzance; at both places I was obliged to preach abroad. Saturday, 22. I crossed over to Redruth, and at six preached to a huge multitude, as usual, from the steps of the market-house. The word seemed to sink deep into every heart. I know not that ever I spent such a week in Cornwall before.

Sun. 23.—I preached there again in the morning, and in the evening at the amphitheatre; I suppose, for the last time; for my voice cannot now command the still increasing multitude. It was supposed they were now more than five-and-twenty thousand. I think it scarce possible that all should hear.

Thurs. Oct. 8.—I am now as well, by the good providence of God, as I am likely to be while I live. My sight is so decayed that I cannot well read by candle-light; but I can write as well as ever : and my strength is much lessened, so that I cannot easily preach above twice a day. But, I bless God, my memory is not much decayed; and my understanding is as clear as it has been these fifty years.

Wesley's Eighty-sixth Christmas

Fri. Dec. 25.—(Being Christmas-day.) We began the service in the new chapel at four o'clock, as usual; where I preached again in the evening, after having officiated in West-street at the common hour. Sunday, 27. I preached in St. Luke's, our parish church, in the afternoon, to a very numerous congregation, on, " The Spirit and the Bride say, Come." So are the tables turned, that I have now more invitations to preach in churches than I can accept of.

Mon. 28.—I retired to Peckham; and at leisure hours read part of a very pretty trifle—the Life of Mrs. Bellamy. Surely never did any, since John Dryden, study more

To make vice pleasing, and damnation shine,

than this lively and elegant writer. Abundance of anecdotes she inserts, which may be true or false. One of them, concerning Mr. Garrick, is curious. She says, "When he was taking ship for England, a lady presented him with a parcel, which she desired him not to open till he was at sea. When he did, he found Wesley's Hymns, which he immediately threw overboard." I cannot believe it. I think Mr. G. had more sense. He knew my brother well; and he knew him to be not only far superior in learning, but in poetry, to Mr. Thomson, and all his theatrical writers put together: none of them can equal him, either in strong, nervous sense, or purity and elegance of language. The musical compositions of his sons are not more excellent than the poetical ones of their father.

Thur. 31.—I preached at the new chapel; but, to avoid the cramp, went to bed at ten o'clock. I was well served. I know not that I ever before felt so much of it in one night.

The Last Year of the Journal

1790. Fri. Jan. 1.—I am now an old man, decayed from head to foot. My eyes are dim; my right hand shakes much; my mouth is hot and dry every morning; I have a lingering fever almost every day; my motion is weak and slow. However, blessed be God, I do not slack my labour: I can preach and write still.

Sun. 17.—In the afternoon I preached in Great St. Helen's, to a large congregation. It is, I believe, fifty years since I preached there before. What has God wrought since that time!

Tues. Feb. 23.—I submitted to importunity, and once more sat for my picture. I could scarce believe myself;—the picture of one in his eighty-seventh year!

Mon. June 28.—This day I enter into my eighty-eighth year. For above eighty-six years, I found none of the infirmities of old age; my eyes did not wax dim, neither was my natural strength abated: but last August

I found almost a sudden change. My eyes were so dim, that no glasses would help me. My strength likewise quite forsook me; and probably will not return in this world. But I feel no pain from head to foot; only it seems nature is exhausted; and, humanly speaking, will sink more and more, till

The weary springs of life stand still at last.

Thur. July 1.—I went to Lincoln. After dinner we took a walk in and around the Minster; which I really think is more elegant than that at York, in various parts of the structure, as well as in its admirable situation. The new house was thoroughly filled in the evening, and with hearers uncommonly serious. There seems to be a remarkable difference between the people of Lincoln, and those of York. They have not so much fire and vigour of spirit; but far more mildness and gentleness; by means of which, if they had the same outward helps, they would probably excel their neighbours.

A Backsliding Innkeeper

Some miles short of Lincoln, our post-boy stopped at an inn on the road, to give his horses a little water. As soon as we went in, the innkeeper burst into tears, as did his wife; wringing her hands, and weeping bitterly. "What!" he said, "are you come into my house! My father is John Lester, of Epworth." I found both he and his wife had been of our society, till they left them. We spent some time in prayer together; and I trust not in vain.

Sat. Sept. 4.—I went on to Bath, and preached in the evening to a serious, but small congregation, for want of notice.

Sun. 5. At ten we had a numerous congregation, and

more communicants than ever I saw here before. This day I cut off that vile custom, I know not when or how it began, of preaching three times a day, by the same preacher to the same congregation; enough to weary out both the bodies and minds of the speaker, as well as his hearers. Surely God is returning to this society! They are now in earnest to make their calling and election sure.

"I Am Become an Honourable Man"

Mon. Oct. 11.—I went (from London) to Colchester, and still found matter of humiliation. The society was lessened, and cold enough; preaching again was discontinued, and the spirit of Methodism quite gone, both from the preachers and the people : yet we had a wonderful congregation in the evening, rich and poor, clergy and laity. So we had likewise on Tuesday evening. So that I trust God will at length build up the waste places.

Wed. 13.—We set out early, but found no horses at Cobdock; so that we were obliged to go round by Ipswich, and wait there half an hour. Nevertheless, we got to Norwich between two and three.

In the evening I preached at Norwich ; but the house would in no wise contain the congregation. How wonderfully is the tide turned! I am become an honourable man at Norwich. God has at length made our enemies to be at peace with us ; and scarce any but Antinomians open their mouth against us.

Thur. 14.—I went to Yarmouth ; and, at length, found a society in peace, and much united together. In the evening the congregation was too large to get into the preaching-house; yet they were far less noisy than usual. After supper a little company went to prayer, and the power of God fell upon us; especially when a young woman broke out into prayer, to the surprise and comfort of us all.

Fri. 15. I went to Lowestoft, to a steady, loving, well-united society. The more strange it is, that they neither increase nor decrease in number.

Sat. 16. I preached at Loddon about one; and at six in Norwich.

Sun. 17. At seven I administered the Lord's supper to about one hundred and fifty persons, near twice as many as we had last year.

Wesley's Last Entries

Mon. 18.—No coach going out for Lynn to-day, I was obliged to take a post-chaise. But at Dereham no horses were to be had; so we were obliged to take the same horses to Swaffham. A congregation was ready here, that filled the house, and seemed quite ready to receive instruction.

But here neither could we procure any post-horses; so that we were obliged to take a single-horse chaise. The wind, with mizzling rain, came full in our faces: and we had nothing to screen us from it; so that I was throughly chilled from head to foot before I came to Lynn. But I soon forgot this little inconvenience; for which the earnestness of the congregation made me large amends.

Tues. 19.—In the evening all the Clergymen in the town, except one, who was lame, were present at the preaching. They are all prejudiced in favour of the Methodists; as indeed are most of the townsmen; who give a fair proof by contributing so much to our Sunday-schools; so that there is near twenty pounds in hand.

Wed. 20.—I had appointed to preach at Diss; a

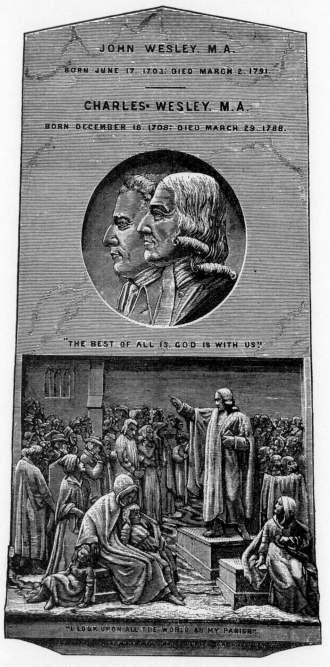

JOHN WESLEY. M.A.
BORN JUNE 17. 1703: DIED MARCH 2. 1791.

CHARLES· WESLEY. M.A.
BORN DECEMBER 18. 1708: DIED MARCH 29. 1788.

"THE BEST OF ALL IS. GOD IS WITH US."

"I LOOK UPON ALL THE WORLD AS MY PARISH".

WESLEY'S MEMORIAL IN WESTMINSTER ABBEY

town near Scoleton; but the difficulty was, where I could preach. The minister was willing I should preach in the church; but feared offending the bishop, who, going up to London, was within a few miles of the town. But a gentleman asking the bishop whether he had any objection to it, was answered, " None at all." I think this church is one of the largest in this county. I suppose it has not been so filled these hundred years. This evening and the next I preached at Bury, to a deeply attentive congregation, many of whom know in whom they have believed. So that here we have not lost all our labour.

Fri. 22.—We returned to London.

Sun. 24.—I explained, to a numerous congregation in Spitalfields church, " the whole armour of God." St. Paul's, Shadwell, was still more crowded in the afternoon, while I enforced that important truth, " One thing is needful"; and I hope many, even then, resolved to choose the better part.

INDEX

THE END